MANDOLIN FRETBOARD ATLAS

GET A BETTER GRIP ON NECK NAVIGATION!

BY JOE CHARUPAKORN

ISBN 978-1-4950-8038-8

Visit Hal Leonard Online at
www.halleonard.com

Contact Us:
Hal Leonard
7777 West Bluemound Road
Milwaukee, WI 53213
Email: info@halleonard.com

In Europe contact:
Hal Leonard Europe Limited
Distribution Centre, Newmarket Road
Bury St Edmunds, Suffolk, IP33 3YB
Email: info@halleonardeurope.com

In Australia contact:
Hal Leonard Australia Pty. Ltd.
4 Lentara Court
Cheltenham, Victoria, 3192 Australia
Email: info@halleonard.com.au

TABLE OF CONTENTS

INTRODUCTION

Mandolin Fretboard Atlas is a collection of roadmaps for the most important scales and chords (up to seventh chords). The material is presented in all 12 keys, using 12-fret neck diagrams with color-coded displays of the most common moveable fingerings. When fingerings share common notes, the colors will overlap. No music reading or understanding of music theory is required.

Mastering the mandolin neck can be challenging, even for very experienced players. There are several obstacles that make learning the mandolin's fretboard difficult. On the mandolin, a note can be played in several different places, unlike many other instruments, where each note has only one location.

The diagrams in *Mandolin Fretboard Atlas* will help you quickly internalize and memorize not only the most common scales and chords, but also others that may have previously seemed impossible to grasp. You'll be able to easily see and understand how scale and chord shapes are laid out and how they connect and overlap across the neck. As an added benefit, once you can see a shape in your mind's eye, you've got all 12 keys covered—just move the shape to start on a different fret, depending on the key you want.

ABOUT THE AUTHOR

New York City native Joe Charupakorn is a guitarist, editor, and best-selling author. He has written over 25 instructional books for Hal Leonard. His books are available worldwide and have been translated into many languages.

Visit him on the web at joecharupakorn.com.

HOW TO USE THIS BOOK

A good plan of attack with *Mandolin Fretboard Atlas* would be to start by learning the most common scales, which are the major, natural minor (Aeolian), minor pentatonic, major pentatonic, and blues scales. After getting comfortable with these (or if the need arises), then add in some of the more complex scales and modes presented in this book.

First, start with one scale shape and work with it for a while in one key until it feels comfortable. When you've internalized that one shape, add in an adjacent shape in the same key. Once you can see both shapes independently and as pieces of a bigger puzzle, then practice going back and forth between the two. Eventually add in more fingerings in the same key, and before long, you'll have the whole neck covered. There are countless ways to put the scale shapes to use. For example, you can run the scales straight up and down, improvise with them, or sight-read, using the shapes as a reference. Do this in all 12 keys.

For the chord section, start with power chords and triads, which are the backbone of virtually any style of music and fall into the "must-know" category. After you've got a firm grasp on these chords, learn the triads with added notes and seventh chords to add harmonic color to your music. To internalize chord shapes, first take some time to get a mental picture of the chord's shape. After committing it to memory, practice getting to the shape quickly without referring to the book, making sure all the notes ring clearly. Then add another voicing of the same chord and practice moving back and forth between the two voicings. Once you are comfortable with this, do it in the remaining keys. To gain flexibility with the new chords, practice a short progression of two or three chords in different keys, using just two voicings for each chord. Then add more voicings as it becomes second nature. Also try creating solo arrangements of some of your favorite tunes and put these new shapes to use.

Beyond the Fingering

For each diagram, every tone of the specific scale or chord is circled, but only the most common moveable shapes are displayed with color codes. The fingerings presented are just a starting point—you shouldn't feel "locked in" to any of the shapes presented. Feel free to experiment! You can take fragments from one fingering and combine it with fragments from an adjacent fingering to create your own shapes that might be more suitable for a specific situation. Use the circled scale and chord tones as a guide and go for it! Because they all interconnect, the idea is that, ultimately, you'll see the mandolin neck as one unit.

NOTATION CONVENTIONS IN THIS BOOK

Any note with an *accidental*—a sharp or flat—can be spelled either as a sharp or flat version of the note. In this book, both the sharp and flat versions of every note (*enharmonic equivalents*) are displayed on the fretboard diagrams. The specific accidentals used in the "proper" spelling of a scale or chord will generally depend on the context.

For example, here is the proper spelling of the G major scale:

G A B C D E F♯ G

And here is an incorrect spelling of the G major scale:

G A B C D E G♭ G

F♯ is the same note as G♭, and, in our diagrams, any note location with that pitch is represented by F♯/G♭ on the fretboard. However, the correct spelling of the G major scale is the one with F♯ because this spelling lets us represent every letter in the music alphabet. In the spelling with G♭, there are no Fs of any kind and two kinds of Gs—a G♭ and a G.

In the headings above the diagrams throughout the book, only the most commonly accepted spellings of the specific scales or chords are displayed.

Exceptions to the Rule

In some cases, it's more practical to suspend the rigidity of the rules and go with a more familiar, if technically "wrong," spelling. This is particularly common in cases involving scales and chords that have double sharps (𝄪) and double flats (𝄫) in their proper spelling.

The fretboard diagrams in *Mandolin Fretboard Atlas* do not include double sharps (𝄪) or double flats (𝄫), or less common accidentals such as F♭, C♭, etc. However, the proper spellings of scales and chords are listed in the headings above the diagrams throughout the book.

For example, the proper spelling of A♭ melodic minor is:

A♭ B♭ C♭ D♭ E♭ F G

While F♭ is enharmonically the same note as E, the dots representing the F♭ notes will be on the fretboard diagram's E notes. Likewise, while C♭ is enharmonically the same note as B, the dots representing the C♭ notes will be on the fretboard diagram's B notes.

If this is all a little confusing, the good news is that, even without any of this information, you'll be able to play any of the scales or chords in any key as long as you can follow the diagrams.

SCALES

THE MAJOR SCALE AND ITS MODES

C IONIAN

C–D–E–F–G–A–B

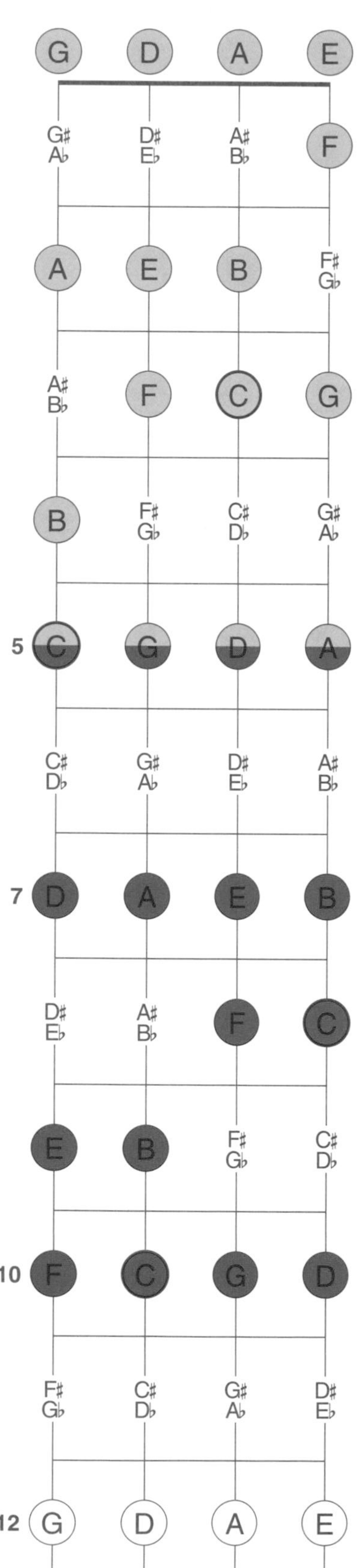

C♯/D♭ IONIAN

C♯–D♯–E♯–F♯–G♯–A♯–B♯
D♭–E♭–F–G♭–A♭–B♭–C

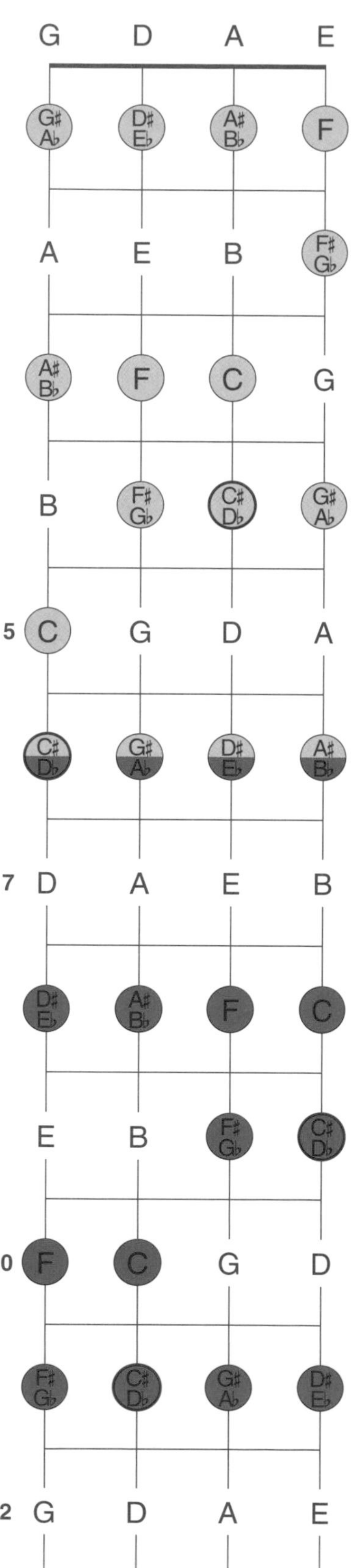

D IONIAN

D–E–F♯–G–A–B–C♯

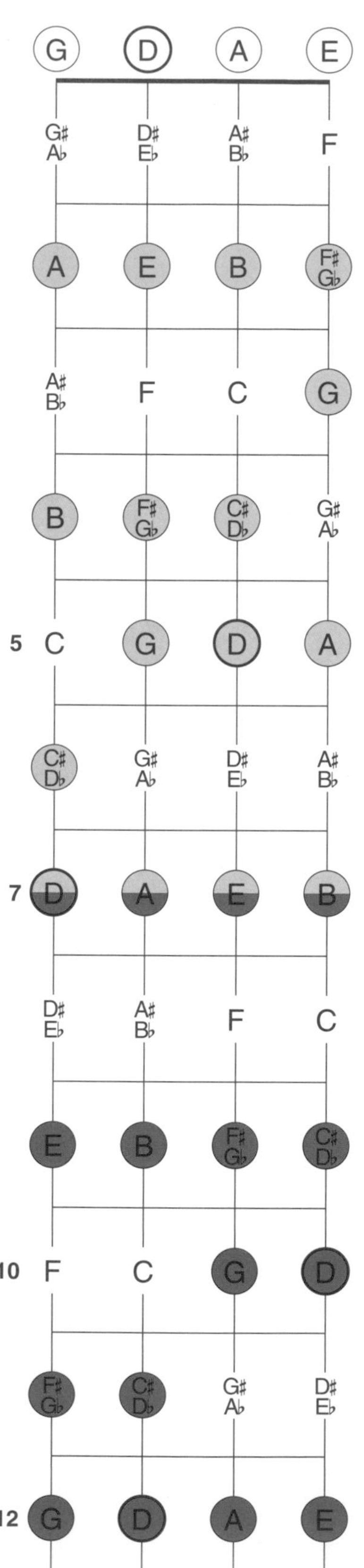

E♭ IONIAN

E♭–F–G–A♭–B♭–C–D

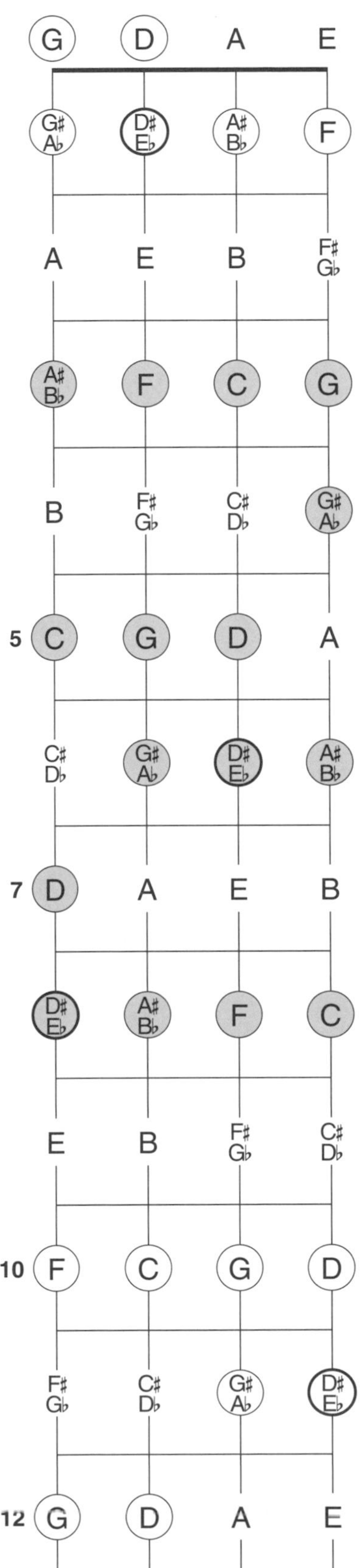

E IONIAN

E–F♯–G♯–A–B–C♯–D♯

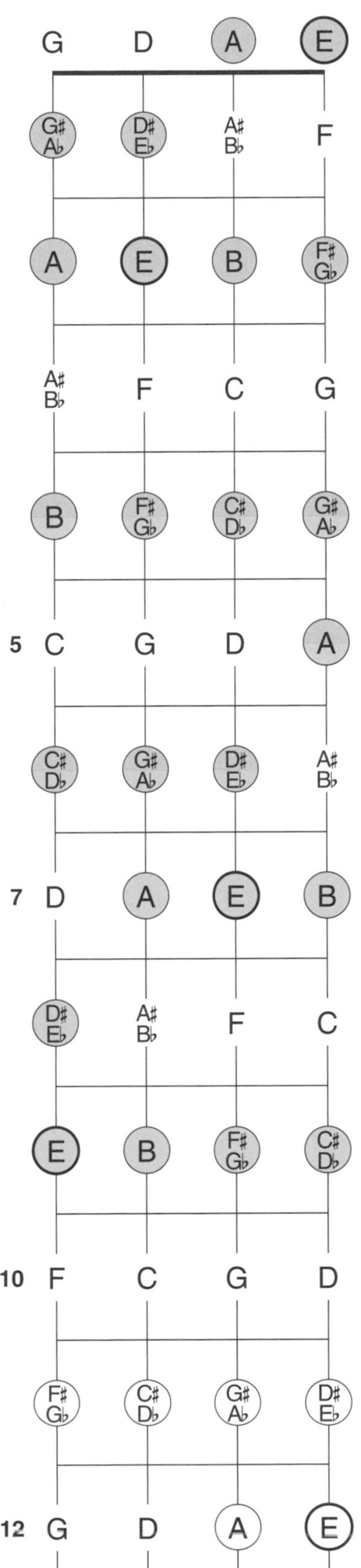

F IONIAN

F–G–A–B♭–C–D–E

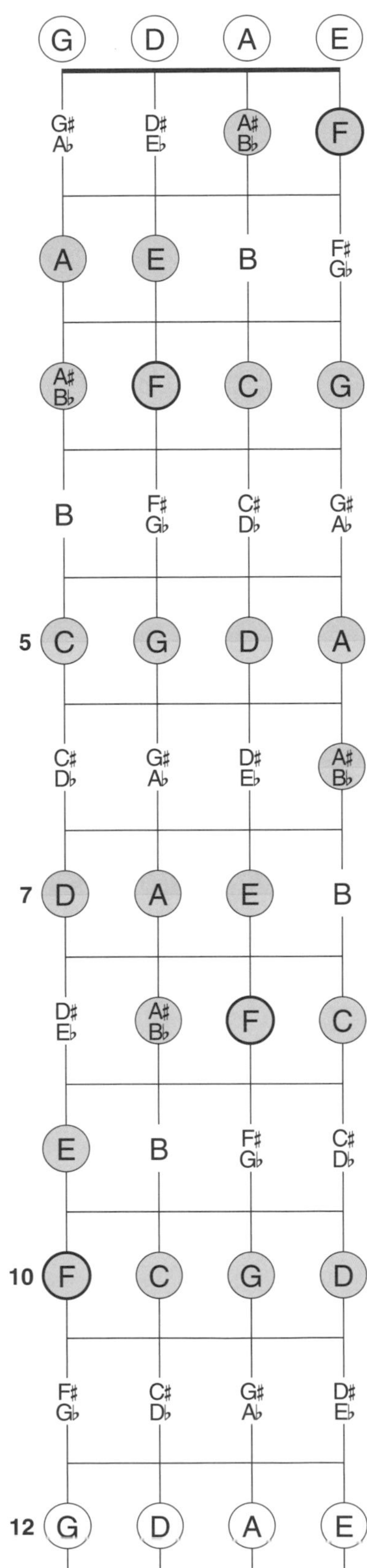

F♯/G♭ IONIAN

F♯–G♯–A♯–B–C♯–D♯–E♯
G♭–A♭–B♭–C♭–D♭–E♭–F

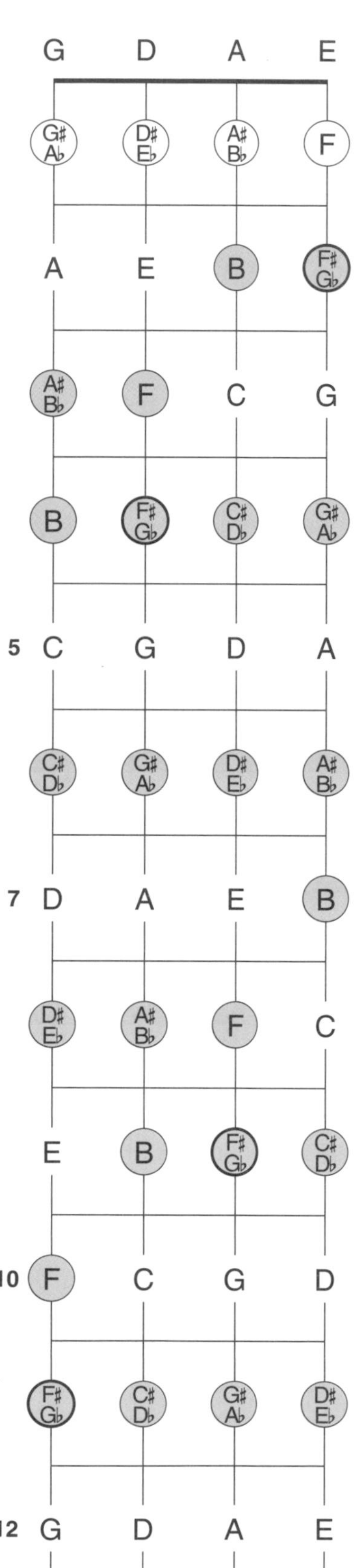

G IONIAN

G–A–B–C–D–E–F♯

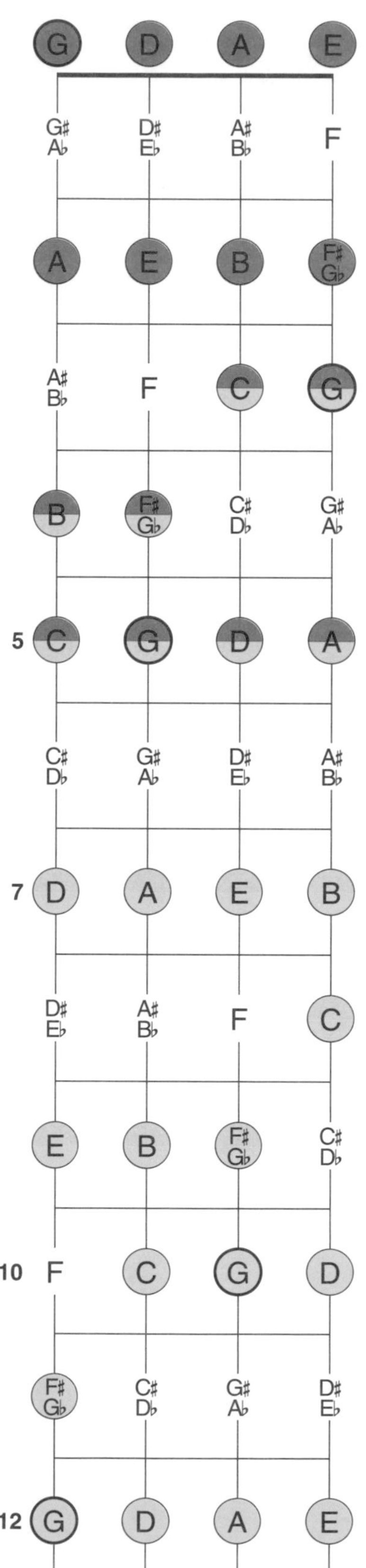

A♭ IONIAN

A♭–B♭–C–D♭–E♭–F–G

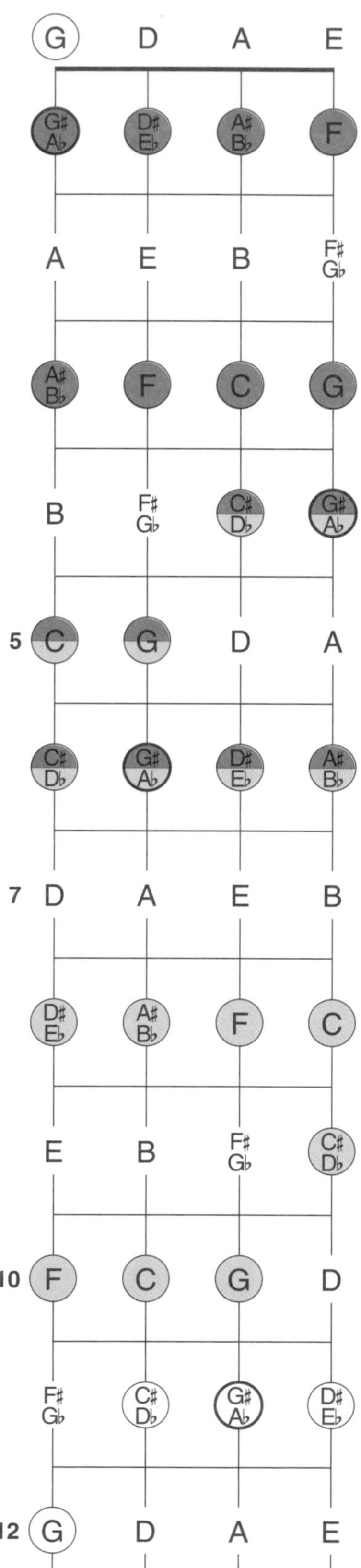

A IONIAN

A–B–C♯–D–E–F♯–G♯

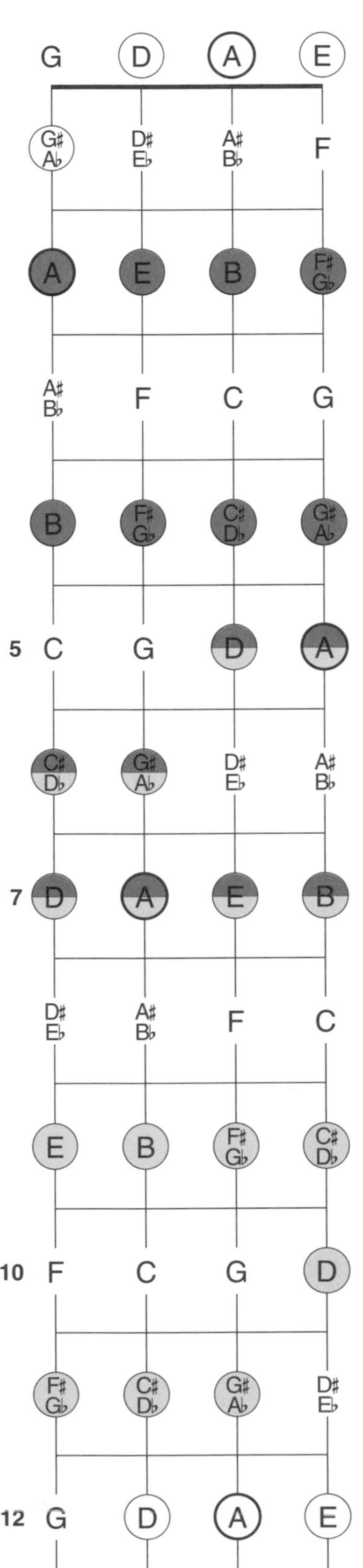

B♭ IONIAN

B♭–C–D–E♭–F–G–A

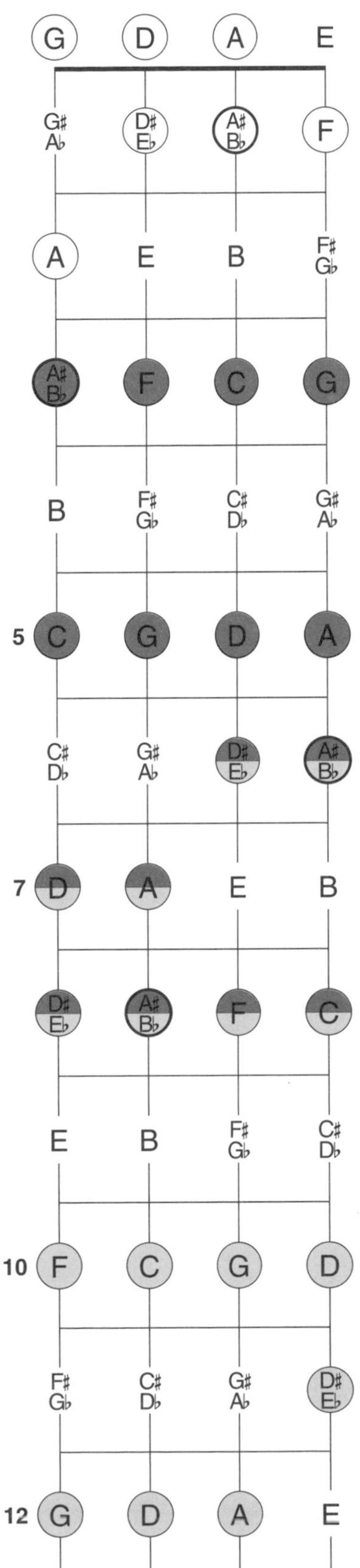

B IONIAN

B–C♯–D♯–E–F♯–G♯–A♯

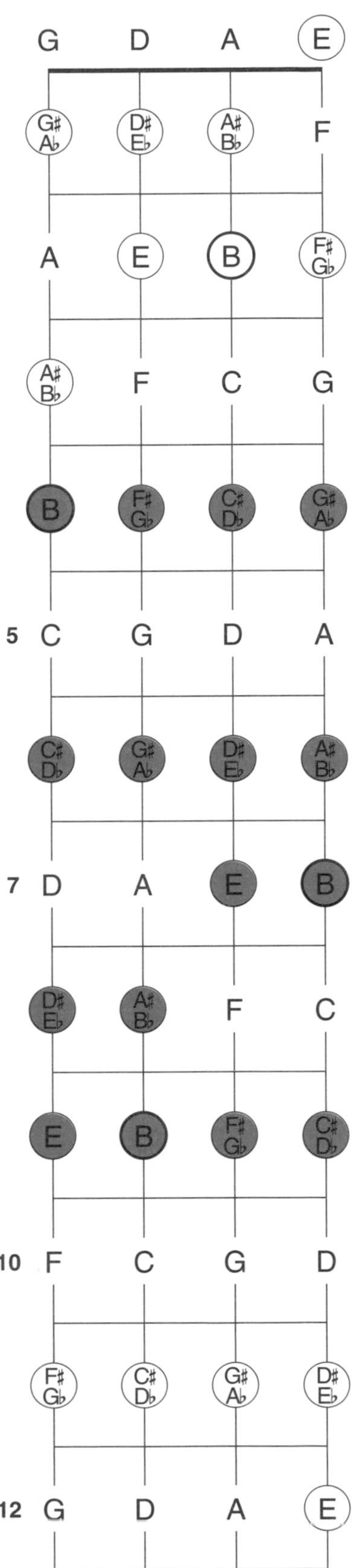

C DORIAN

C–D–E♭–F–G–A–B♭

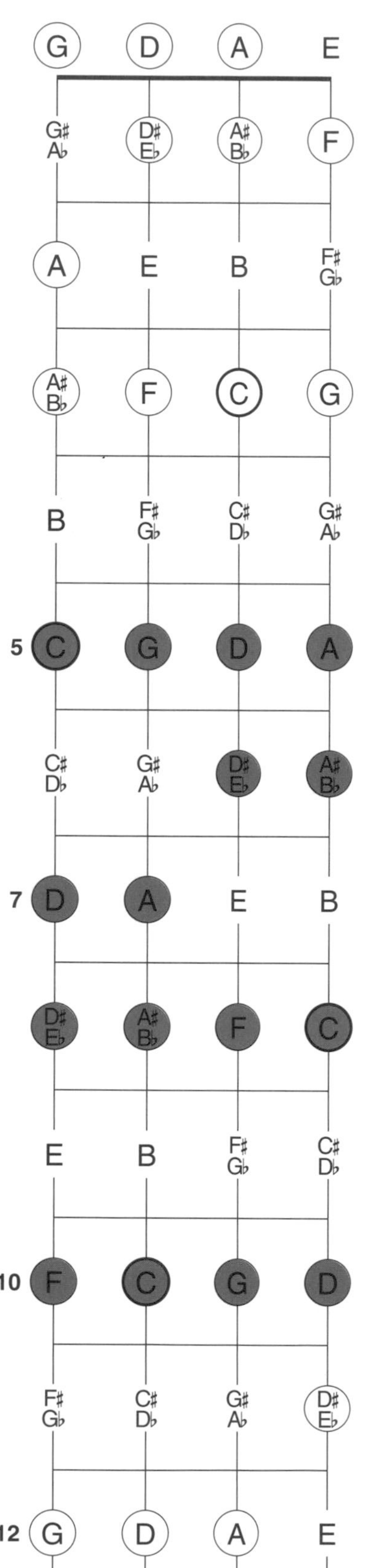

C♯ DORIAN

C♯–D♯–E–F♯–G♯–A♯–B

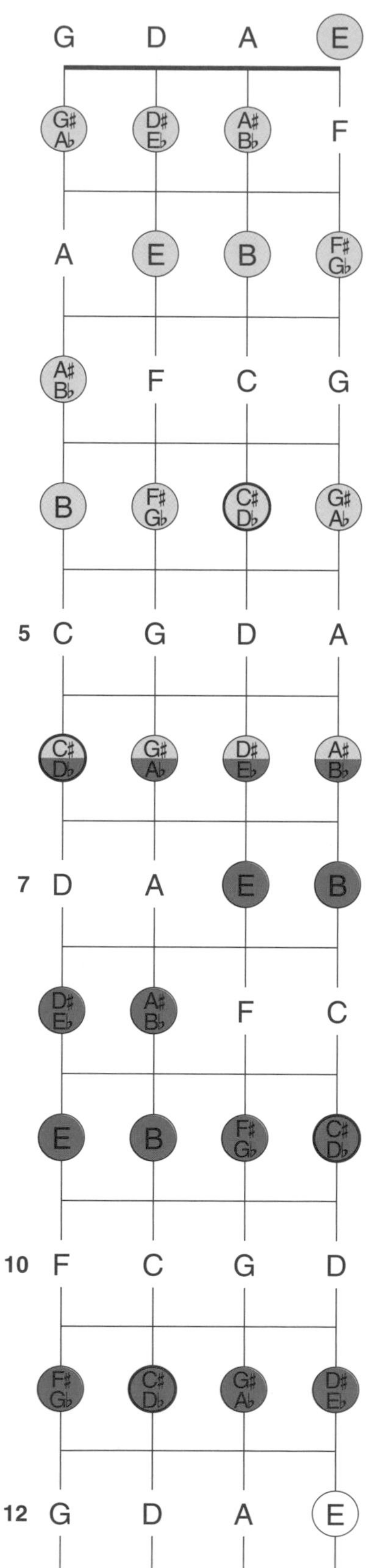

D DORIAN

D–E–F–G–A–B–C

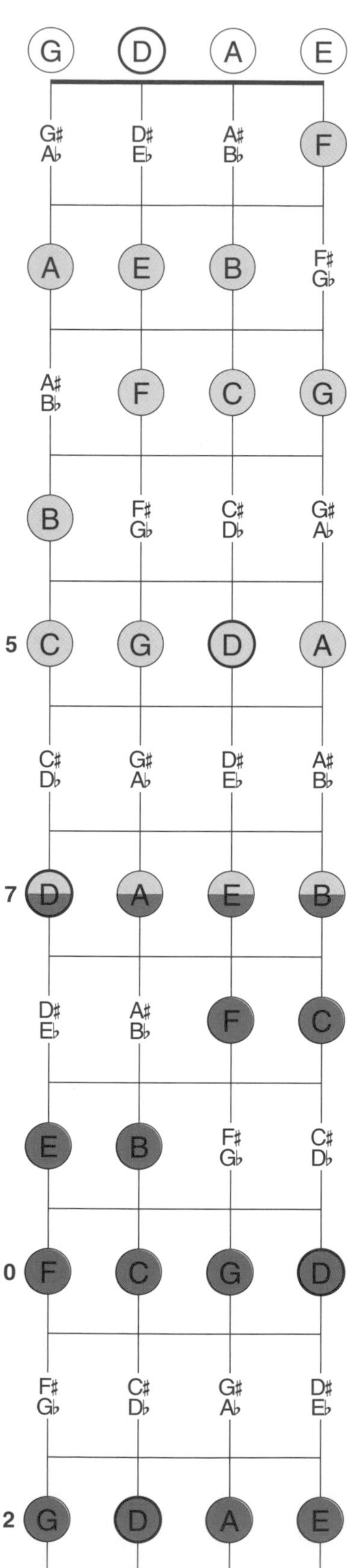

E♭ DORIAN

E♭–F–G♭–A♭–B♭–C–D♭

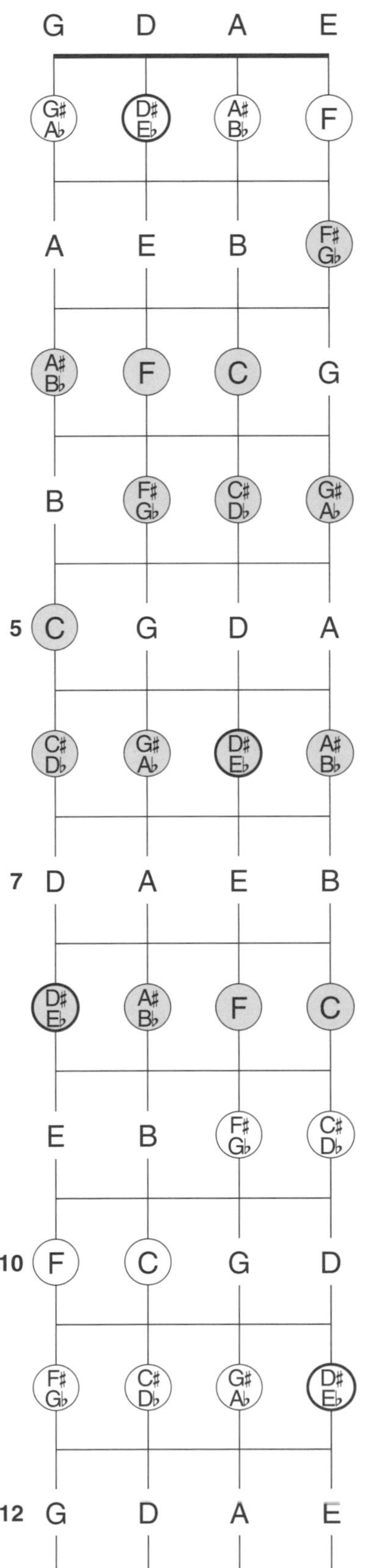

E DORIAN

E–F♯–G–A–B–C♯–D

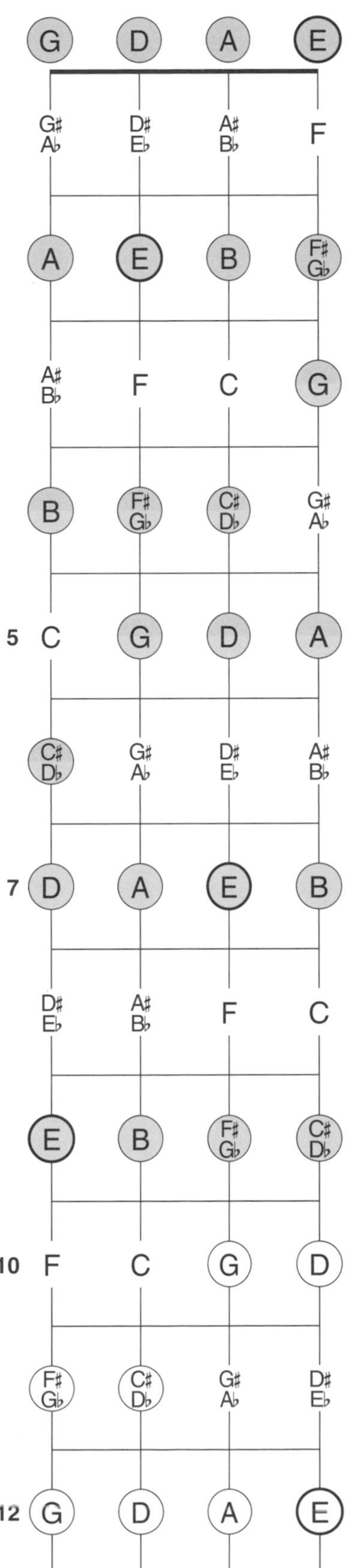

F DORIAN

F–G–A♭–B♭–C–D–E♭

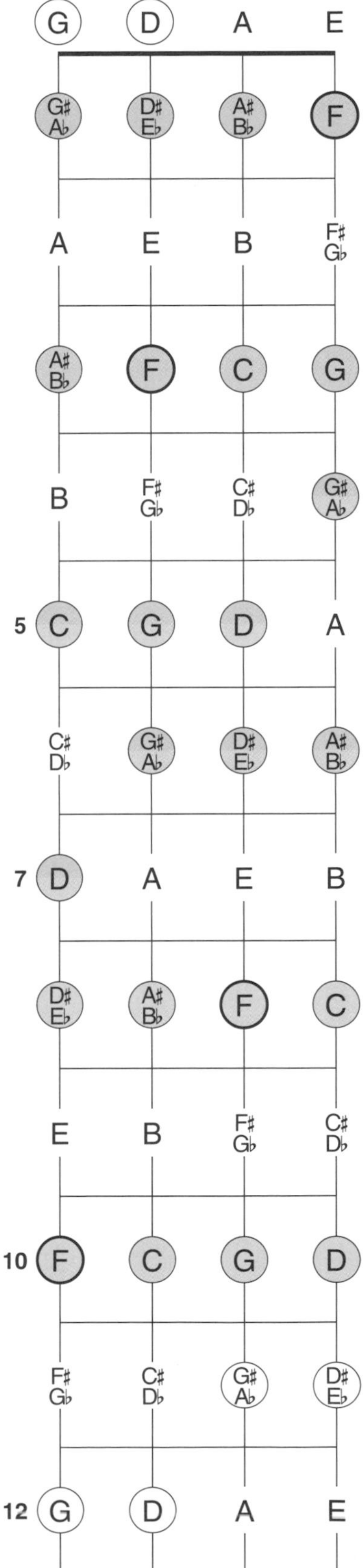

F♯ DORIAN

F♯–G♯–A–B–C♯–D♯–E

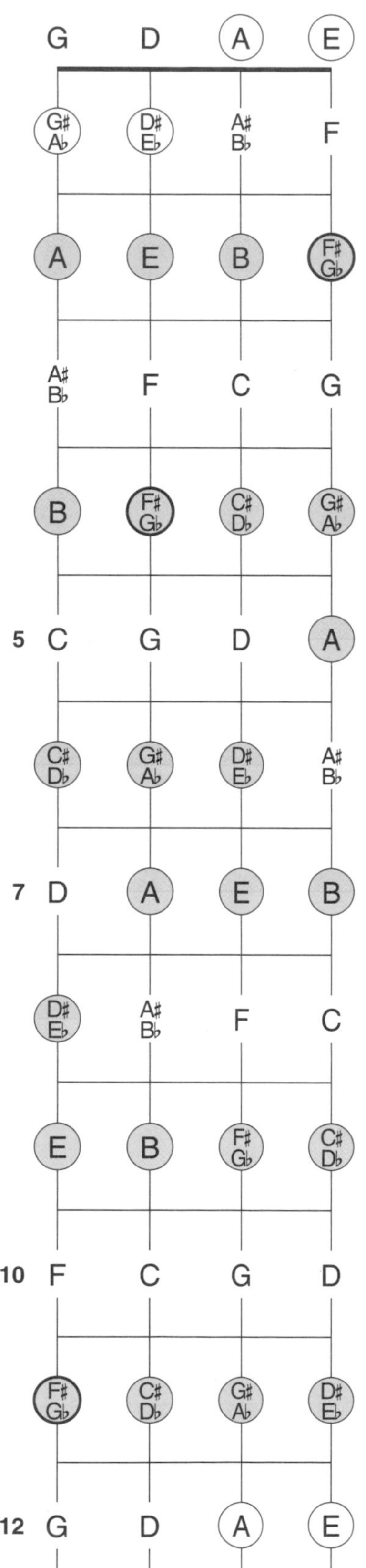

G DORIAN

G–A–B♭–C–D–E–F

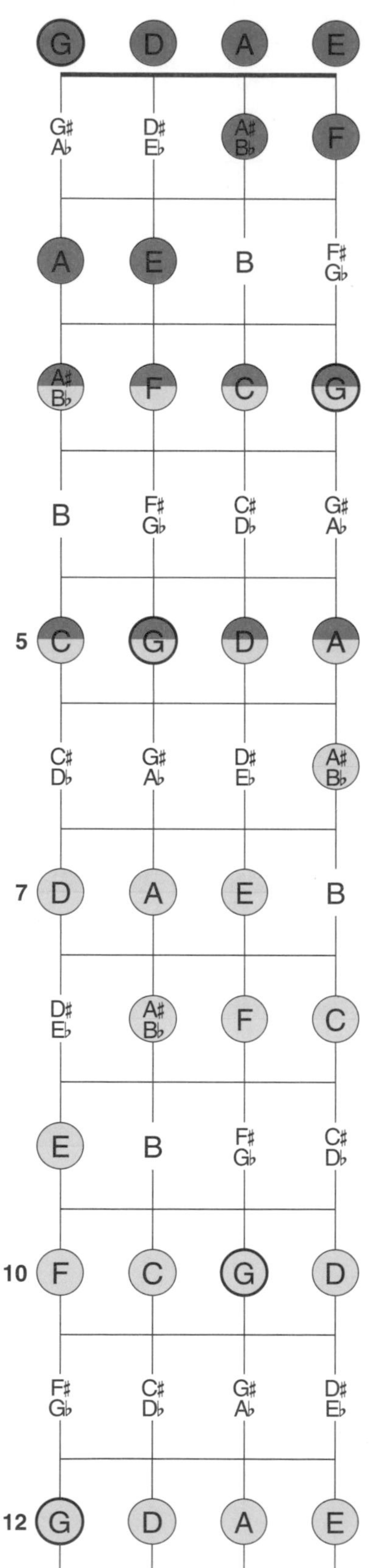

A♭ DORIAN

A♭–B♭–C♭–D♭–E♭–F–G♭

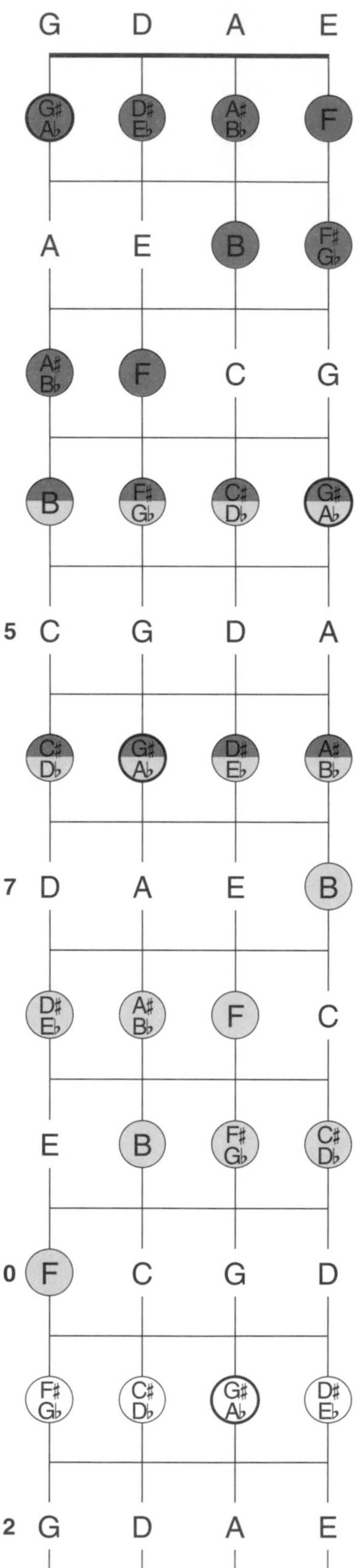

A DORIAN

A–B–C–D–E–F♯–G

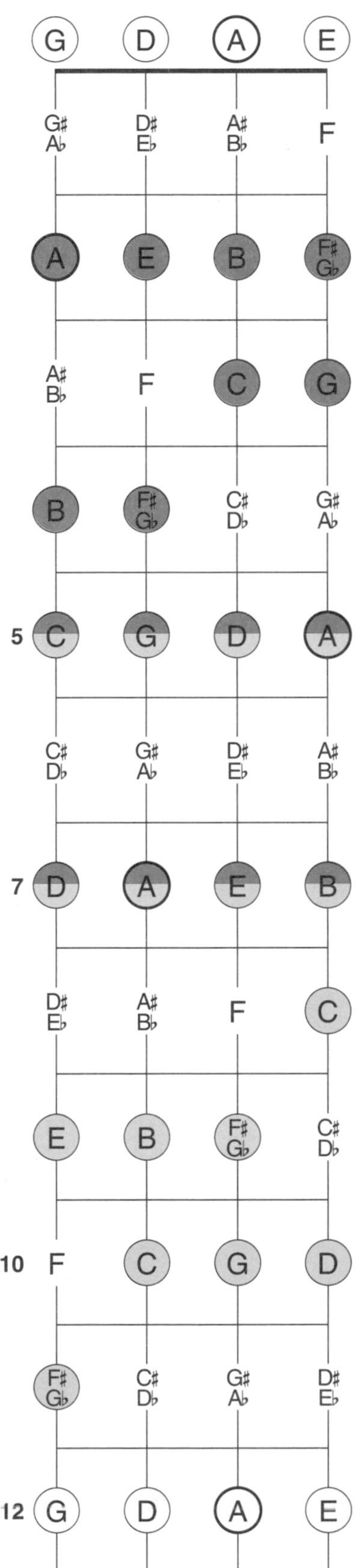

B♭ DORIAN

B♭–C–D♭–E♭–F–G–A♭

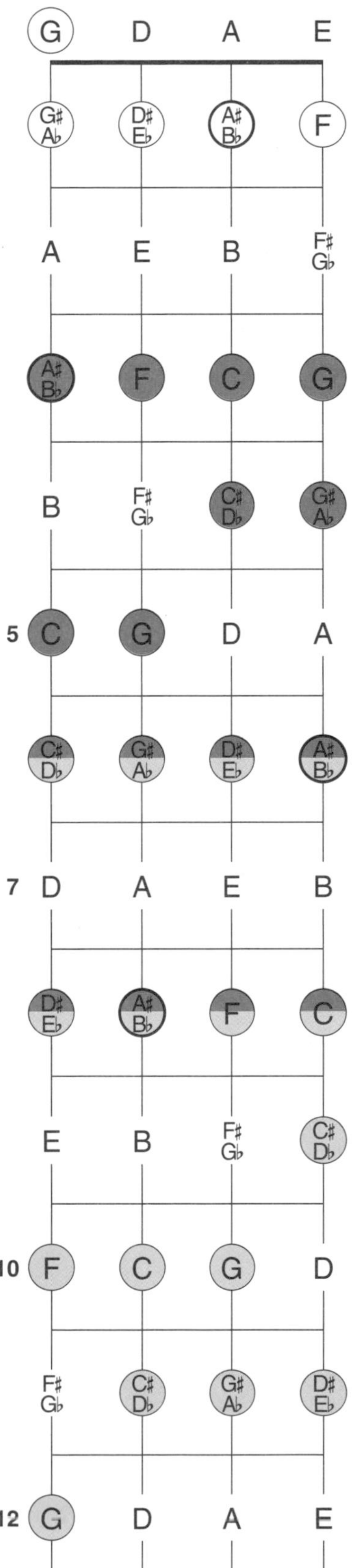

B DORIAN

B–C♯–D–E–F♯–G♯–A

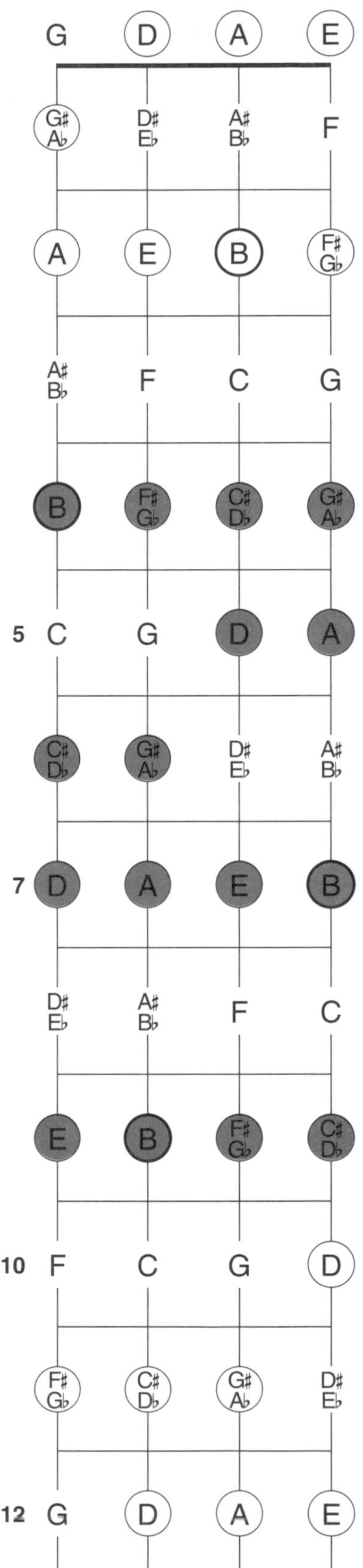

C PHRYGIAN

C–D♭–E♭–F–G–A♭–B♭

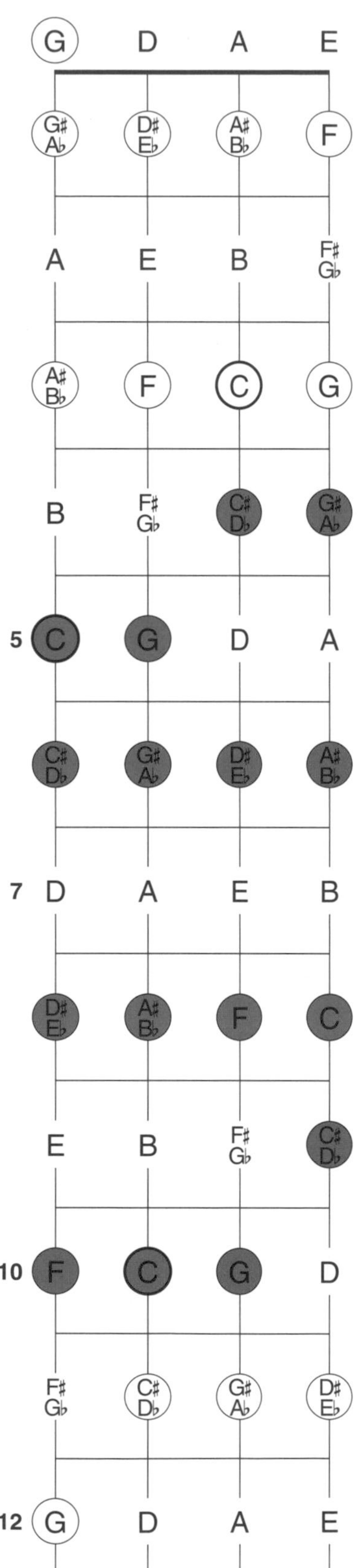

C♯ PHRYGIAN

C♯–D–E–F♯–G♯–A–B

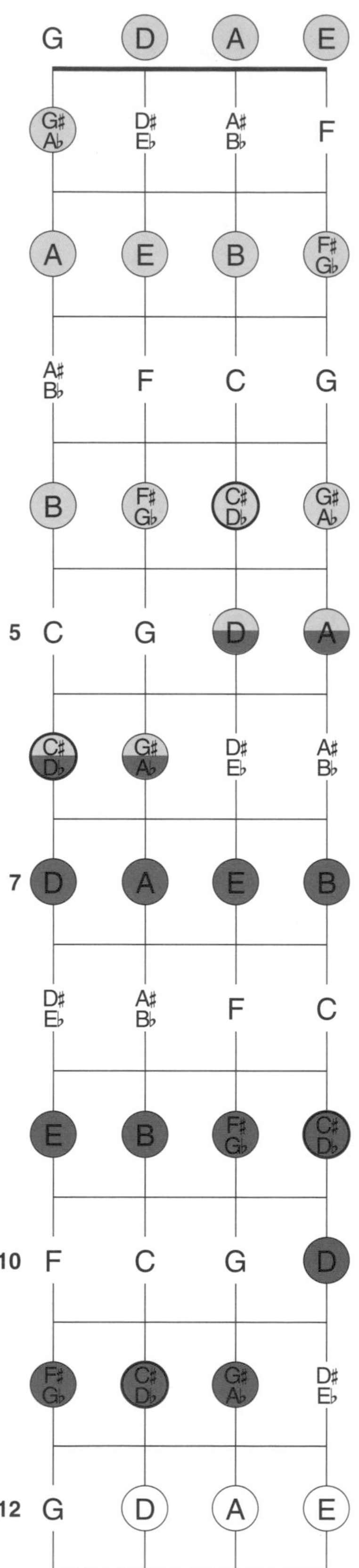

D PHRYGIAN

D–E♭–F–G–A–B♭–C

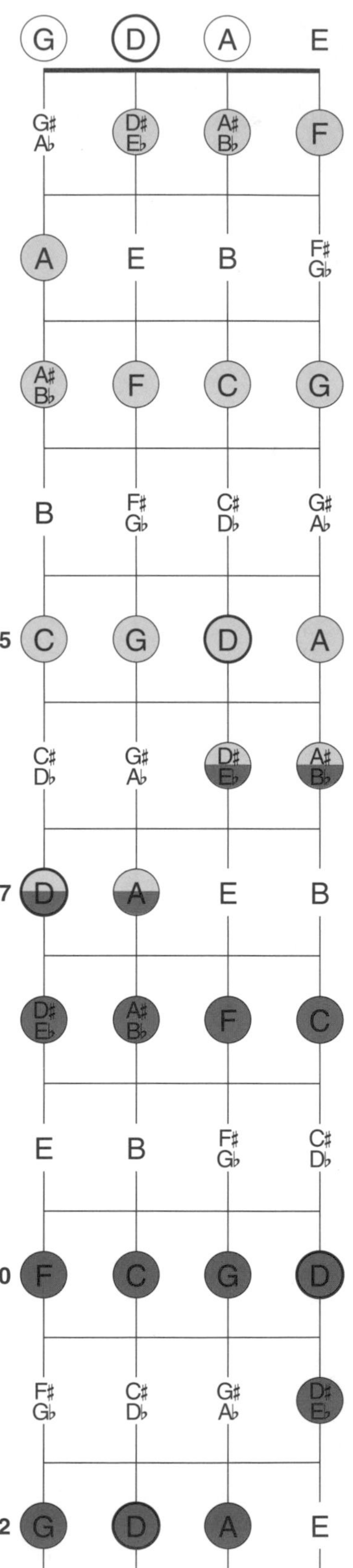

D♯ PHRYGIAN

D♯–E–F♯–G♯–A♯–B–C♯

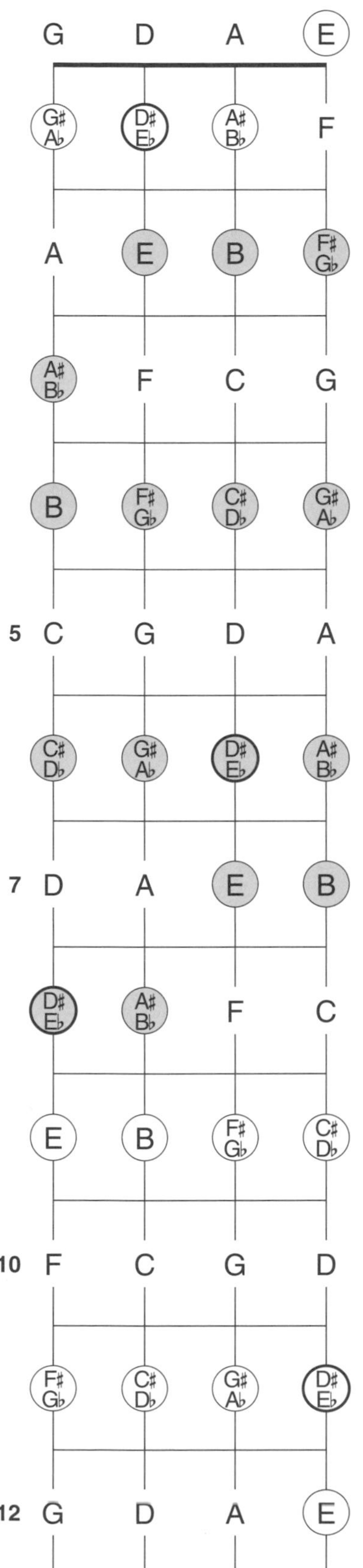

E PHRYGIAN

E–F–G–A–B–C–D

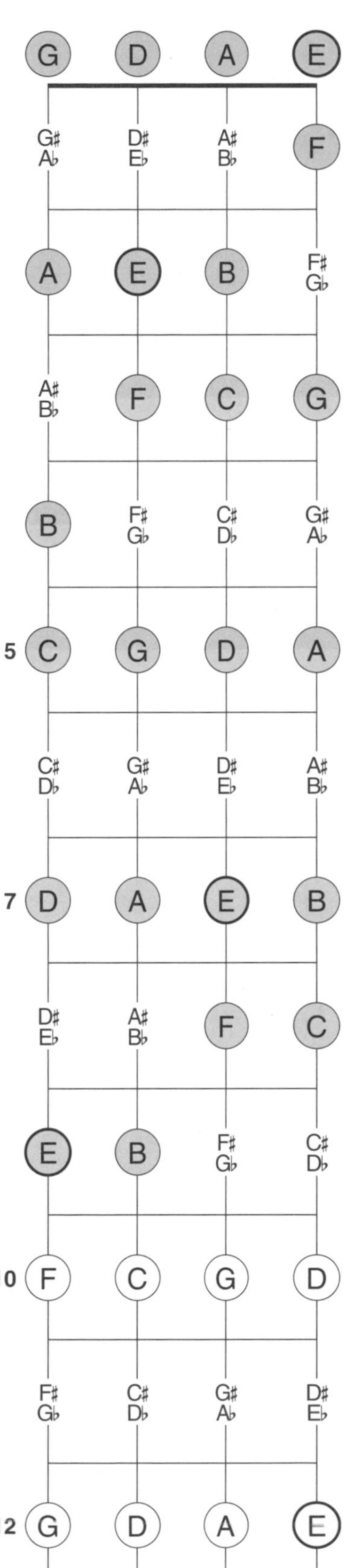

F PHRYGIAN

F–G♭–A♭–B♭–C–D♭–E♭

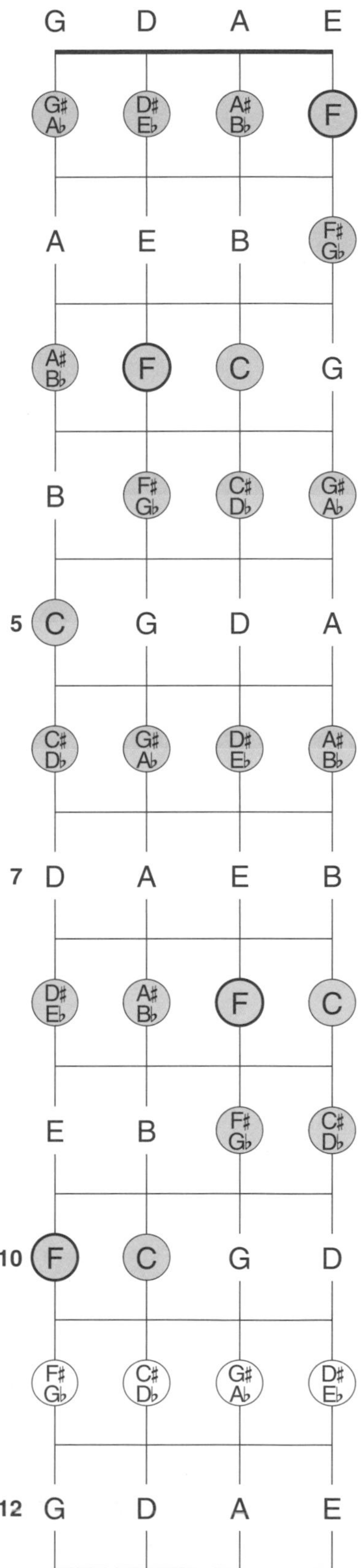

F♯ PHRYGIAN

F♯–G–A–B–C♯–D–E

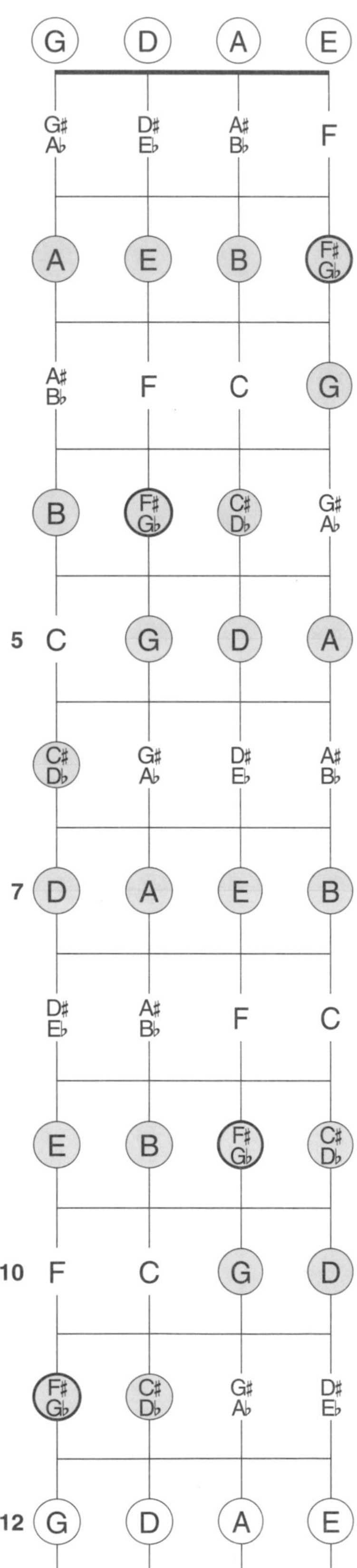

G PHRYGIAN

G–A♭–B♭–C–D–E♭–F

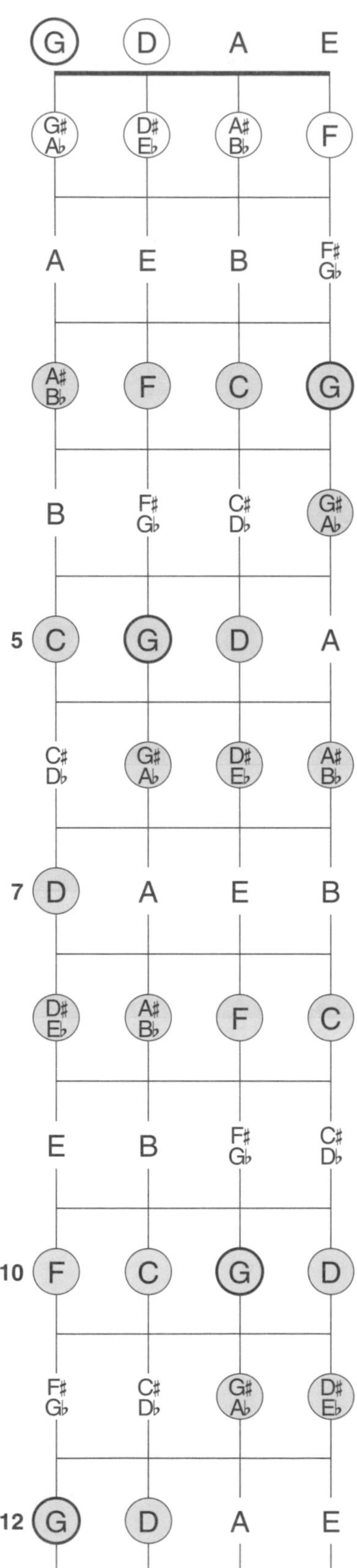

G♯ PHRYGIAN

G♯–A–B–C♯–D♯–E–F♯

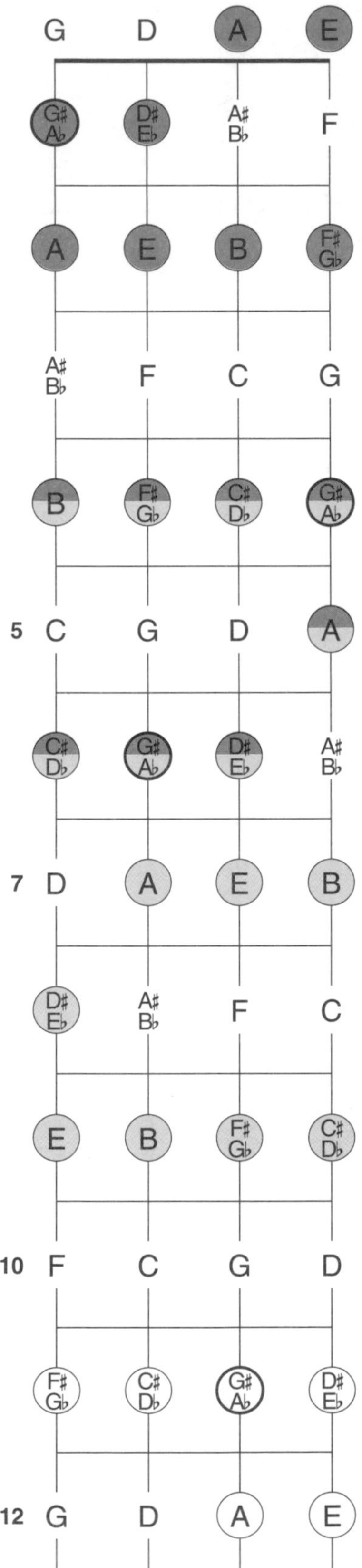

A PHRYGIAN

A–B♭–C–D–E–F–G

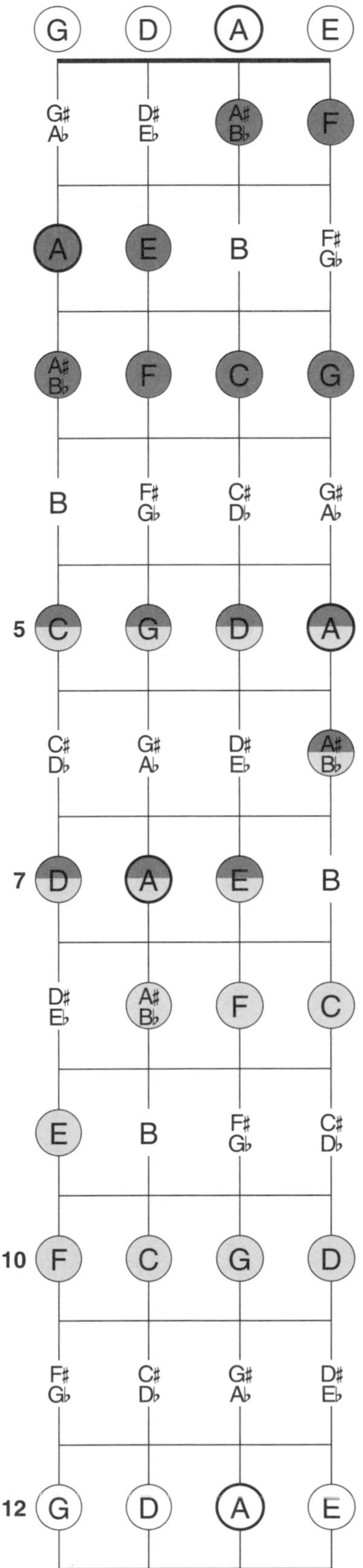

B♭ PHRYGIAN

B♭–C♭–D♭–E♭–F–G♭–A♭

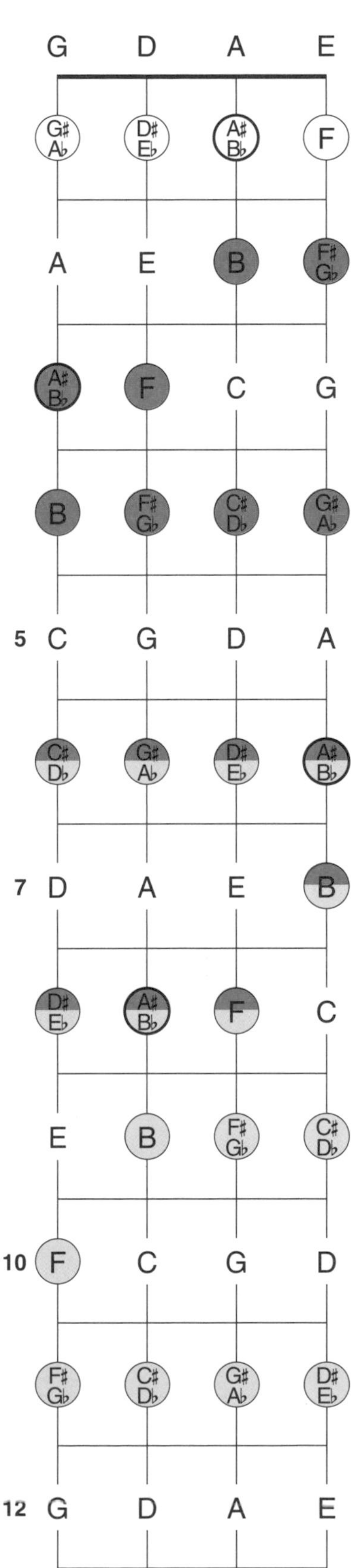

B PHRYGIAN

B–C–D–E–F♯–G–A

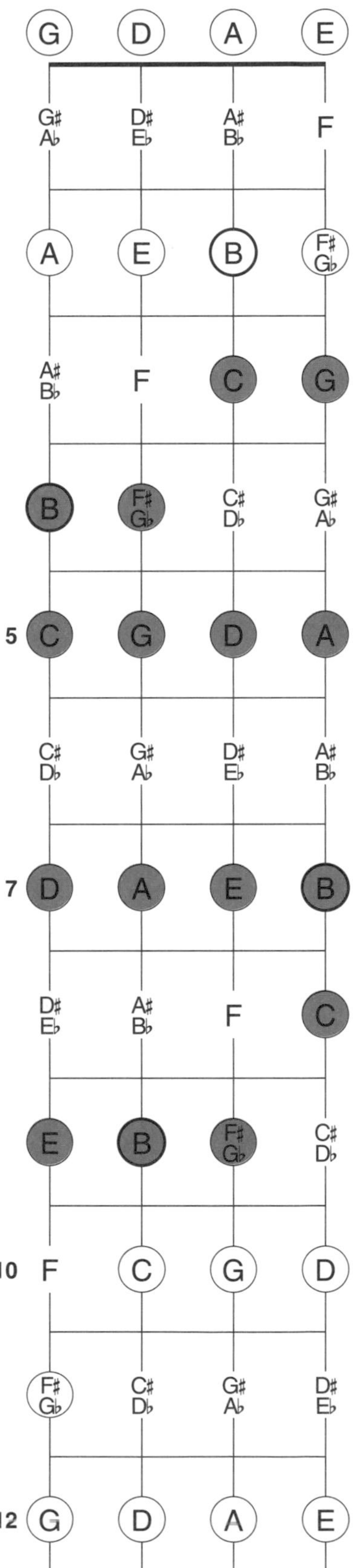

C LYDIAN

C–D–E–F♯–G–A–B

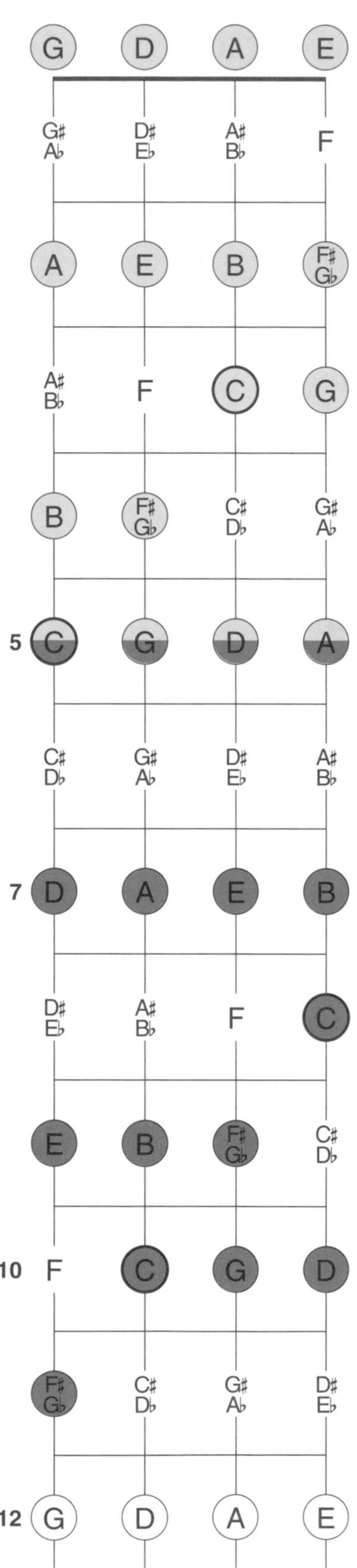

D♭ LYDIAN

D♭–E♭–F–G–A♭–B♭–C

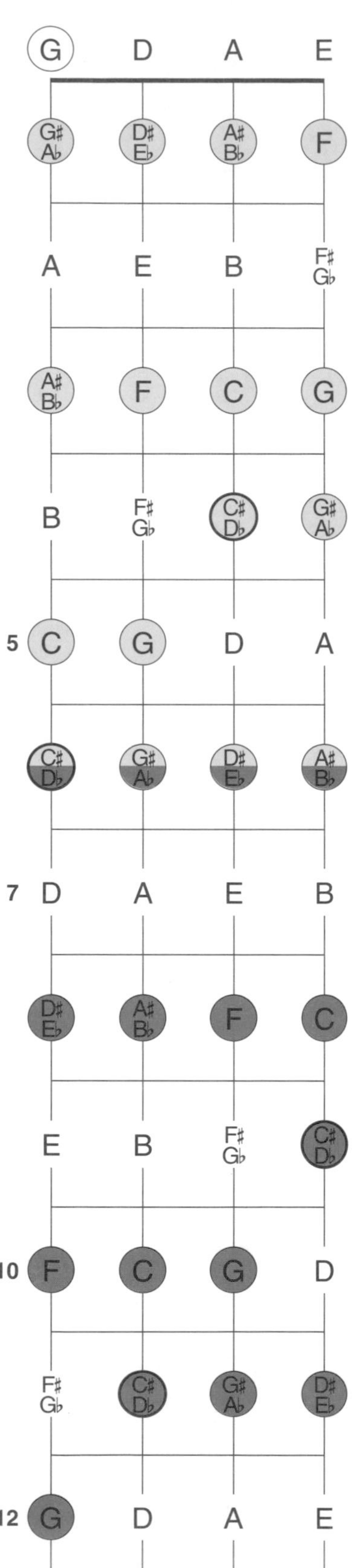

D LYDIAN

D–E–F♯–G♯–A–B–C♯

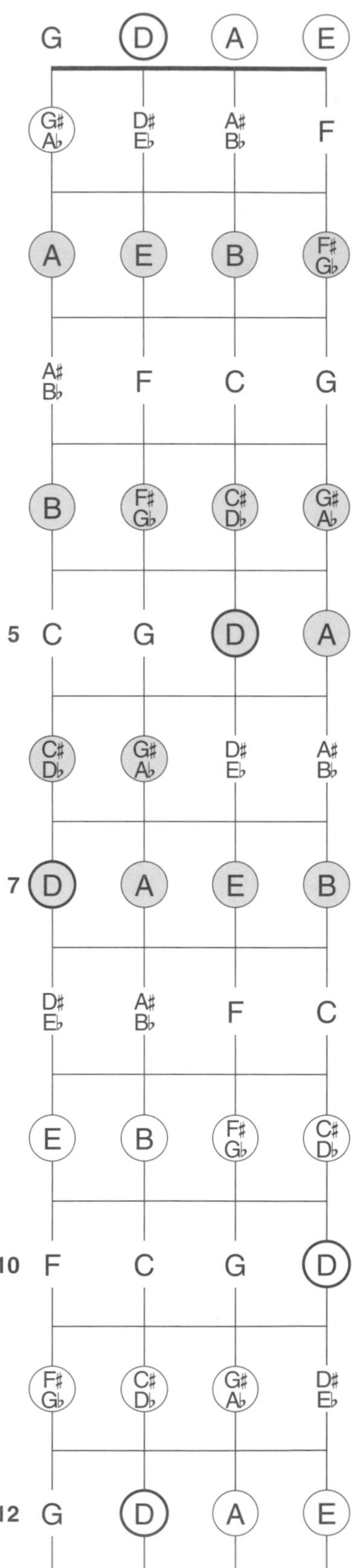

E♭ LYDIAN

E♭–F–G–A–B♭–C–D

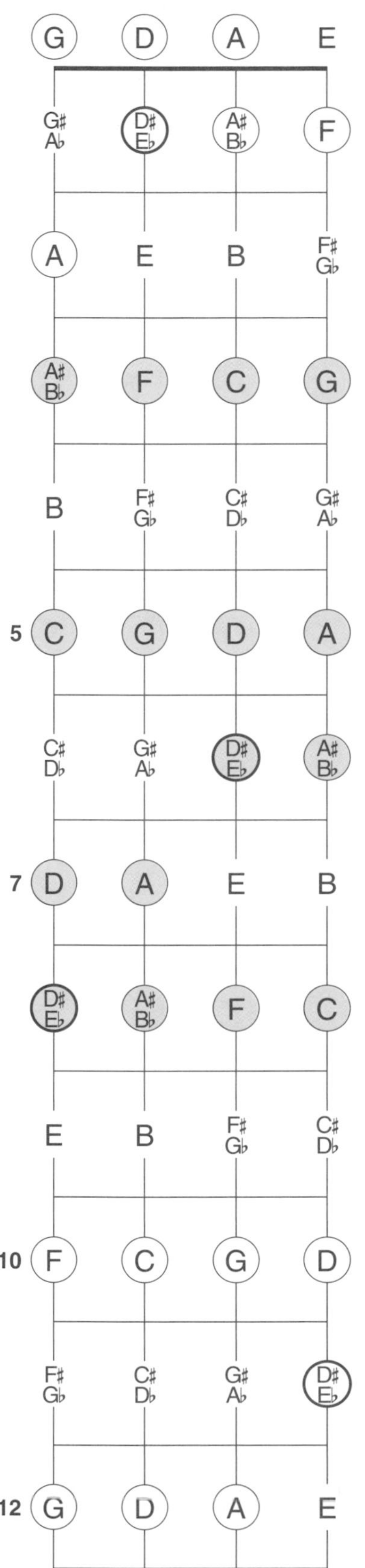

E LYDIAN

E–F♯–G♯–A♯–B–C♯–D♯

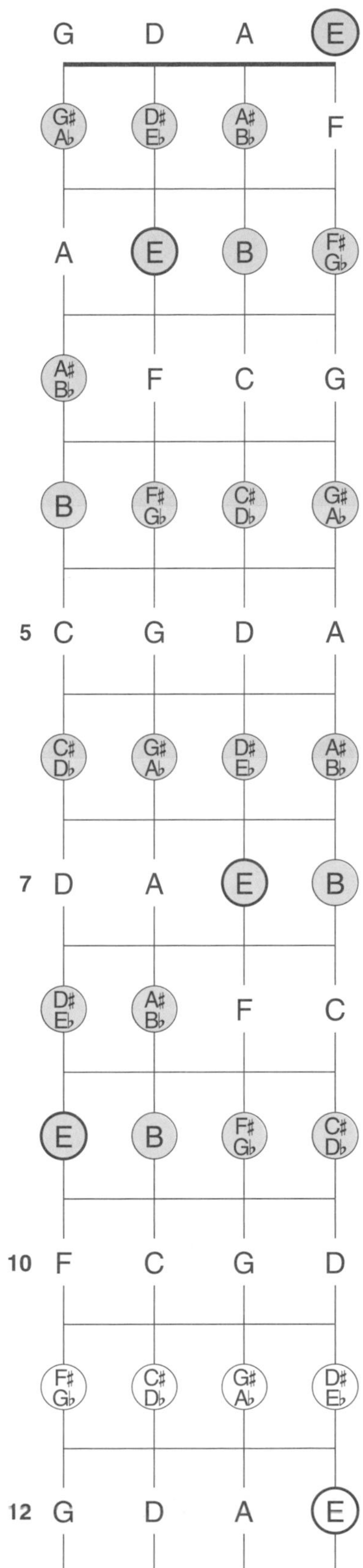

F LYDIAN

F–G–A–B–C–D–E

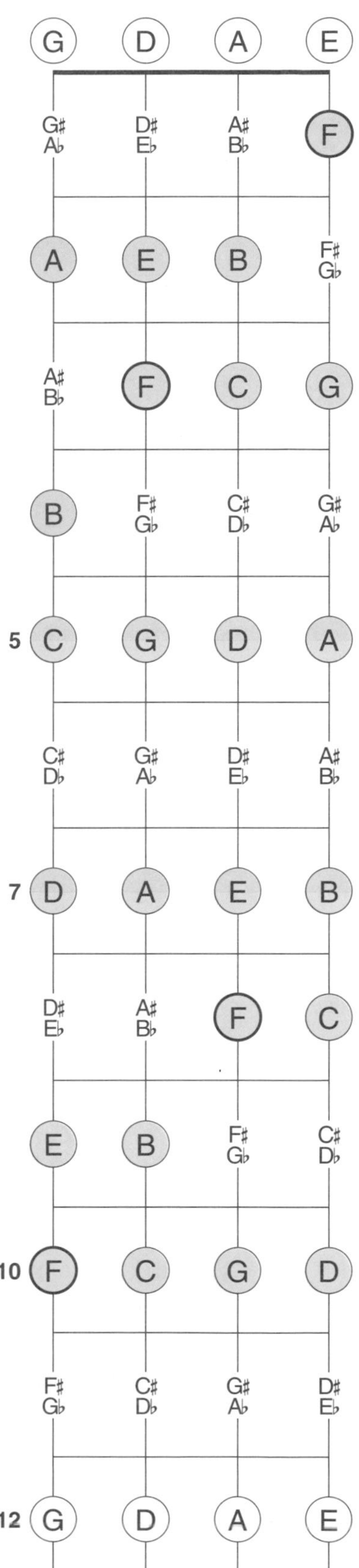

F♯/G♭ LYDIAN

F♯–G♯–A♯–B♯–C♯–D♯–E♯
G♭–A♭–B♭–C–D♭–E♭–F

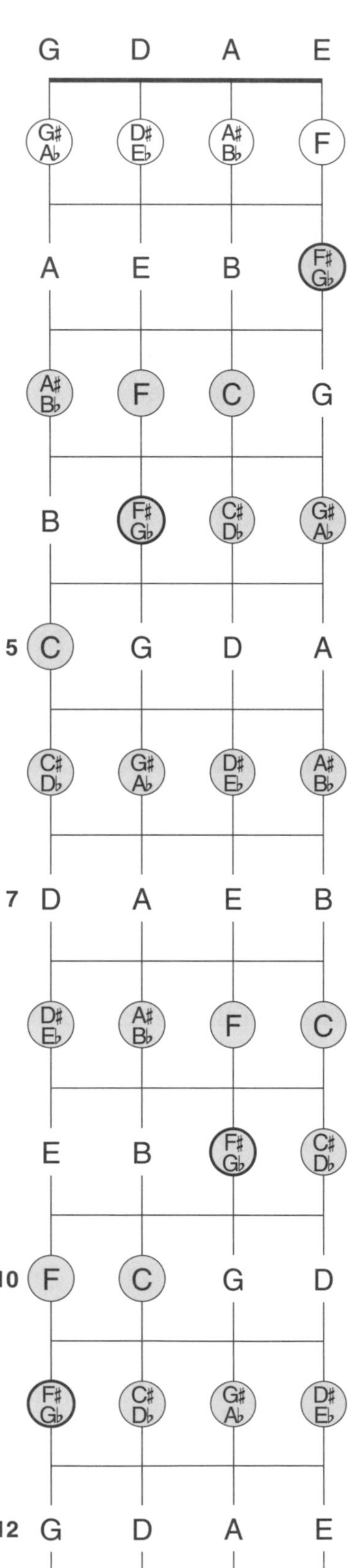

G LYDIAN

G–A–B–C♯–D–E–F♯

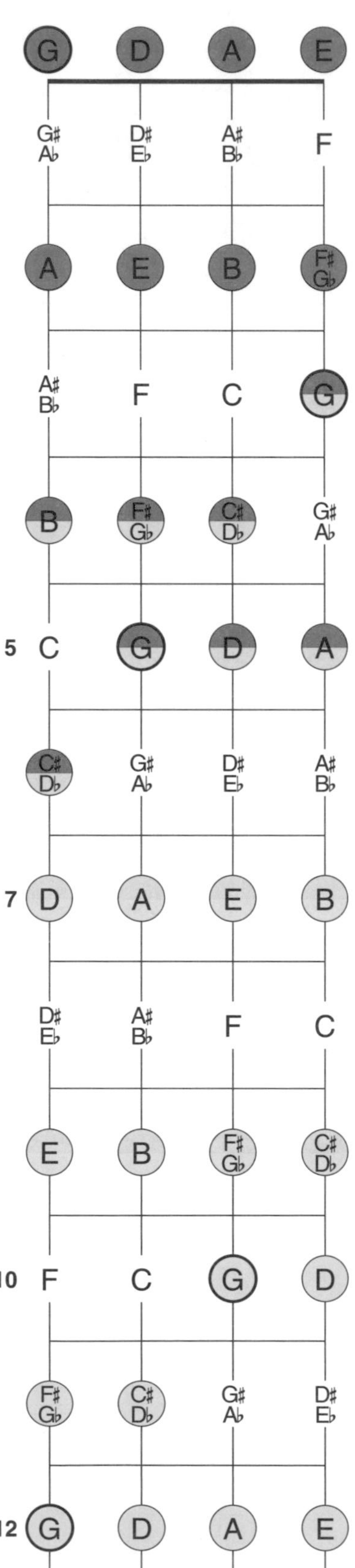

A♭ LYDIAN

A♭–B♭–C–D–E♭–F–G

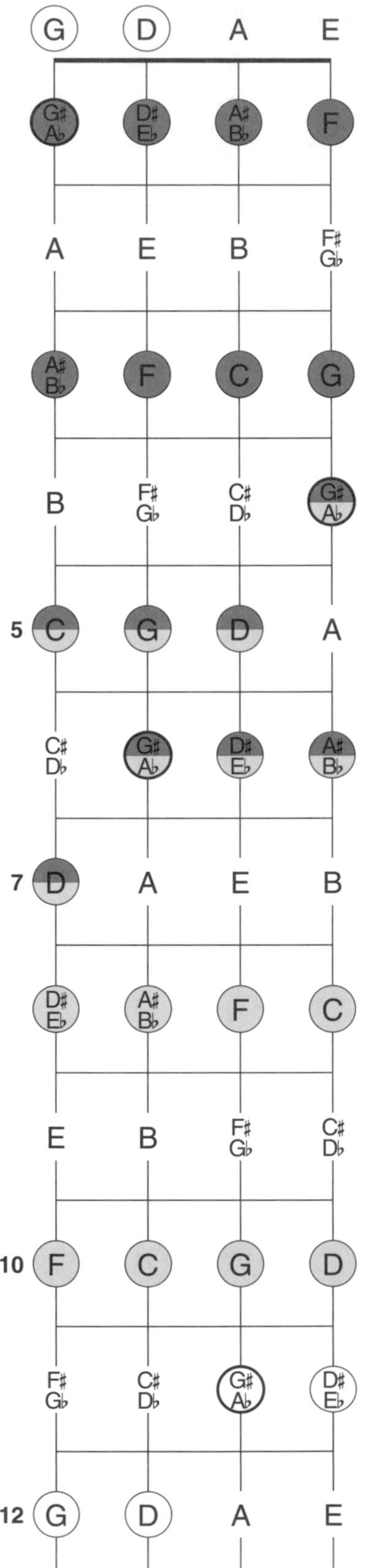

A LYDIAN

A–B–C♯–D♯–E–F♯–G♯

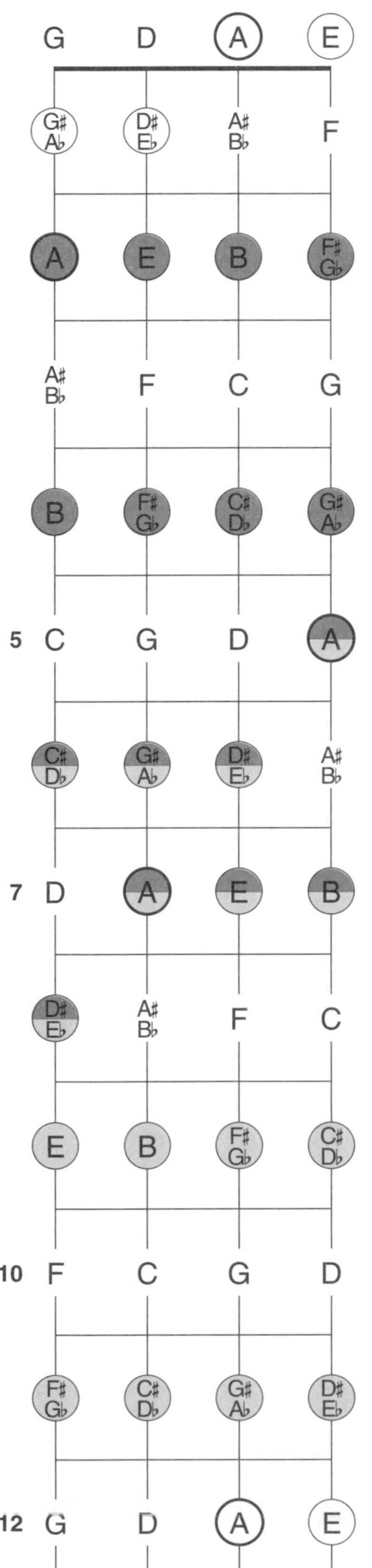

B♭ LYDIAN

B♭–C–D–E–F–G–A

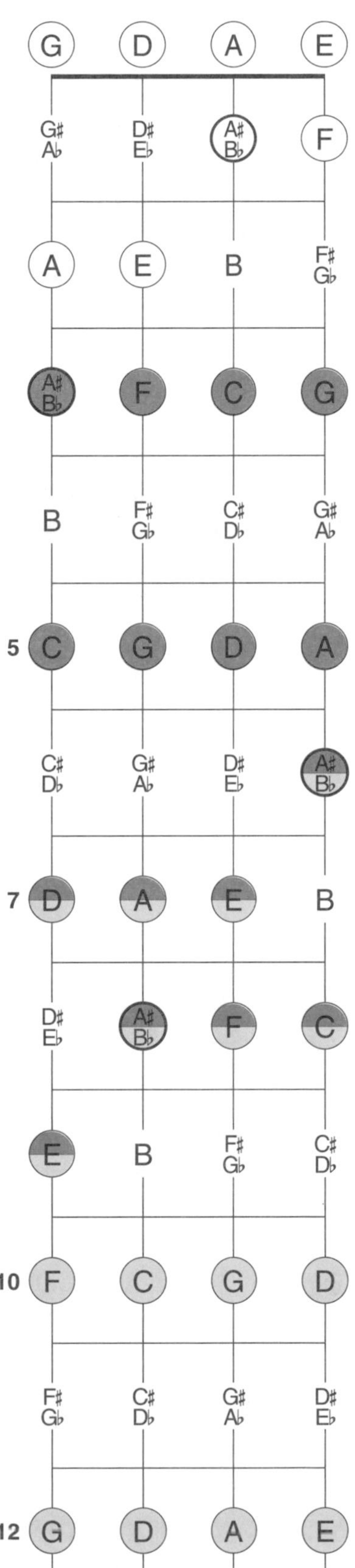

B LYDIAN

B–C♯–D♯–E♯–F♯–G♯–A♯

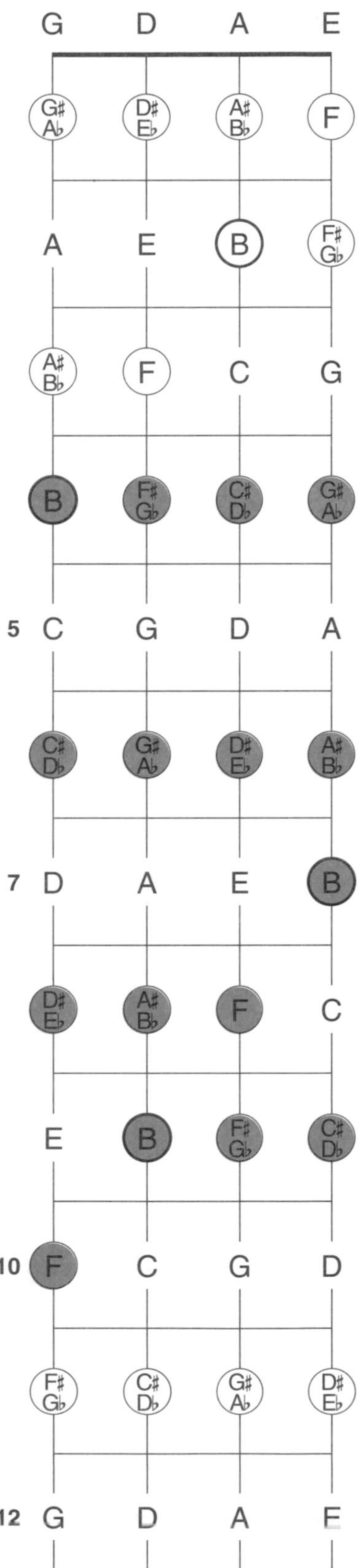

C MIXOLYDIAN

C–D–E–F–G–A–B♭

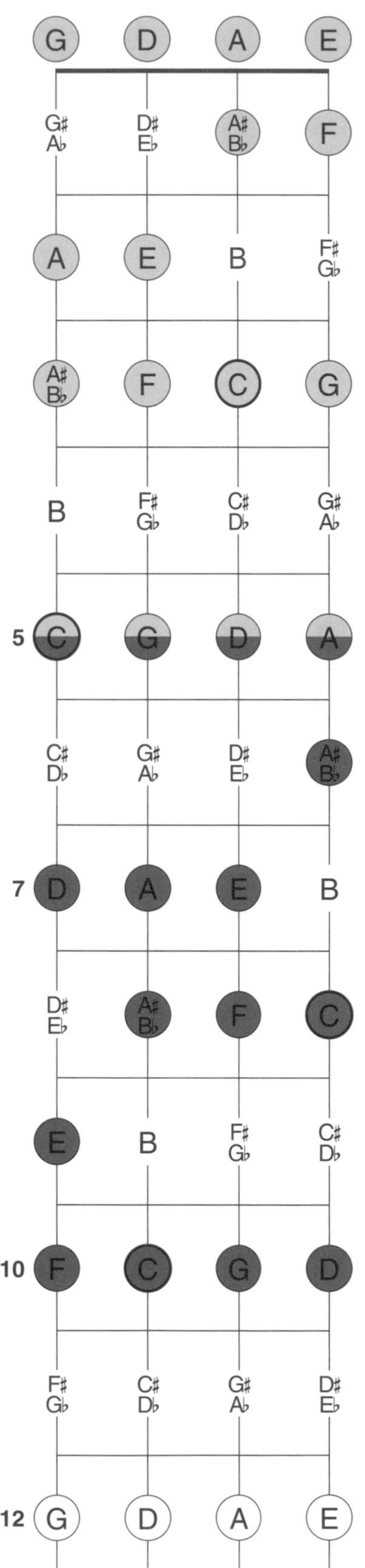

C♯/D♭ MIXOLYDIAN

C♯–D♯–E♯–F♯–G♯–A♯–B
D♭–E♭–F–G♭–A♭–B♭–C♭

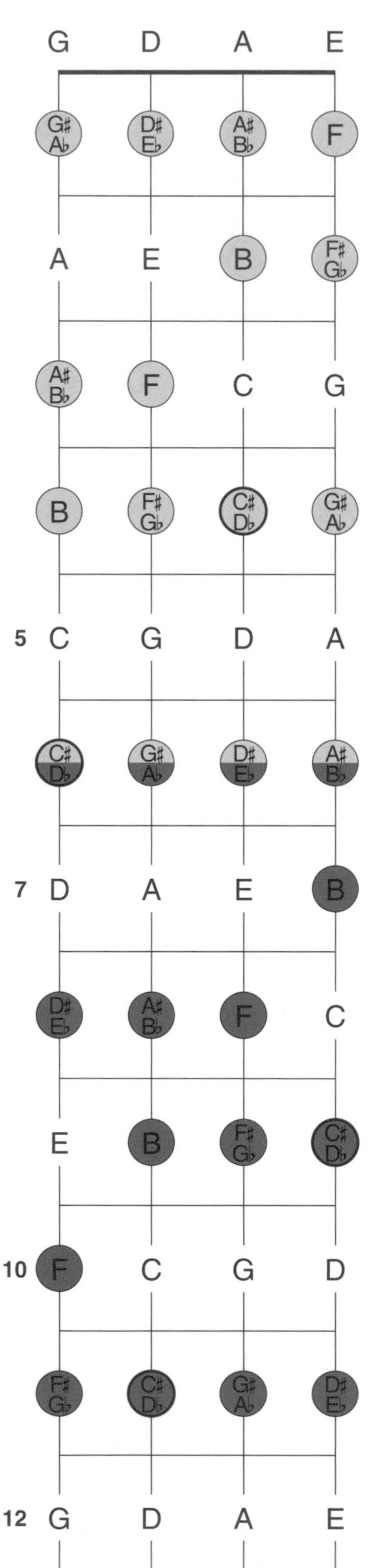

D MIXOLYDIAN

D–E–F♯–G–A–B–C

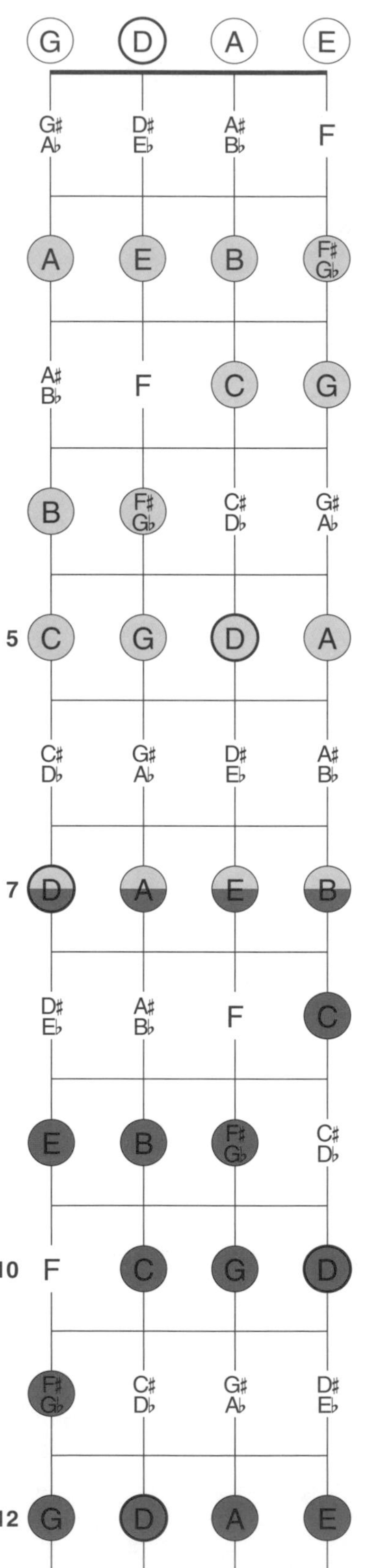

E♭ MIXOLYDIAN

E♭–F–G–A♭–B♭–C–D♭

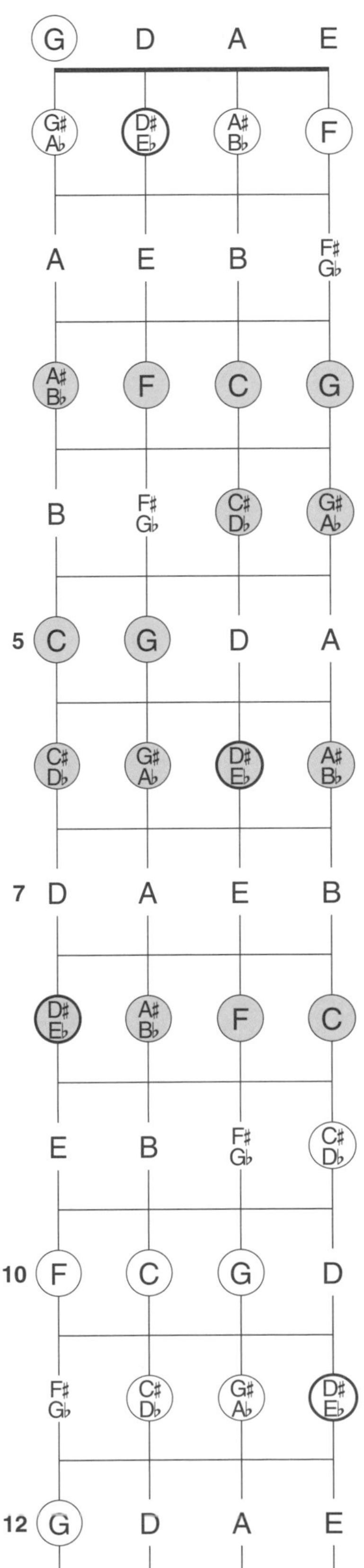

E MIXOLYDIAN

E–F♯–G♯–A–B–C♯–D

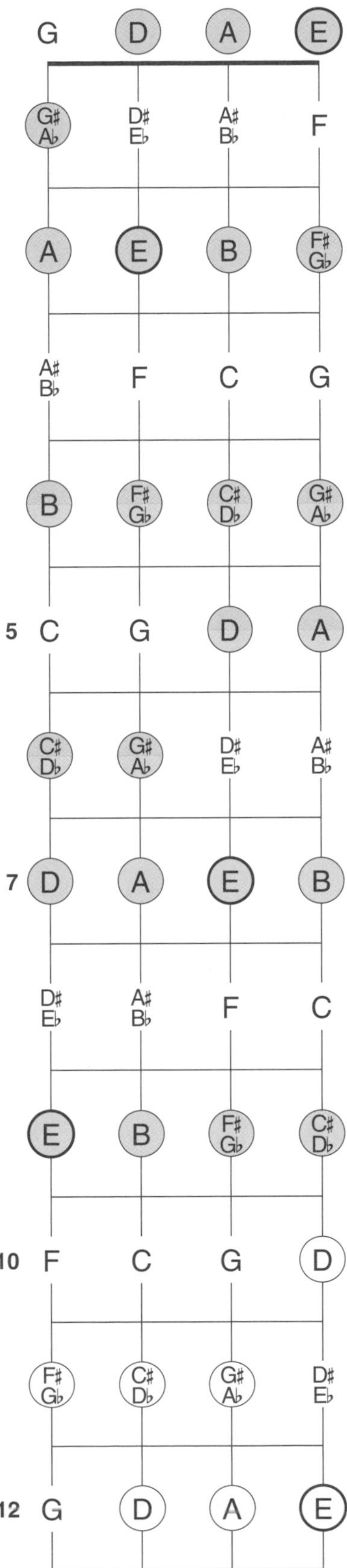

F MIXOLYDIAN

F–G–A–B♭–C–D–E♭

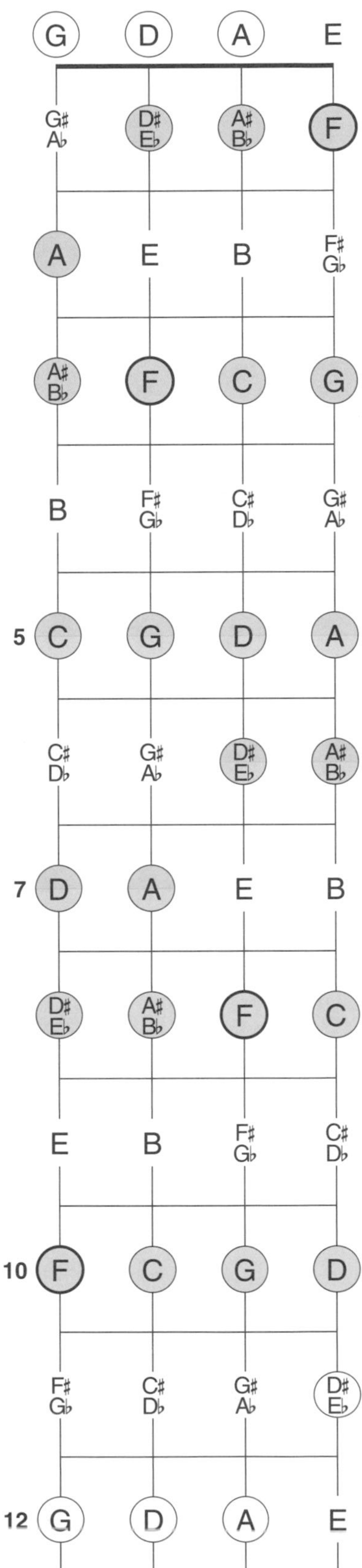

F♯/G♭ MIXOLYDIAN

F♯–G♯–A♯–B–C♯–D♯–E
G♭–A♭–B♭–C♭–D♭–E♭–F♭

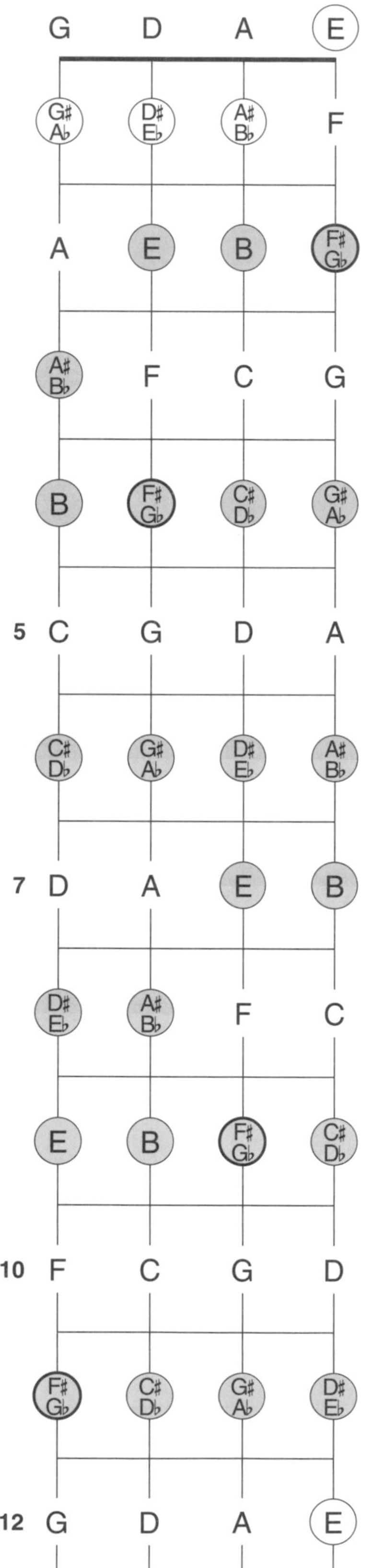

G MIXOLYDIAN

G–A–B–C–D–E–F

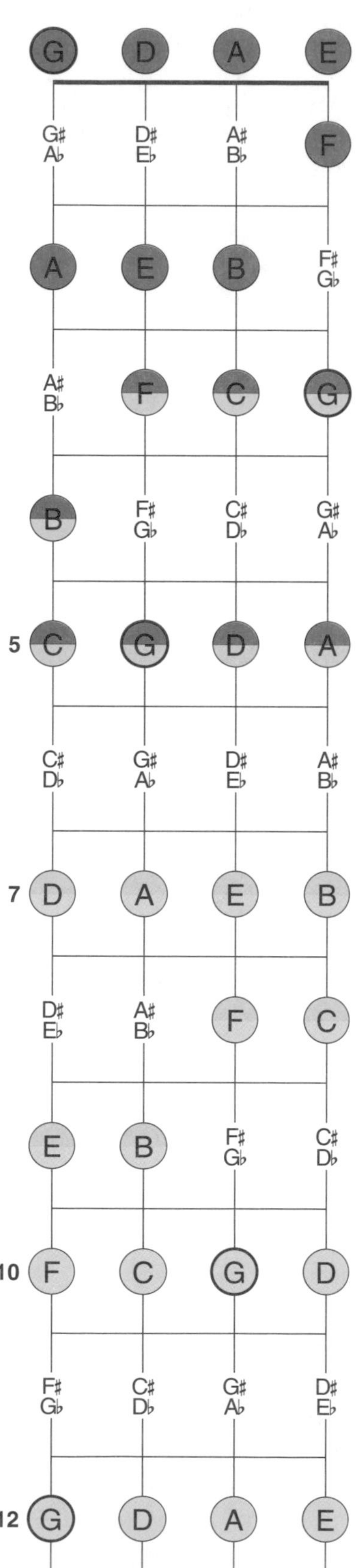

A♭ MIXOLYDIAN

A♭–B♭–C–D♭–E♭–F–G♭

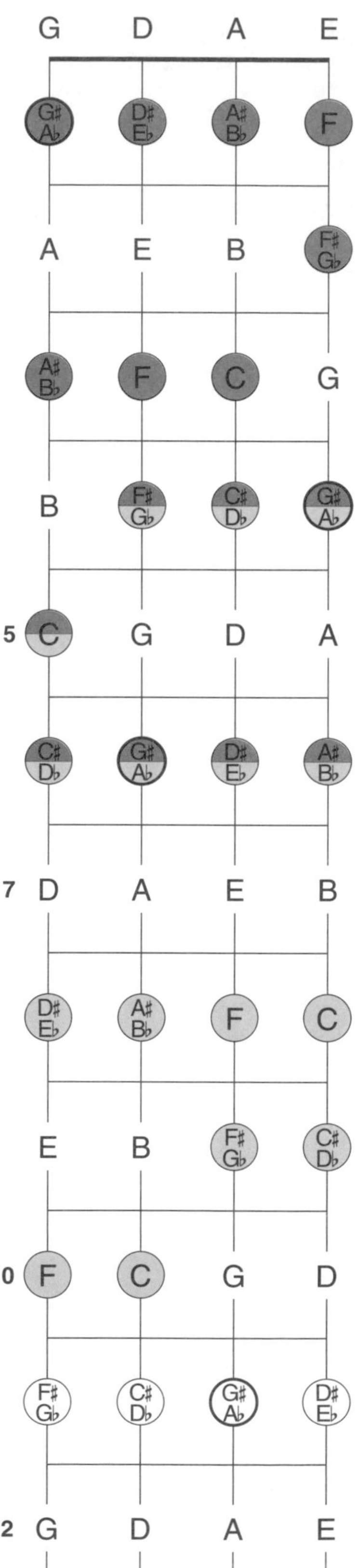

A MIXOLYDIAN

A–B–C♯–D–E–F♯–G

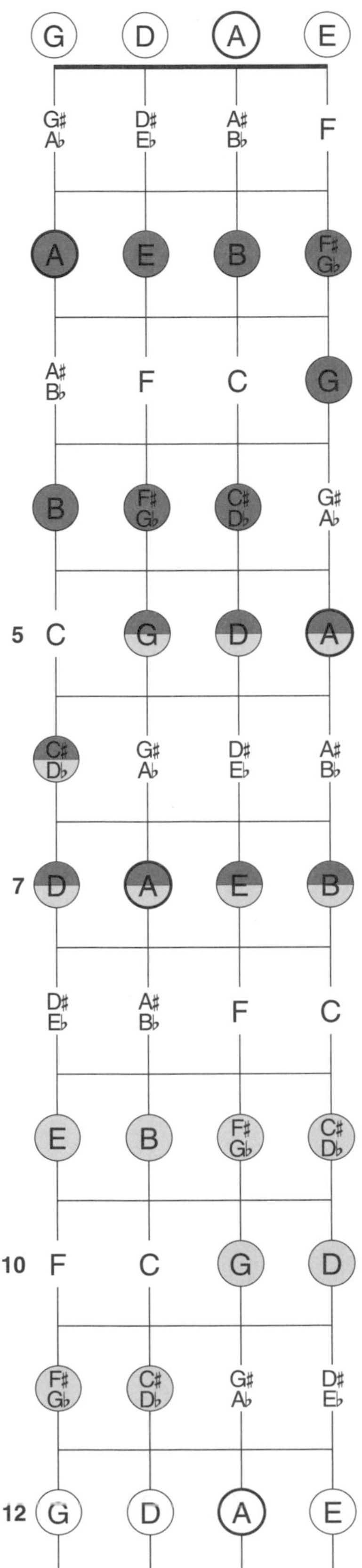

B♭ MIXOLYDIAN

B♭–C–D–E♭–F–G–A♭

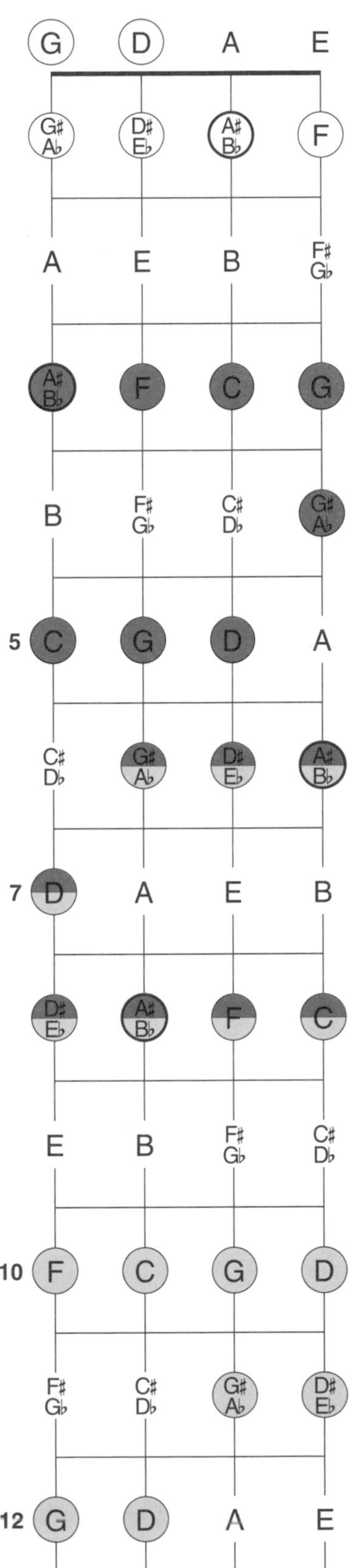

B MIXOLYDIAN

B–C♯–D♯–E–F♯–G♯–A

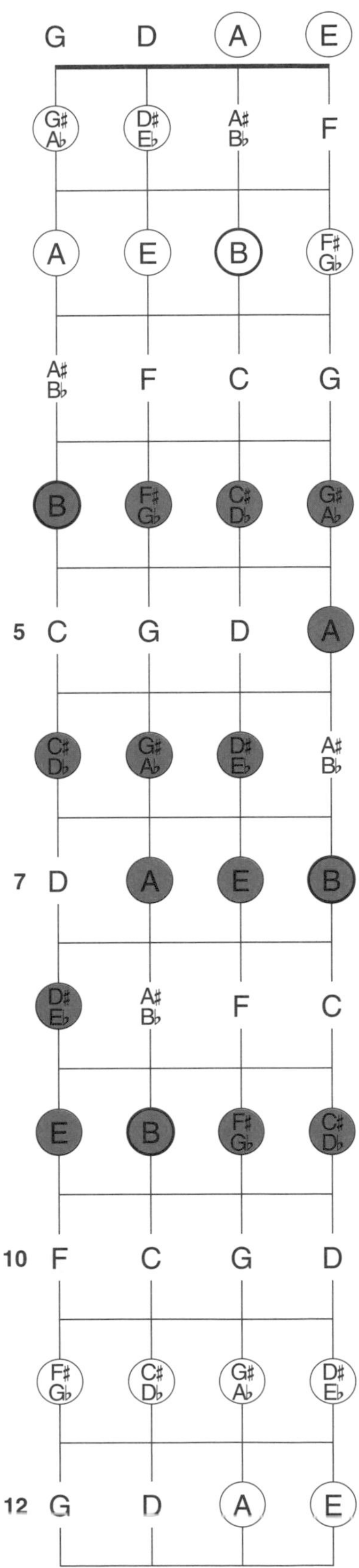

C AEOLIAN

C–D–E♭–F–G–A♭–B♭

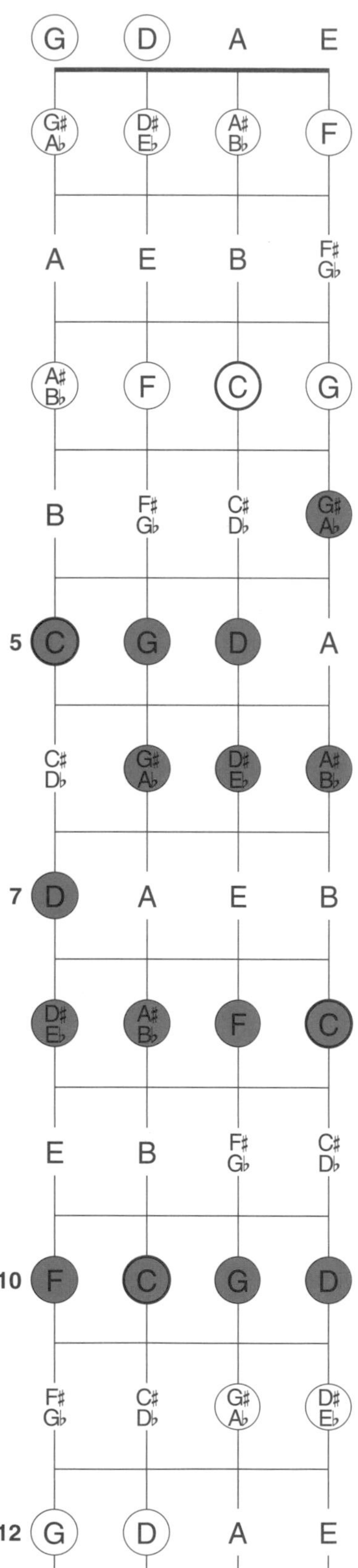

C♯ AEOLIAN

C♯–D♯–E–F♯–G♯–A–B

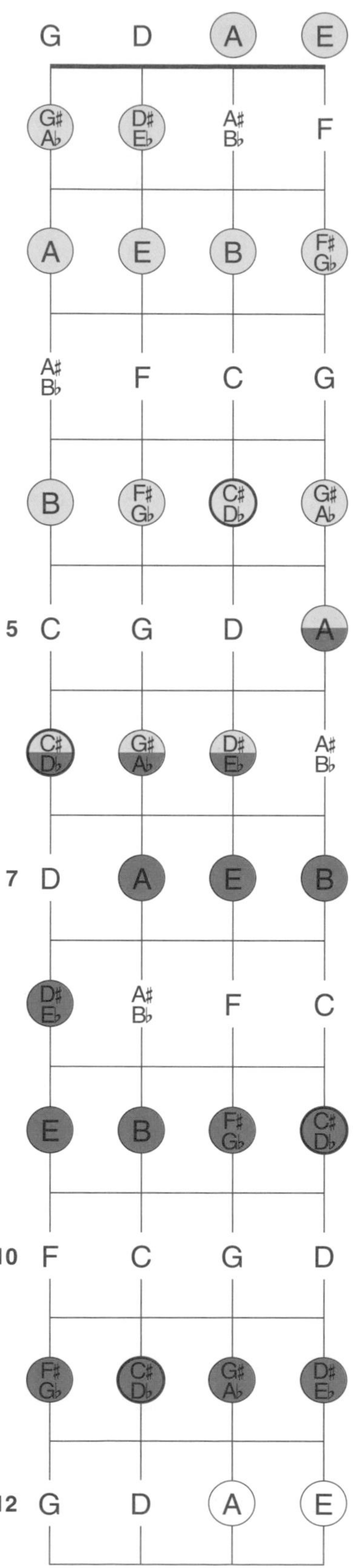

D AEOLIAN

D–E–F–G–A–B♭–C

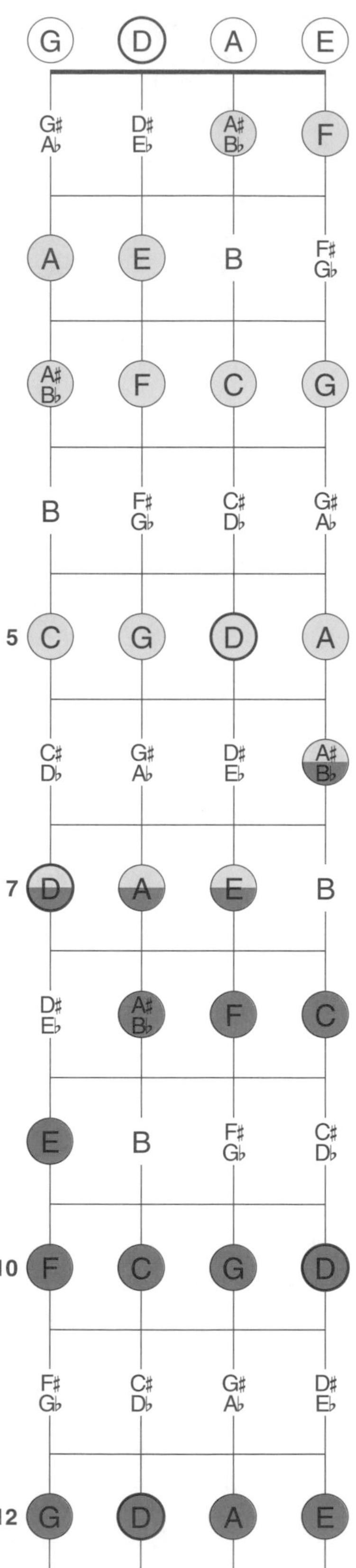

D♯/E♭ AEOLIAN

D♯–E♯–F♯–G♯–A♯–B–C♯
E♭–F–G♭–A♭–B♭–C♭–D♭

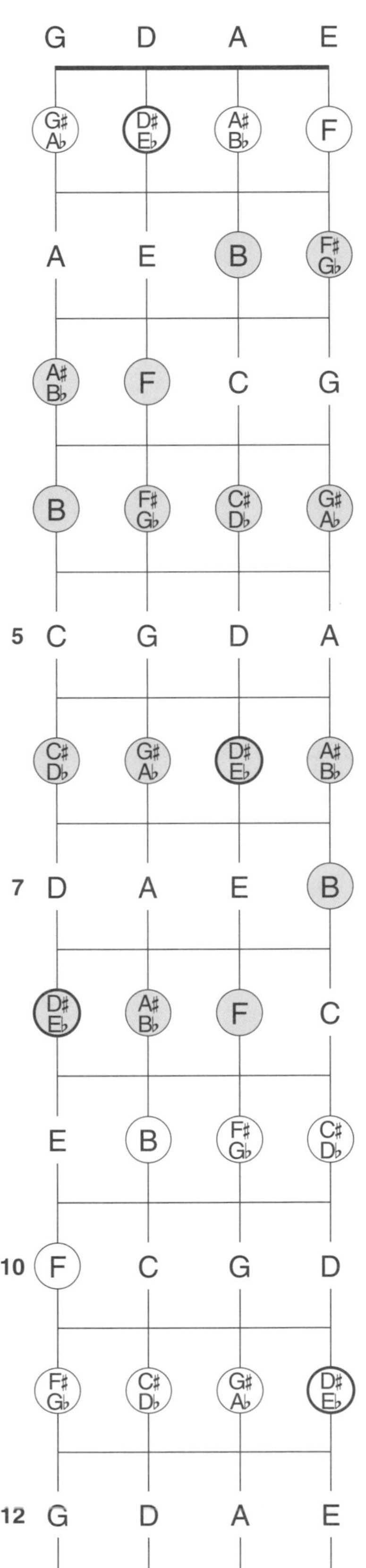

E AEOLIAN

E–F♯–G–A–B–C–D

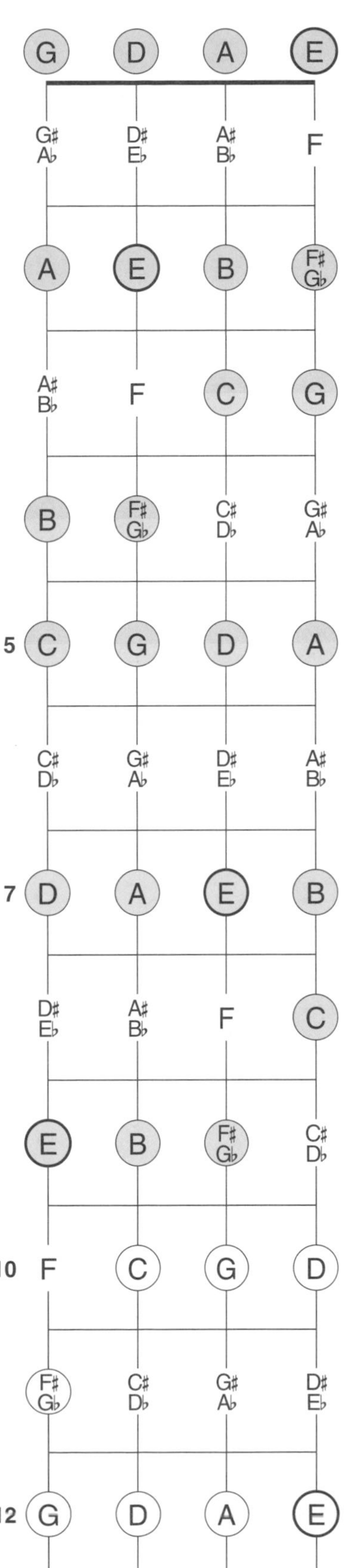

F AEOLIAN

F–G–A♭–B♭–C–D♭–E♭

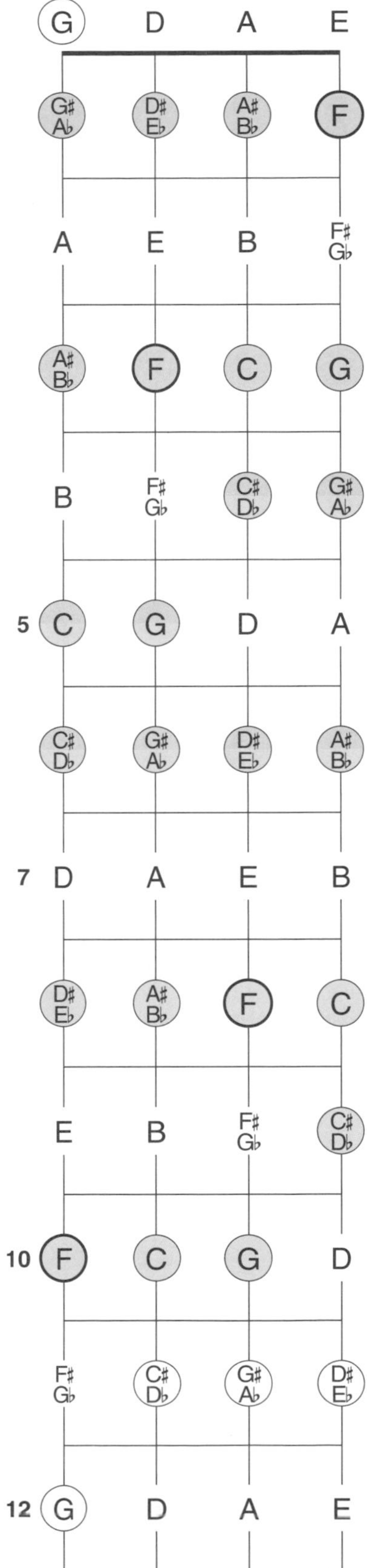

F♯ AEOLIAN

F♯–G♯–A–B–C♯–D–E

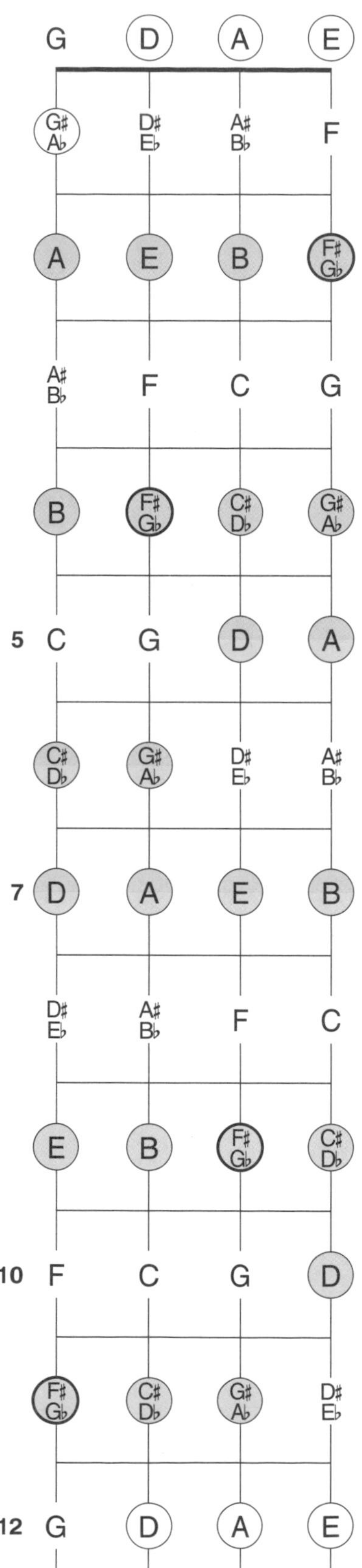

G AEOLIAN

G–A–B♭–C–D–E♭–F

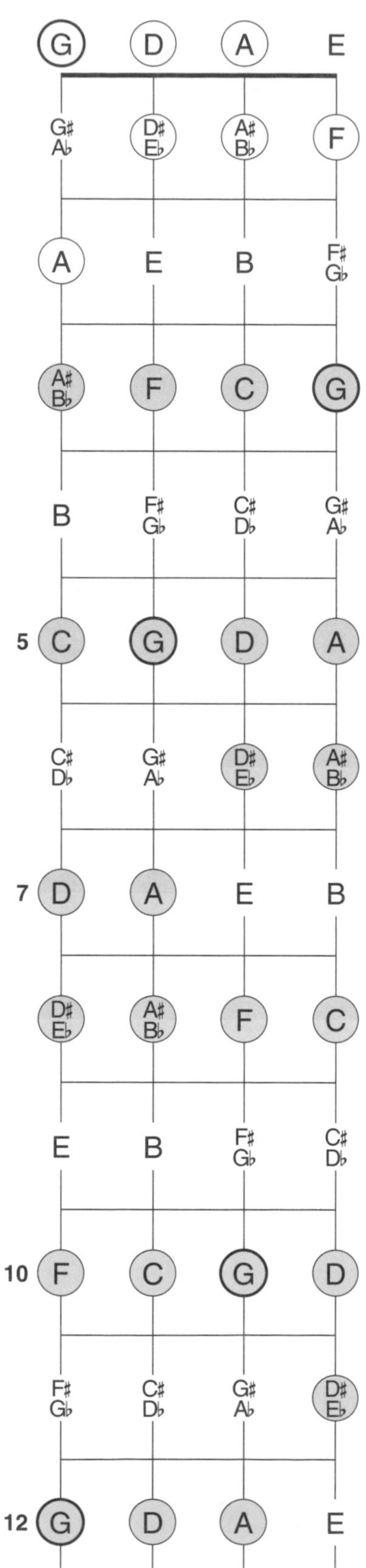

G♯/A♭ AEOLIAN

G♯–A♯–B–C♯–D♯–E–F♯
A♭–B♭–C♭–D♭–E♭–F♭–G♭

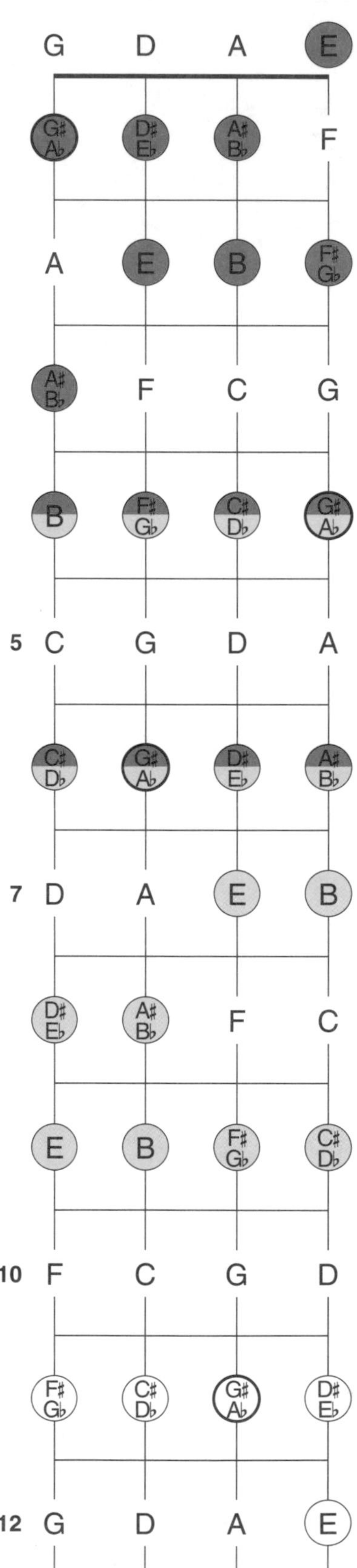

A AEOLIAN

A–B–C–D–E–F–G

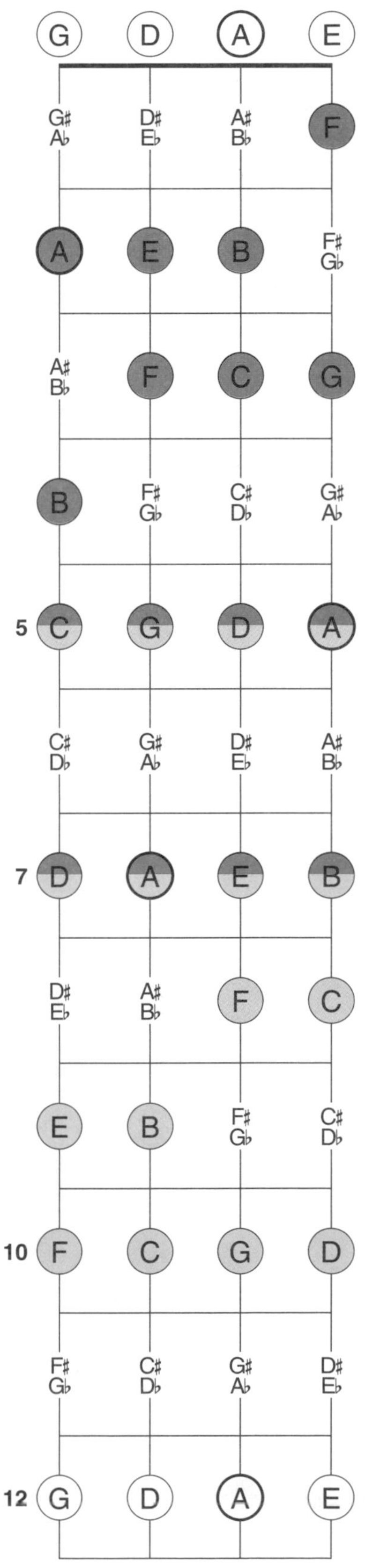

B♭ AEOLIAN

B♭–C–D♭–E♭–F–G♭–A♭

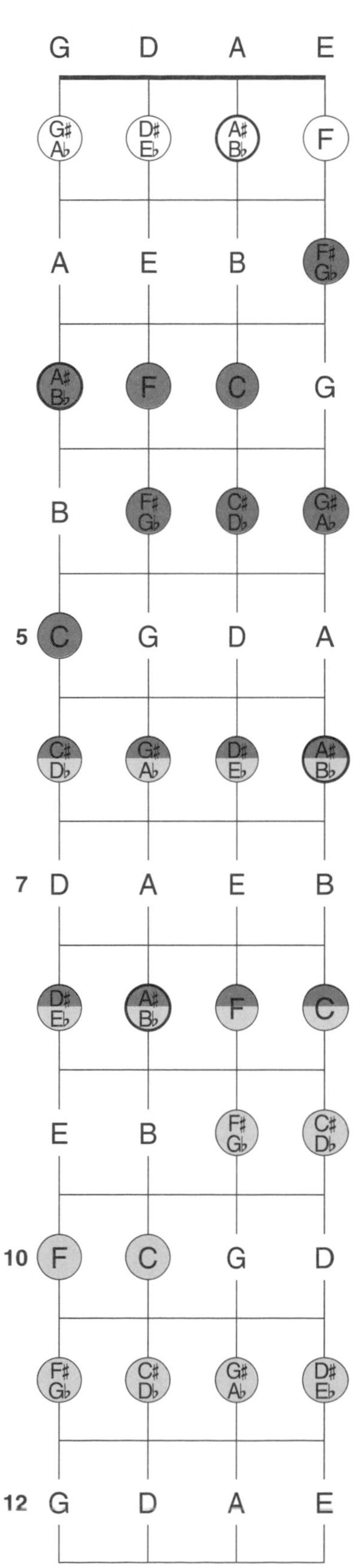

B AEOLIAN

B–C♯–D–E–F♯–G–A

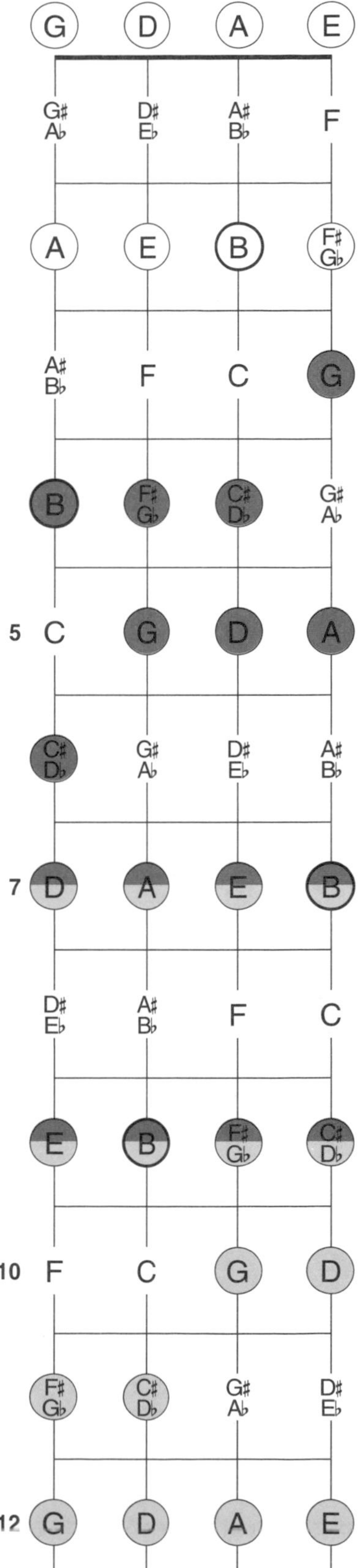

C LOCRIAN

C–D♭–E♭–F–G♭–A♭–B♭

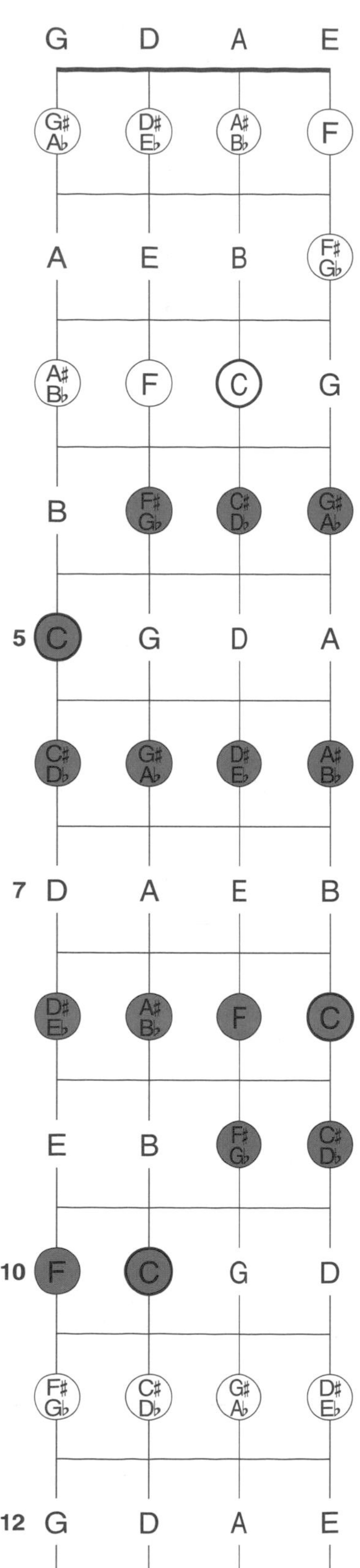

C♯ LOCRIAN

C♯–D–E–F♯–G–A–B

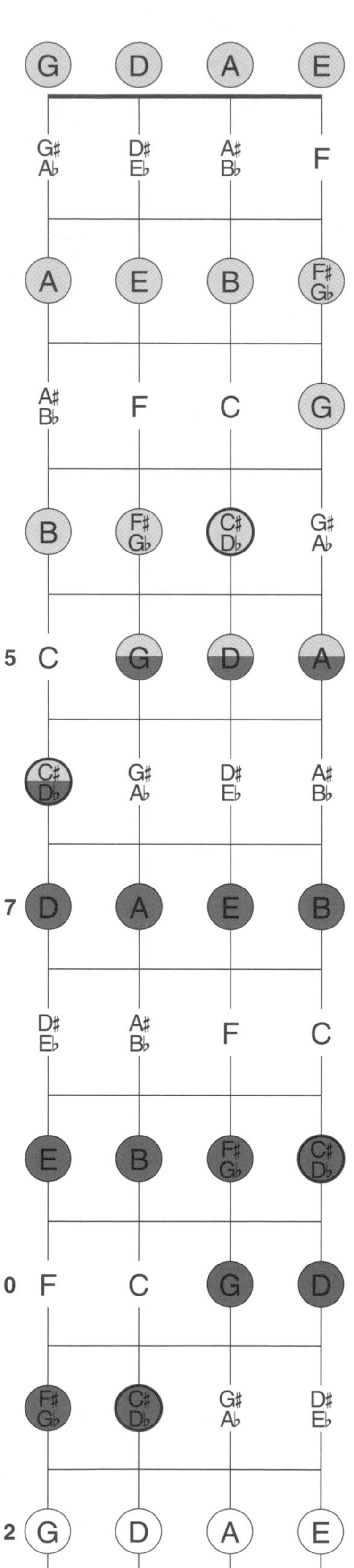

D LOCRIAN

D–E♭–F–G–A♭–B♭–C

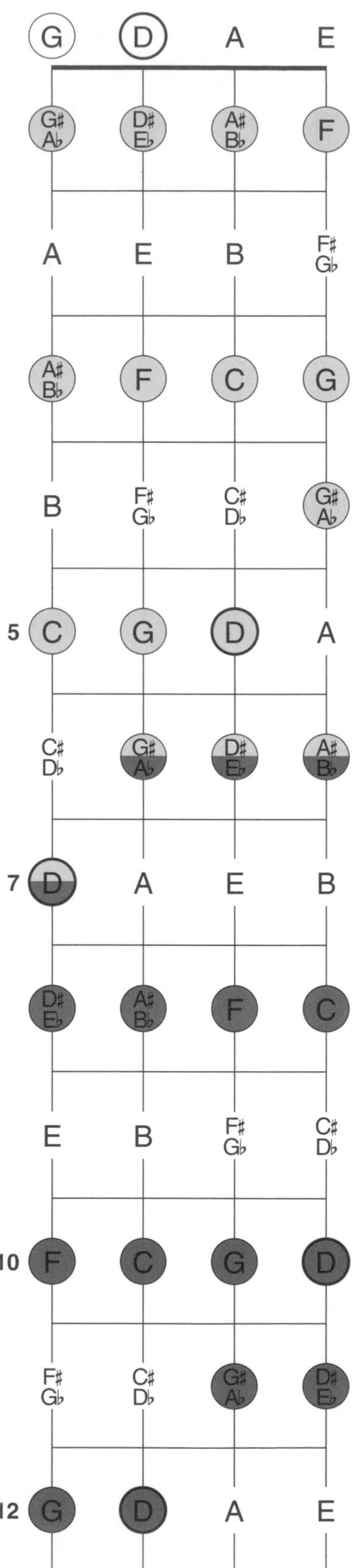

D♯ LOCRIAN

D♯–E–F♯–G♯–A–B–C♯

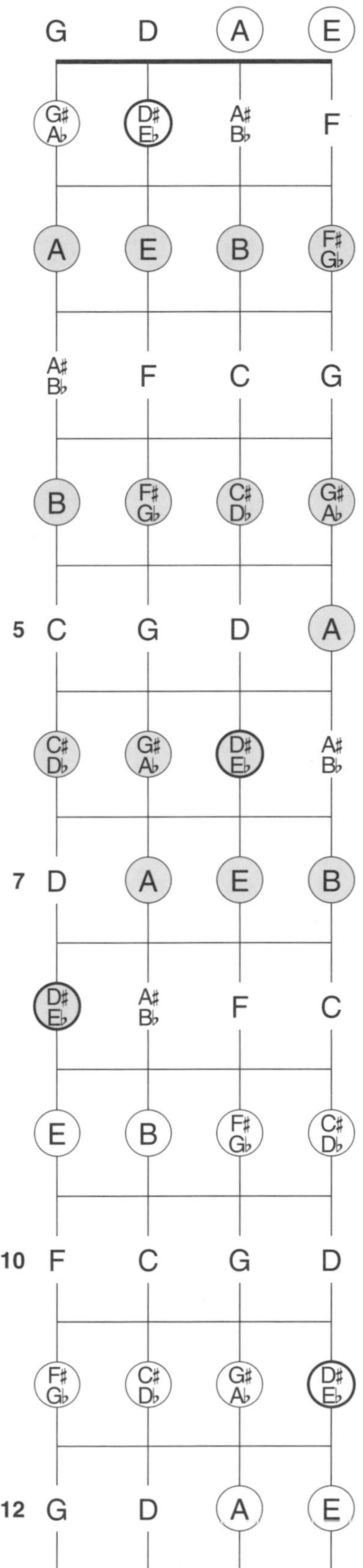

E LOCRIAN

E–F–G–A–B♭–C–D

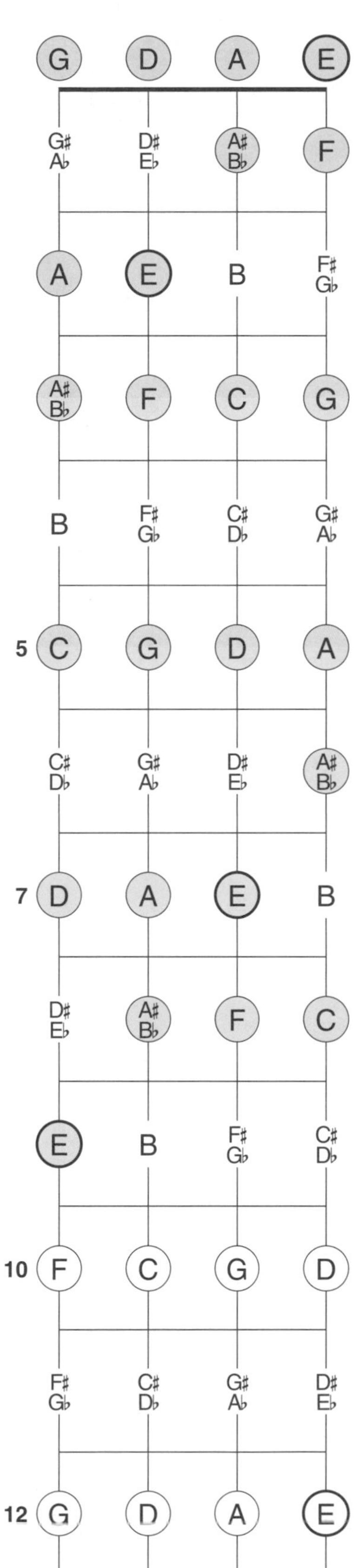

F LOCRIAN

F–G♭–A♭–B♭–C♭–D♭–E♭

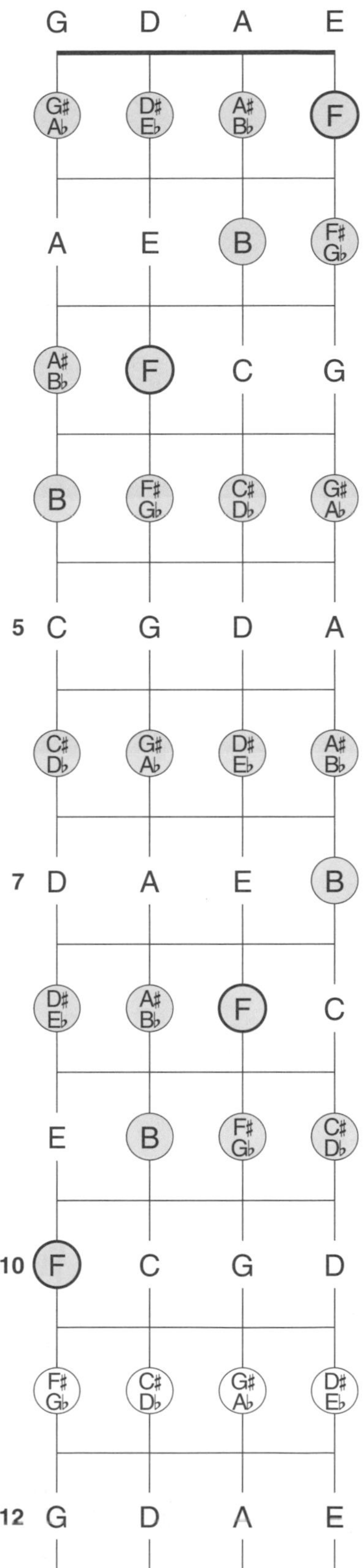

F♯ LOCRIAN

F♯–G–A–B–C–D–E

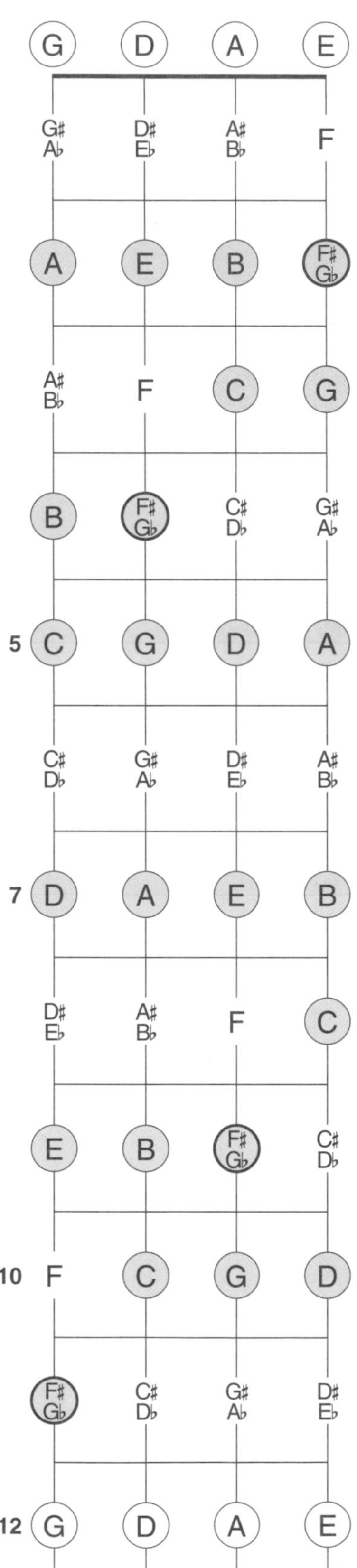

G LOCRIAN

G–A♭–B♭–C–D♭–E♭–F

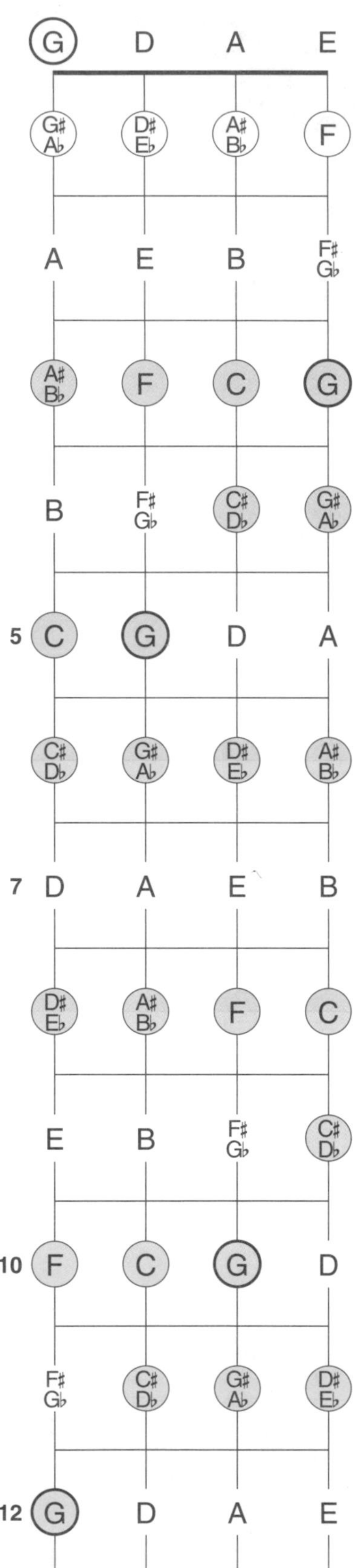

G♯ LOCRIAN

G♯–A–B–C♯–D–E–F♯

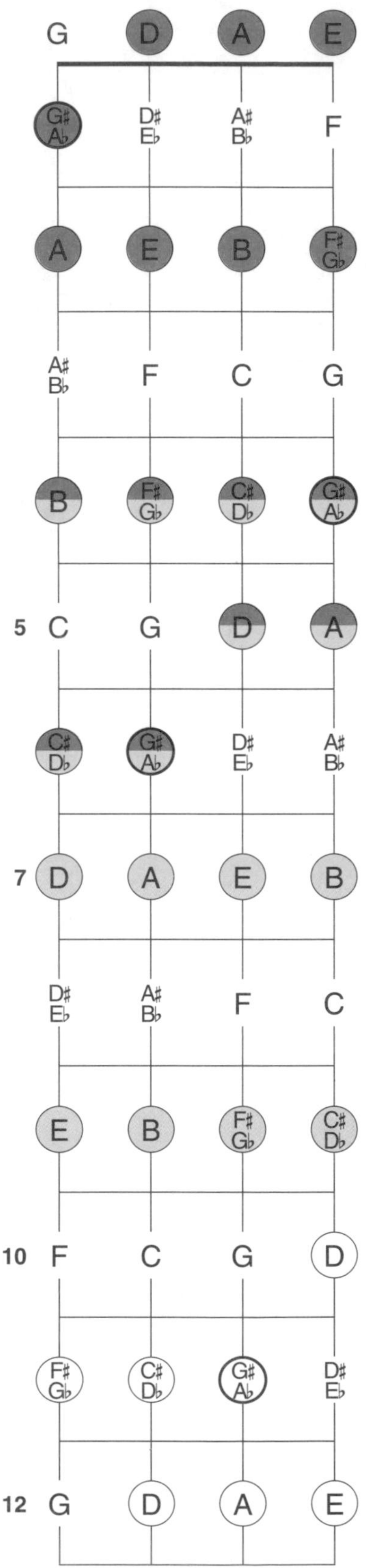

A LOCRIAN

A–B♭–C–D–E♭–F–G

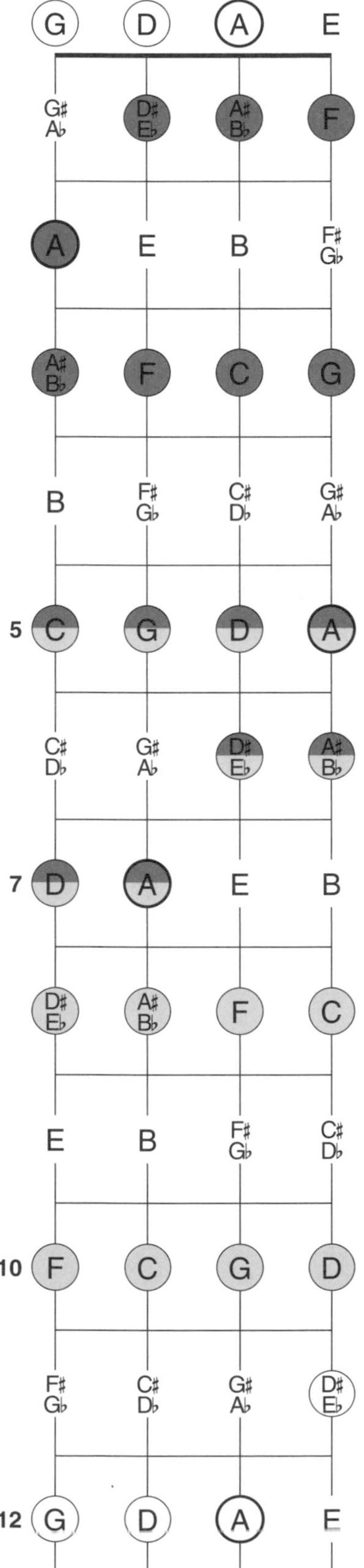

A♯ LOCRIAN

A♯–B–C♯–D♯–E–F♯–G♯

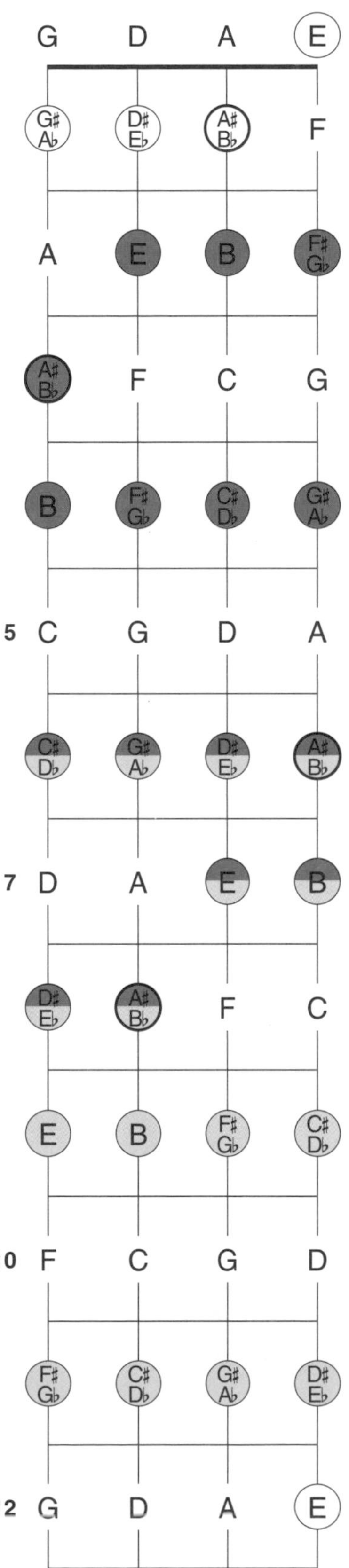

B LOCRIAN

B–C–D–E–F–G–A

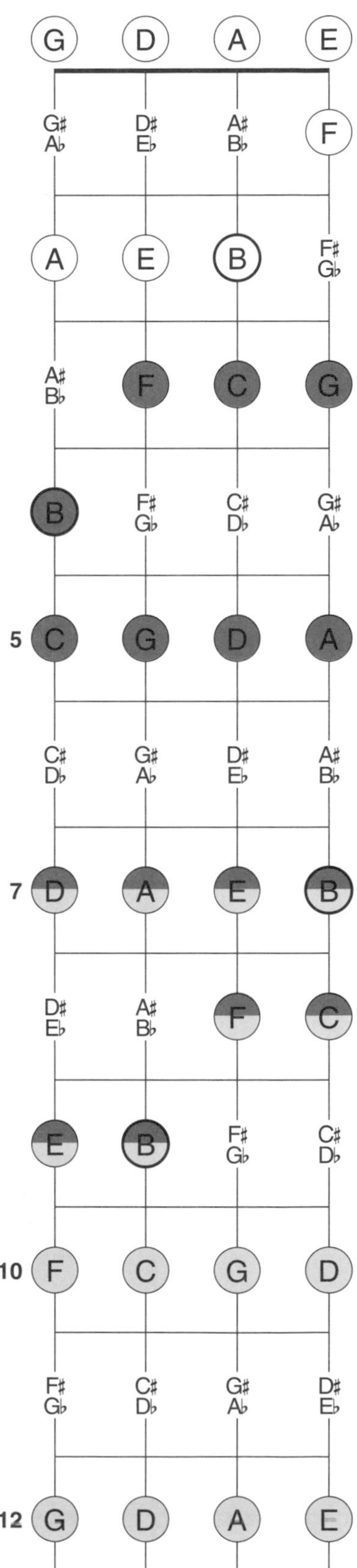

SCALES

PENTATONIC AND BLUES SCALES

C MAJOR PENTATONIC

C–D–E–G–A

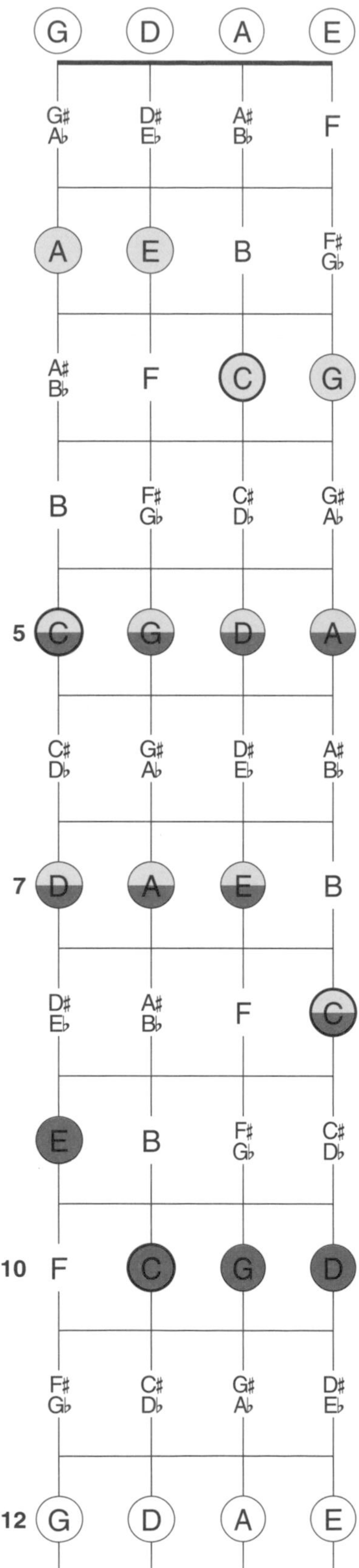

D♭ MAJOR PENTATONIC

D♭–E♭–F–A♭–B♭

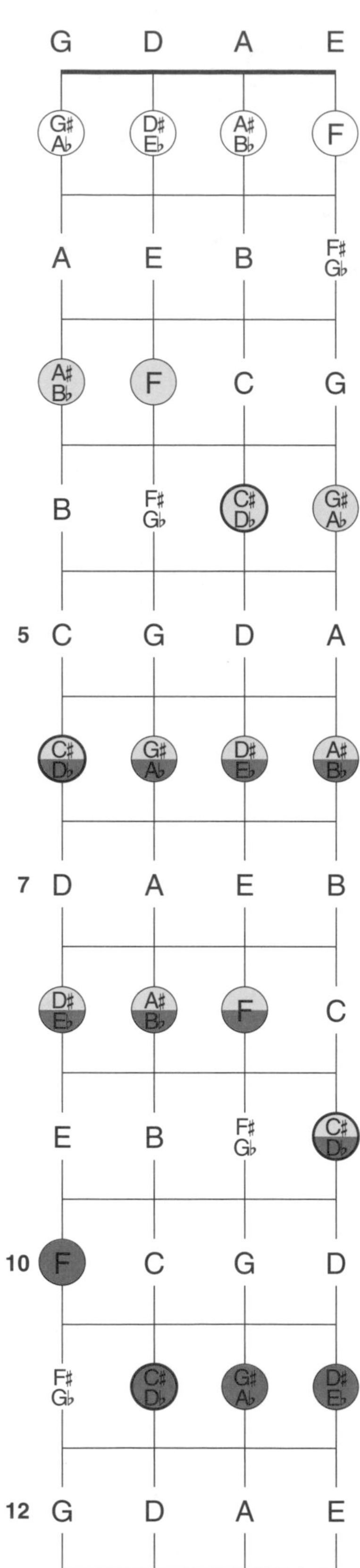

D MAJOR PENTATONIC

D–E–F♯–A–B

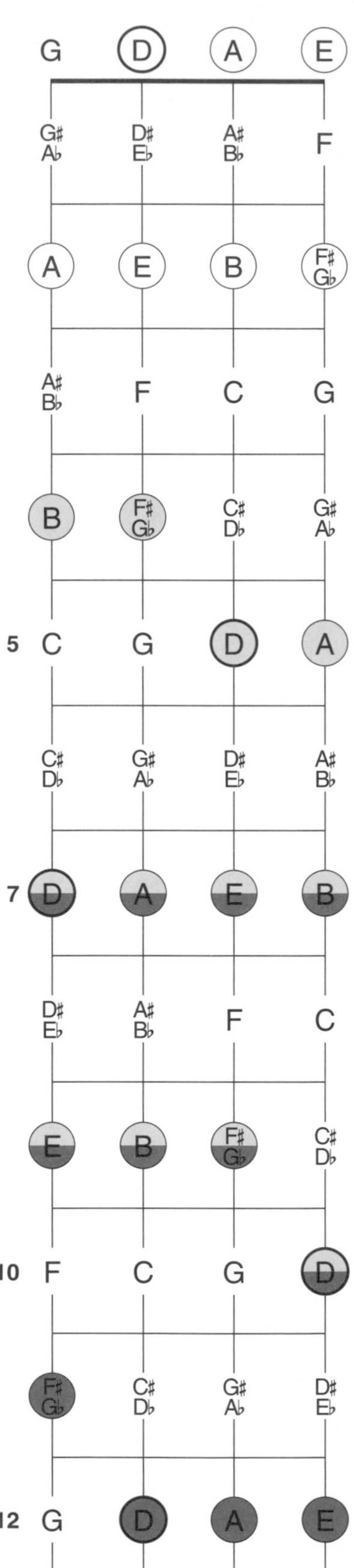

E♭ MAJOR PENTATONIC

E♭–F–G–B♭–C

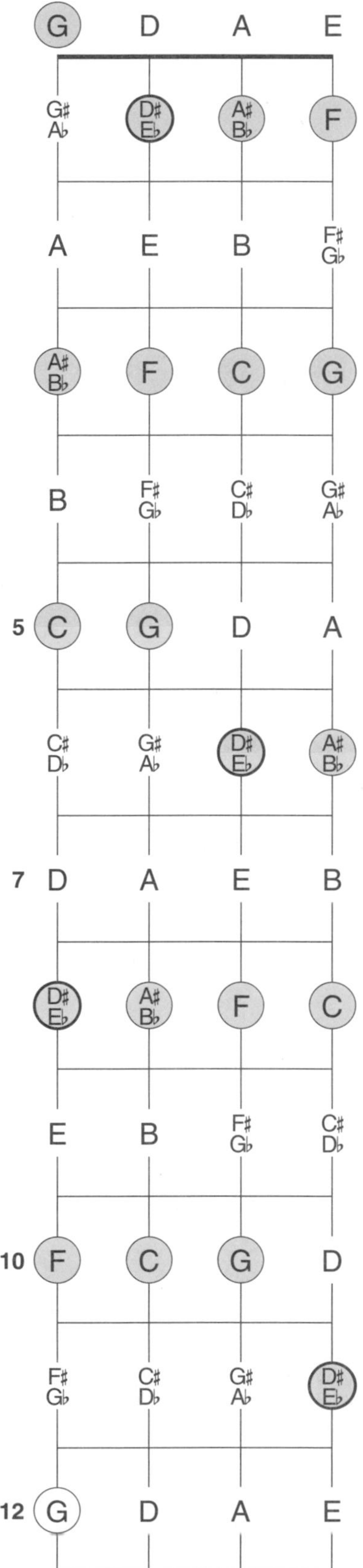

E MAJOR PENTATONIC

E–F♯–G♯–B–C♯

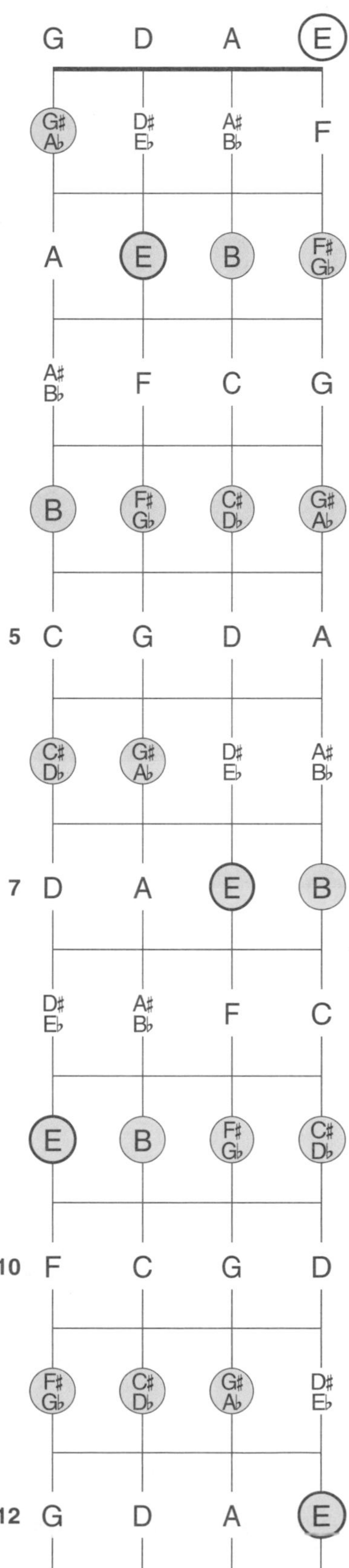

F MAJOR PENTATONIC

F–G–A–C–D

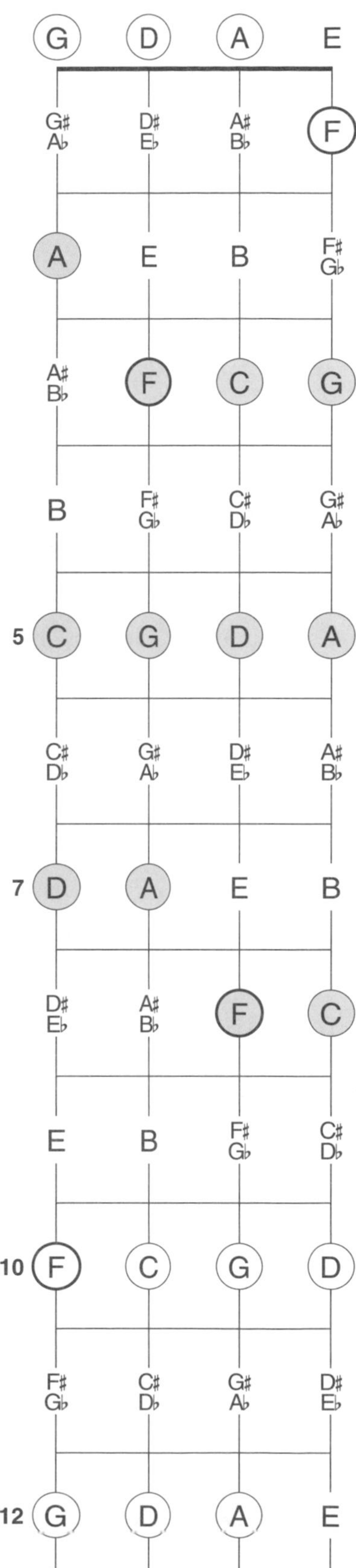

F♯/G♭ MAJOR PENTATONIC

F♯–G♯–A♯–C♯–D♯
G♭–A♭–B♭–D♭–E♭

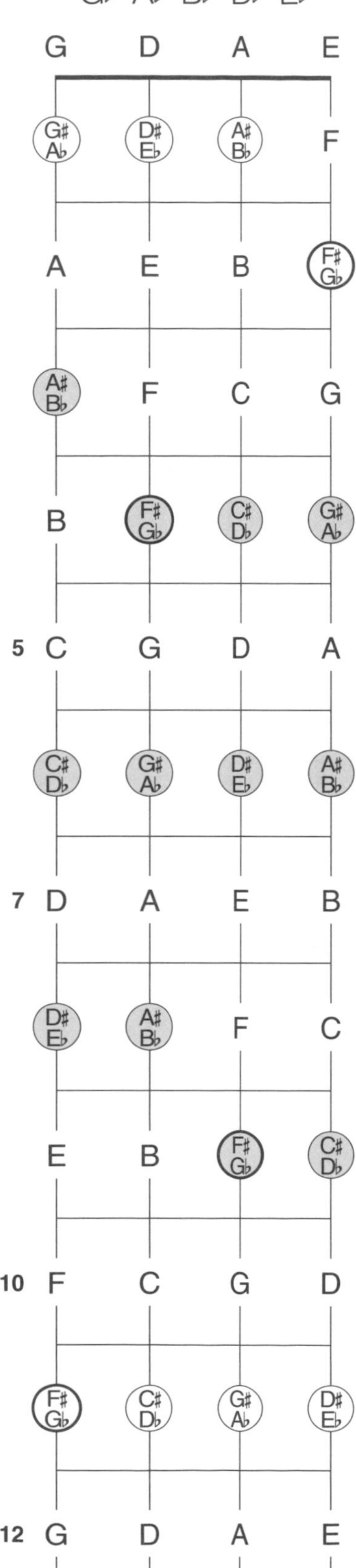

G MAJOR PENTATONIC

G–A–B–D–E

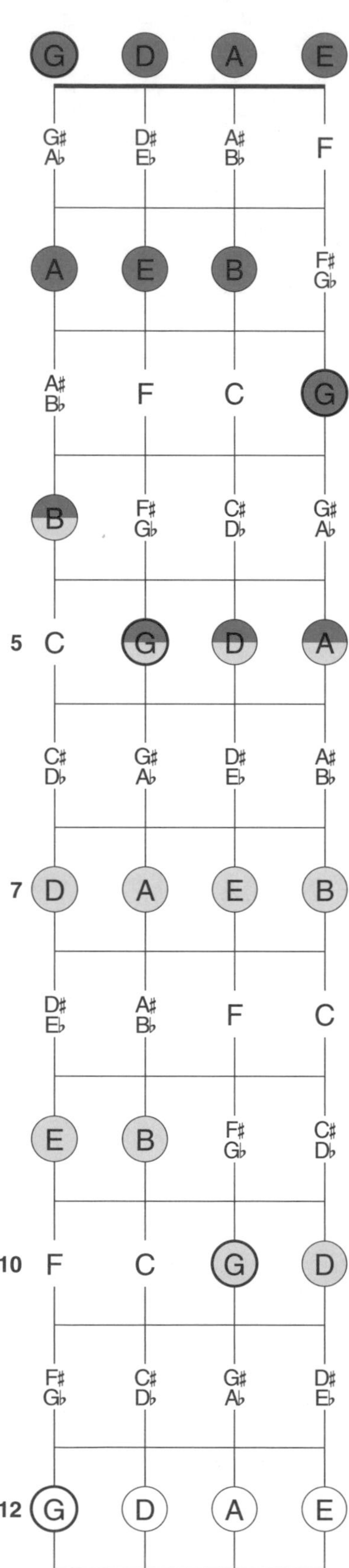

A♭ MAJOR PENTATONIC

A♭–B♭–C–E♭–F

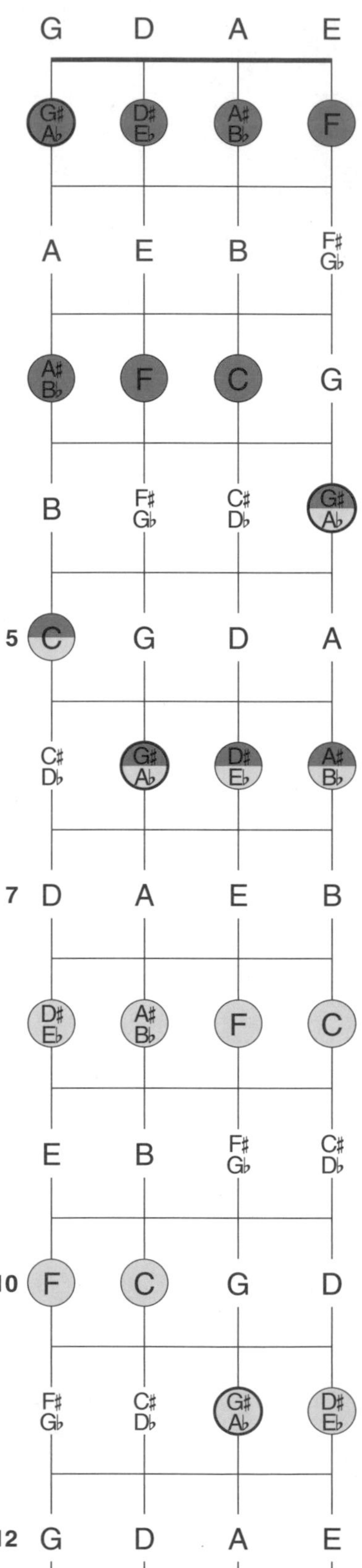

A MAJOR PENTATONIC

A–B–C♯–E–F♯

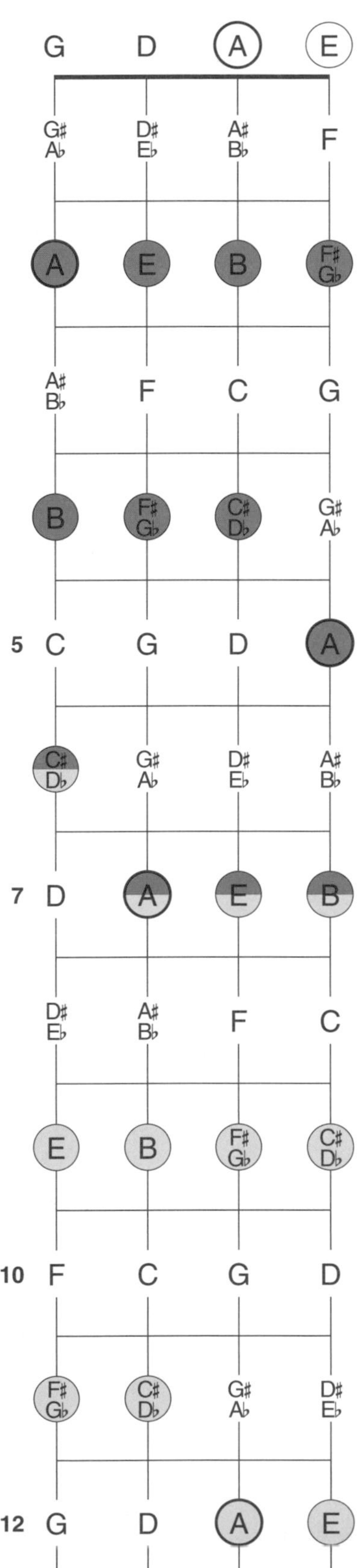

B♭ MAJOR PENTATONIC

B♭–C–D–F–G

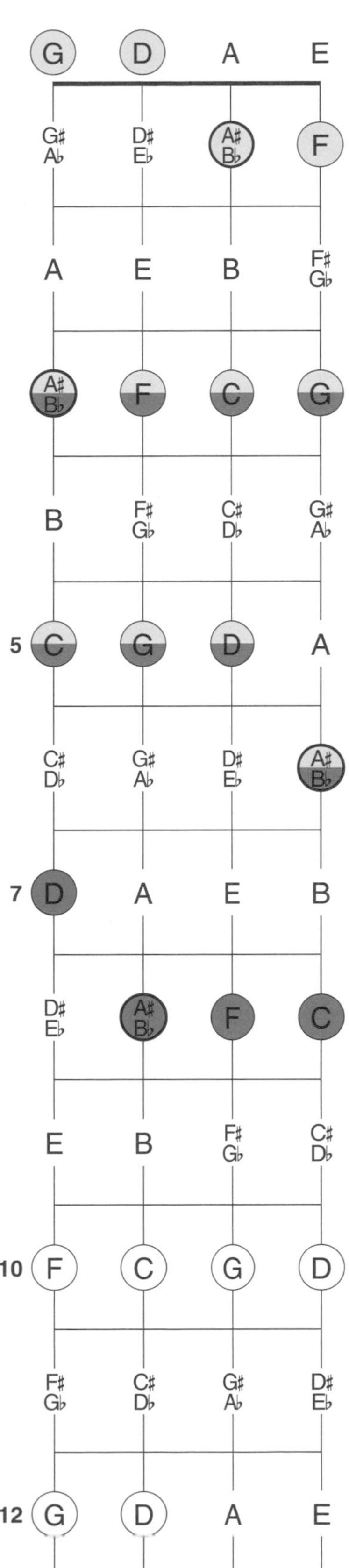

B MAJOR PENTATONIC

B–C♯–D♯–F♯–G♯

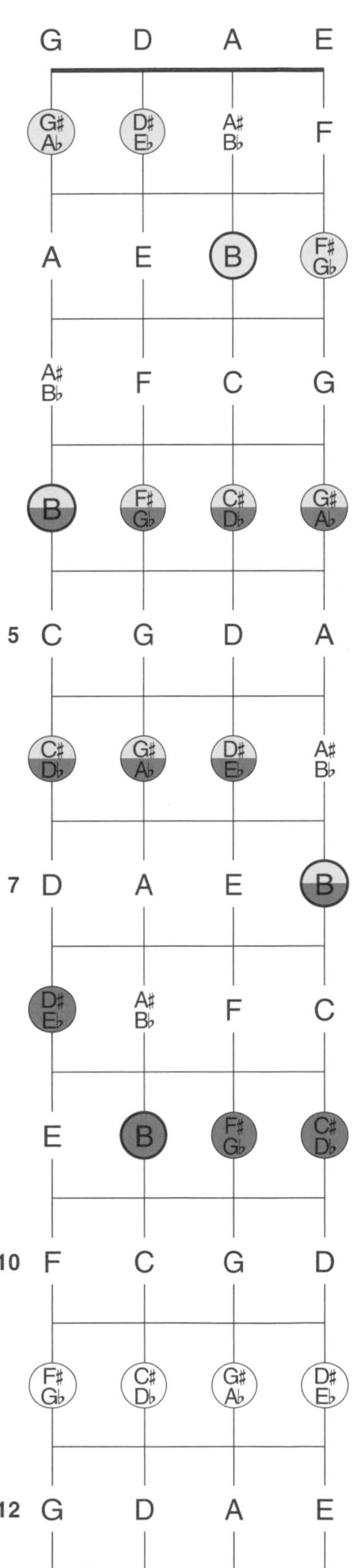

C MINOR PENTATONIC

C–E♭–F–G–B♭

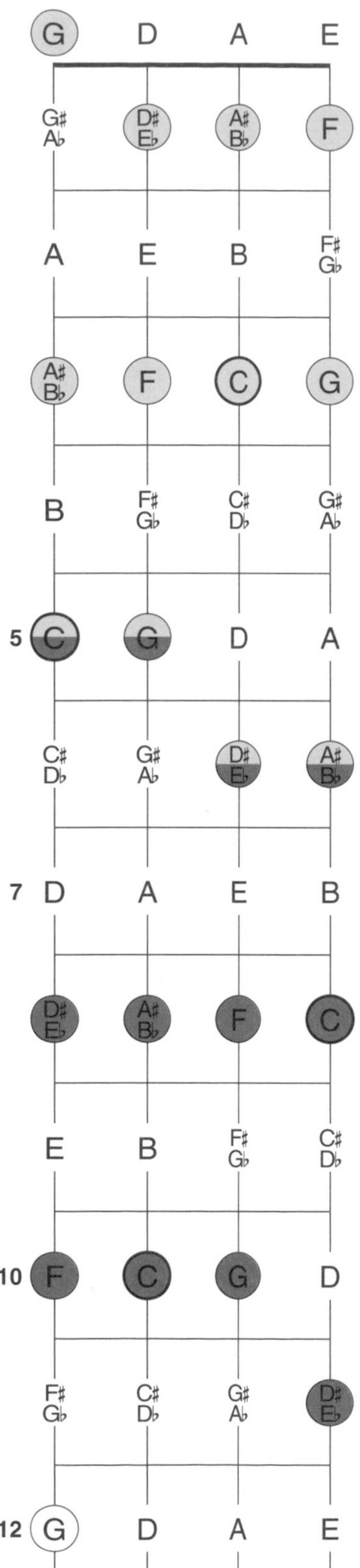

C♯ MINOR PENTATONIC

C♯–E–F♯–G♯–B

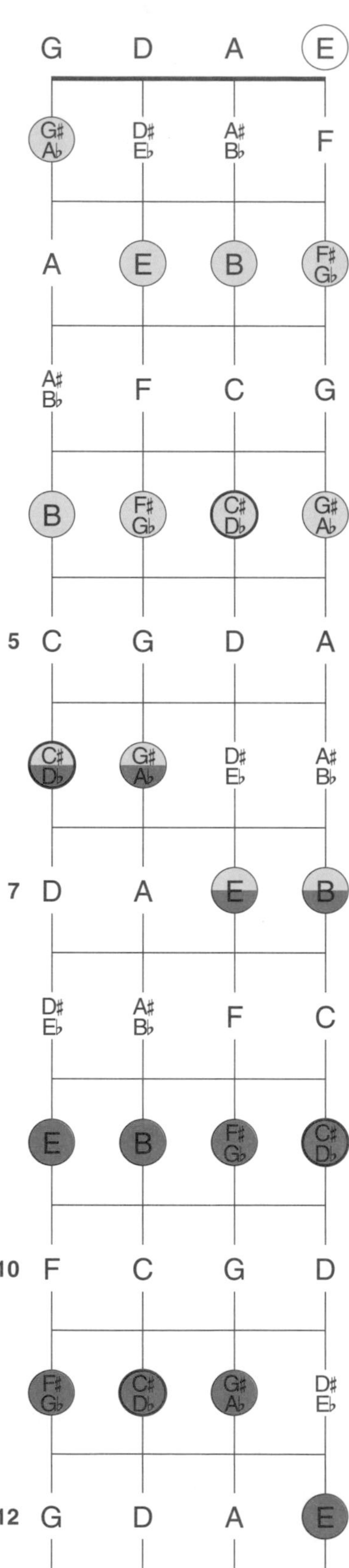

D MINOR PENTATONIC

D–F–G–A–C

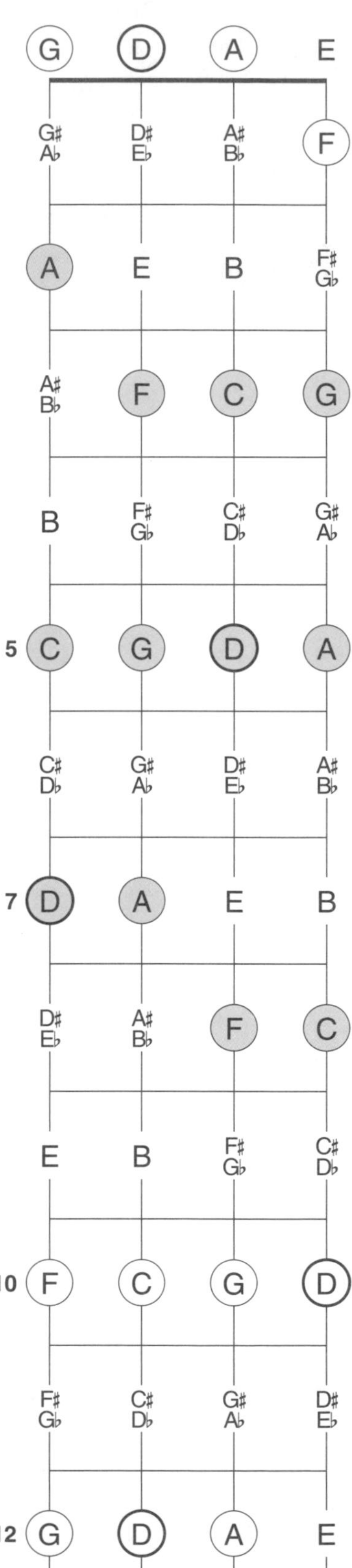

D♯/E♭ MINOR PENTATONIC

D♯–F♯–G♯–A♯–C♯
E♭–G♭–A♭–B♭–D♭

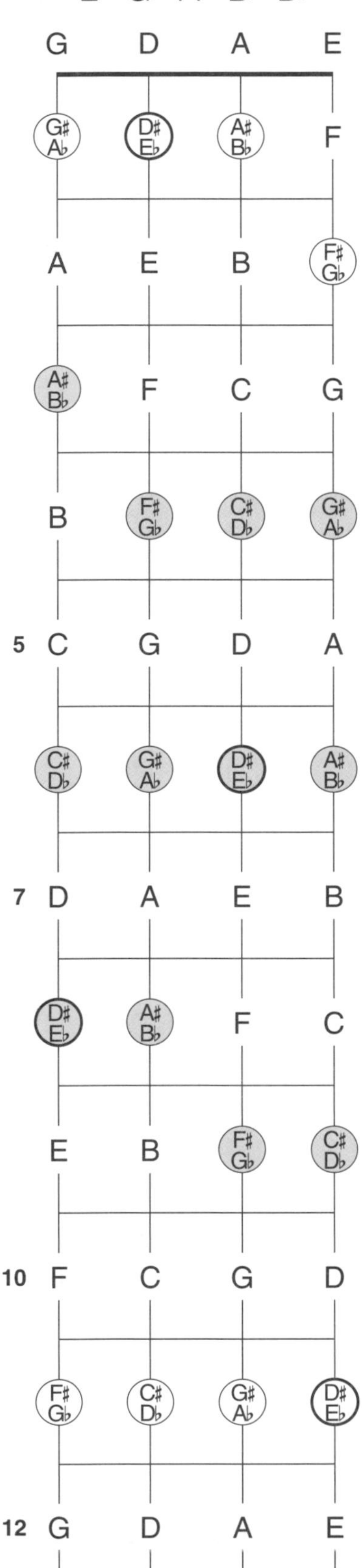

E MINOR PENTATONIC

E–G–A–B–D

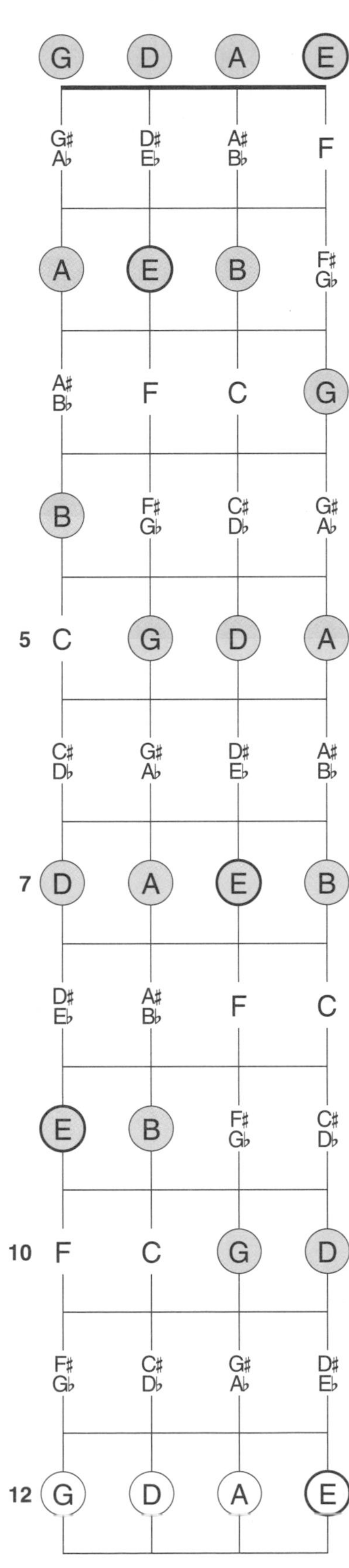

F MINOR PENTATONIC

F–A♭–B♭–C–E♭

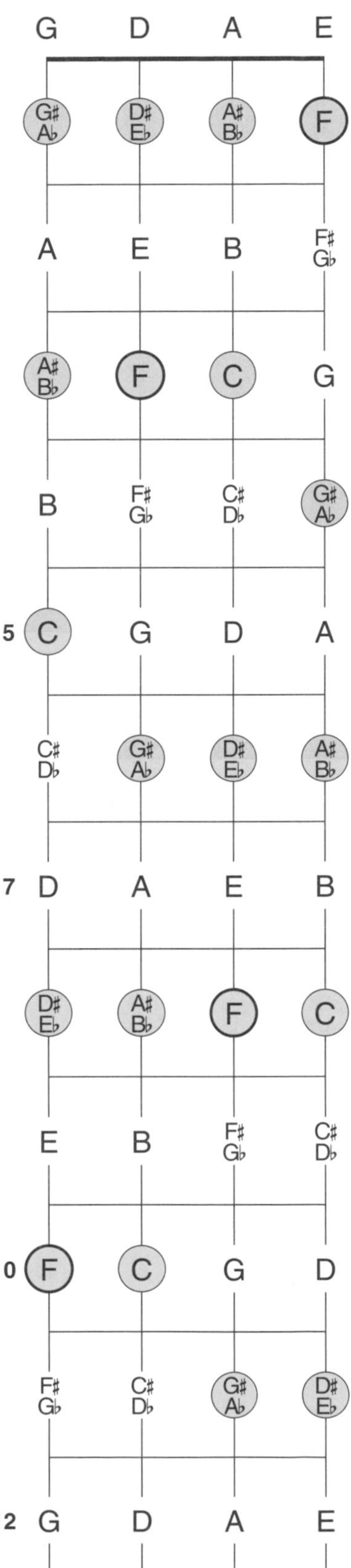

F♯ MINOR PENTATONIC

F♯–A–B–C♯–E

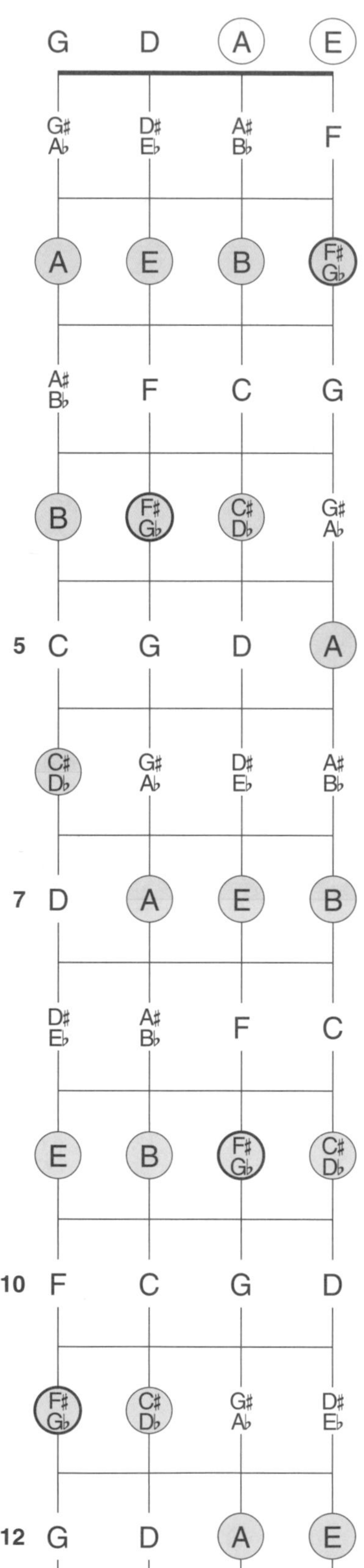

G MINOR PENTATONIC

G–B♭–C–D–F

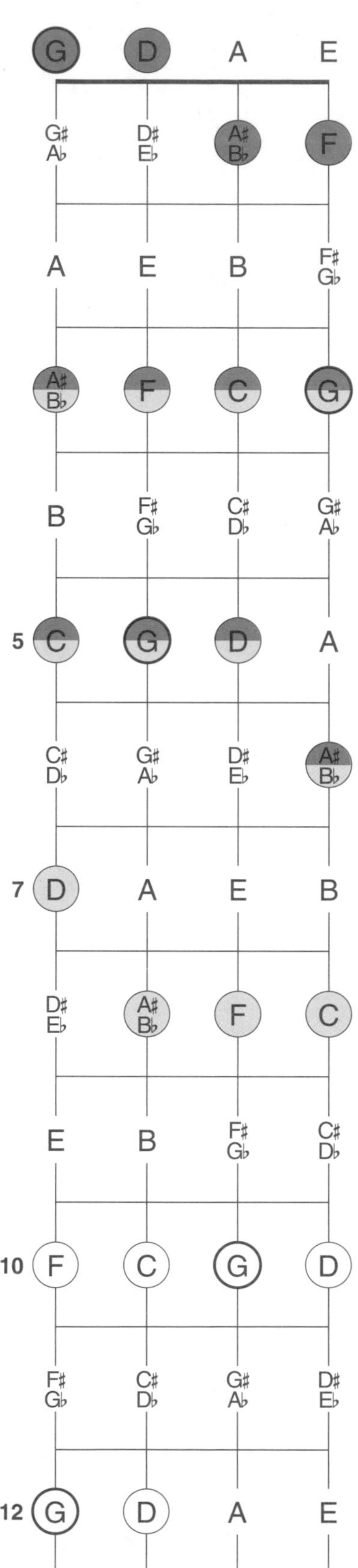

G♯/A♭ MINOR PENTATONIC

G♯–B–C♯–D♯–F♯
A♭–C♭–D♭–E♭–G♭

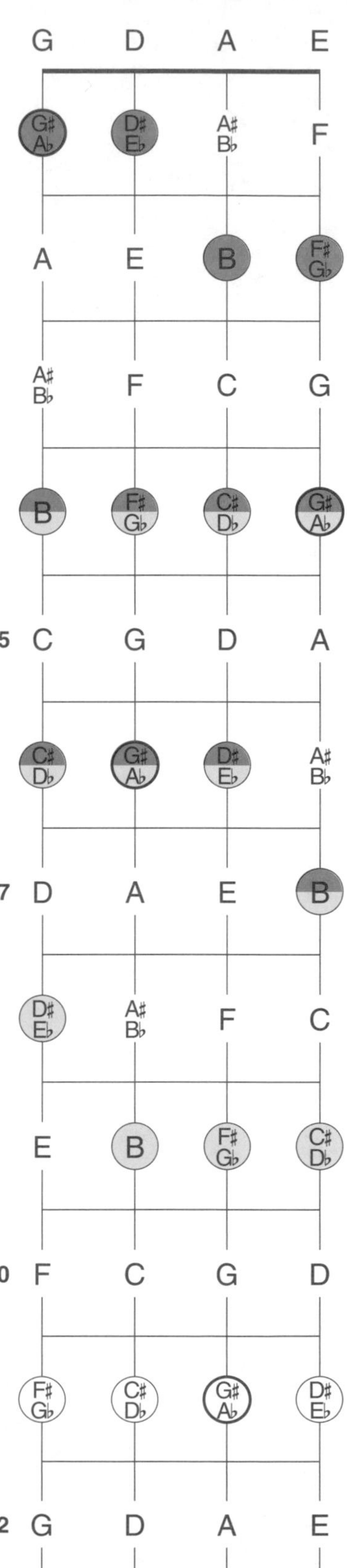

A MINOR PENTATONIC

A–C–D–E–G

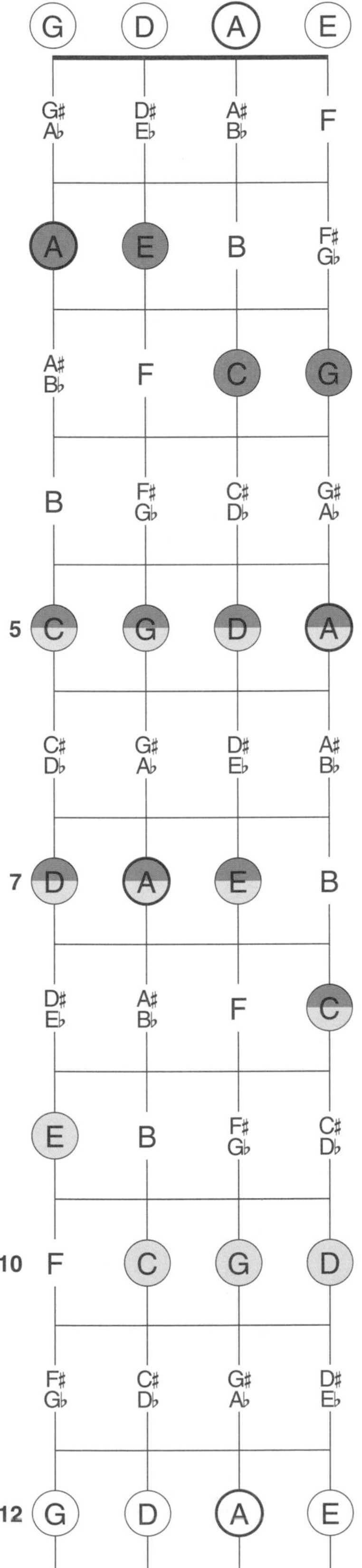

B♭ MINOR PENTATONIC

B♭–D♭–E♭–F–A♭

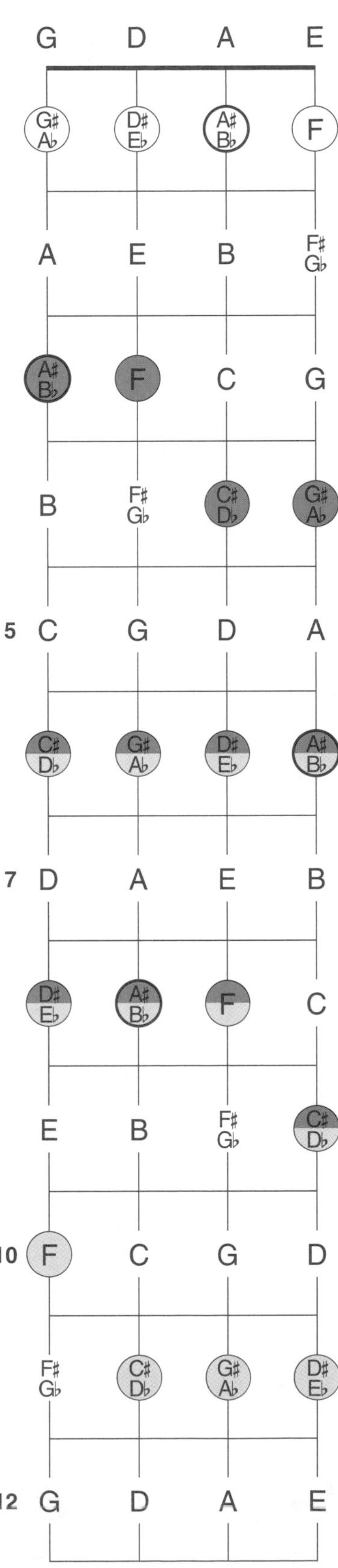

B MINOR PENTATONIC

B–D–E–F♯–A

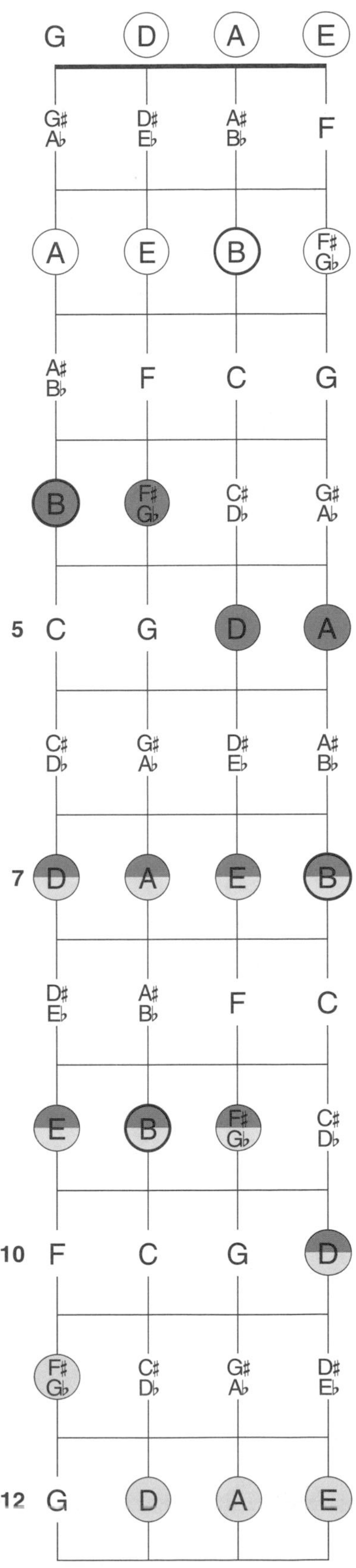

C BLUES

C–E♭–F–G♭–G–B♭

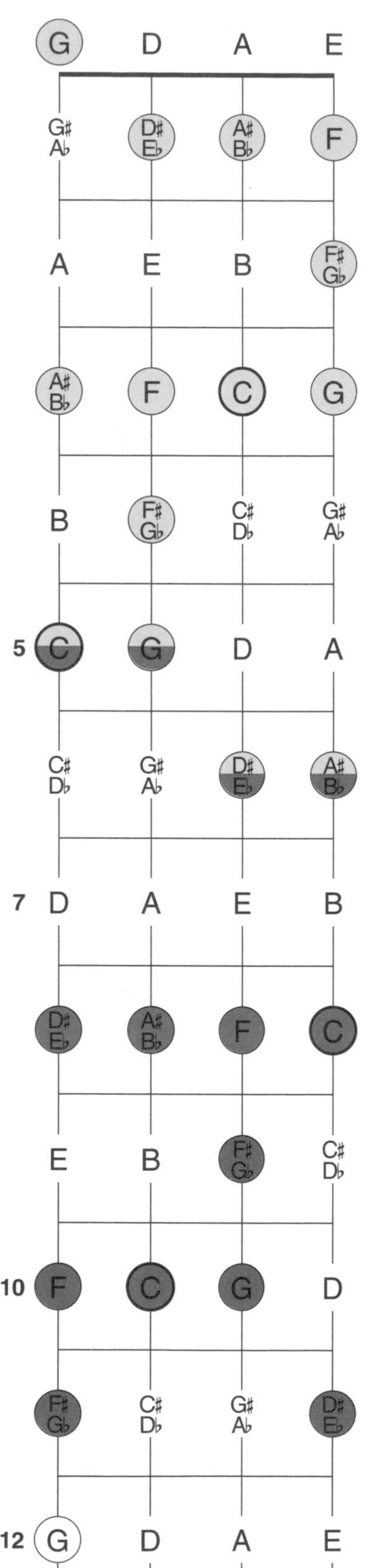

C♯ BLUES

C♯–E–F♯–G–G♯–B

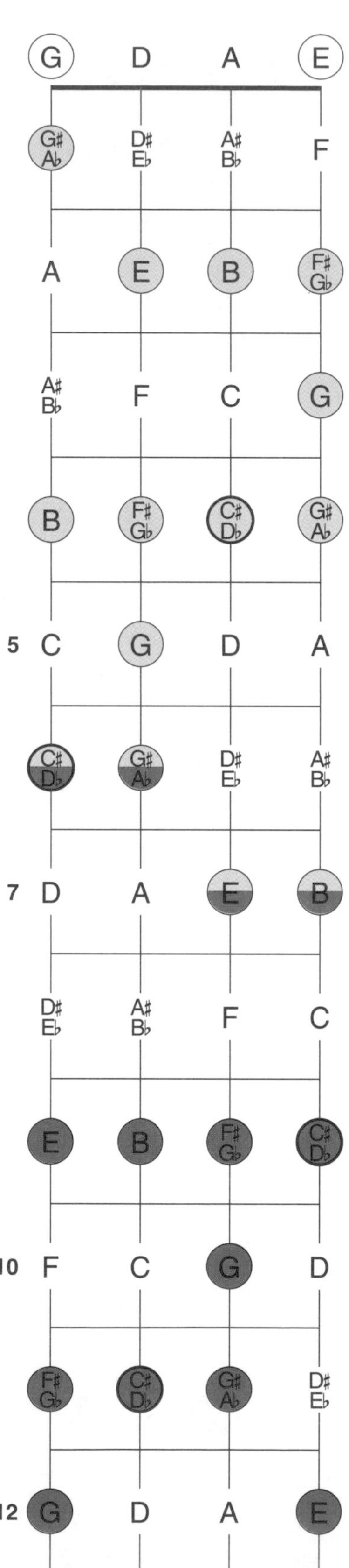

D BLUES

D–F–G–A♭–A–C

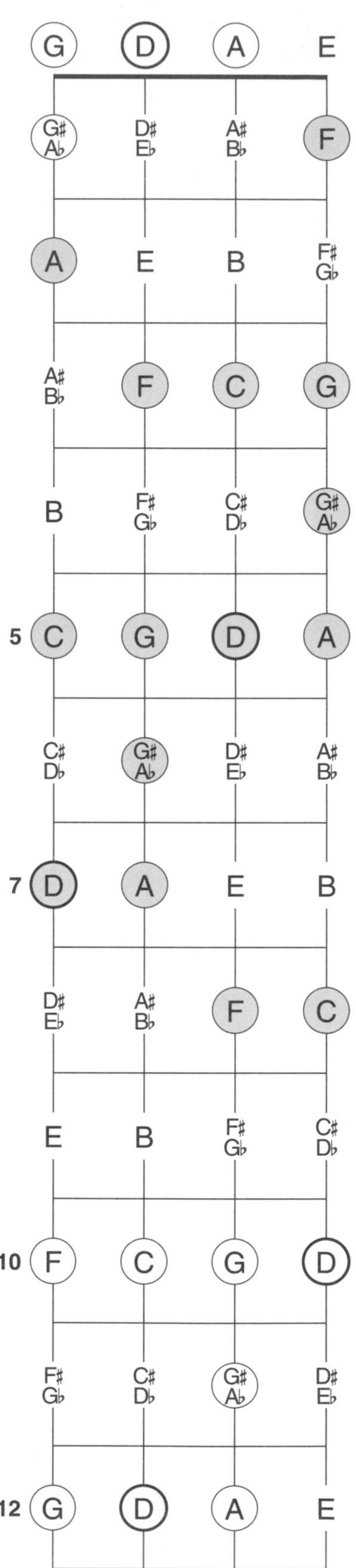

D♯/E♭ BLUES

D♯–F♯–G♯–A–A♯–C♯
E♭–G♭–A♭–A–B♭–D♭

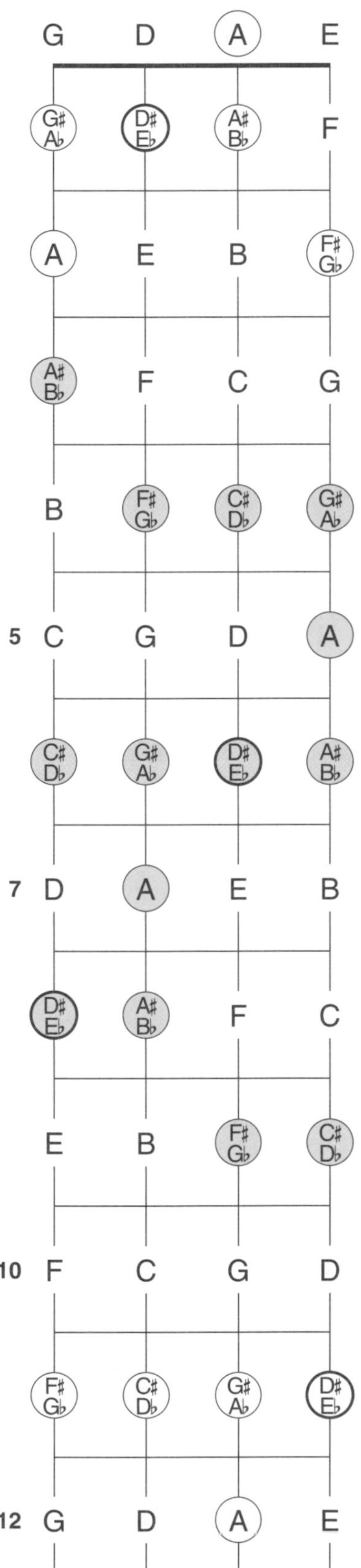

E BLUES

E–G–A–B♭–B–D

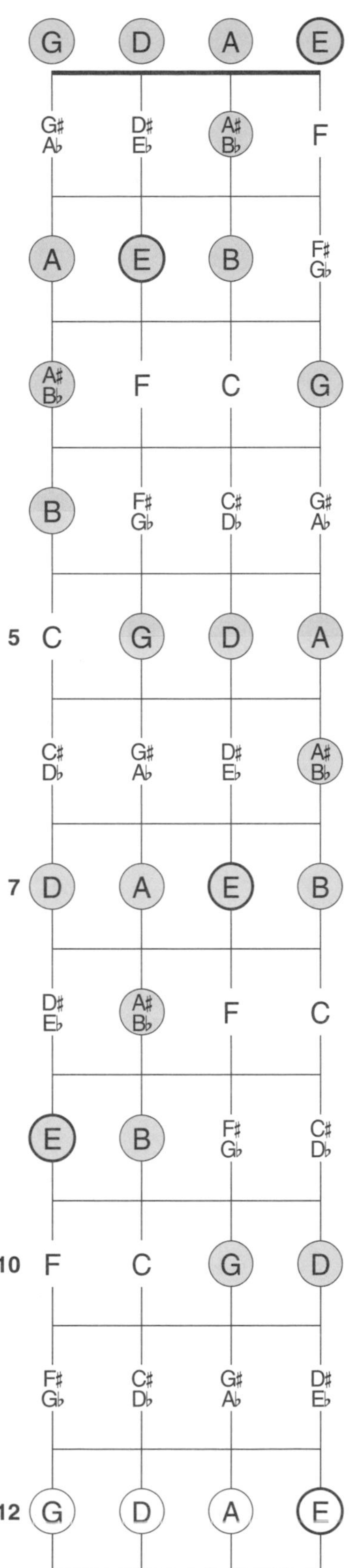

F BLUES

F–A♭–B♭–B–C–E♭

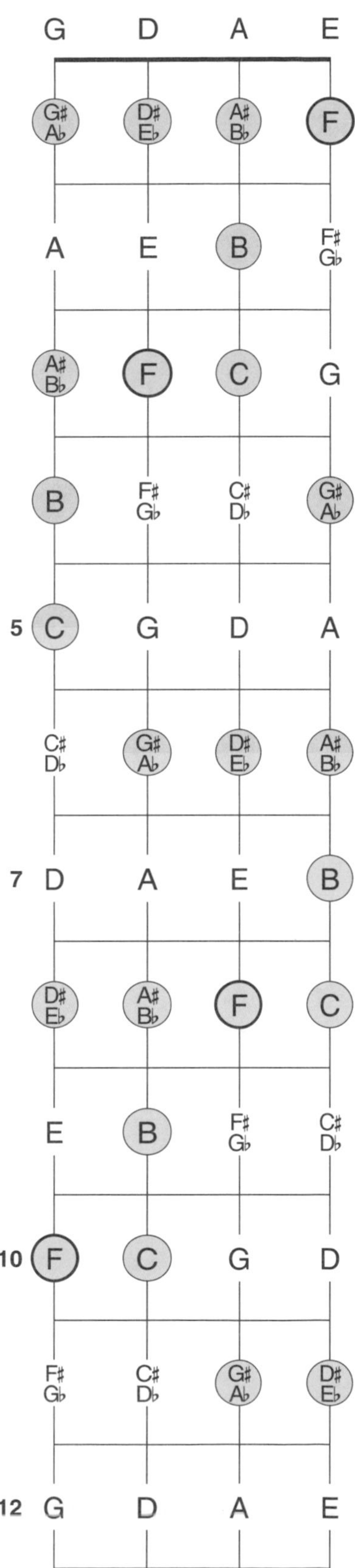

F♯ BLUES

F♯–A–B–C–C♯–E

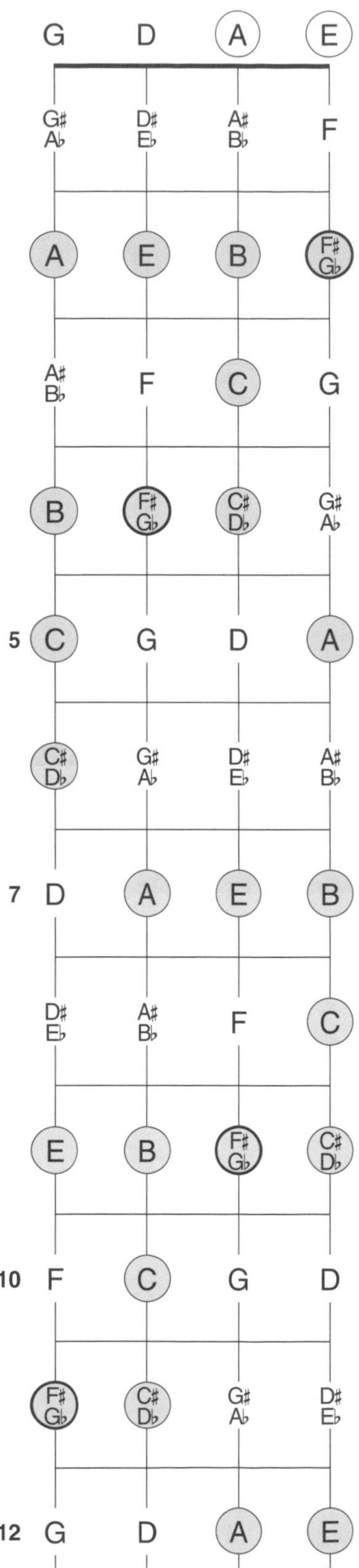

G BLUES

G–B♭–C–D♭–D–F

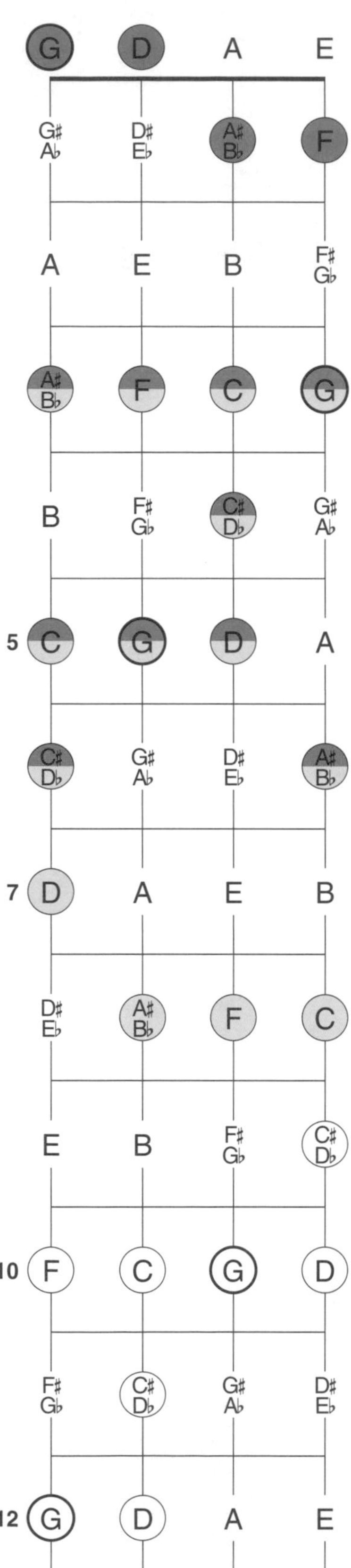

A♭ BLUES

A♭–C♭–D♭–D–E♭–G♭

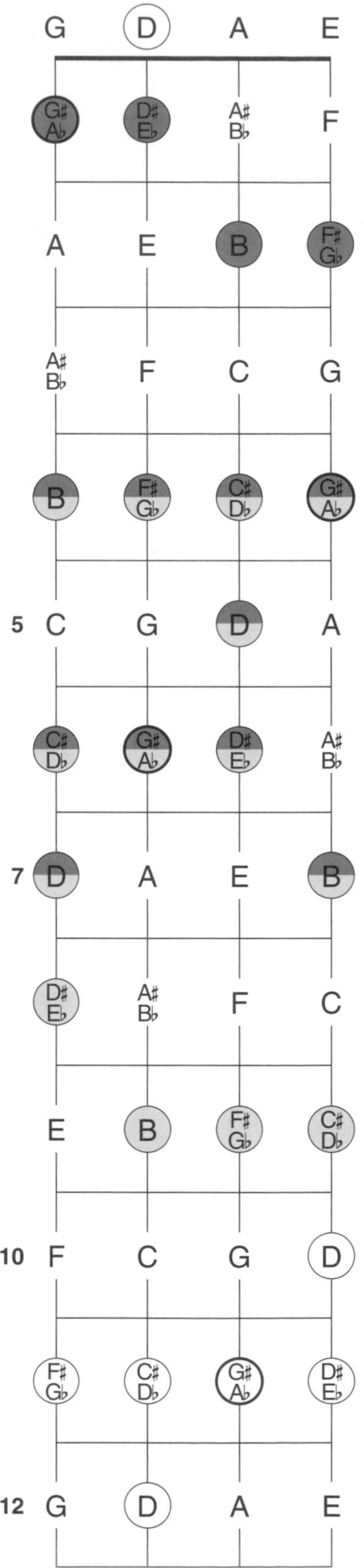

A BLUES

A–C–D–E♭–E–G

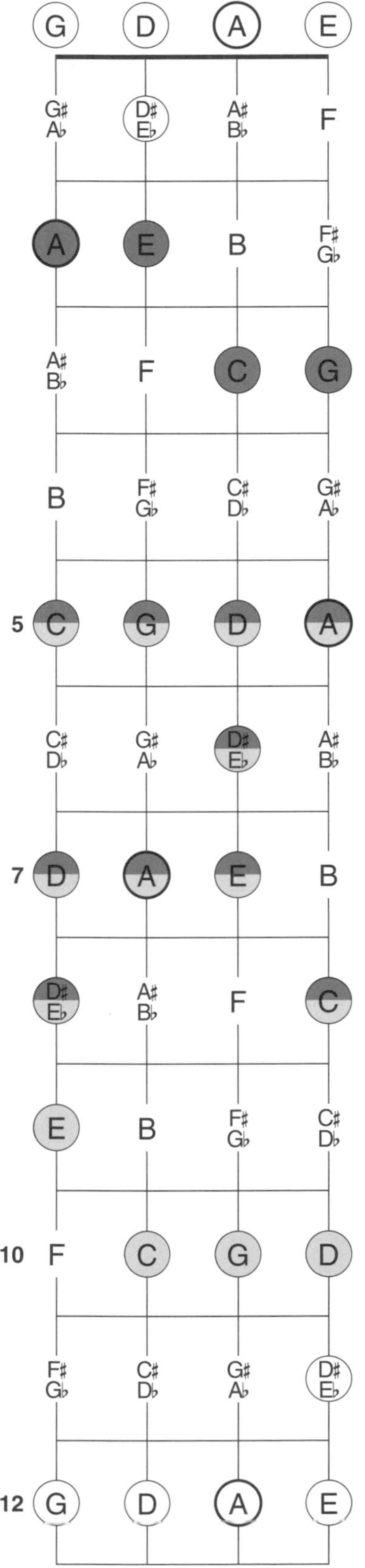

B♭ BLUES

B♭–D♭–E♭–E–F–A♭

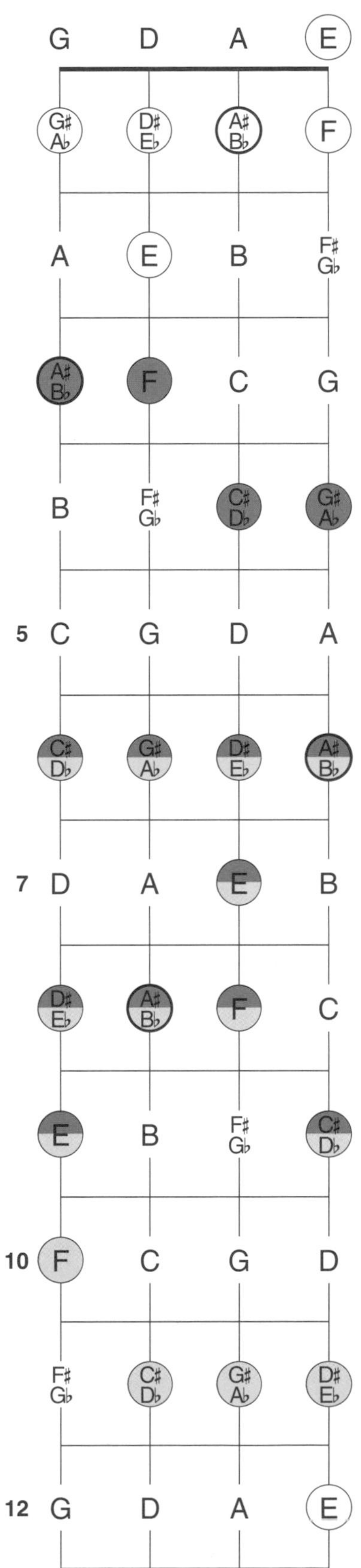

B BLUES

B–D–E–F–F♯–A

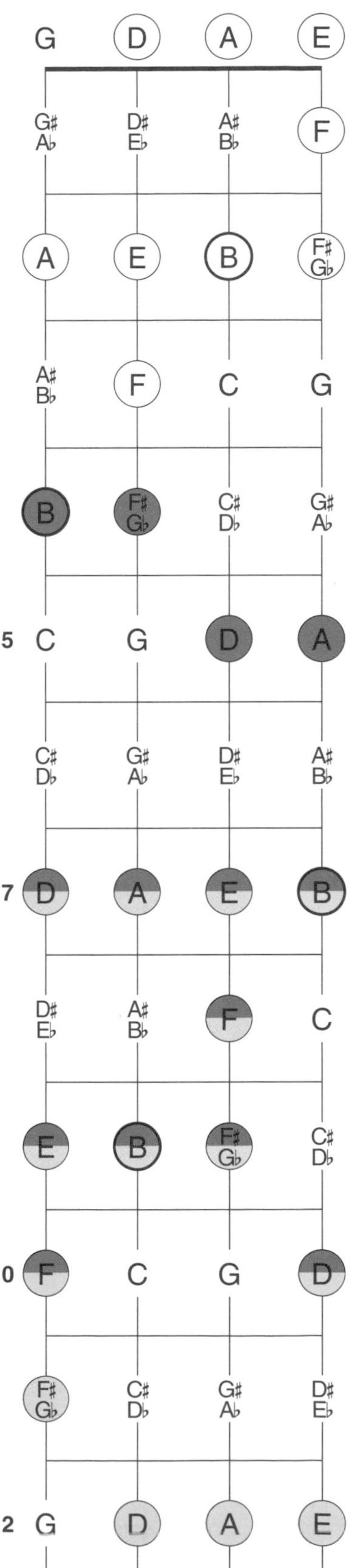

SCALES

THE MELODIC MINOR SCALE AND SELECT MODES

C MELODIC MINOR

C–D–E♭–F–G–A–B

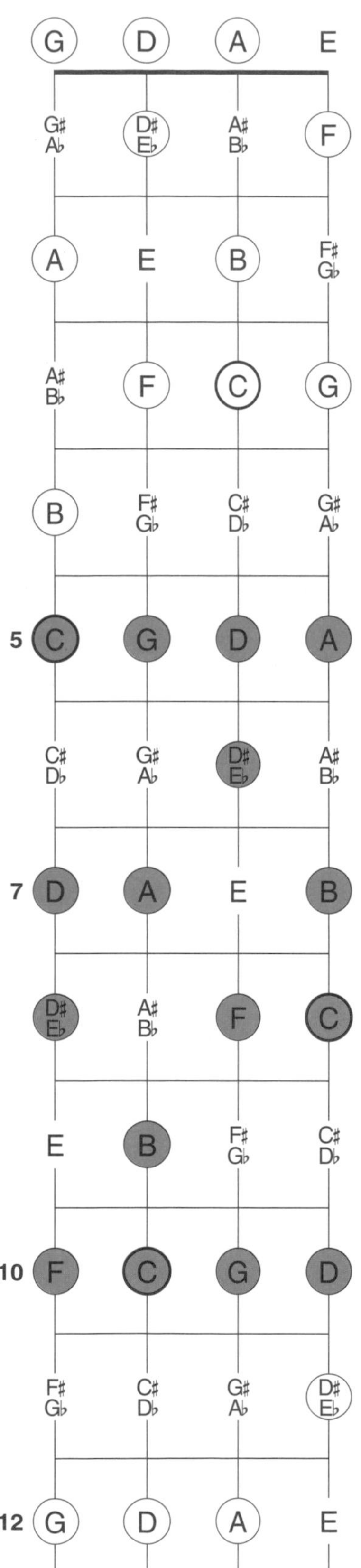

C♯ MELODIC MINOR

C♯–D♯–E–F♯–G♯–A♯–B♯

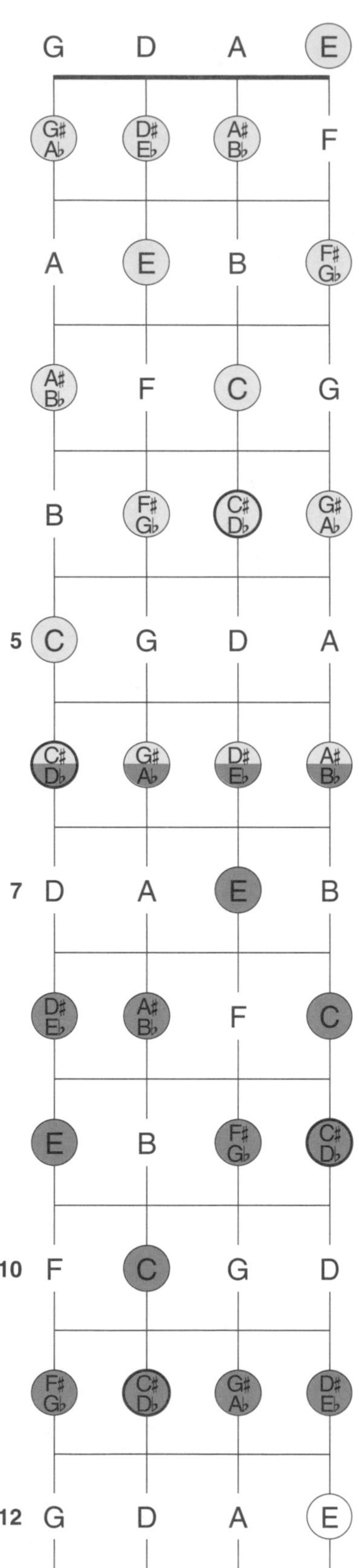

D MELODIC MINOR

D–E–F–G–A–B–C♯

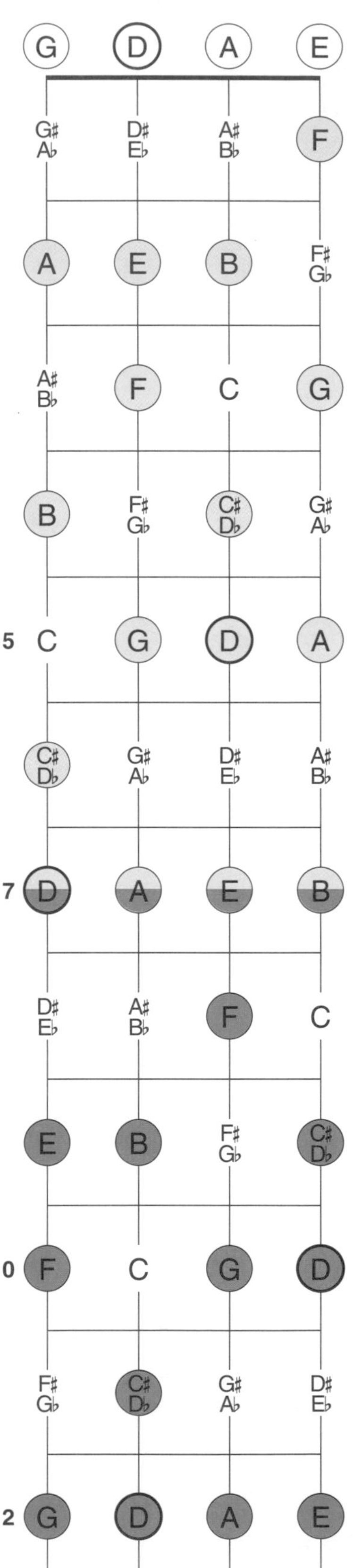

D♯/E♭ MELODIC MINOR

D♯–E♯–F♯–G♯–A♯–B♯–C𝄪
E♭–F–G♭–A♭–B♭–C–D

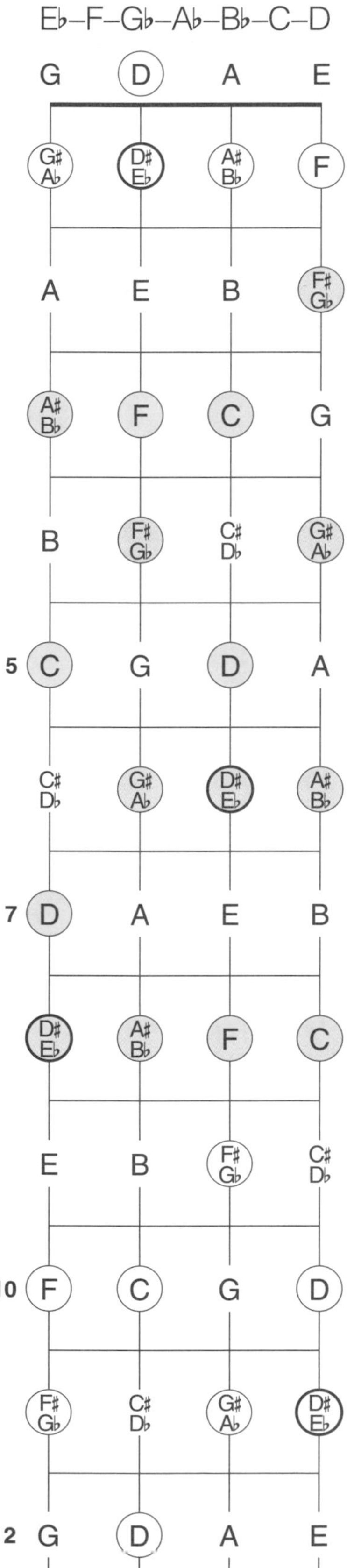

E MELODIC MINOR

E–F♯–G–A–B–C♯–D♯

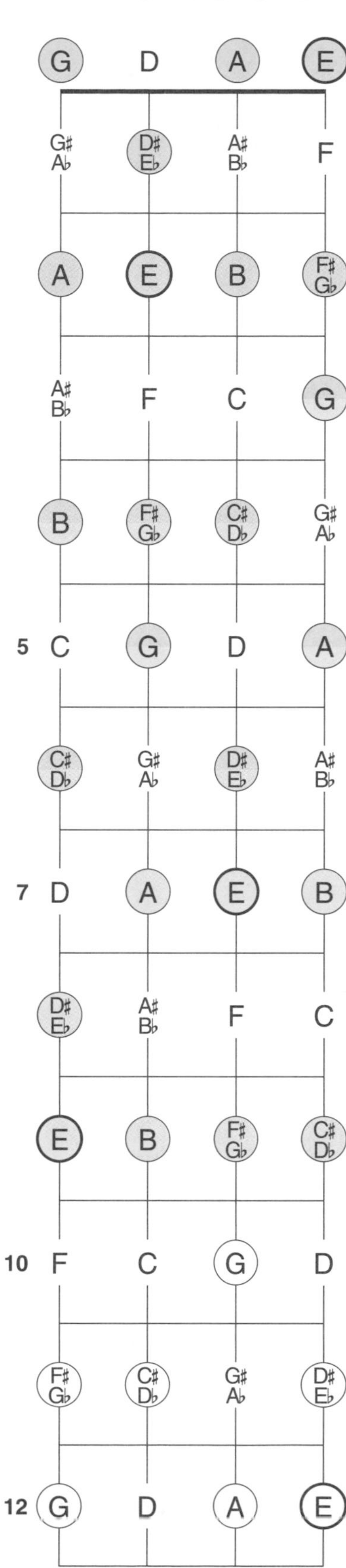

F MELODIC MINOR

F–G–A♭–B♭–C–D–E

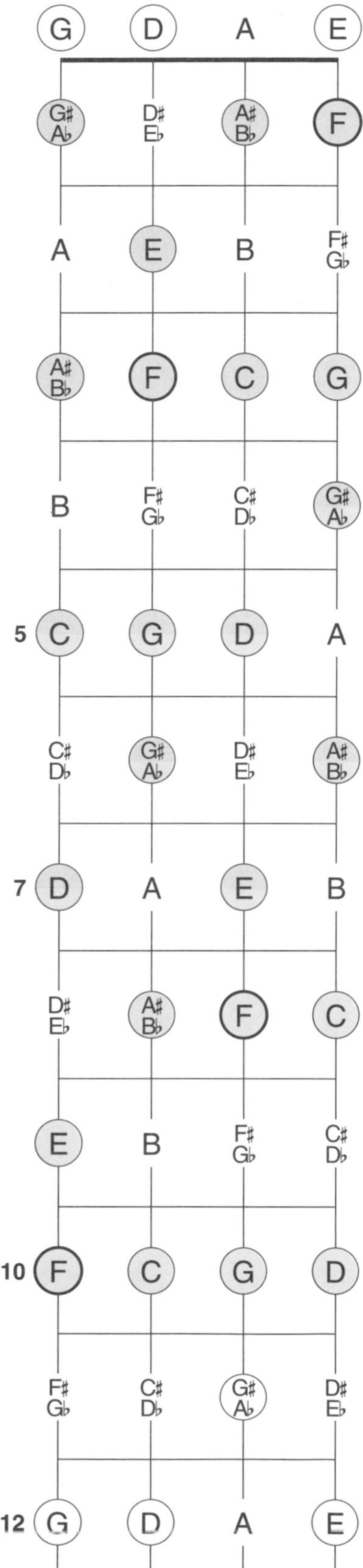

F♯ MELODIC MINOR

F♯–G♯–A–B–C♯–D♯–E♯

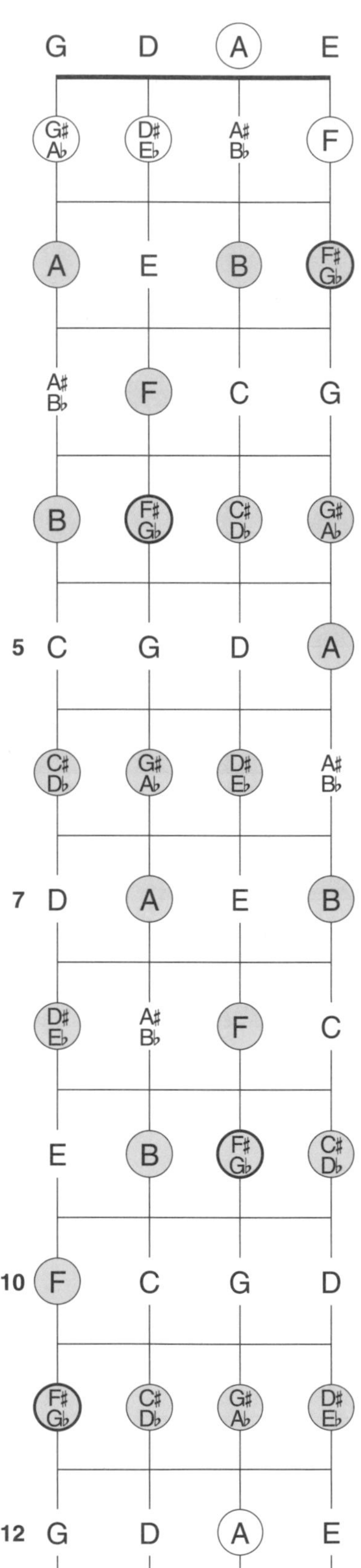

G MELODIC MINOR

G–A–B♭–C–D–E–F♯

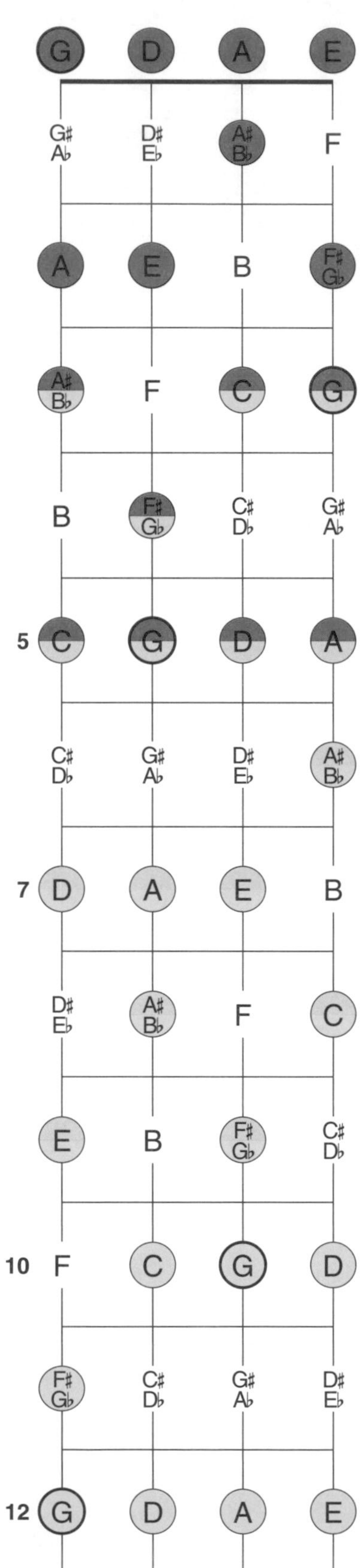

G♯/A♭ MELODIC MINOR

G♯–A♯–B–C♯–D♯–E♯–F𝄪

A♭–B♭–C♭–D♭–E♭–F–G

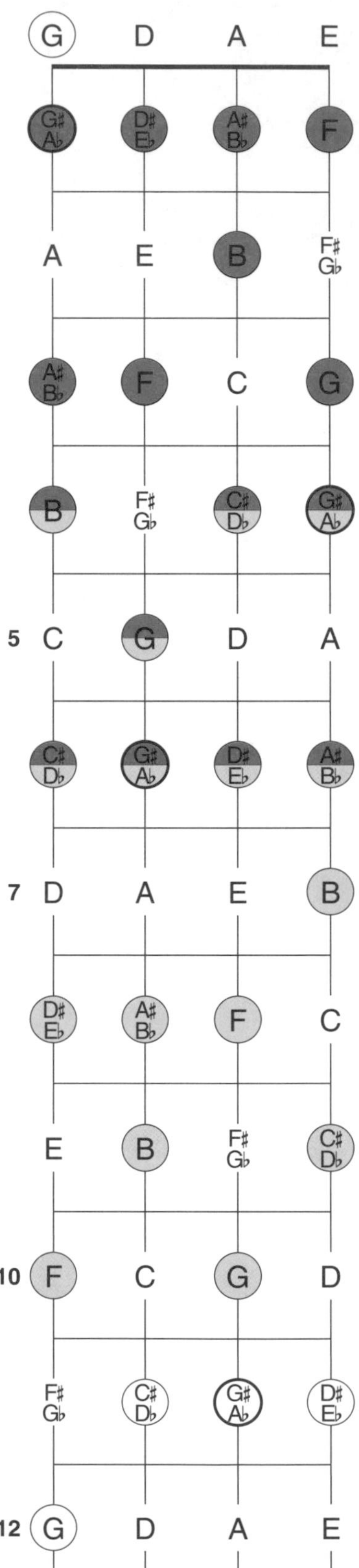

A MELODIC MINOR

A–B–C–D–E–F♯–G♯

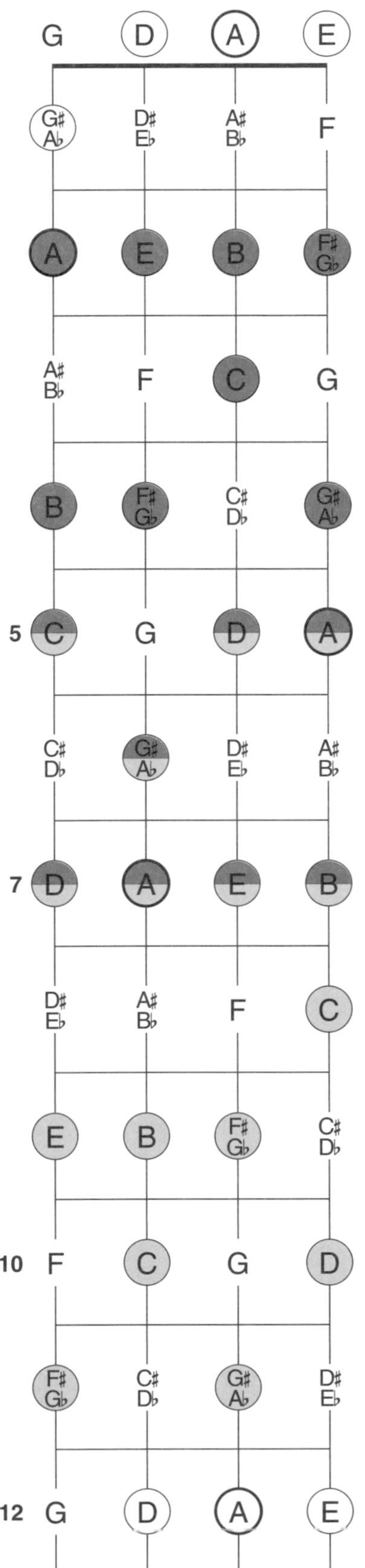

B♭ MELODIC MINOR

B♭–C–D♭–E♭–F–G–A

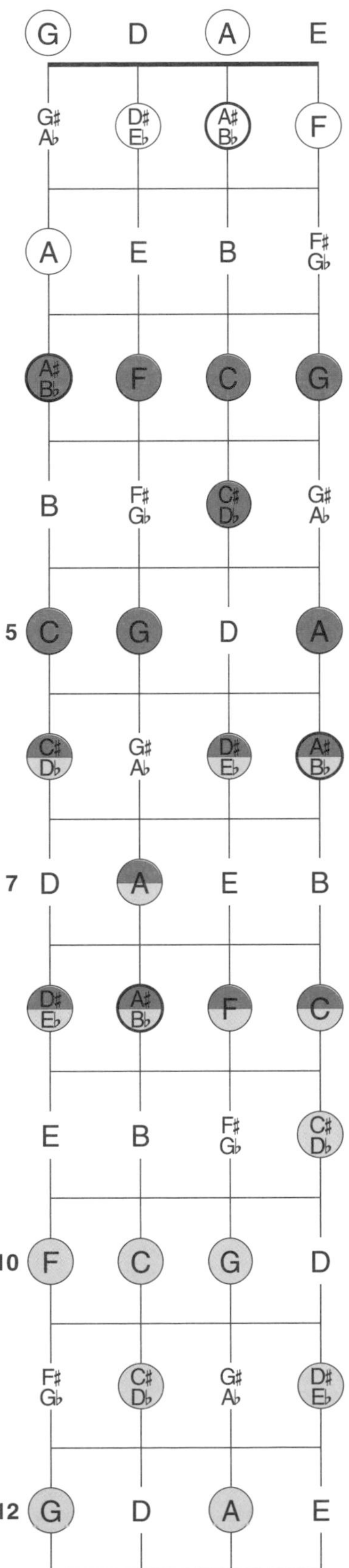

B MELODIC MINOR

B–C♯–D–E–F♯–G♯–A♯

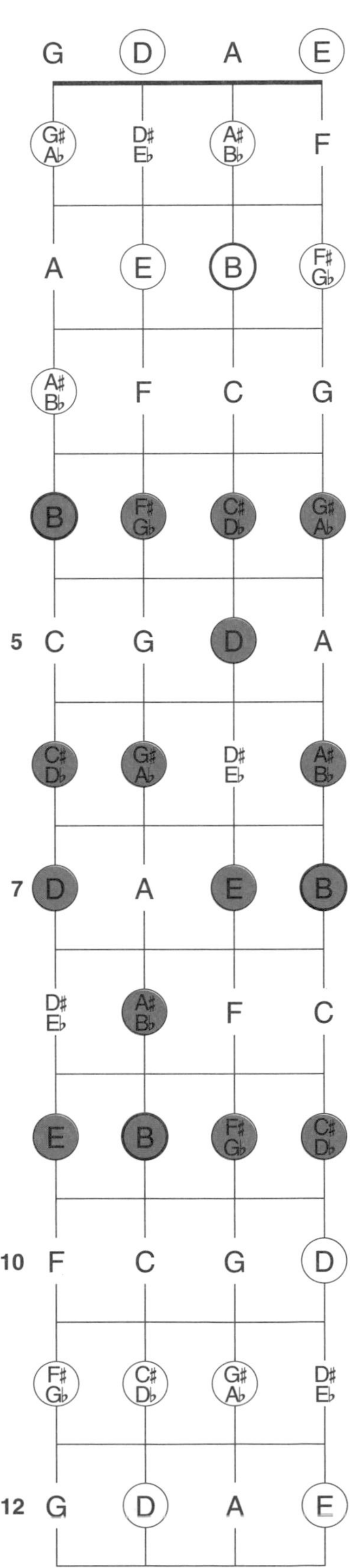

C LYDIAN DOMINANT

C–D–E–F♯–G–A–B♭

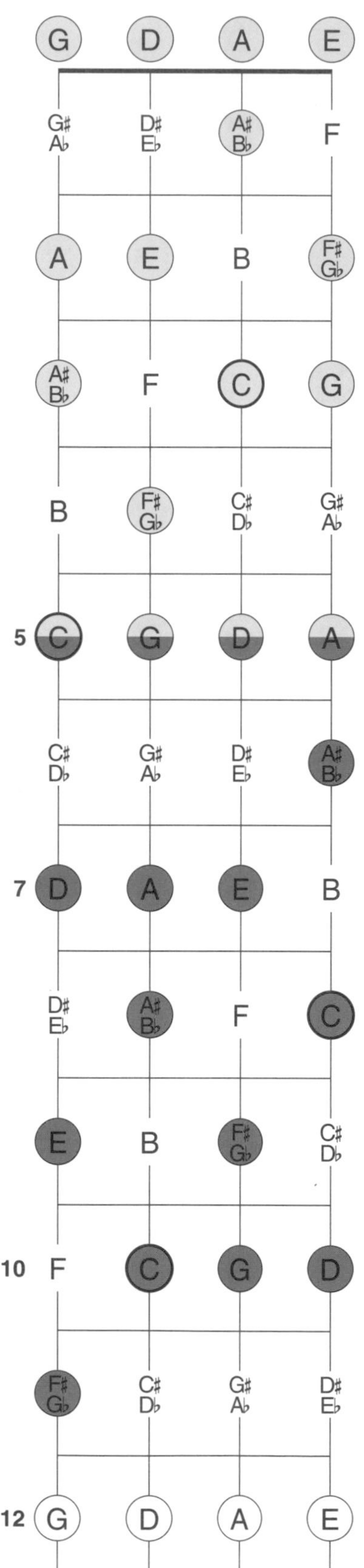

D♭ LYDIAN DOMINANT

D♭–E♭–F–G–A♭–B♭–C♭

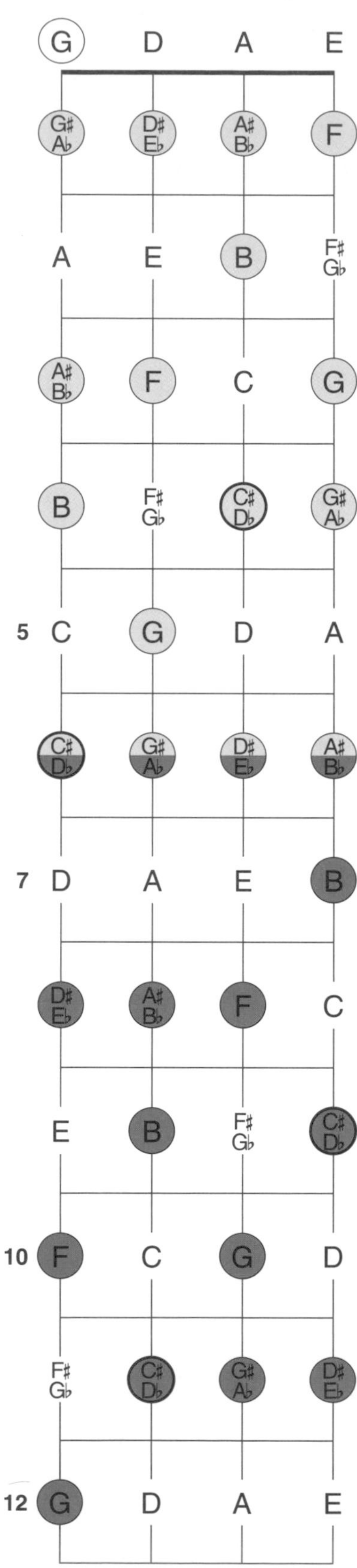

D LYDIAN DOMINANT

D–E–F♯–G♯–A–B–C

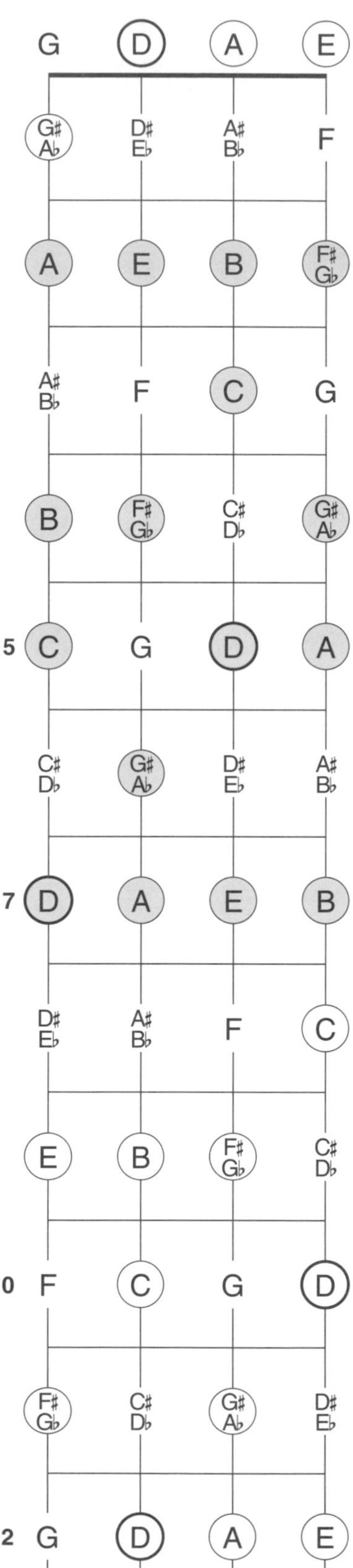

E♭ LYDIAN DOMINANT

E♭–F–G–A–B♭–C–D♭

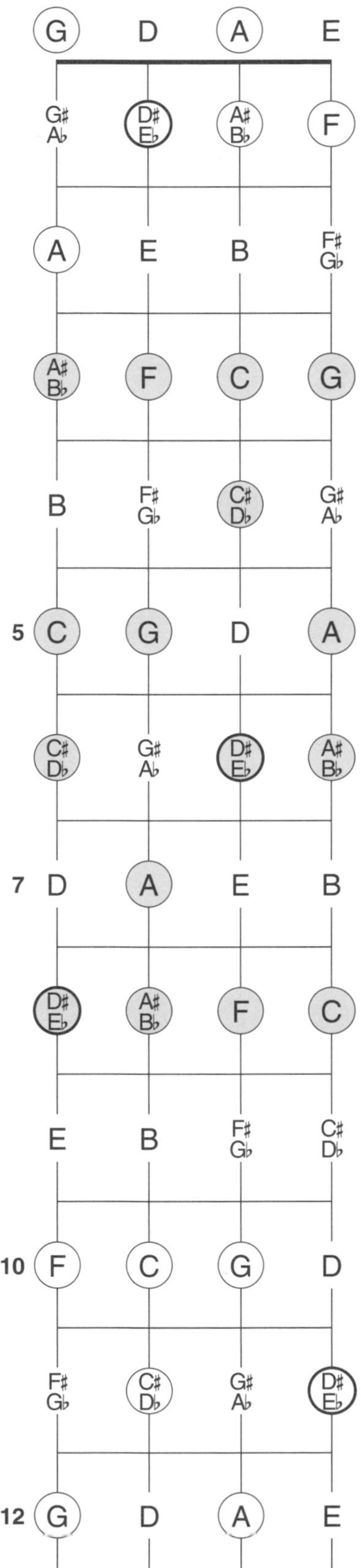

E LYDIAN DOMINANT

E–F♯–G♯–A♯–B–C♯–D

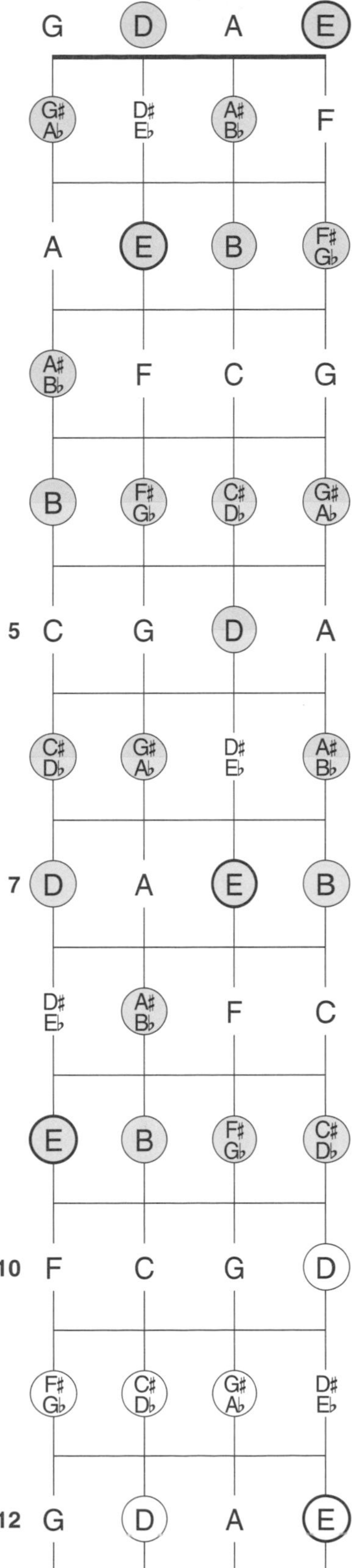

F LYDIAN DOMINANT

F–G–A–B–C–D–E♭

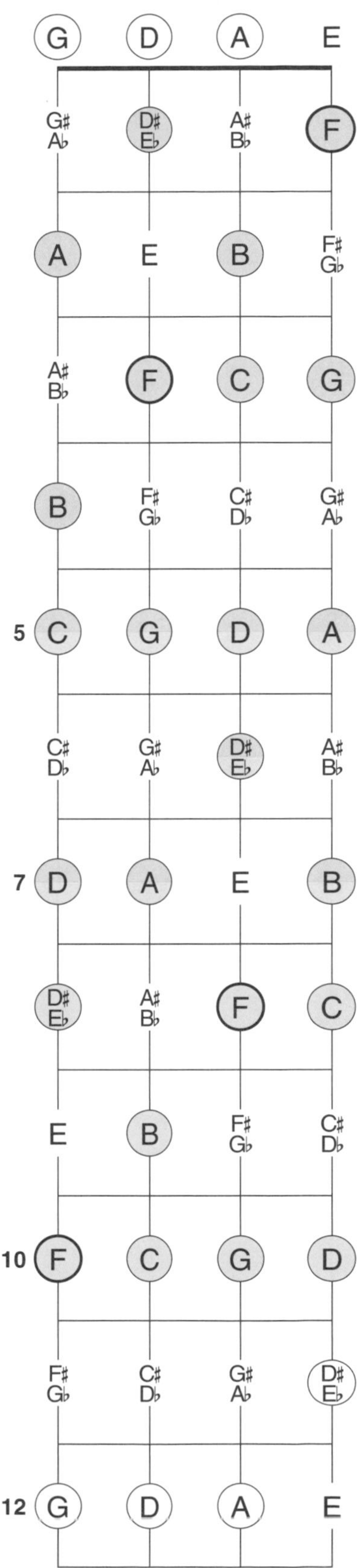

F♯/G♭ LYDIAN DOMINANT

F♯–G♯–A♯–B♯–C♯–D♯–E
G♭–A♭–B♭–C–D♭–E♭–F♭

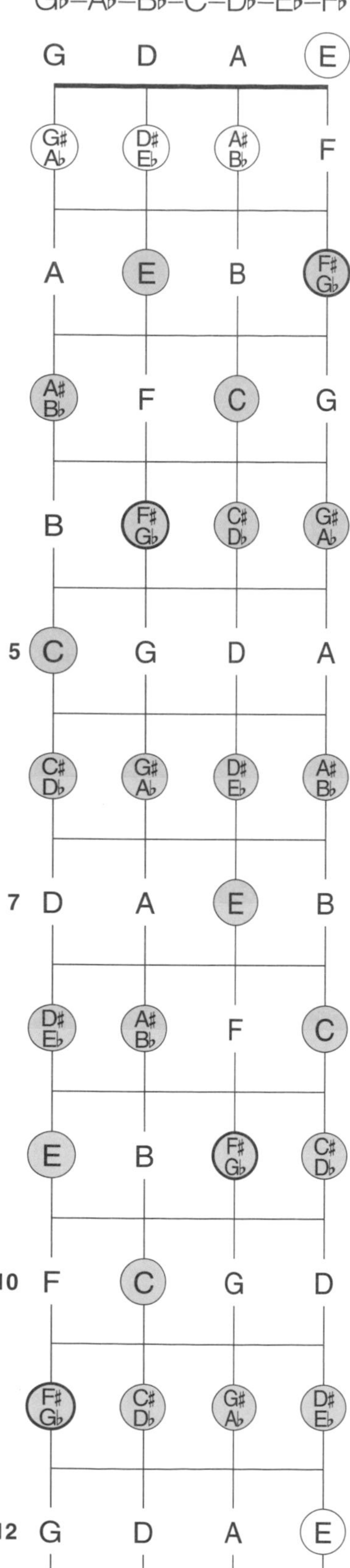

G LYDIAN DOMINANT

G–A–B–C♯–D–E–F

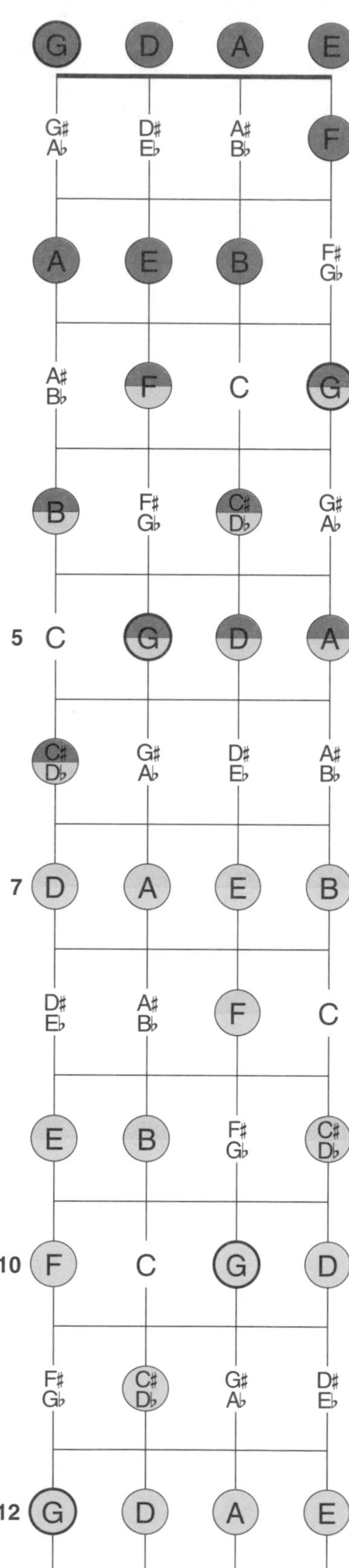

A♭ LYDIAN DOMINANT

A♭–B♭–C–D–E♭–F–G♭

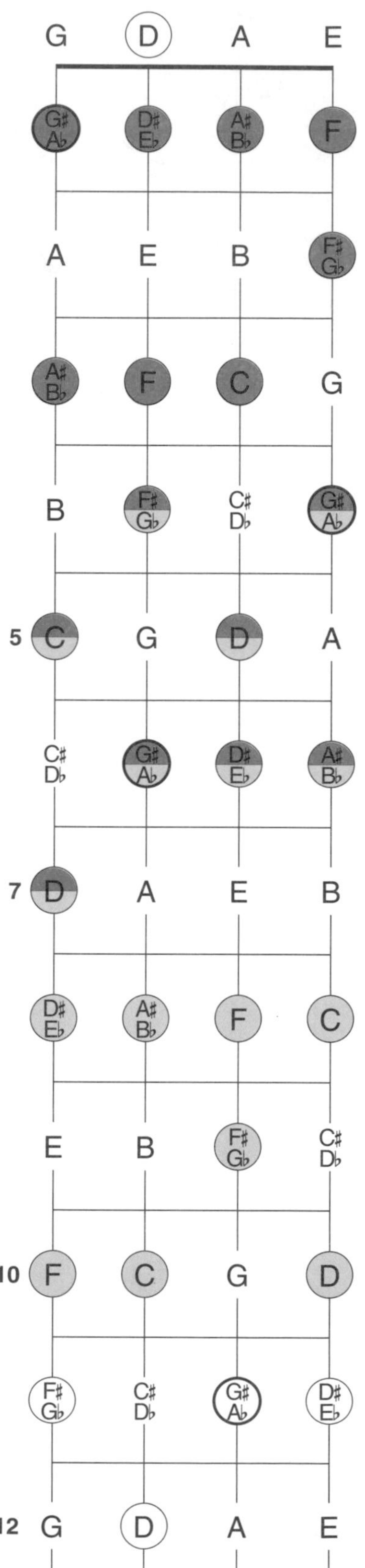

A LYDIAN DOMINANT

A–B–C♯–D♯–E–F♯–G

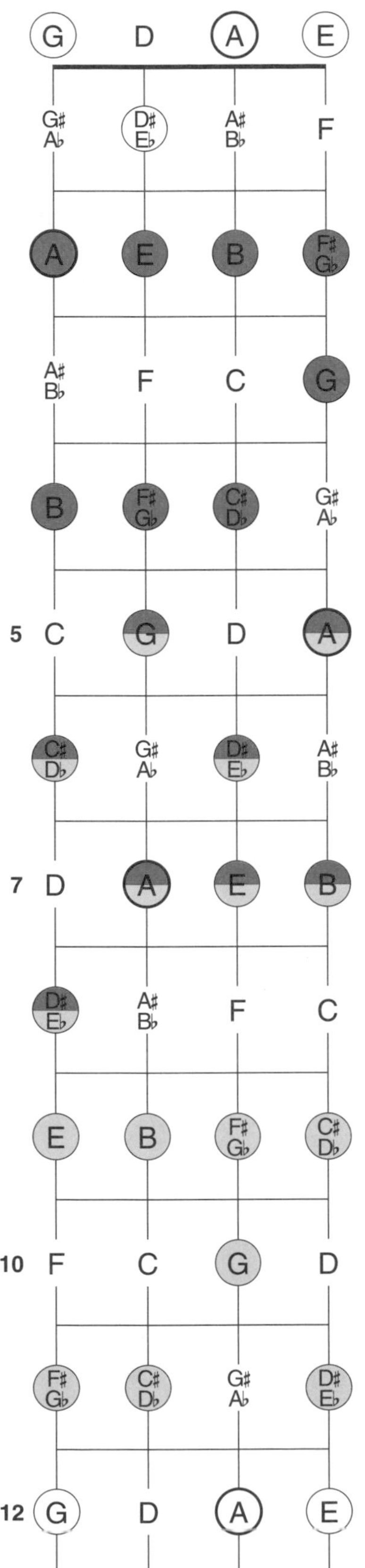

B♭ LYDIAN DOMINANT

B♭–C–D–E–F–G–A♭

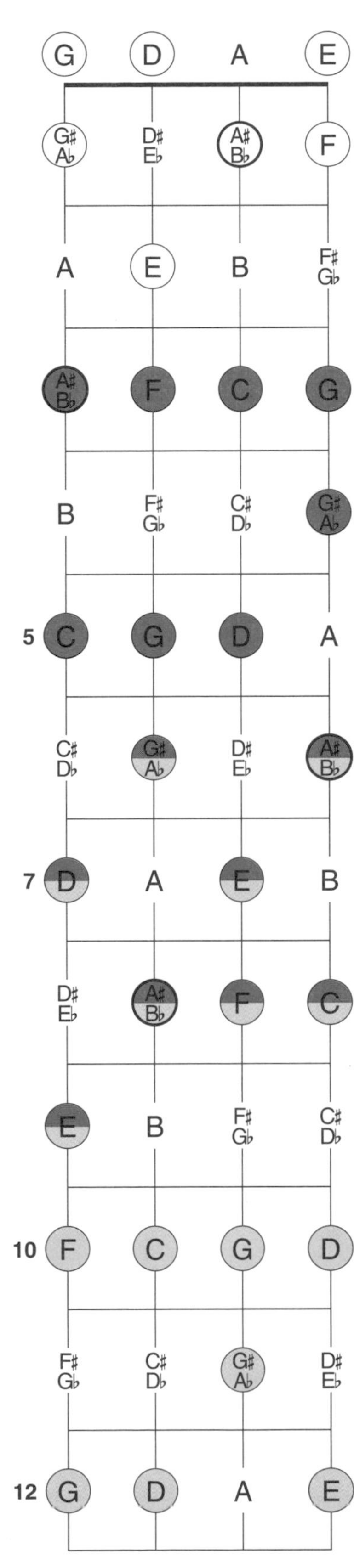

B LYDIAN DOMINANT

B–C♯–D♯–E♯–F♯–G♯–A

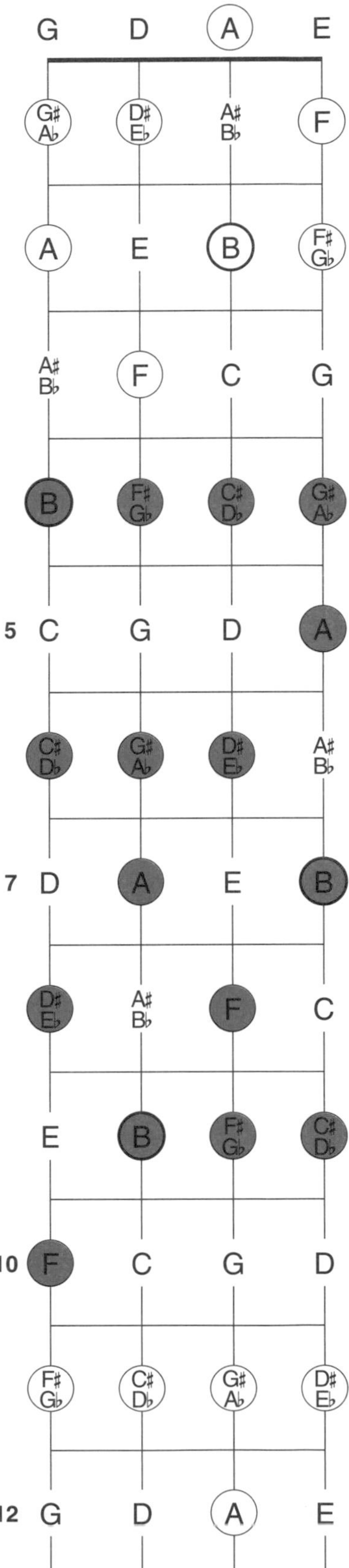

C SUPER LOCRIAN

C–D♭–E♭–F♭–G♭–A♭–B♭

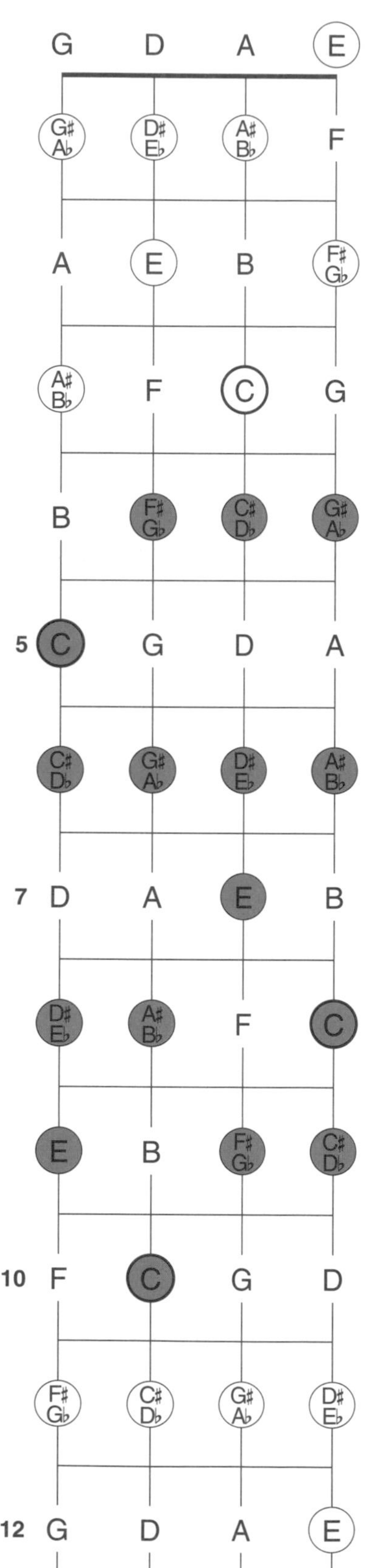

C♯ SUPER LOCRIAN

C♯–D–E–F–G–A–B

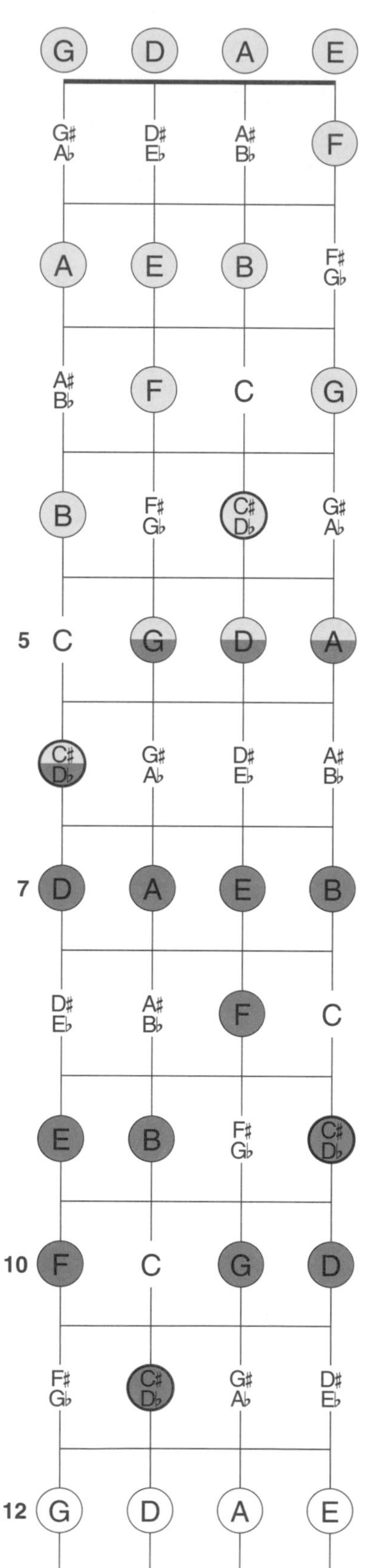

D SUPER LOCRIAN

D–E♭–F–G♭–A♭–B♭–C

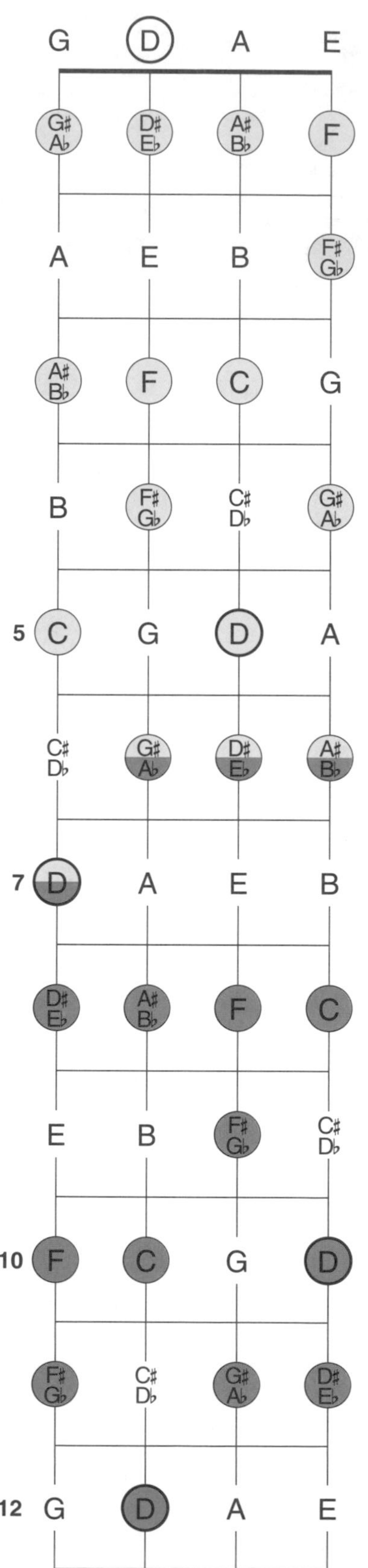

D♯ SUPER LOCRIAN

D♯–E–F♯–G–A–B–C♯

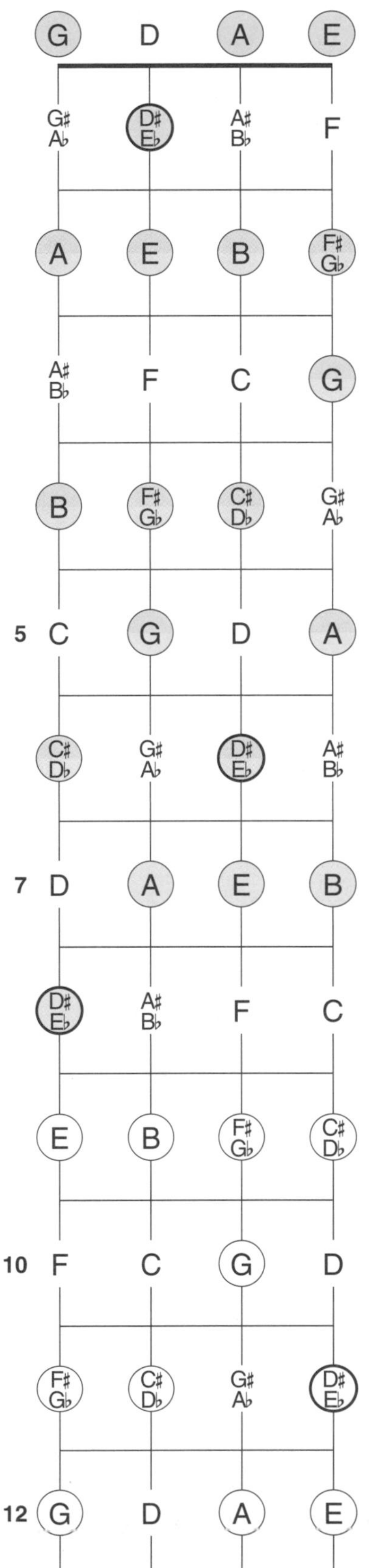

E SUPER LOCRIAN

E–F–G–A♭–B♭–C–D

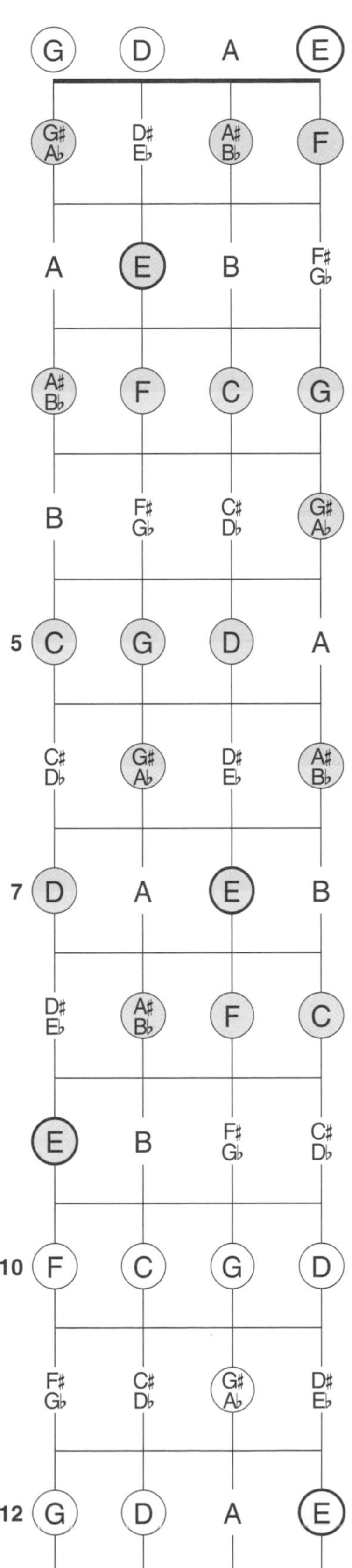

F SUPER LOCRIAN

F–G♭–A♭–B𝄫–C♭–D♭–E♭

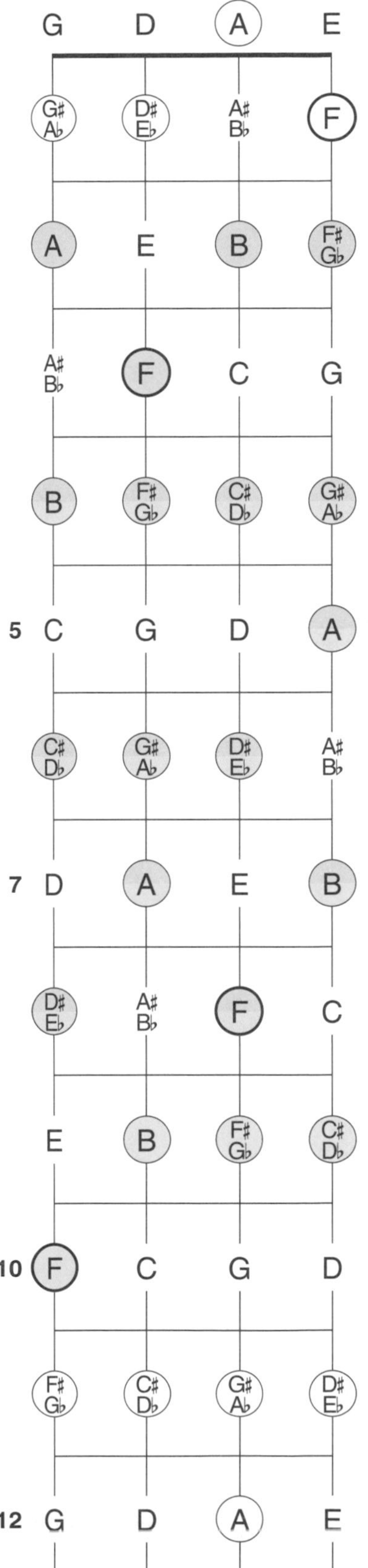

F♯ SUPER LOCRIAN

F♯–G–A–B♭–C–D–E

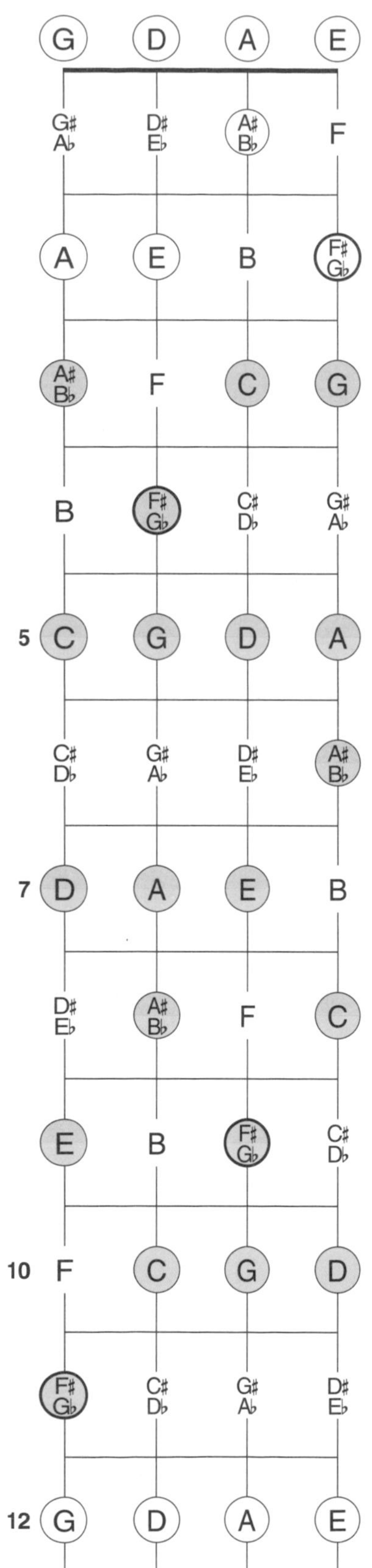

G SUPER LOCRIAN

G–A♭–B♭–C♭–D♭–E♭–F

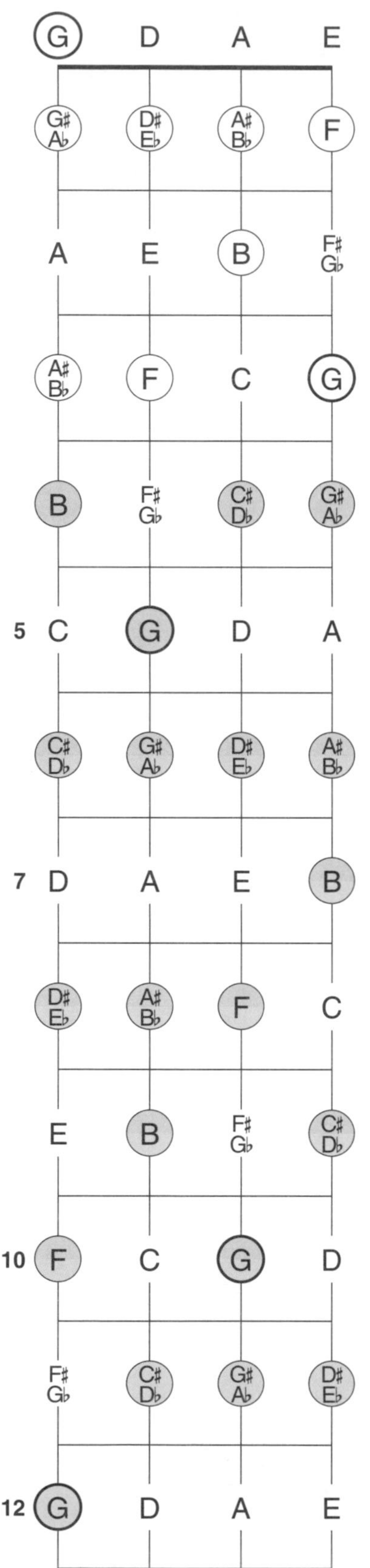

G♯ SUPER LOCRIAN

G♯–A–B–C–D–E–F♯

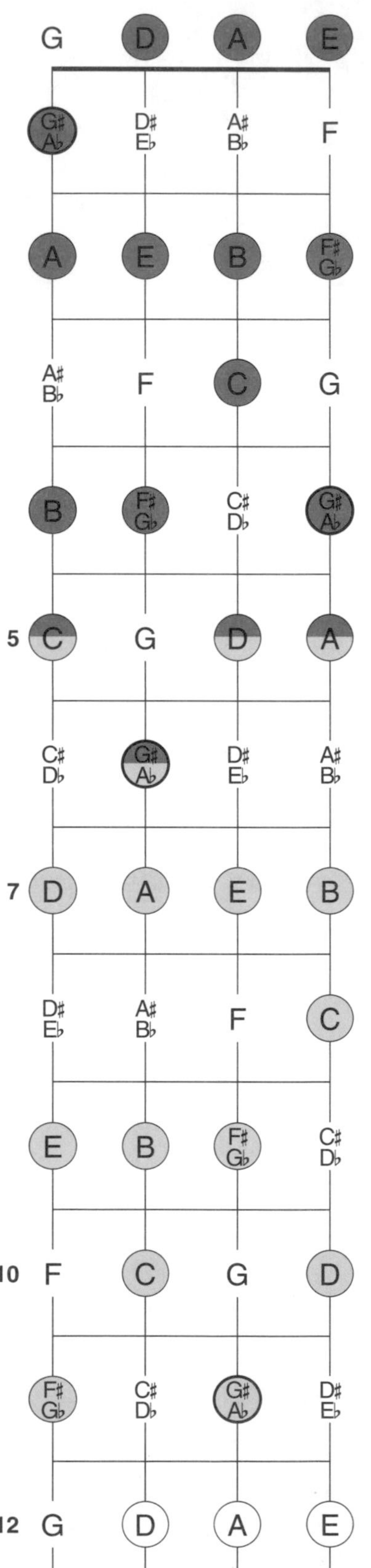

A SUPER LOCRIAN

A–B♭–C–D♭–E♭–F–G

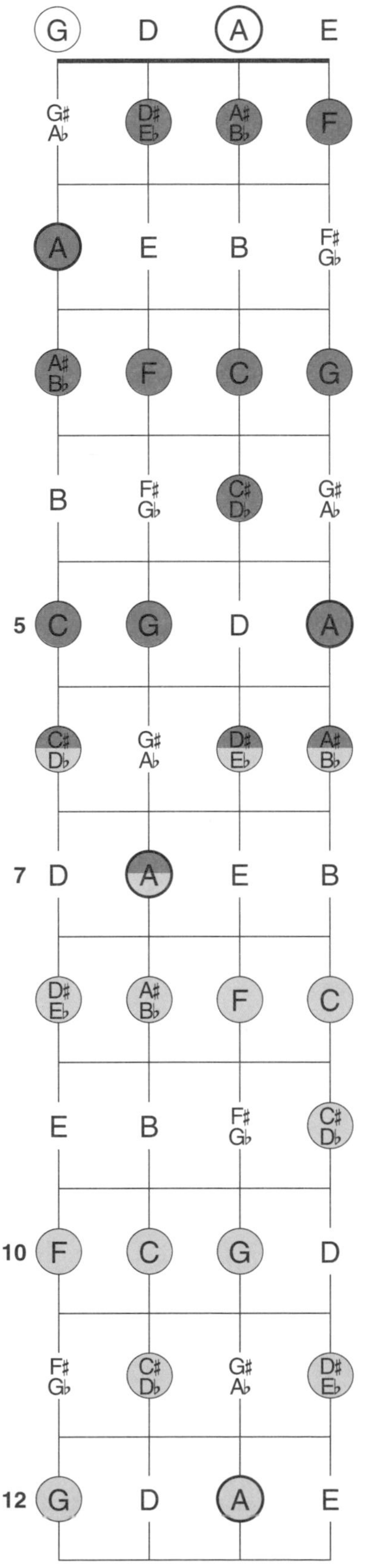

A♯ SUPER LOCRIAN

A♯–B–C♯–D–E–F♯–G♯

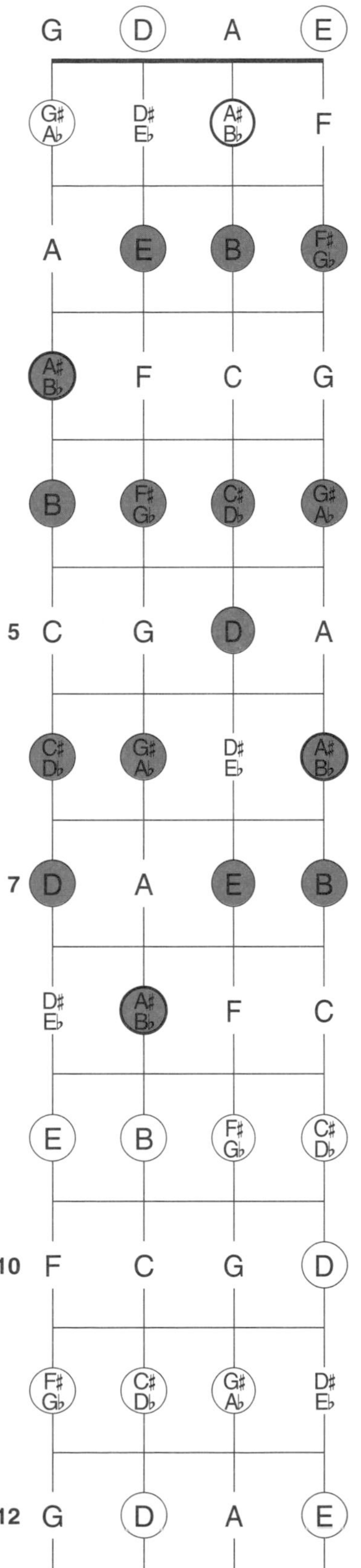

B SUPER LOCRIAN

B–C–D–E♭–F–G–A

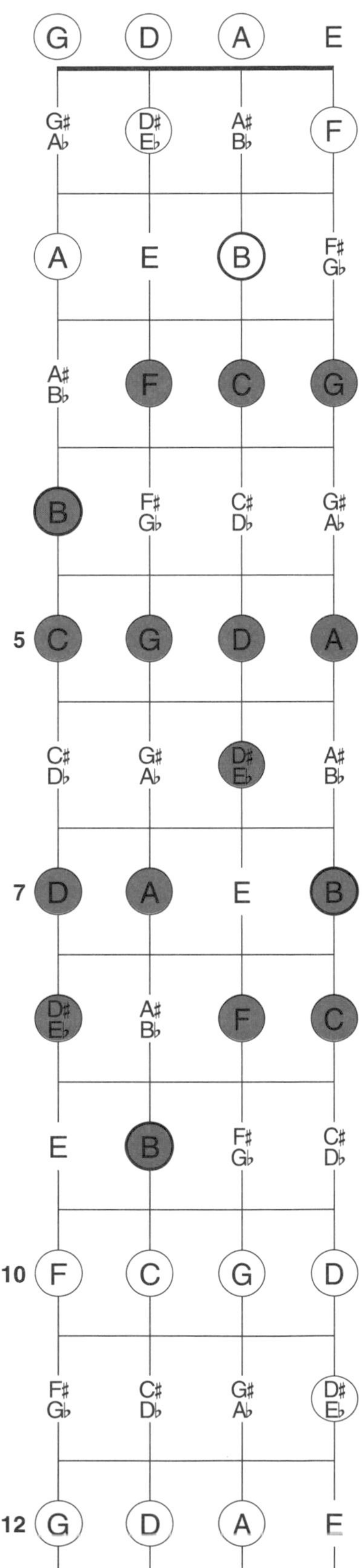

SCALES

THE HARMONIC MINOR SCALE AND SELECT MODE

C HARMONIC MINOR

C–D–E♭–F–G–A♭–B

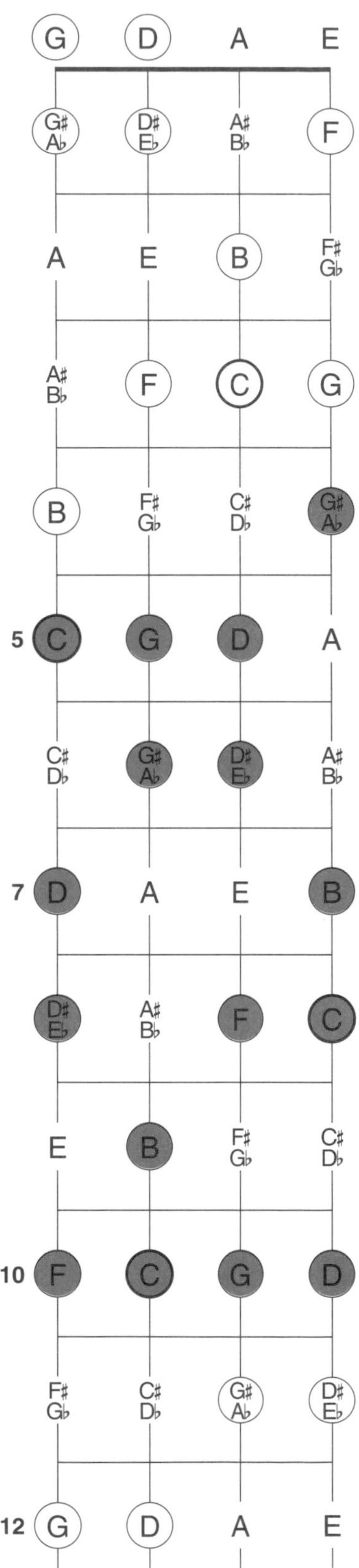

C♯ HARMONIC MINOR

C♯–D♯–E–F♯–G♯–A–B♯

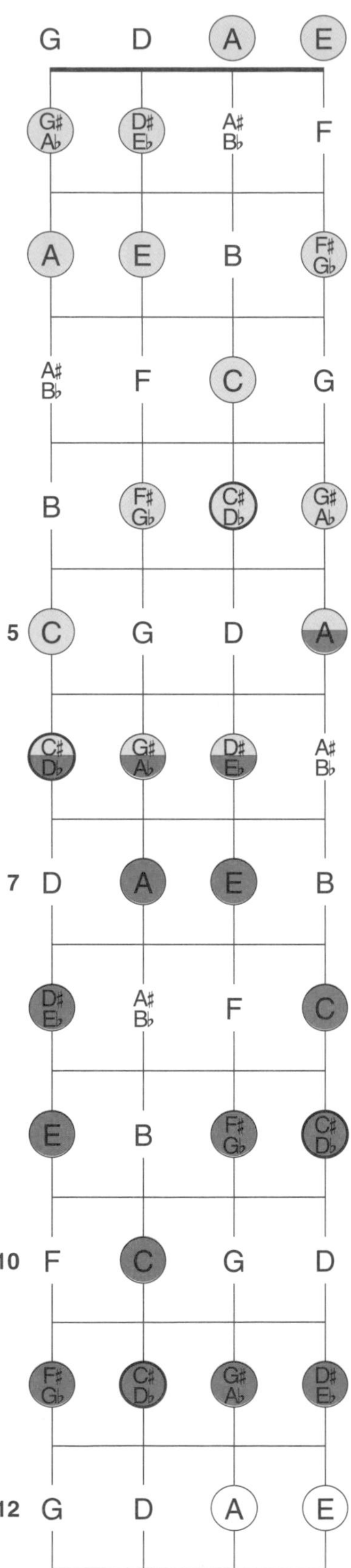

D HARMONIC MINOR

D–E–F–G–A–B♭–C♯

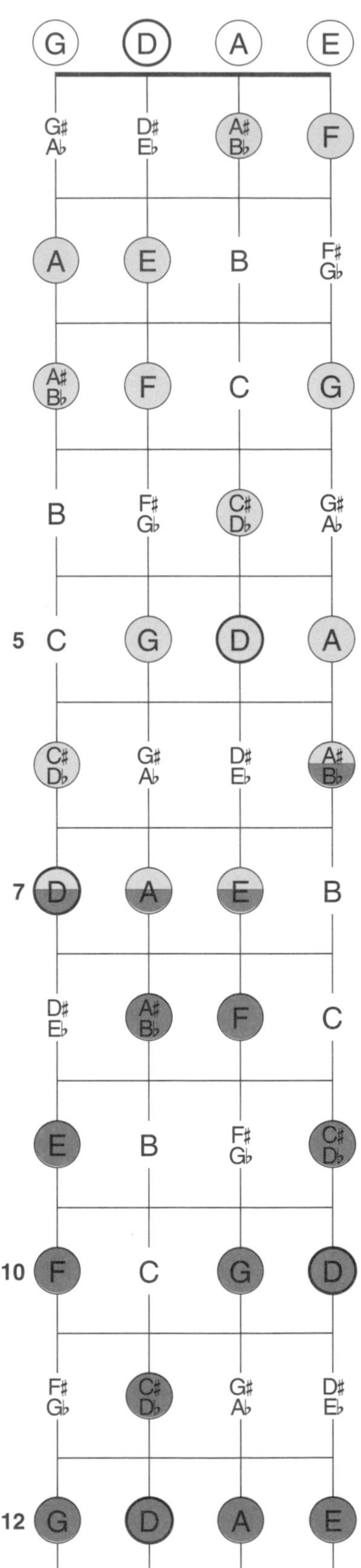

E♭ HARMONIC MINOR

E♭–F–G♭–A♭–B♭–C♭–D

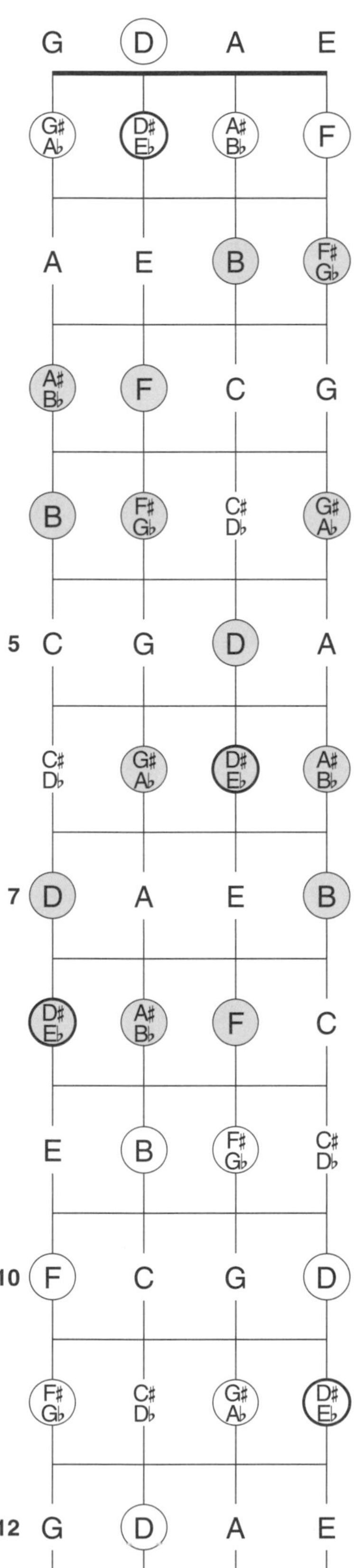

E HARMONIC MINOR

E–F♯–G–A–B–C–D♯

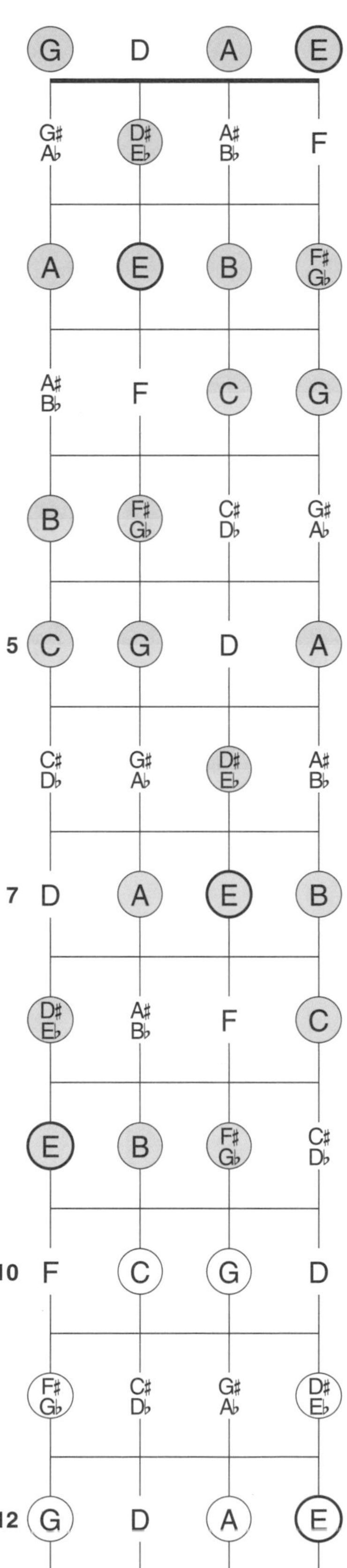

F HARMONIC MINOR

F–G–A♭–B♭–C–D♭–E

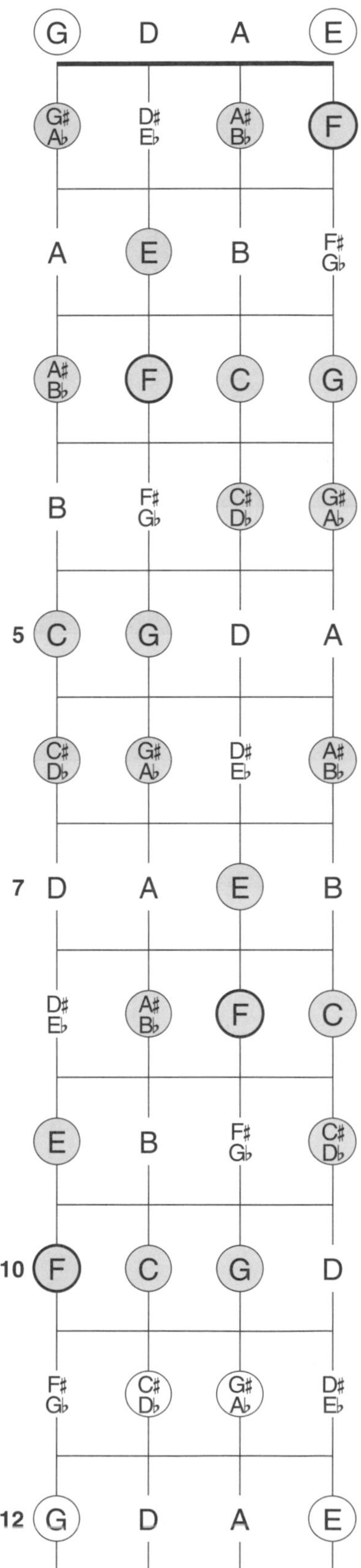

F♯ HARMONIC MINOR

F♯–G♯–A–B–C♯–D–E♯

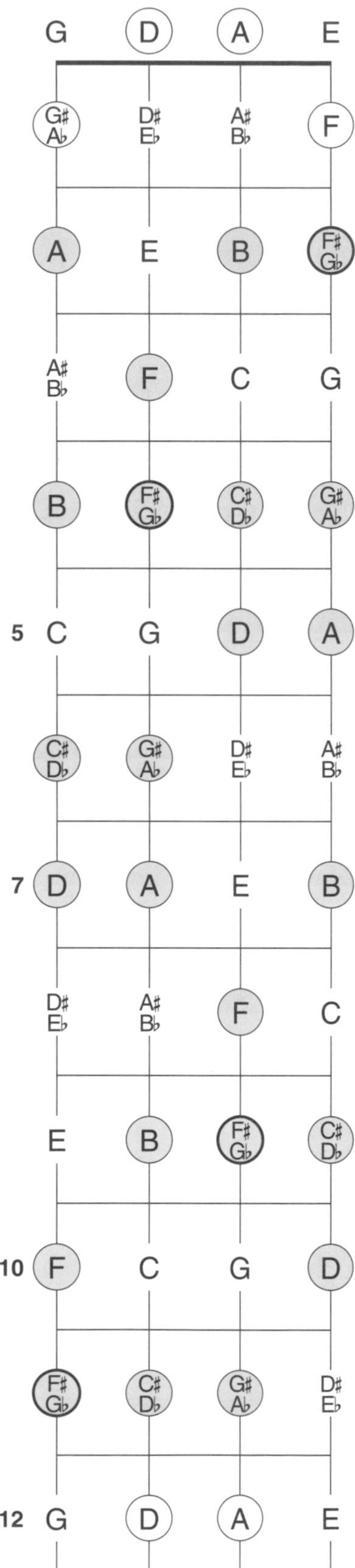

G HARMONIC MINOR

G–A–B♭–C–D–E♭–F♯

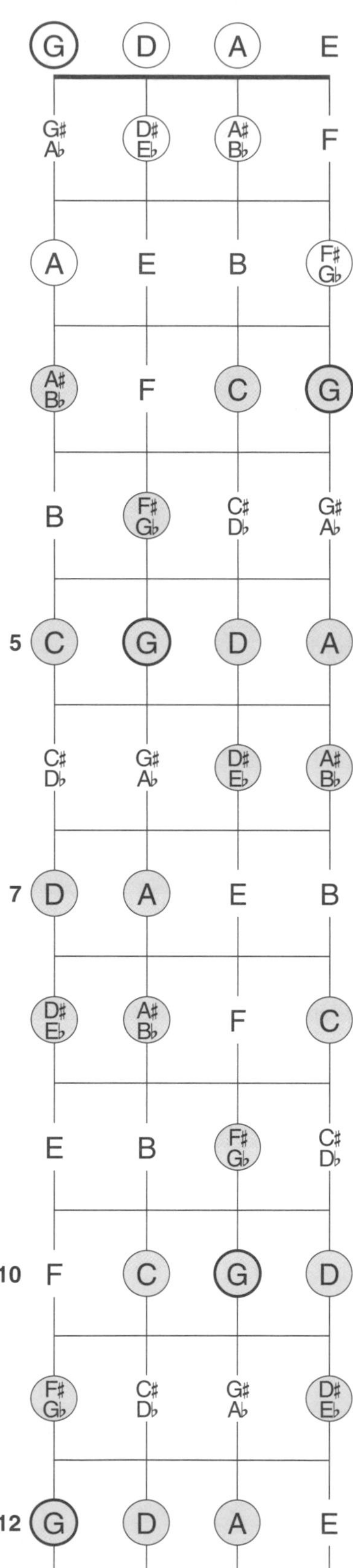

A♭ HARMONIC MINOR

A♭–B♭–C♭–D♭–E♭–F♭–G

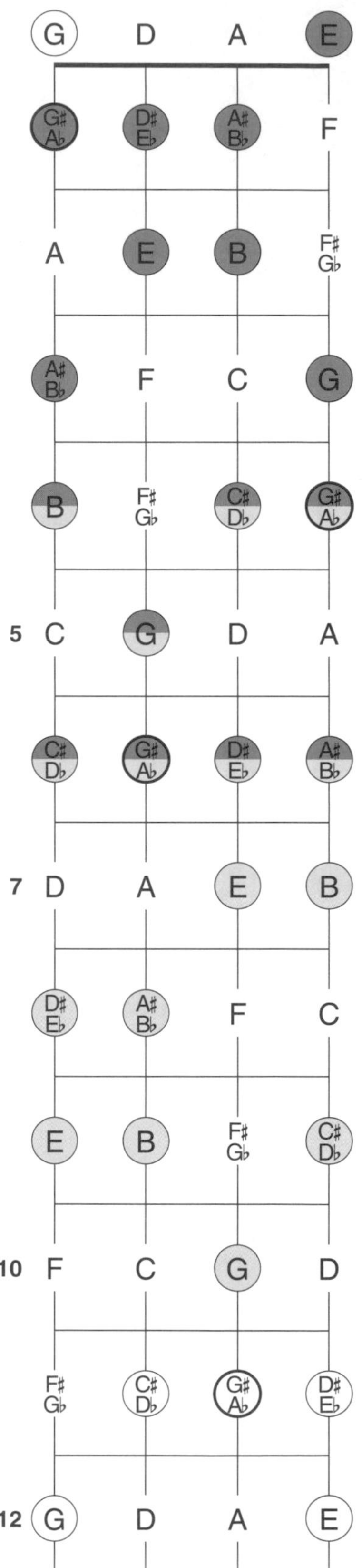

A HARMONIC MINOR

A–B–C–D–E–F–G♯

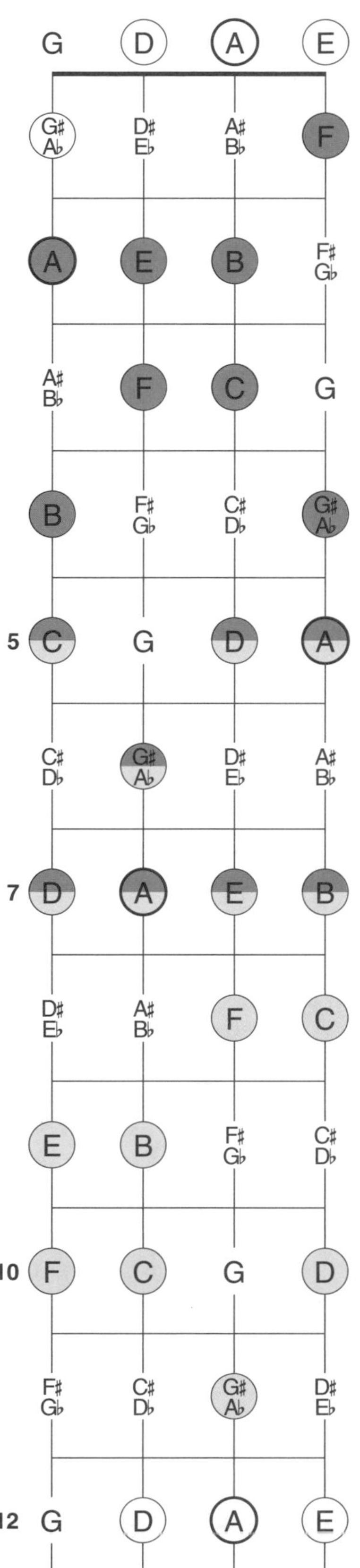

B♭ HARMONIC MINOR

B♭–C–D♭–E♭–F–G♭–A

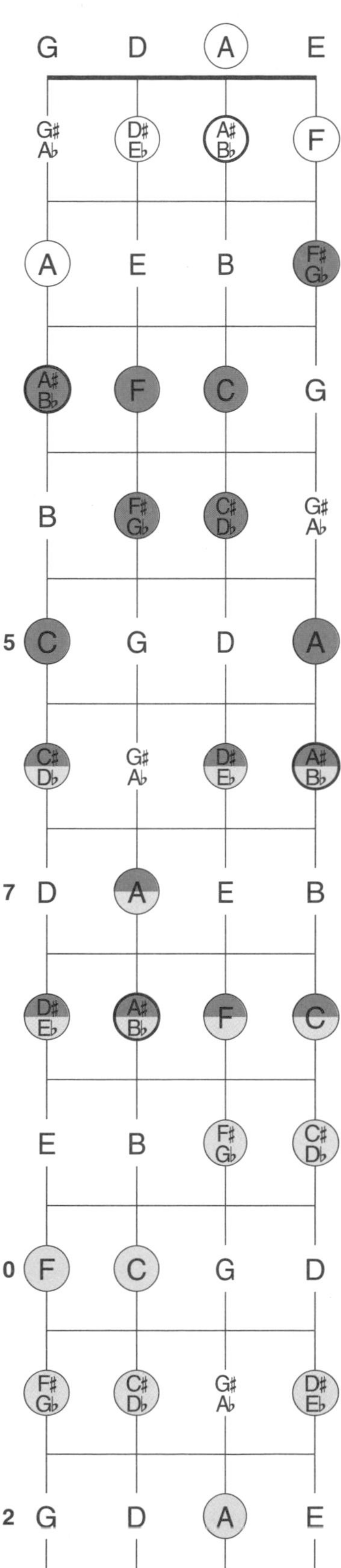

B HARMONIC MINOR

B–C♯–D–E–F♯–G–A♯

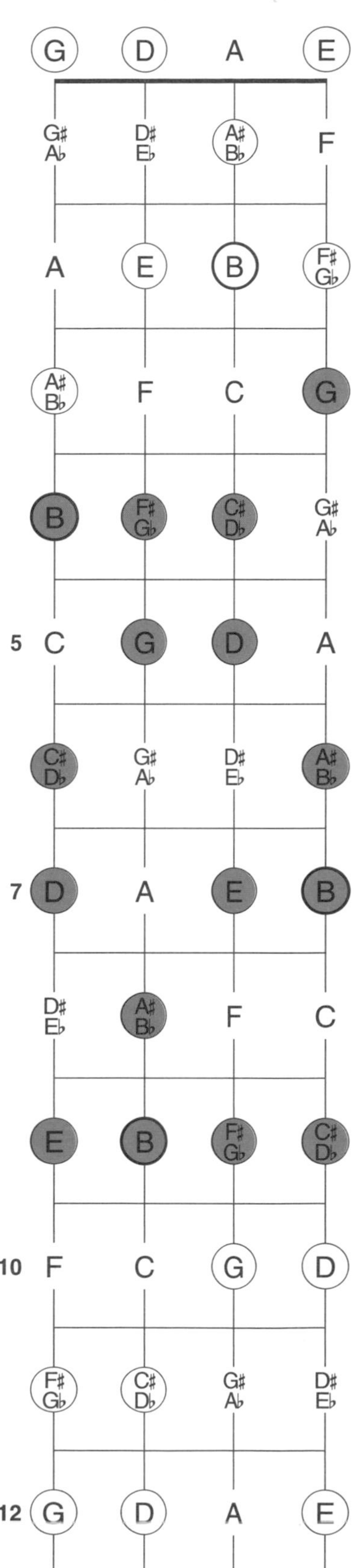

C PHRYGIAN DOMINANT

C–D♭–E–F–G–A♭–B♭

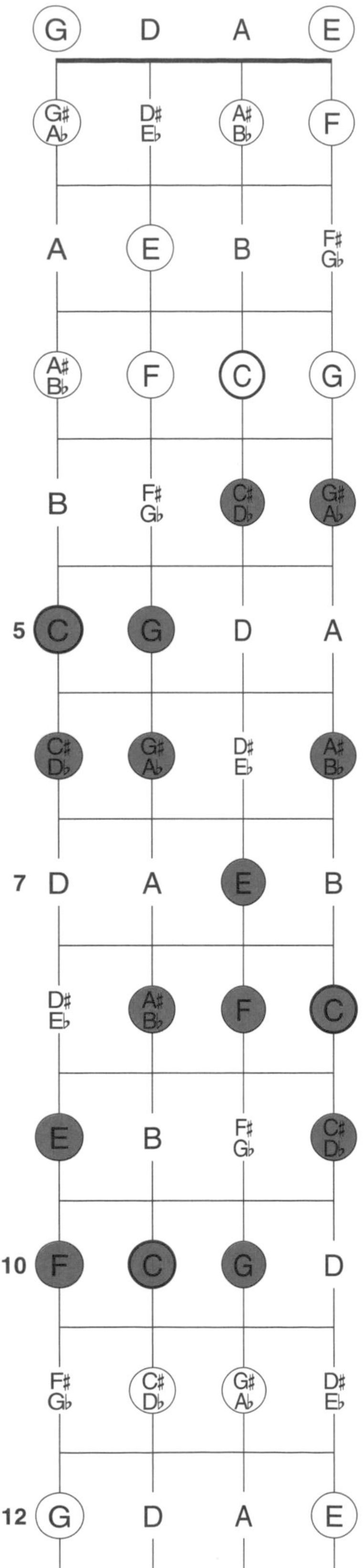

C♯ PHRYGIAN DOMINANT

C♯–D–E♯–F♯–G♯–A–B

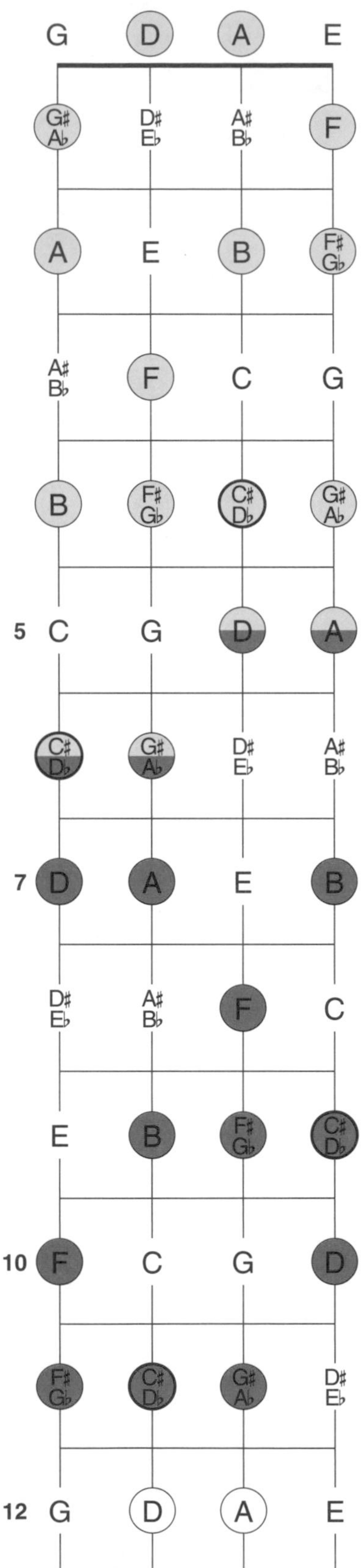

D PHRYGIAN DOMINANT

D–E♭–F♯–G–A–B♭–C

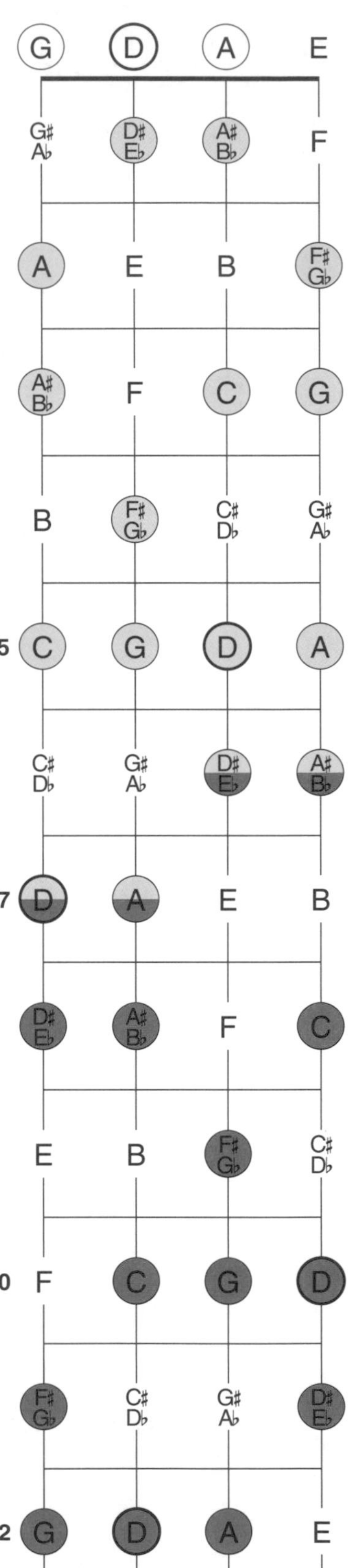

E♭ PHRYGIAN DOMINANT

E♭–F♭–G–A♭–B♭–C♭–D♭

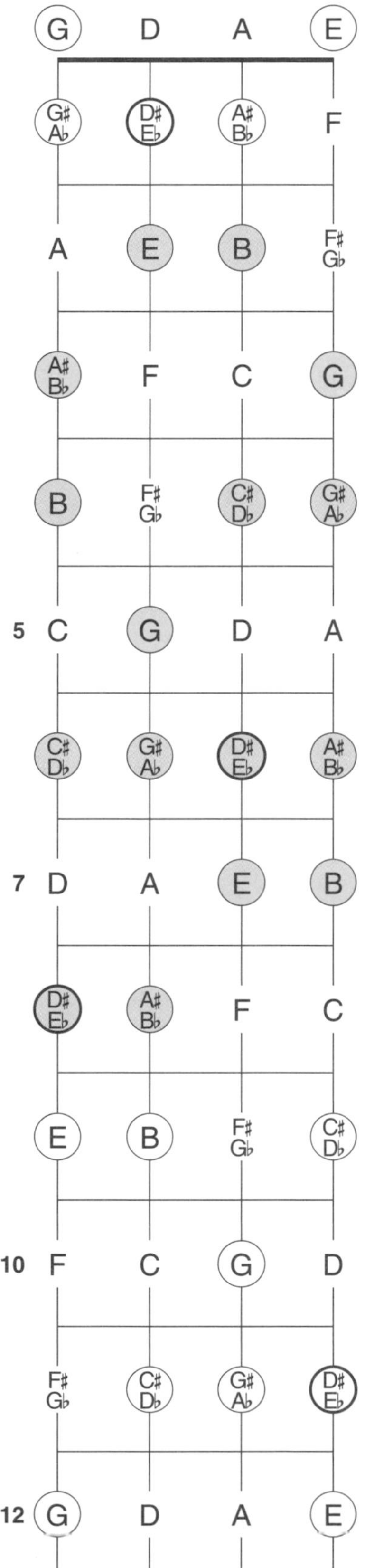

E PHRYGIAN DOMINANT

E–F–G♯–A–B–C–D

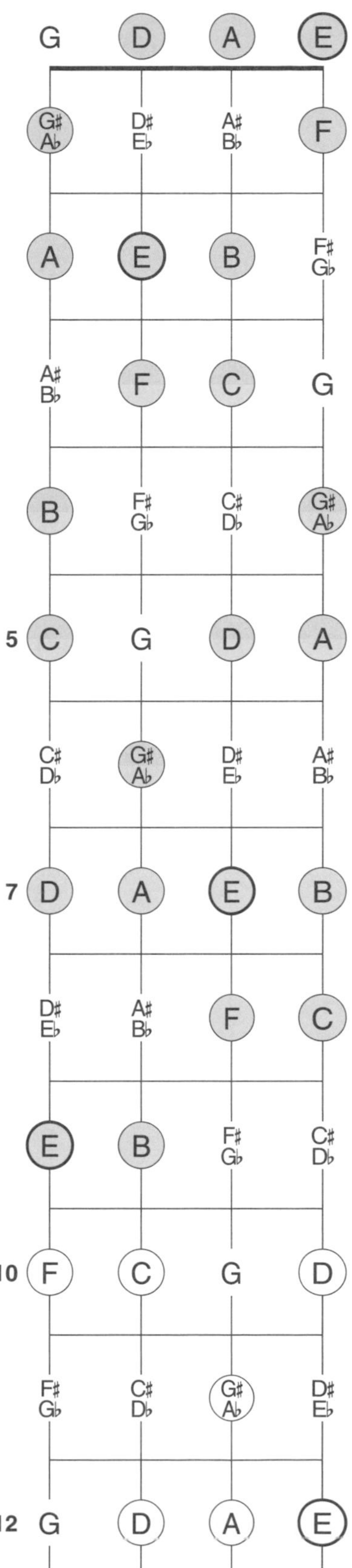

F PHRYGIAN DOMINANT

F–G♭–A–B♭–C–D♭–E♭

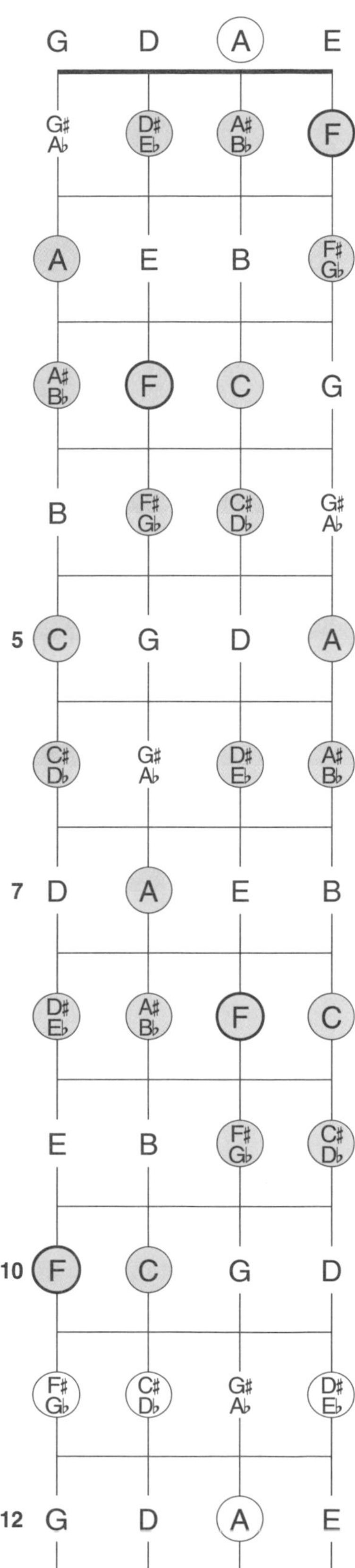

F♯ PHRYGIAN DOMINANT

F♯–G–A♯–B–C♯–D–E

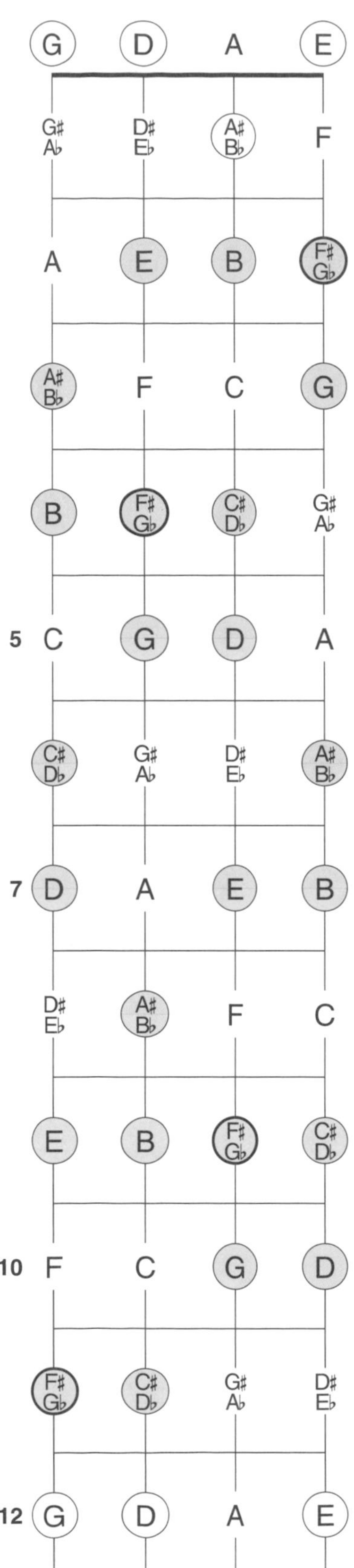

G PHRYGIAN DOMINANT

G–A♭–B–C–D–E♭–F

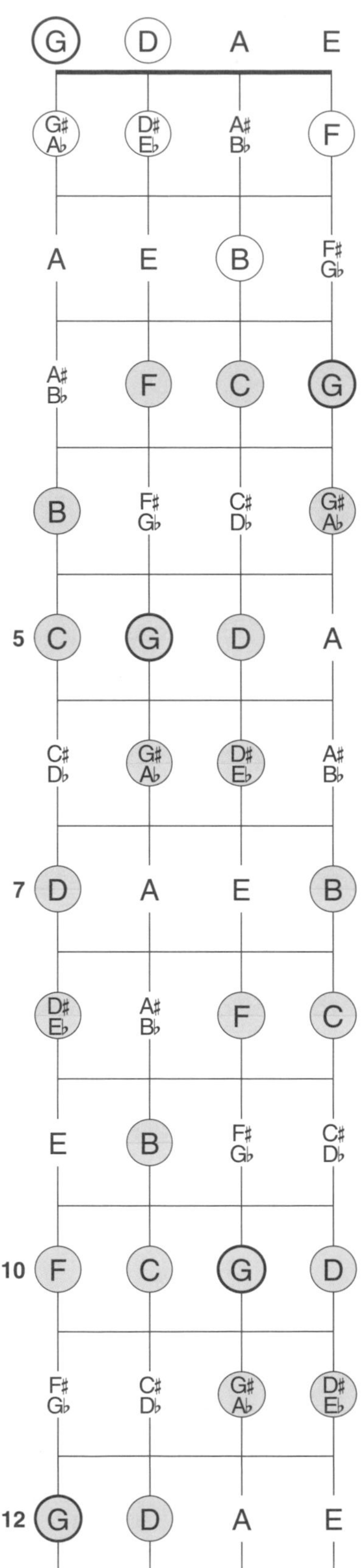

G♯ PHRYGIAN DOMINANT

G♯–A–B♯–C♯–D♯–E–F♯

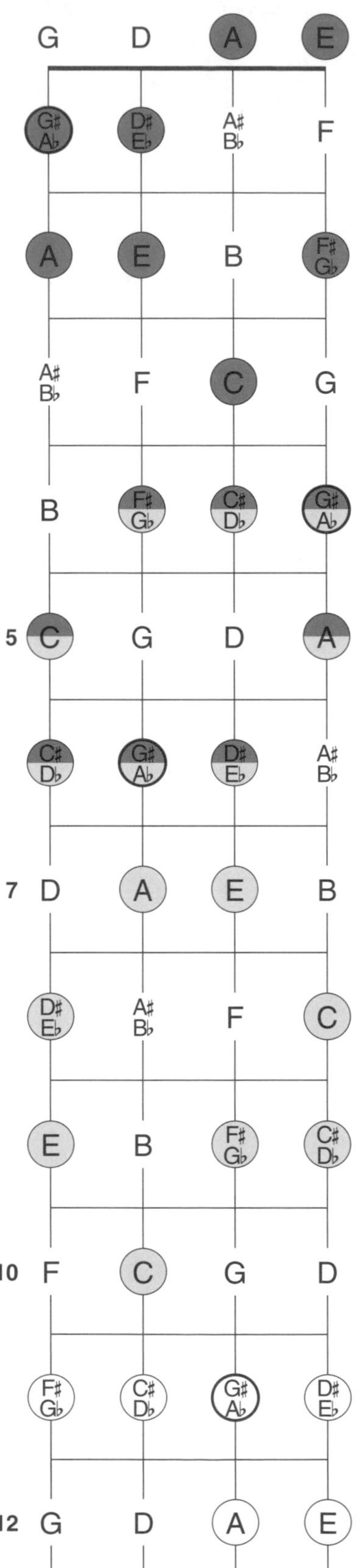

A PHRYGIAN DOMINANT

A–B♭–C♯–D–E–F–G

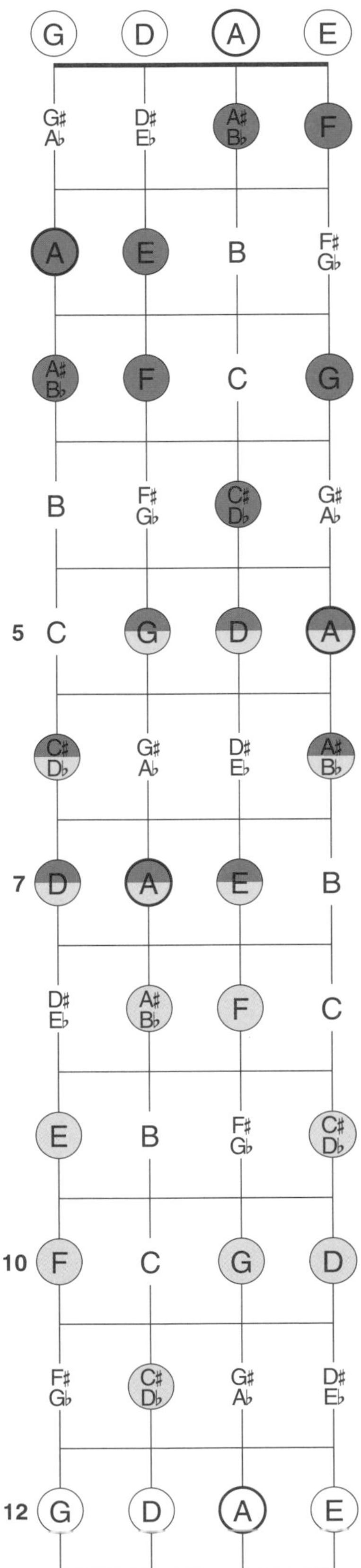

B♭ PHRYGIAN DOMINANT

B♭–C♭–D–E♭–F–G♭–A♭

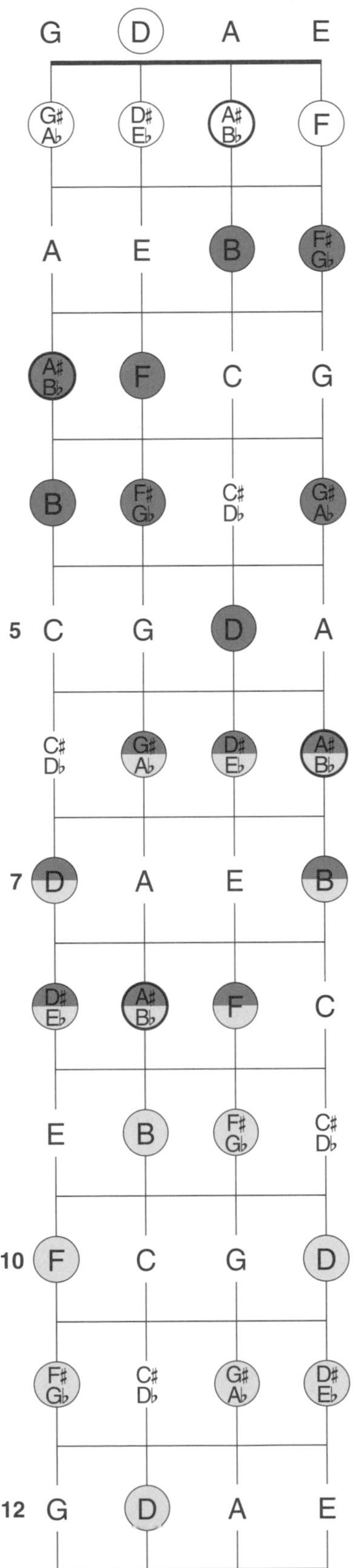

B PHRYGIAN DOMINANT

B–C–D♯–E–F♯–G–A

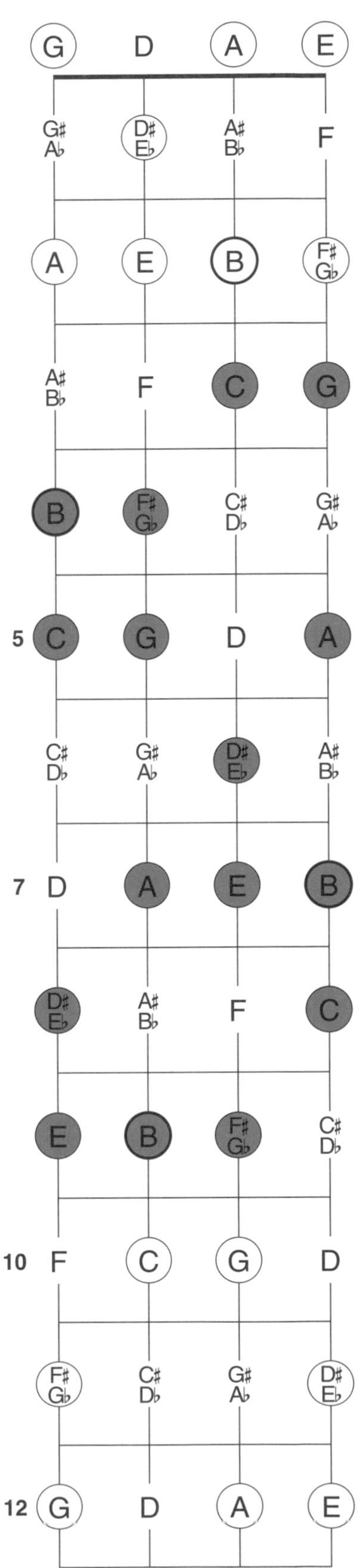

CHORDS

POWER CHORDS

C5

C–G

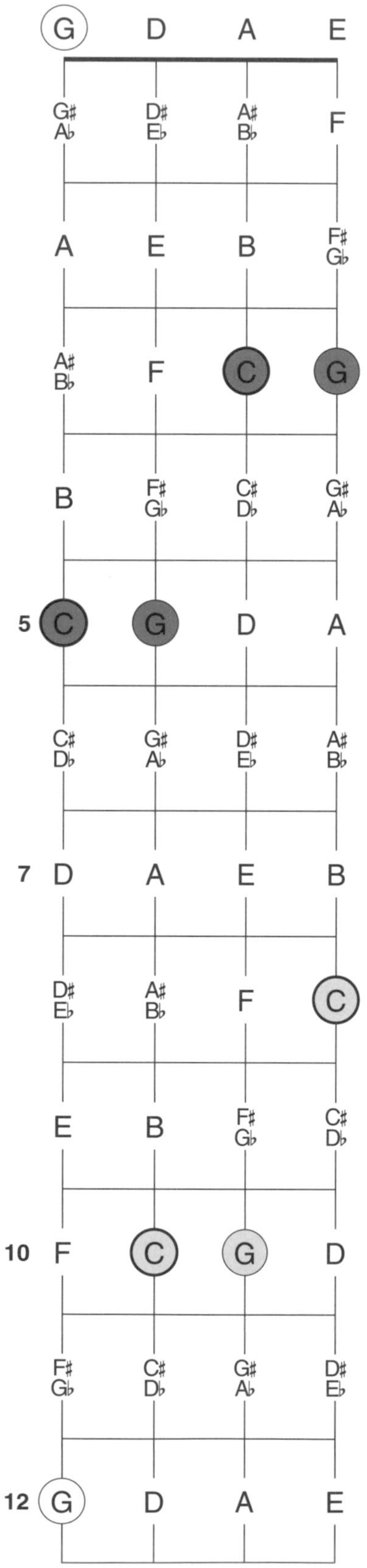

C♯/D♭5

C♯–G♯/D♭–A♭

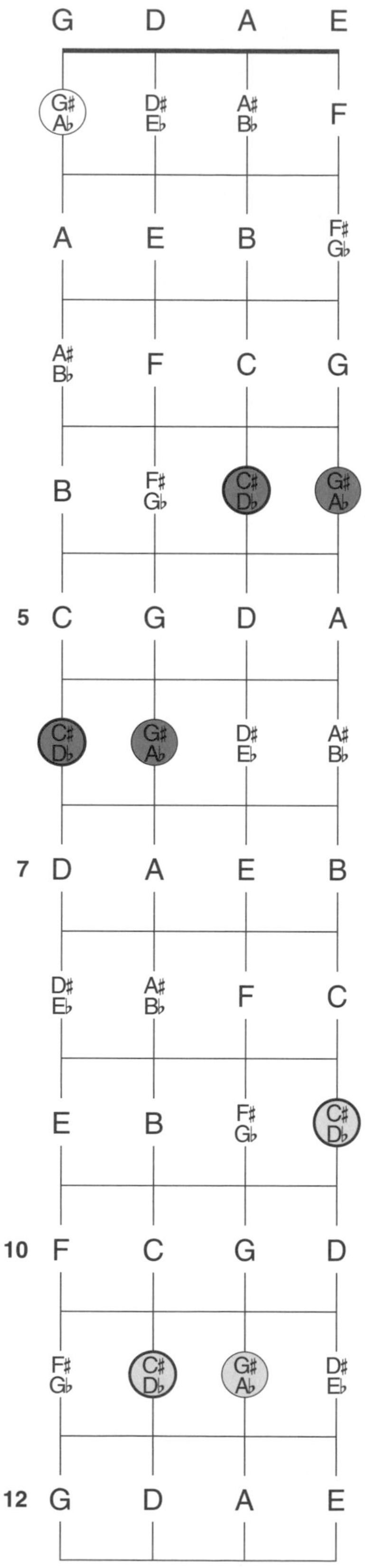

D5

D–A

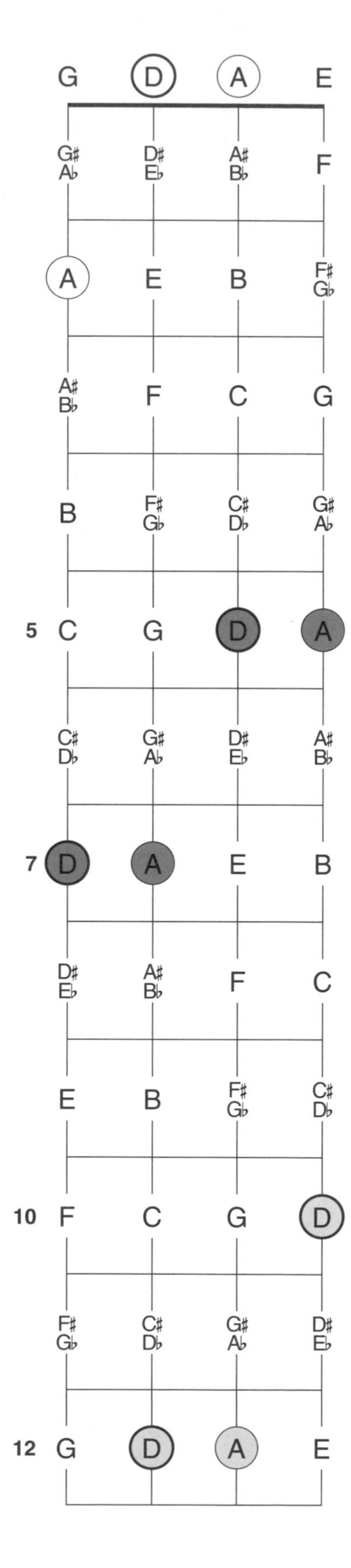

E♭5

E♭–B♭

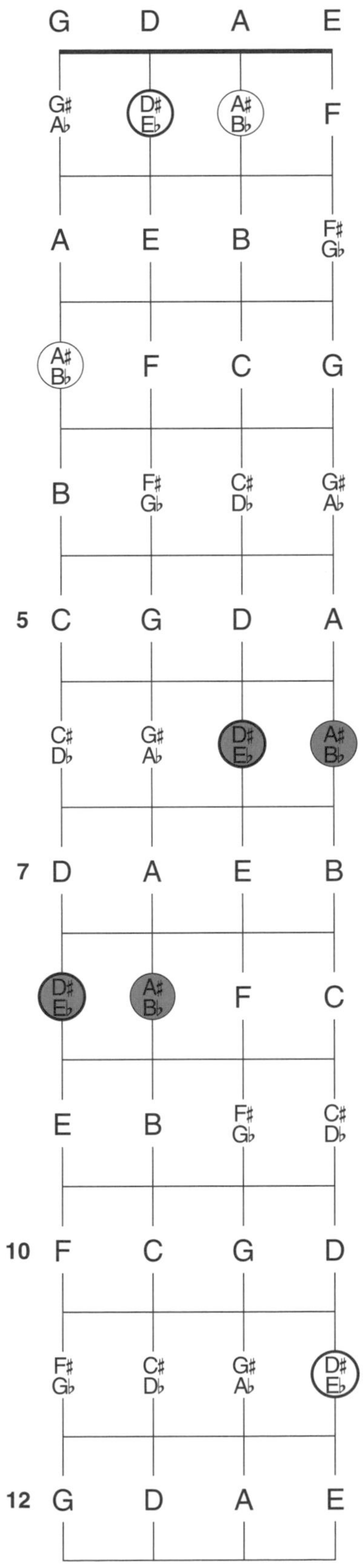

E5

E–B

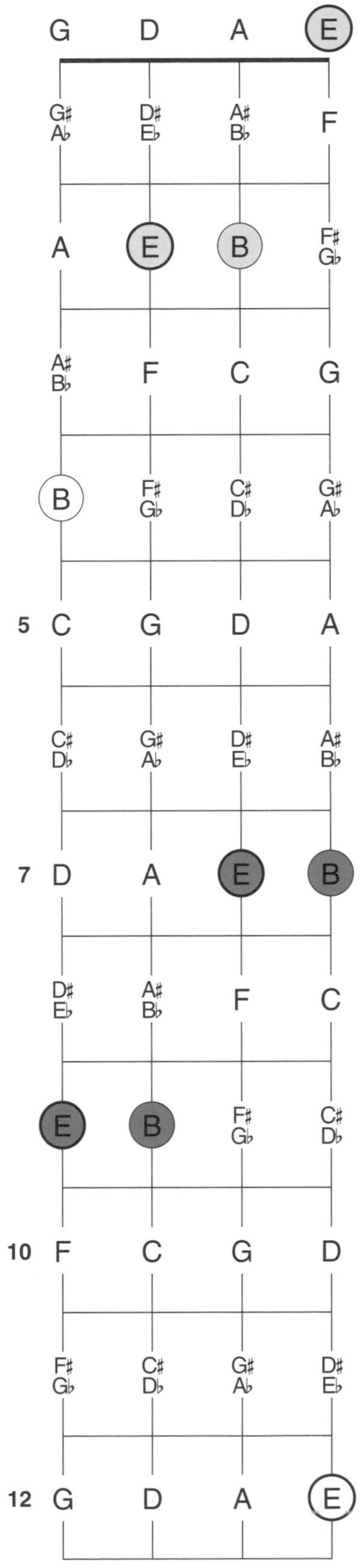

F5

F–C

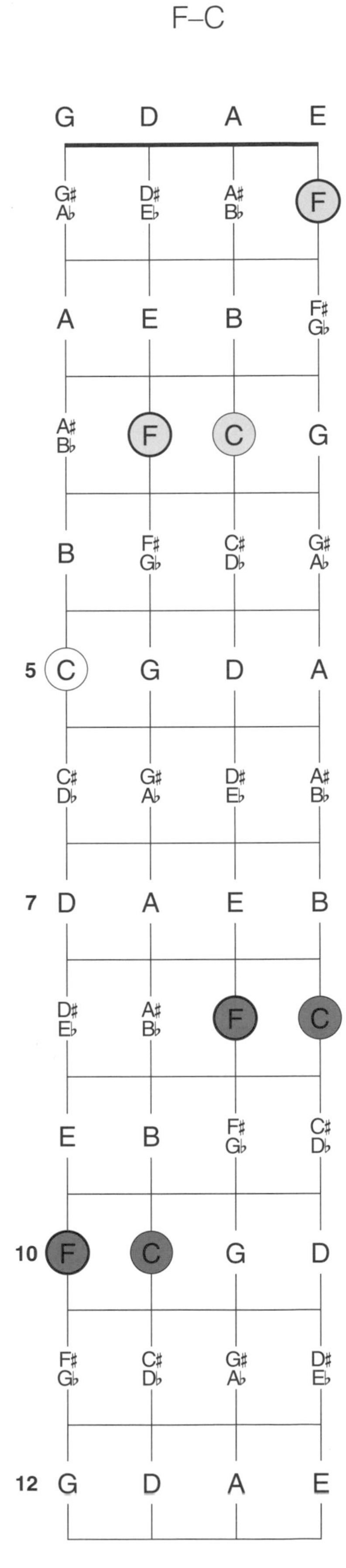

F♯/G♭5

F♯–C♯/G♭–D♭

G5

G–D

G♯/A♭5

G♯–D♯/A♭–E♭

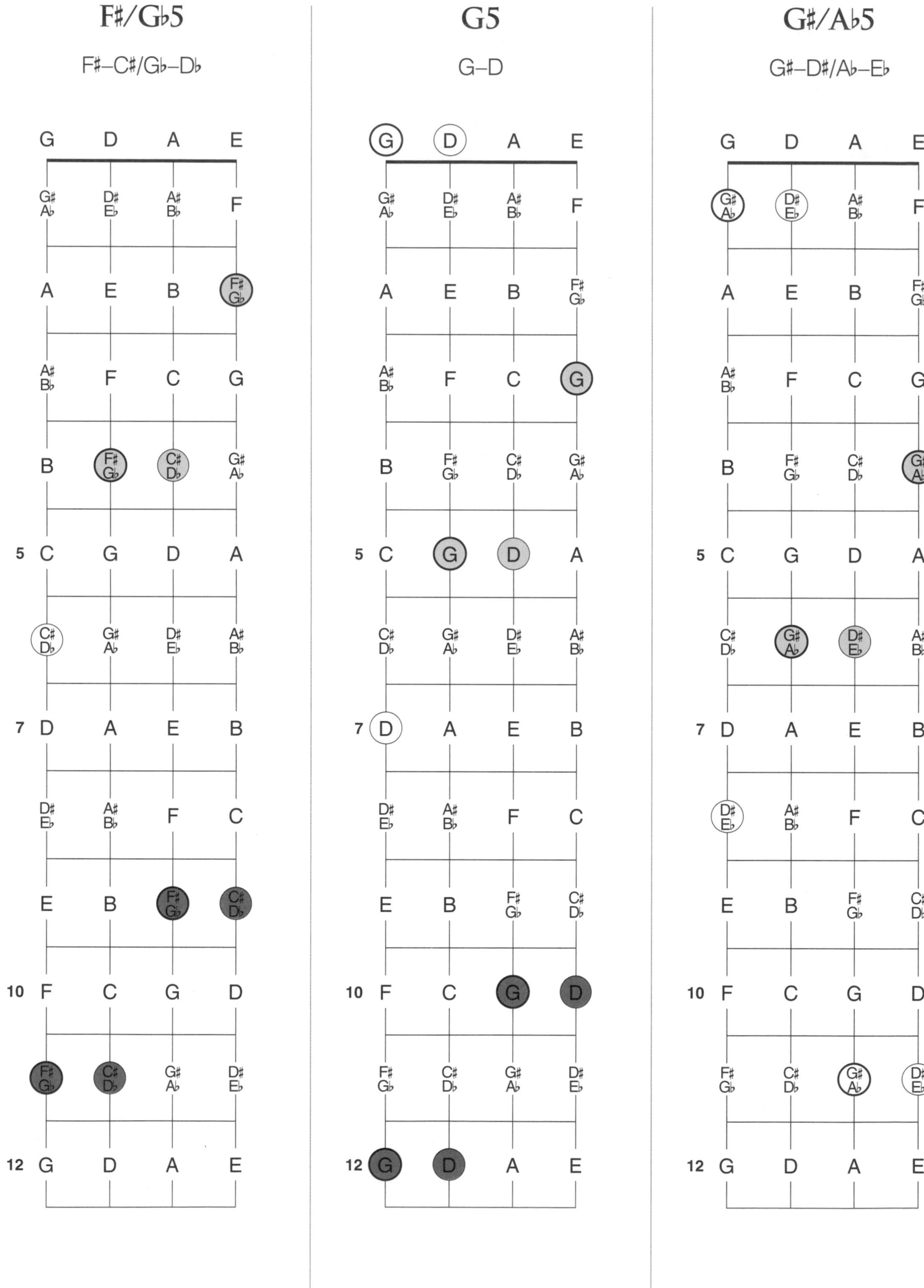

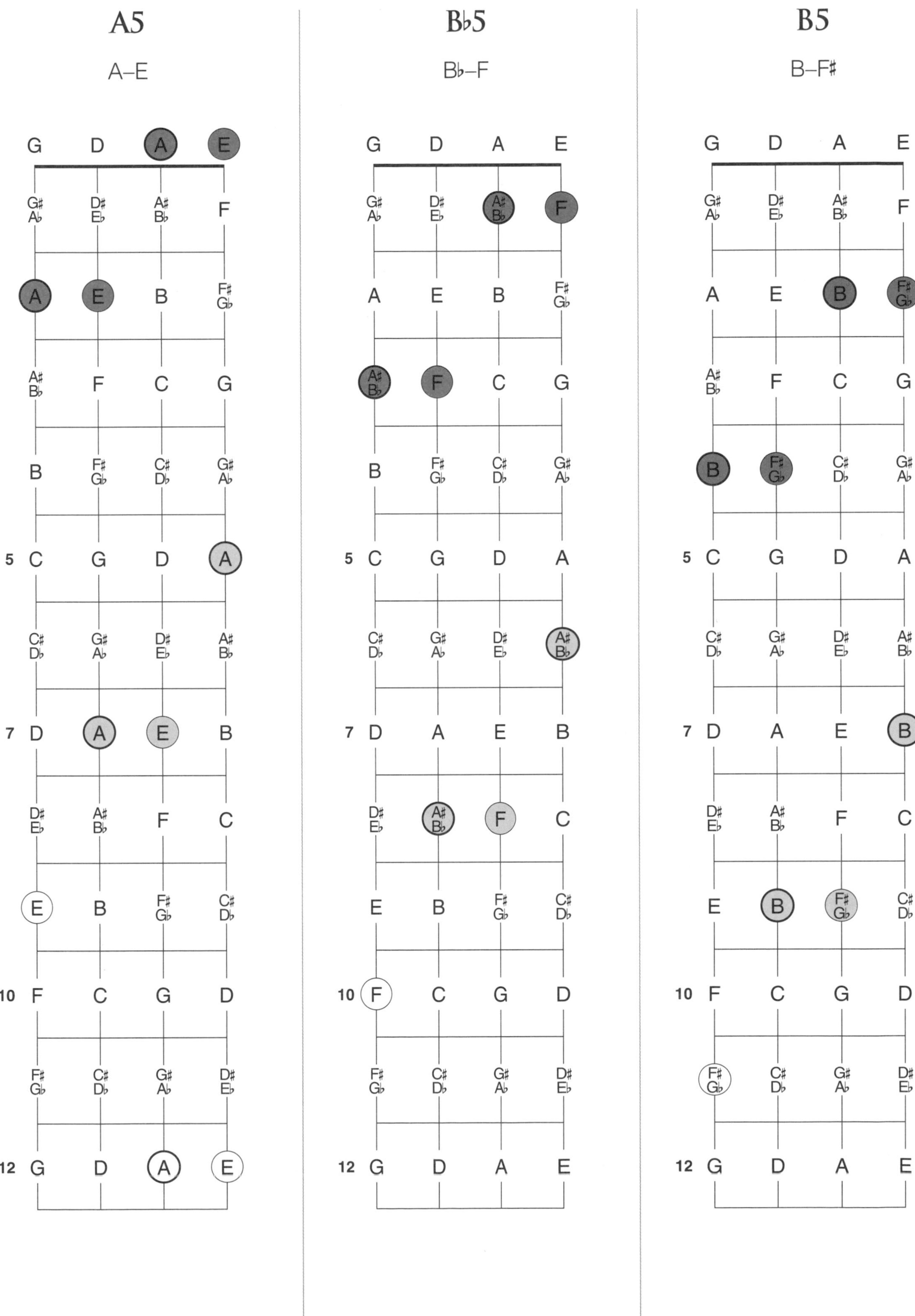
A5
A–E
B♭5
B♭–F
B5
B–F♯

CHORDS

TRIADS

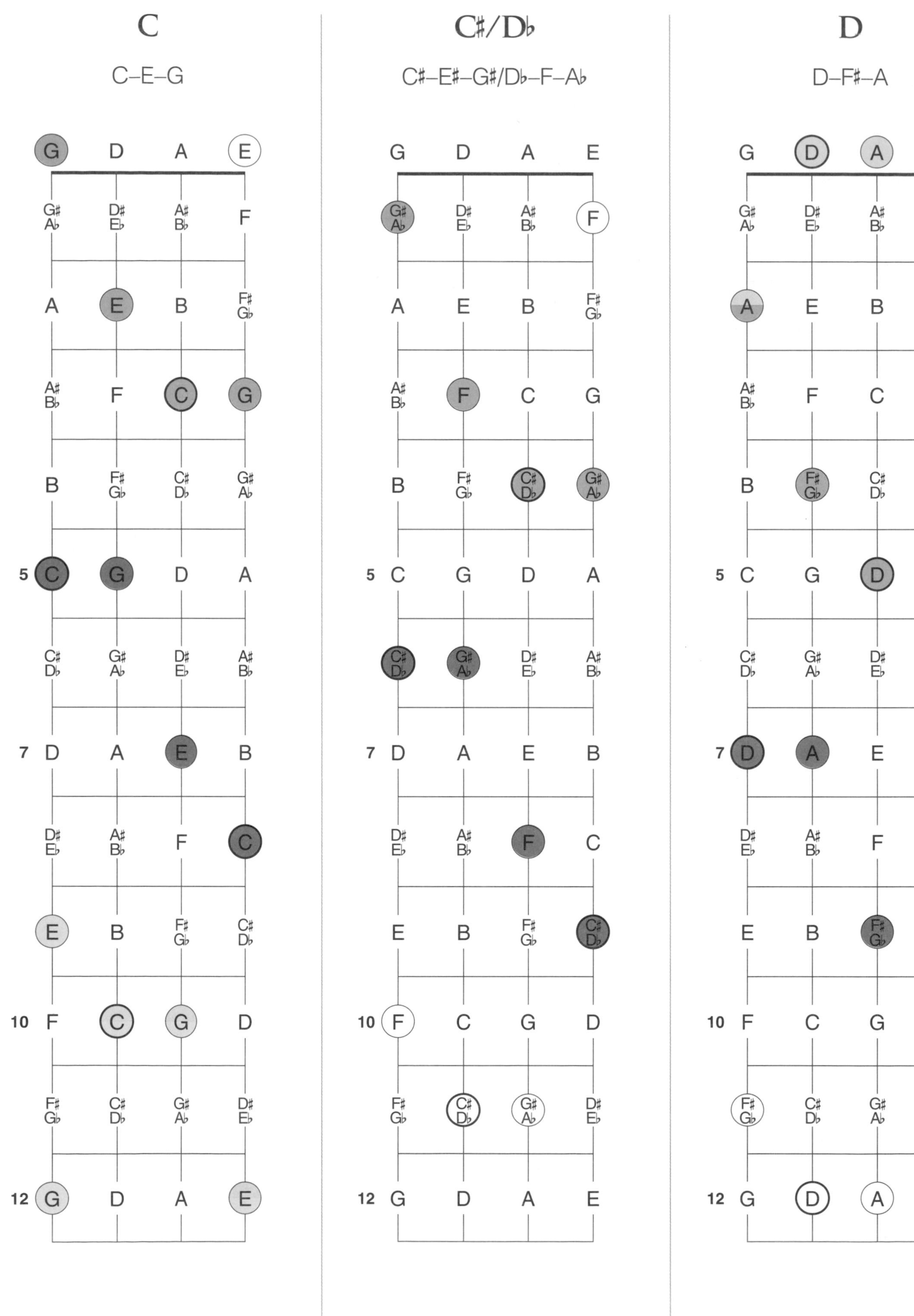

C
C–E–G
C♯/D♭
C♯–E♯–G♯/D♭–F–A♭
D
D–F♯–A

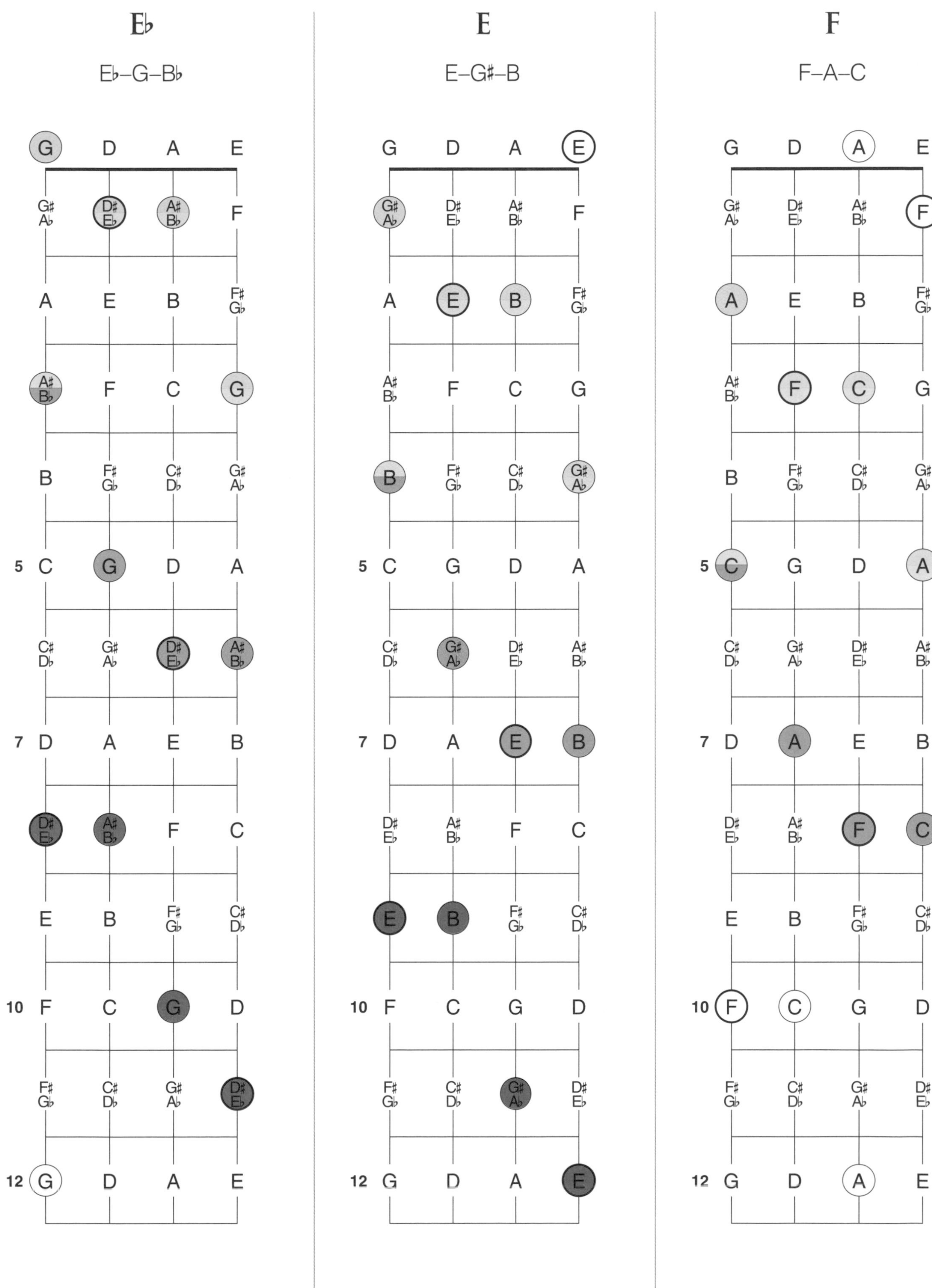
E♭
E♭–G–B♭
E
E–G♯–B
F
F–A–C
G D A E
5
7
10
12

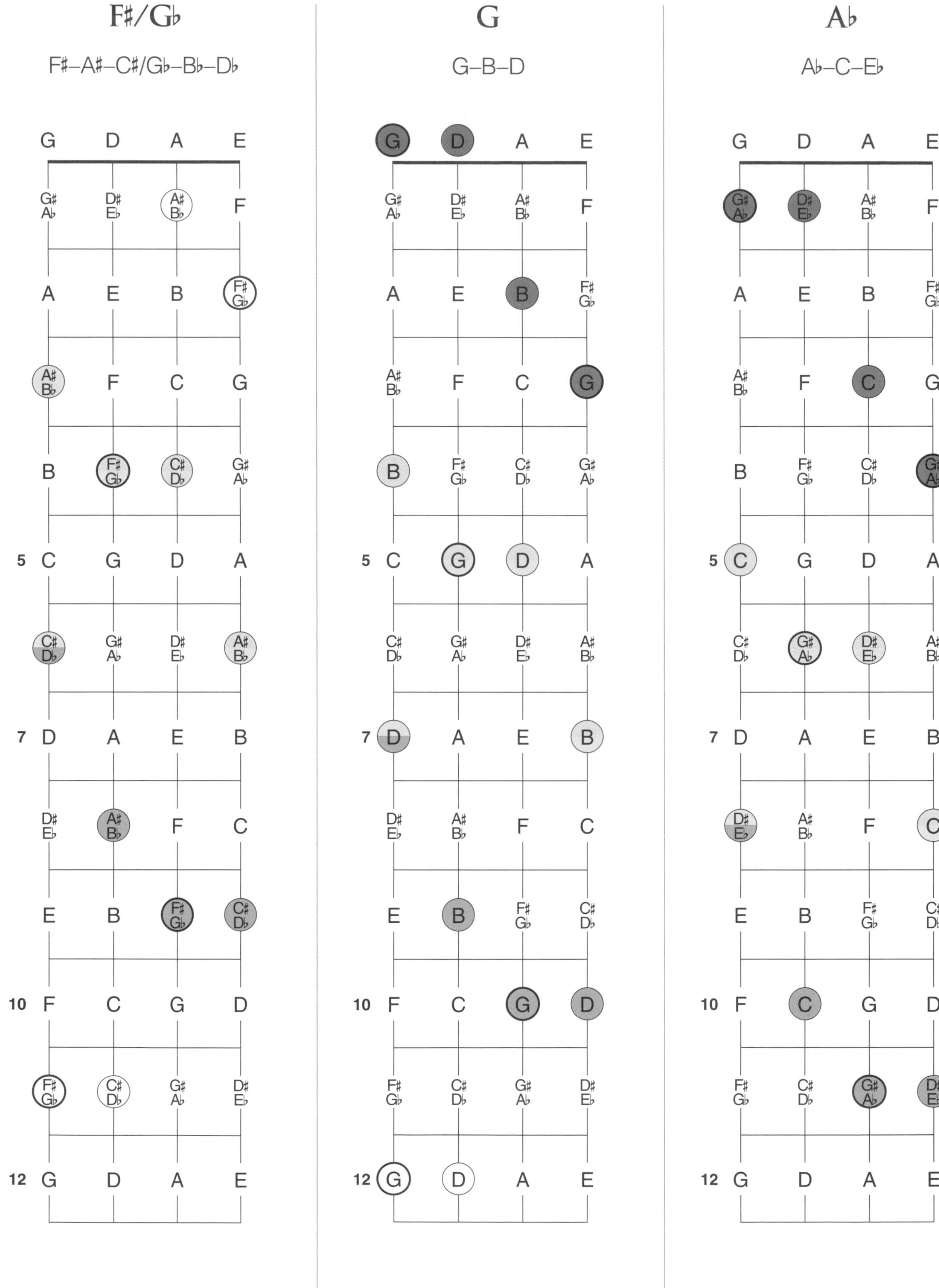
F♯/G♭
F♯–A♯–C♯/G♭–B♭–D♭
G
G–B–D
A♭
A♭–C–E♭
G D A E
5
7
10
12

A

A–C♯–E

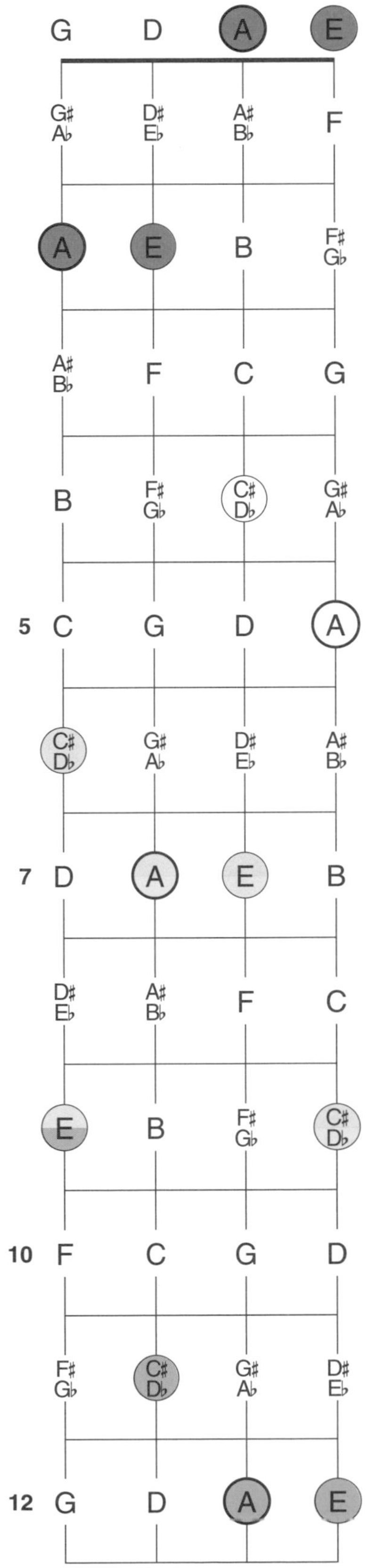

G D A E
G♯ A♭ D♯ E♭ A♯ B♭ F
A E B F♯ G♭
A♯ B♭ F C G
B F♯ G♭ C♯ D♭ G♯ A♭
5 C G D A
C♯ D♭ G♯ A♭ D♯ E♭ A♯ B♭
7 D A E B
D♯ E♭ A♯ B♭ F C
E B F♯ G♭ C♯ D♭
10 F C G D
F♯ G♭ C♯ D♭ G♯ A♭ D♯ E♭
12 G D A E

B♭

B♭–D–F

G D A E
G♯ A♭ D♯ E♭ A♯ B♭ F
A E B F♯ G♭
A♯ B♭ F C G
B F♯ G♭ C♯ D♭ G♯ A♭
5 C G D A
C♯ D♭ G♯ A♭ D♯ E♭ A♯ B♭
7 D A E B
D♯ E♭ A♯ B♭ F C
E B F♯ G♭ C♯ D♭
10 F C G D
F♯ G♭ C♯ D♭ G♯ A♭ D♯ E♭
12 G D A E

B

B–D♯–F♯

G D A E
G♯ A♭ D♯ E♭ A♯ B♭ F
A E B F♯ G♭
A♯ B♭ F C G
B F♯ G♭ C♯ D♭ G♯ A♭
5 C G D A
C♯ D♭ G♯ A♭ D♯ E♭ A♯ B♭
7 D A E B
D♯ E♭ A♯ B♭ F C
E B F♯ G♭ C♯ D♭
10 F C G D
F♯ G♭ C♯ D♭ G♯ A♭ D♯ E♭
12 G D A E

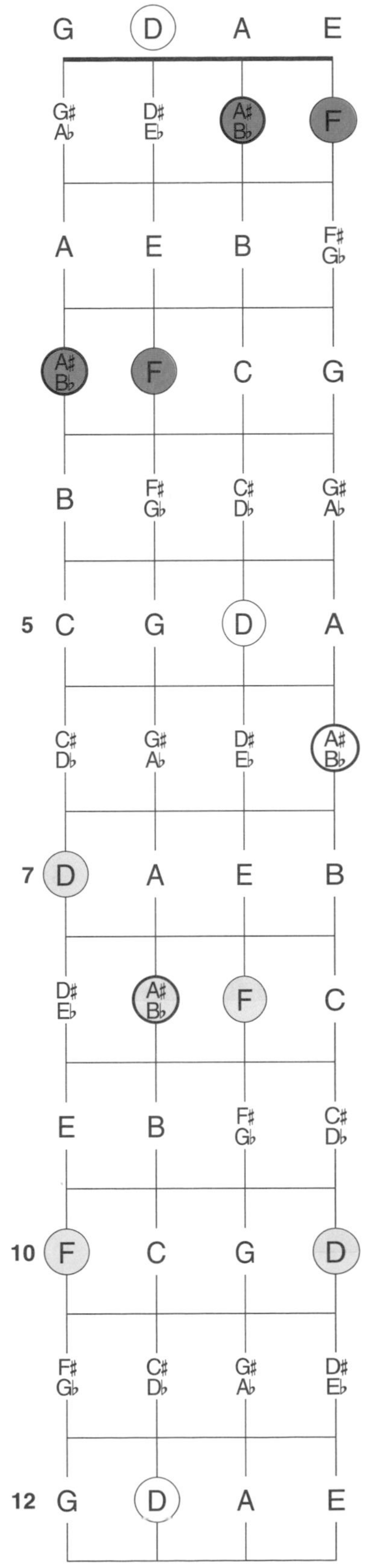

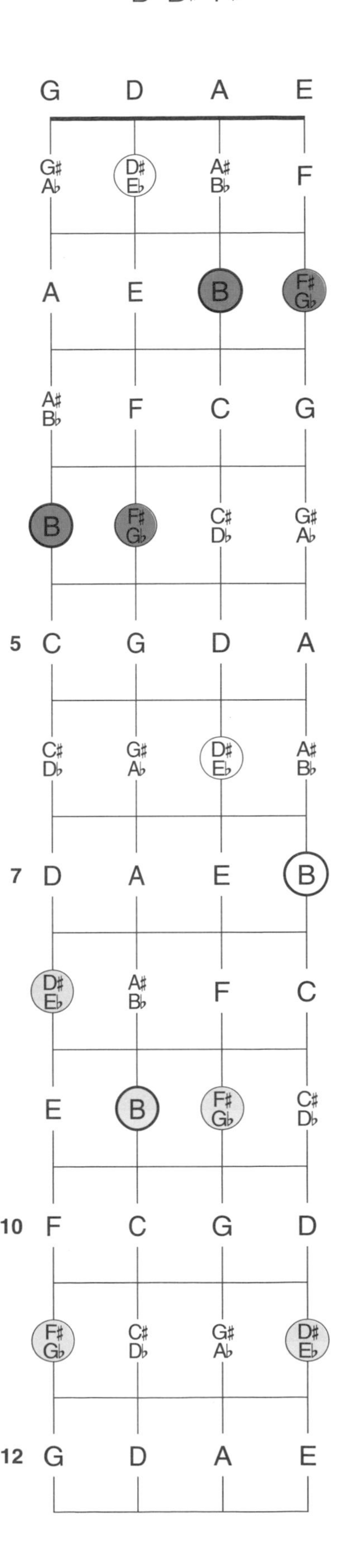

Csus4

C–F–G

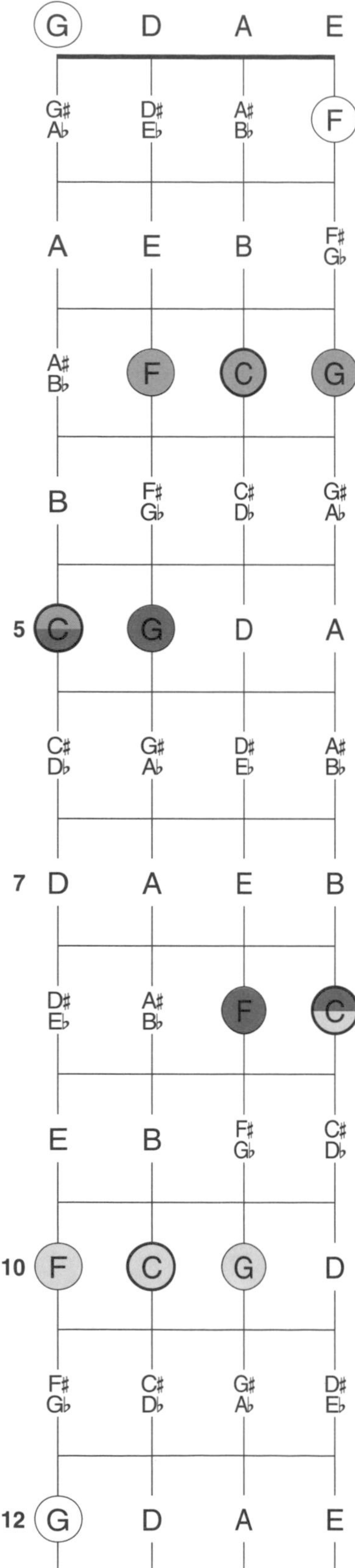

C♯/D♭sus4

C♯–F♯–G♯/D♭–G♭–A♭

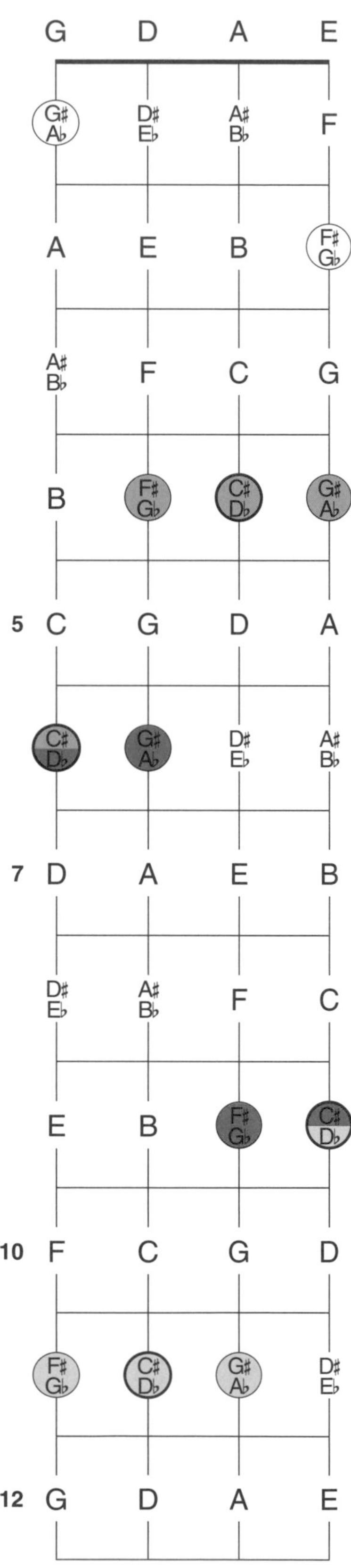

Dsus4

D–G–A

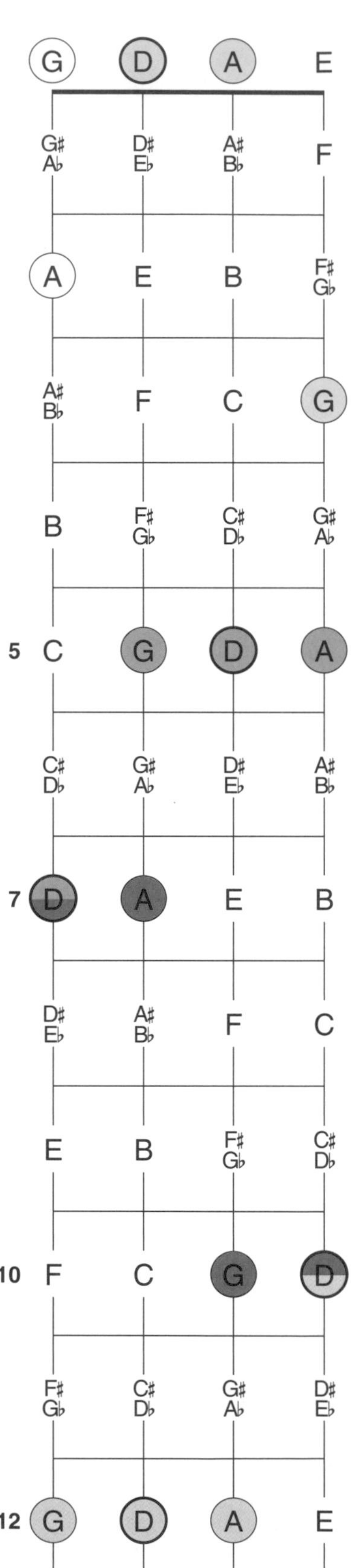

E♭sus4

E♭–A♭–B♭

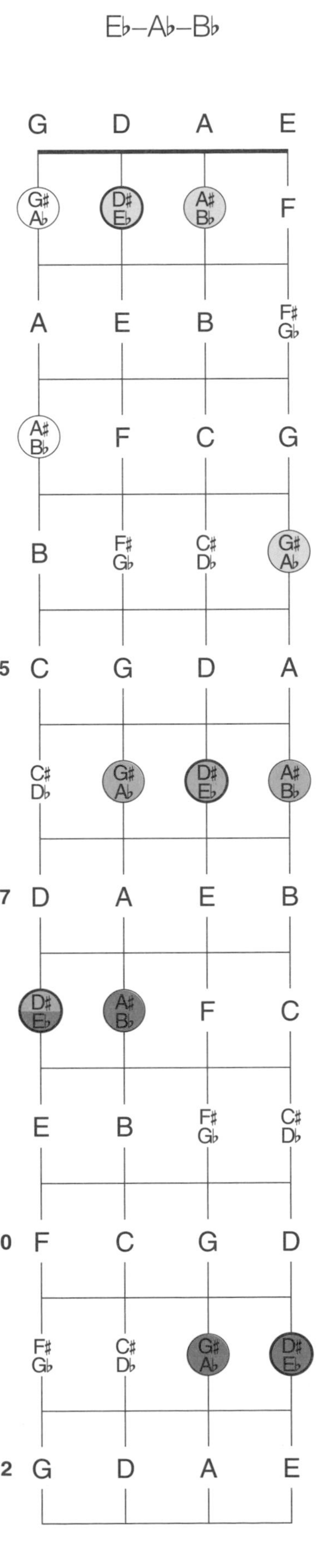

Esus4

E–A–B

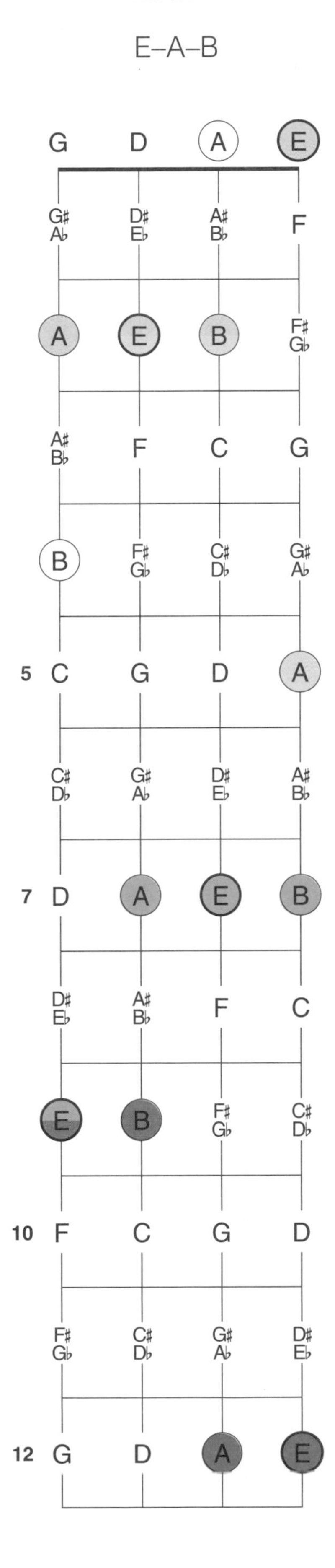

Fsus4

F–B♭–C

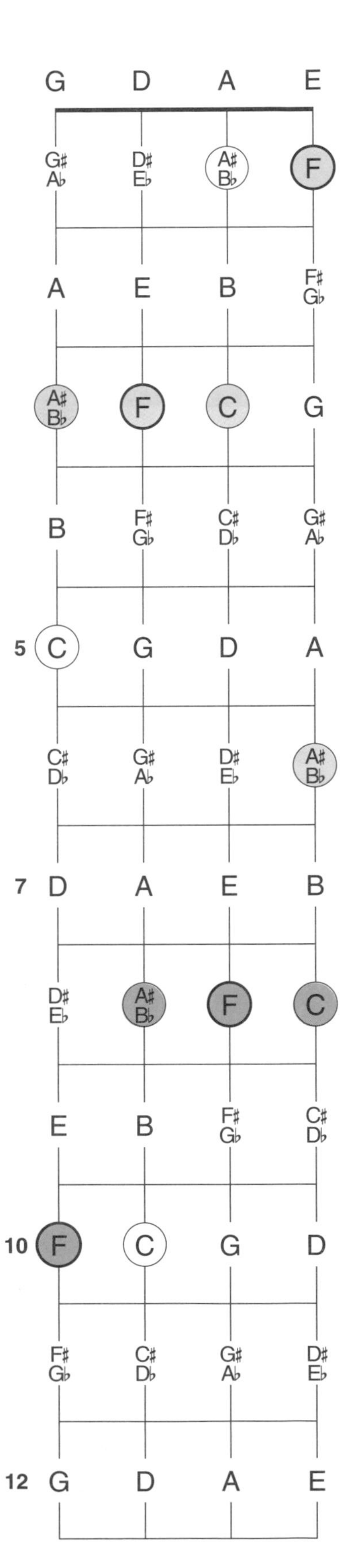

F♯/G♭sus4

F♯–B–C♯/G♭–C♭–D♭

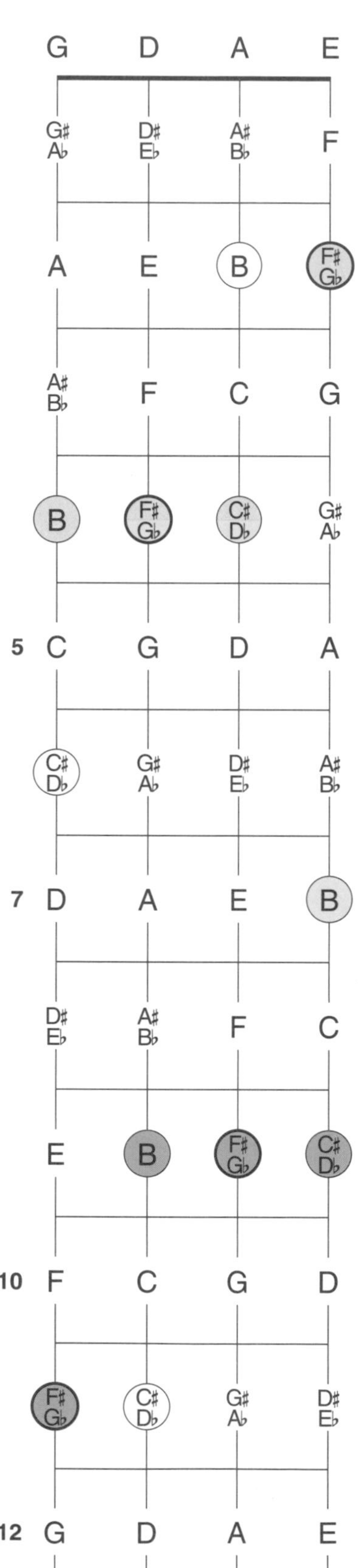

Gsus4

G–C–D

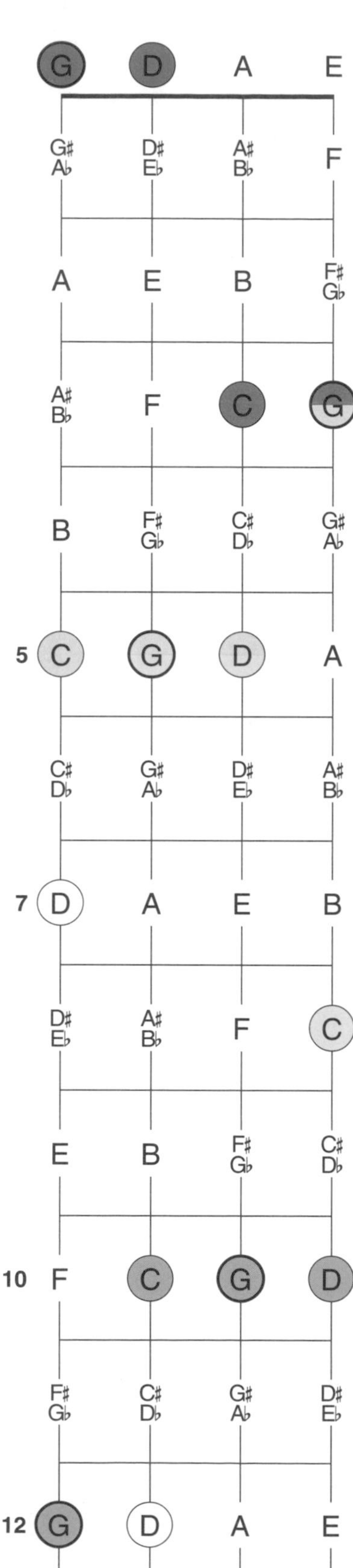

A♭sus4

A♭–D♭–E♭

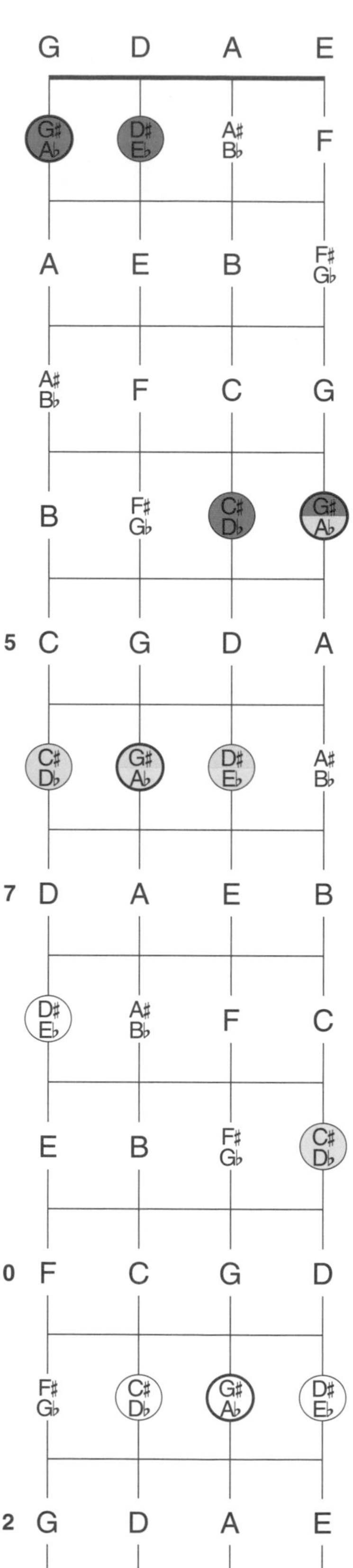

Asus4

A–D–E

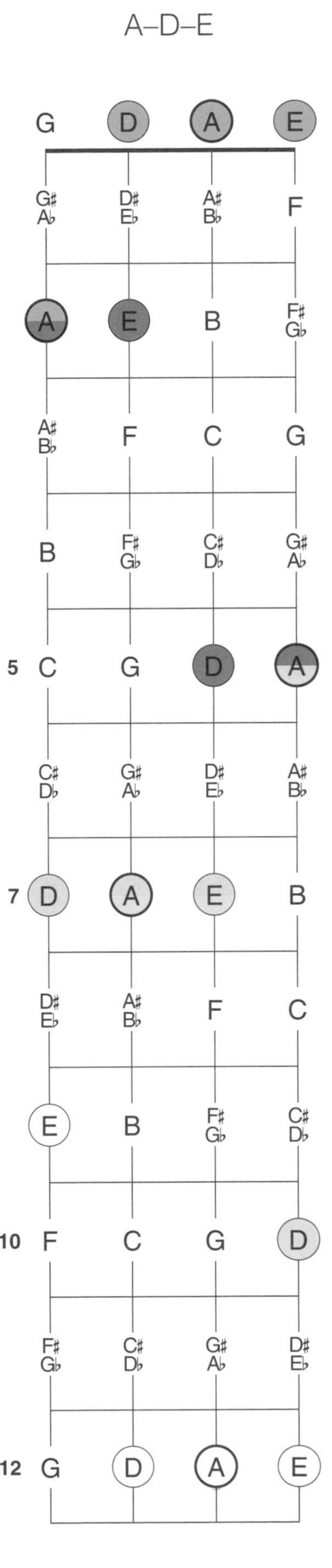

B♭sus4

B♭–E♭–F

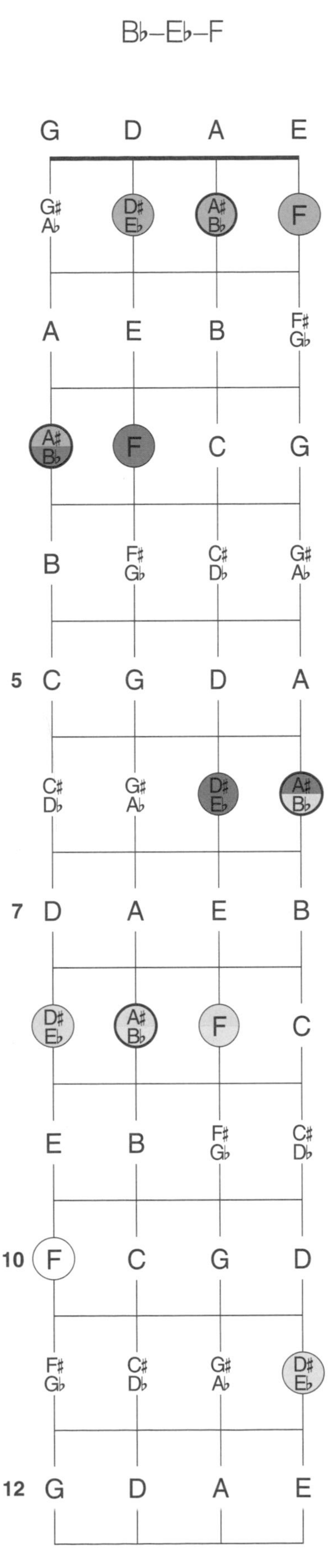

Bsus4

B–E–F♯

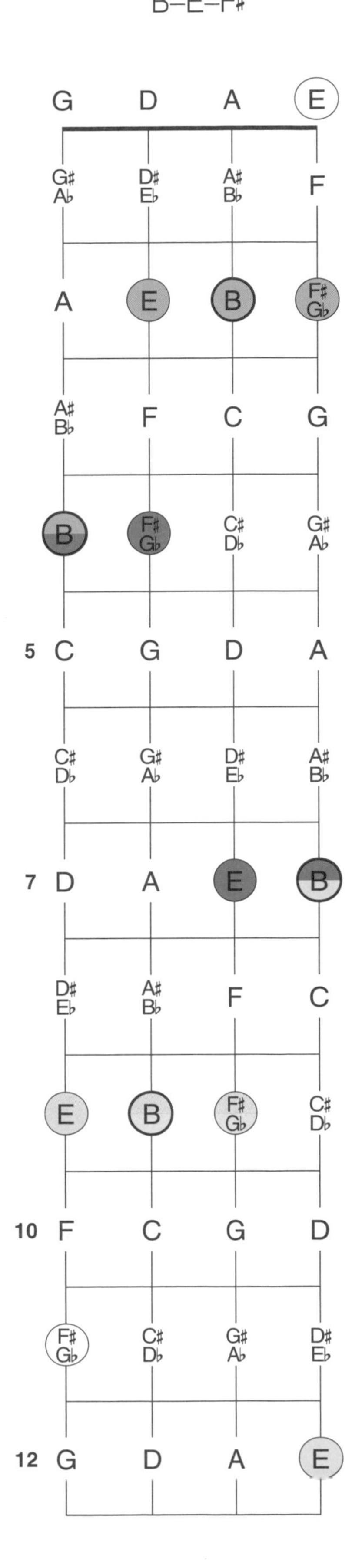

Cm

C–E♭–G

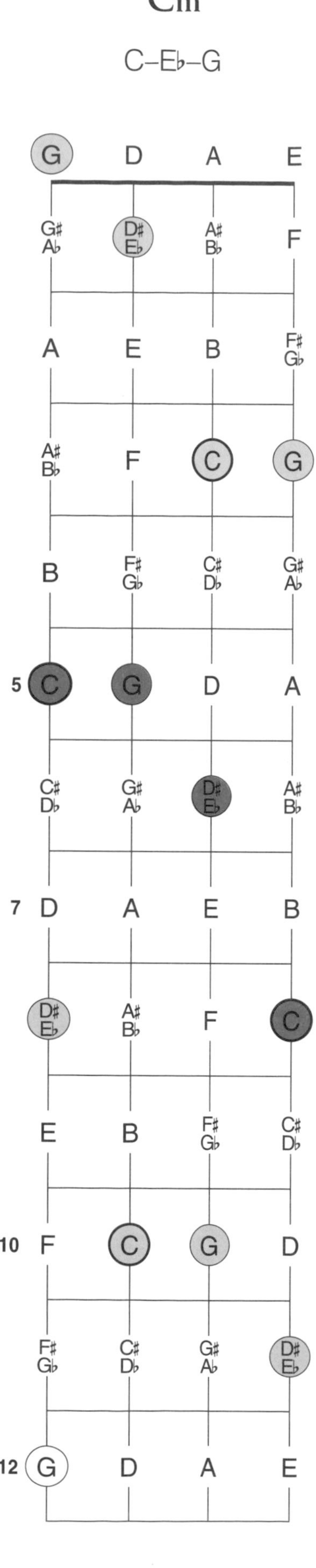

C♯m

C♯–E–G♯

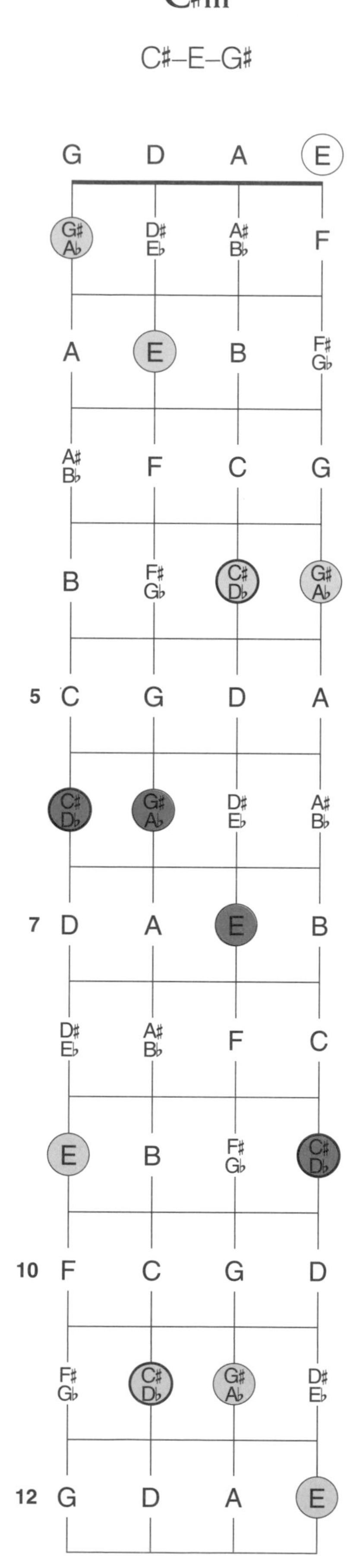

Dm

D–F–A

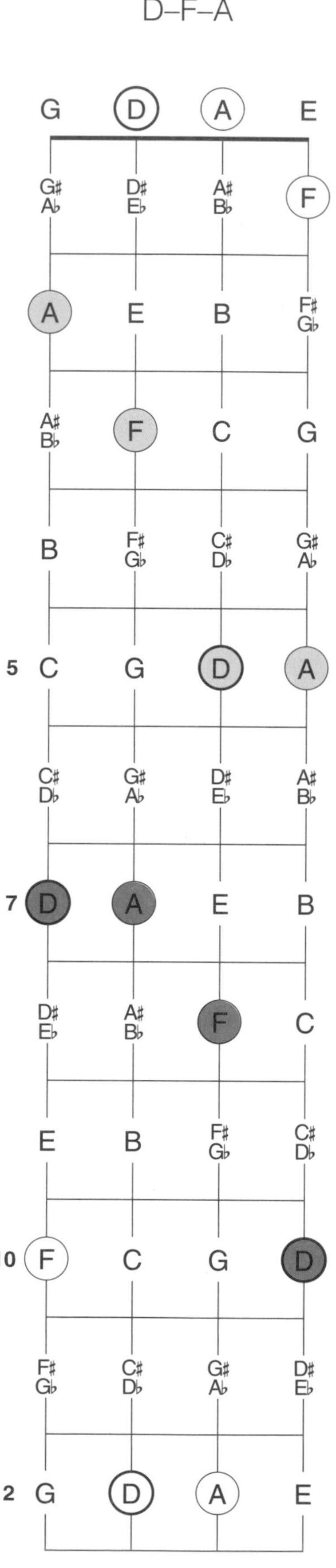

D♯/E♭m

D♯–F♯–A♯/E♭–G♭–B♭

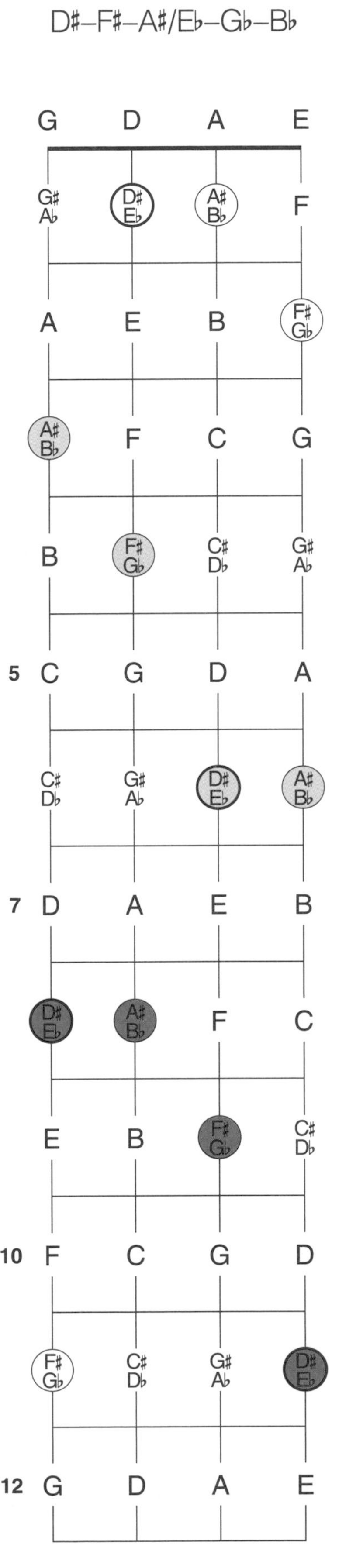

Em

E–G–B

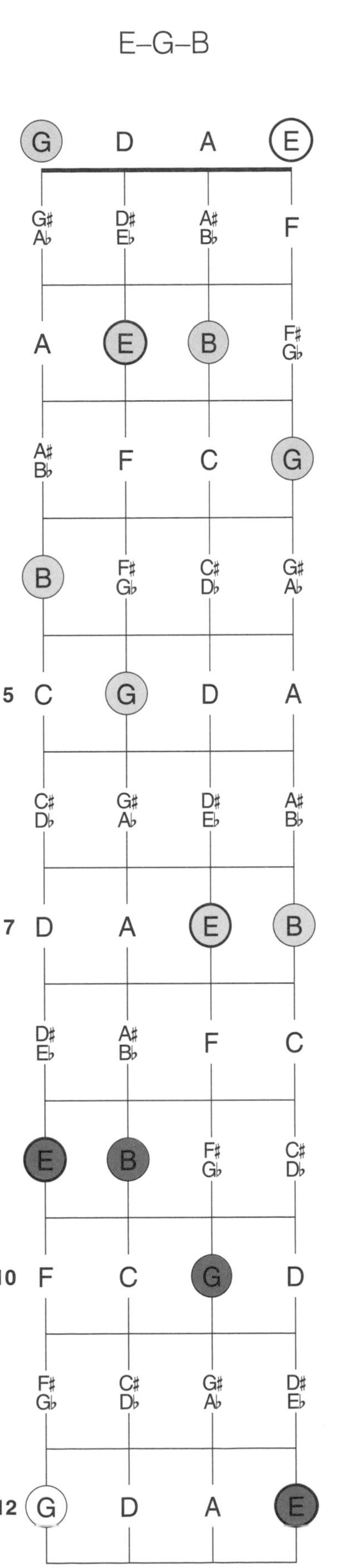

Fm

F–A♭–C

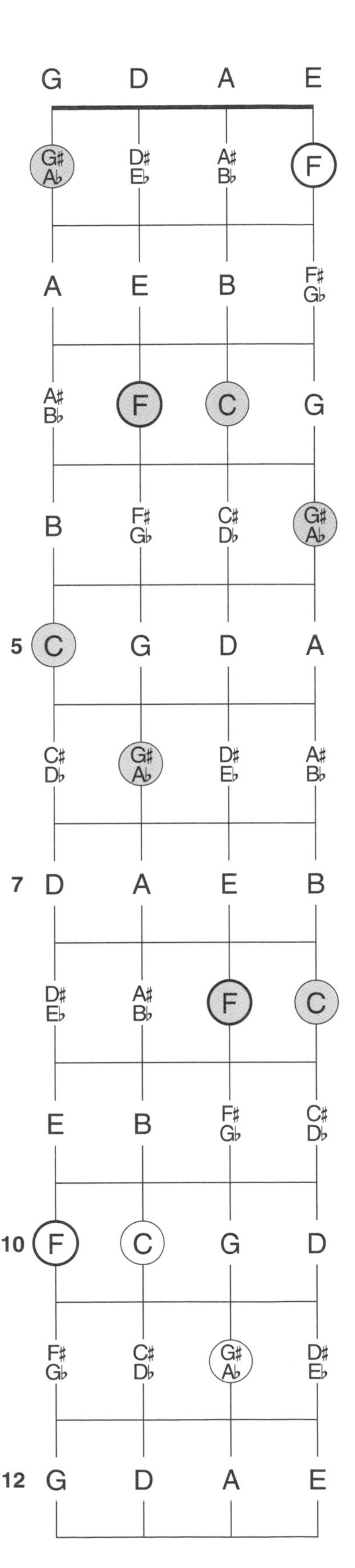

F♯m

F♯–A–C♯

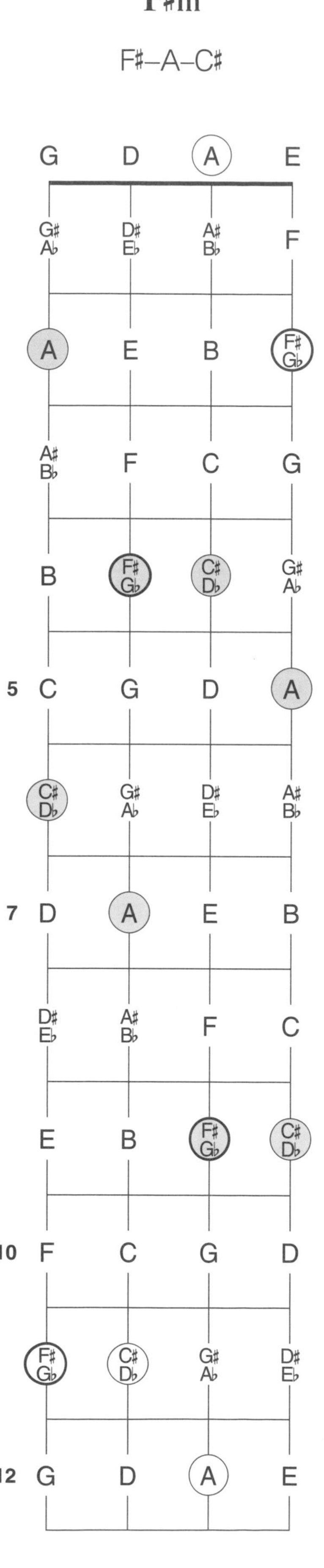

Gm

G–B♭–D

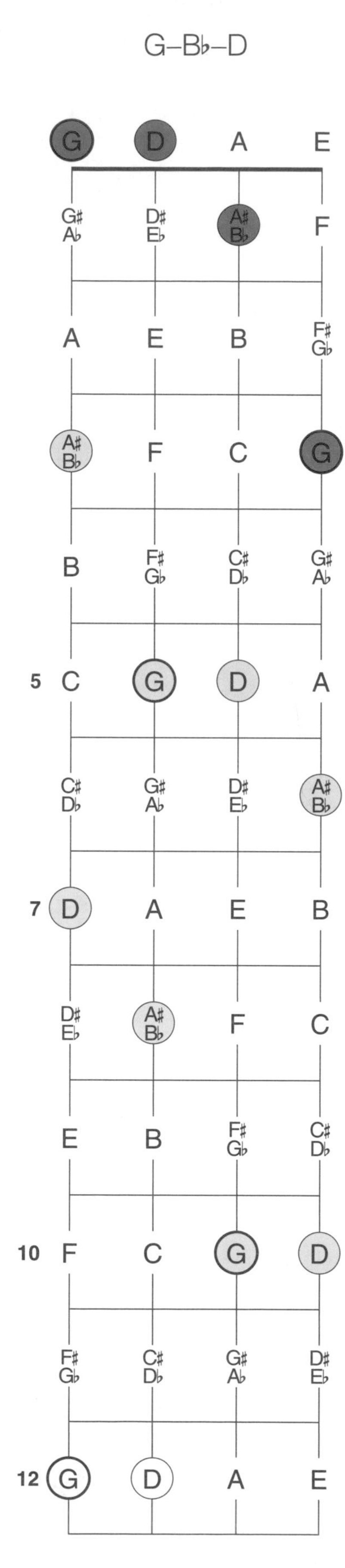

G♯/A♭m

G♯–B–D♯/A♭–C♭–E♭

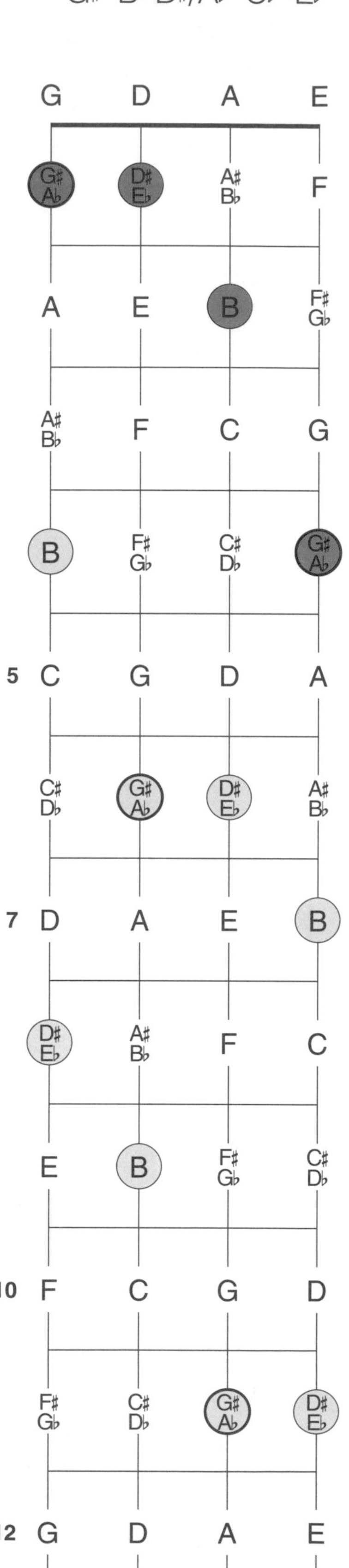

Am

A–C–E

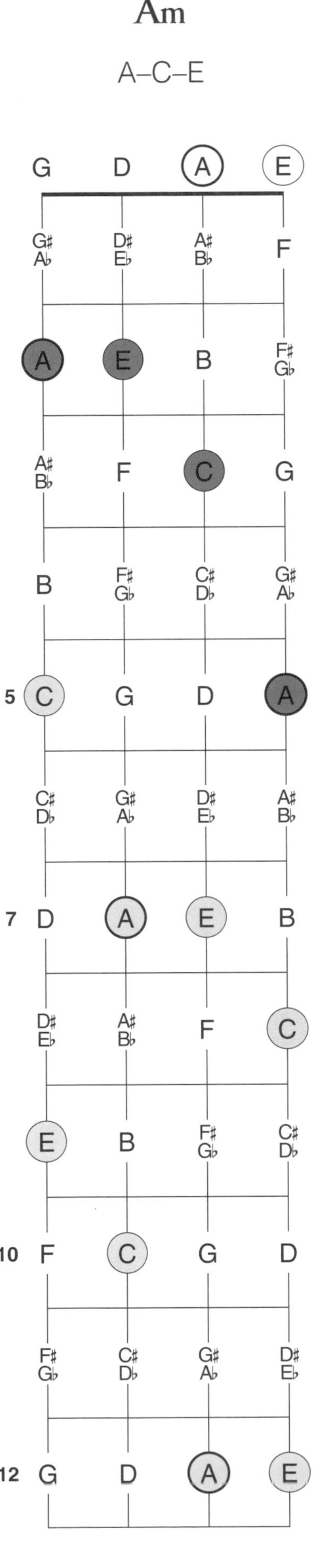

B♭m

B♭–D♭–F

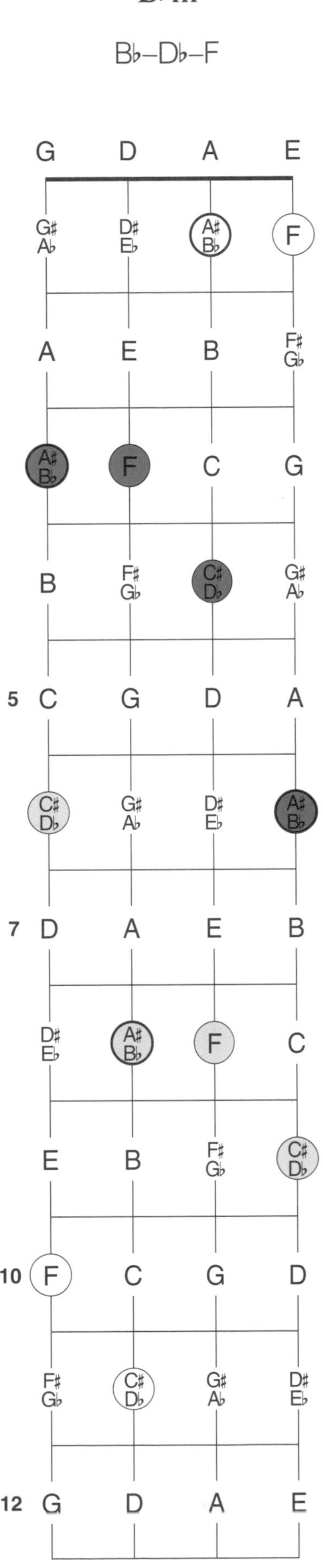

Bm

B–D–F♯

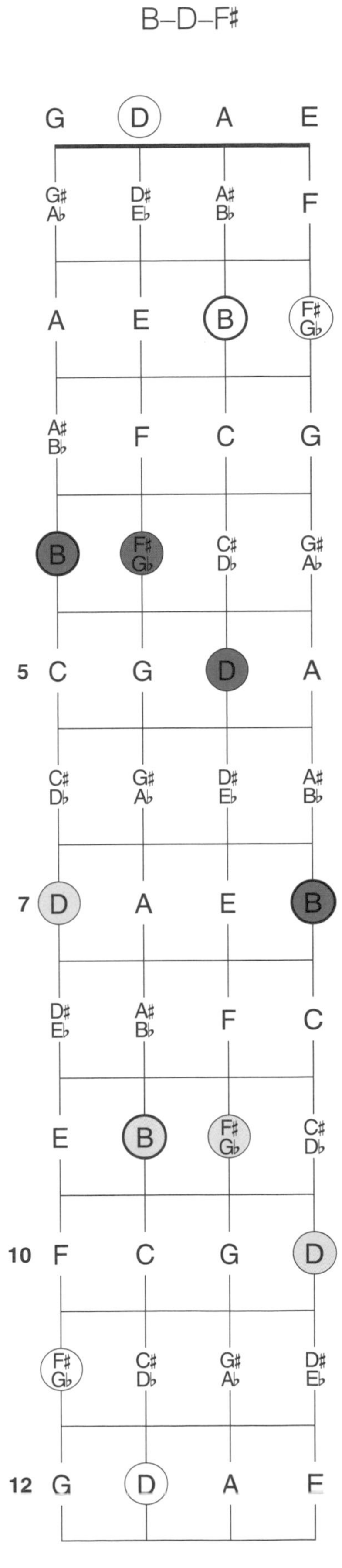

C+

C–E–G♯

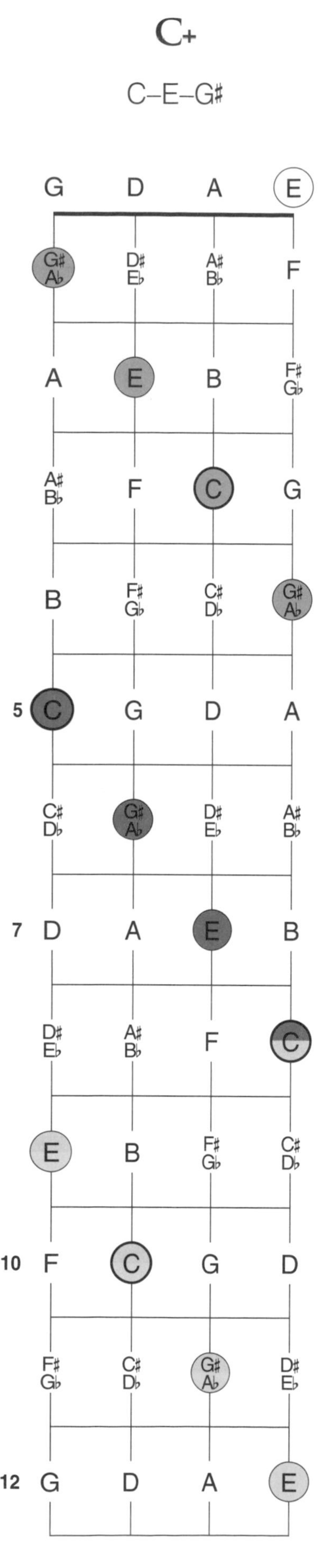

C♯/D♭+

C♯–E♯–G𝄪/D♭–F–A

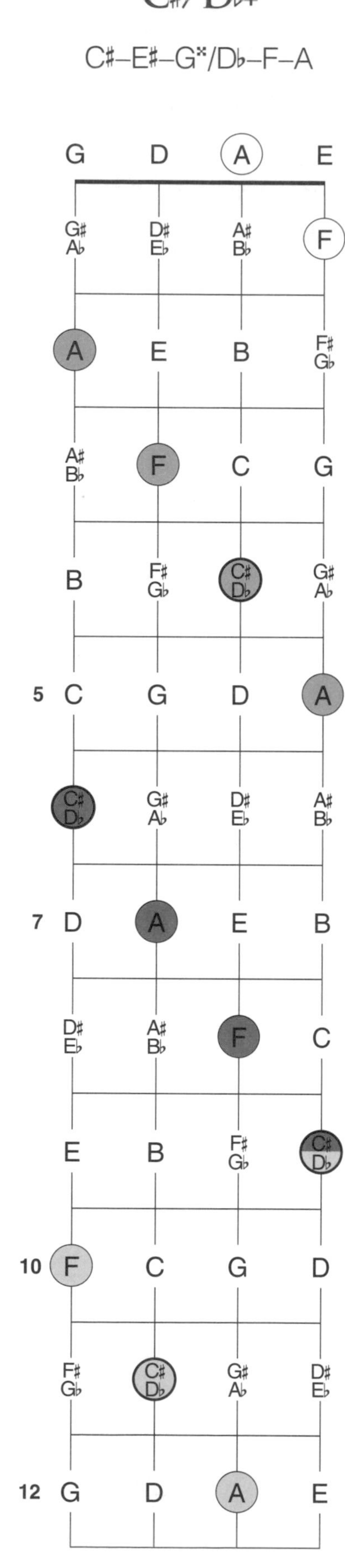

D+

D–F♯–A♯

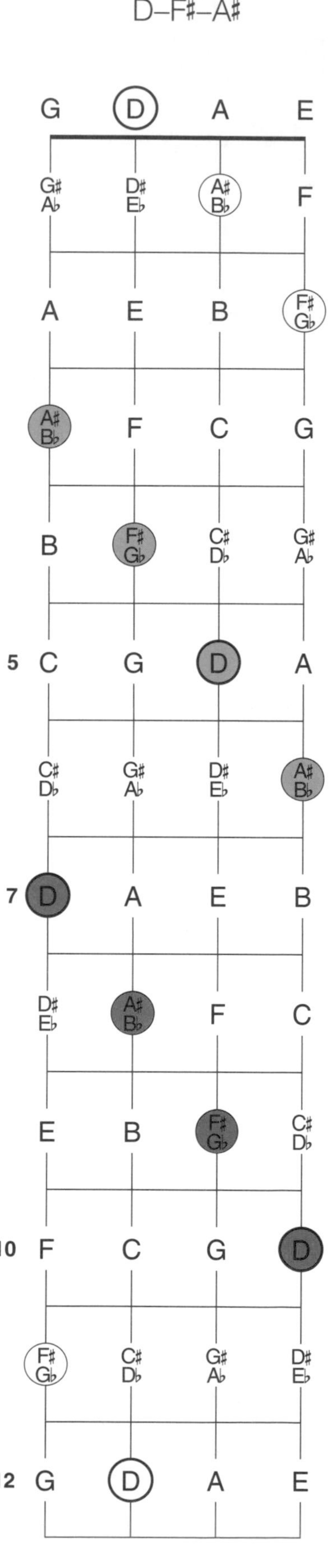

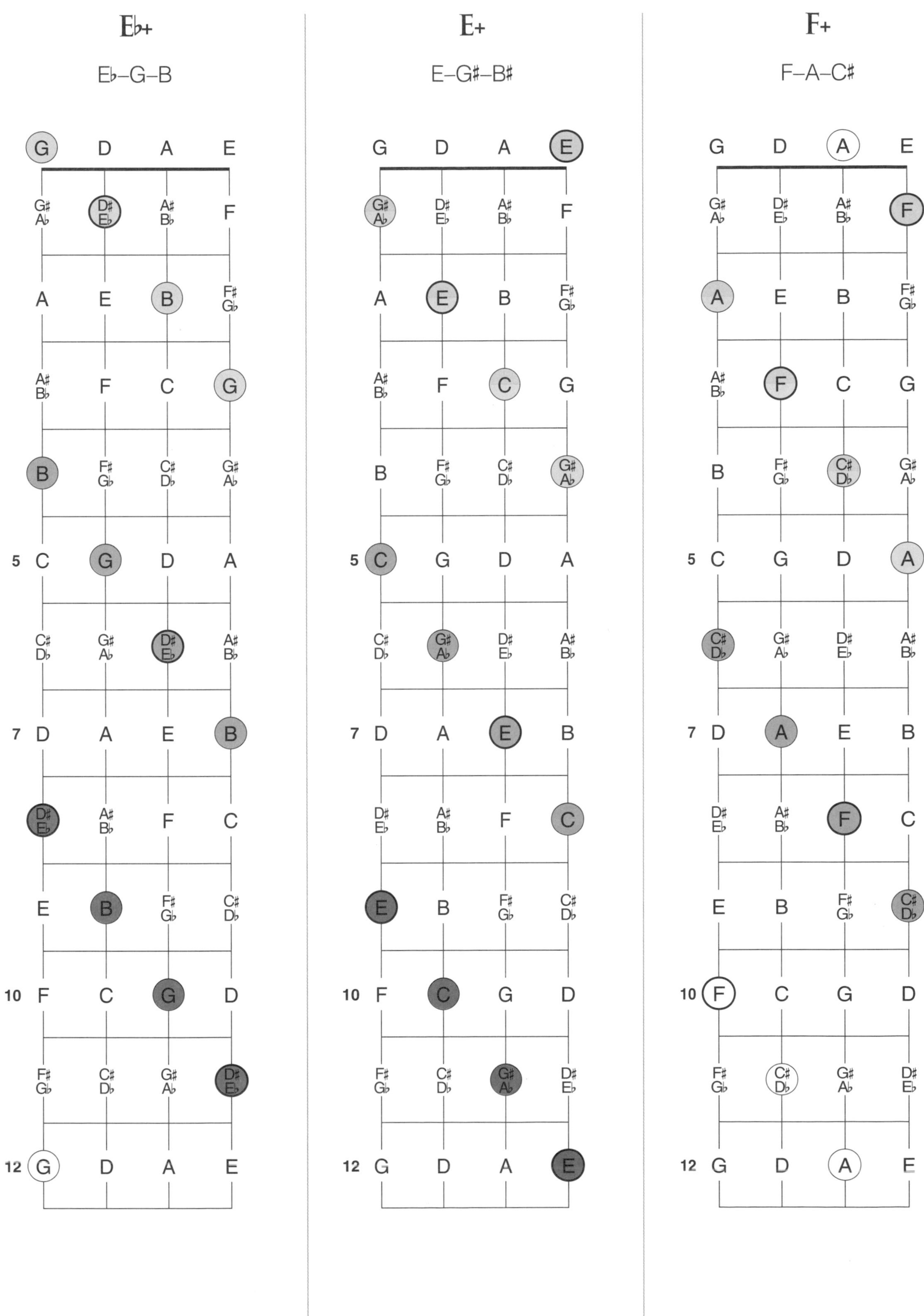
E♭+
E♭–G–B
E+
E–G♯–B♯
F+
F–A–C♯

G♭+

G♭–B♭–D

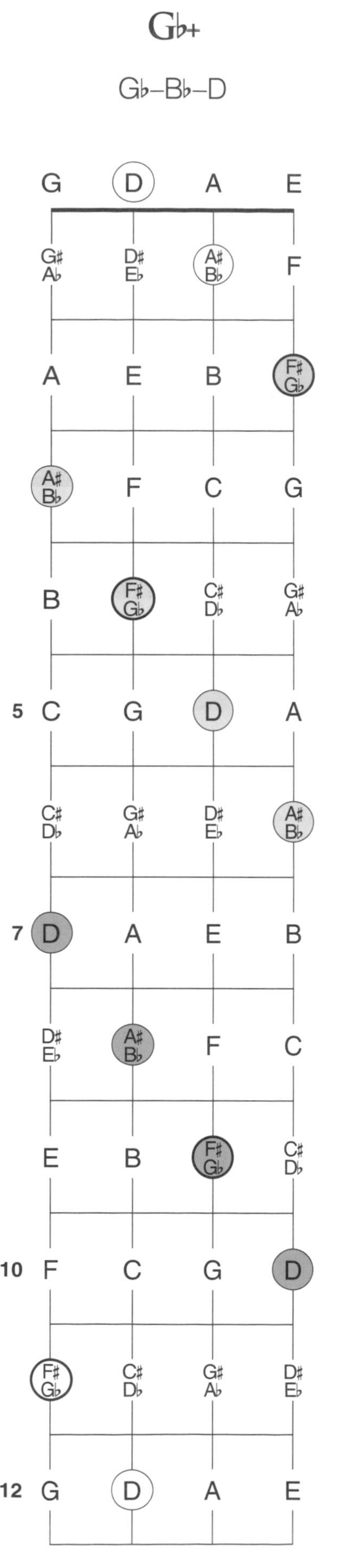

G+

G–B–D♯

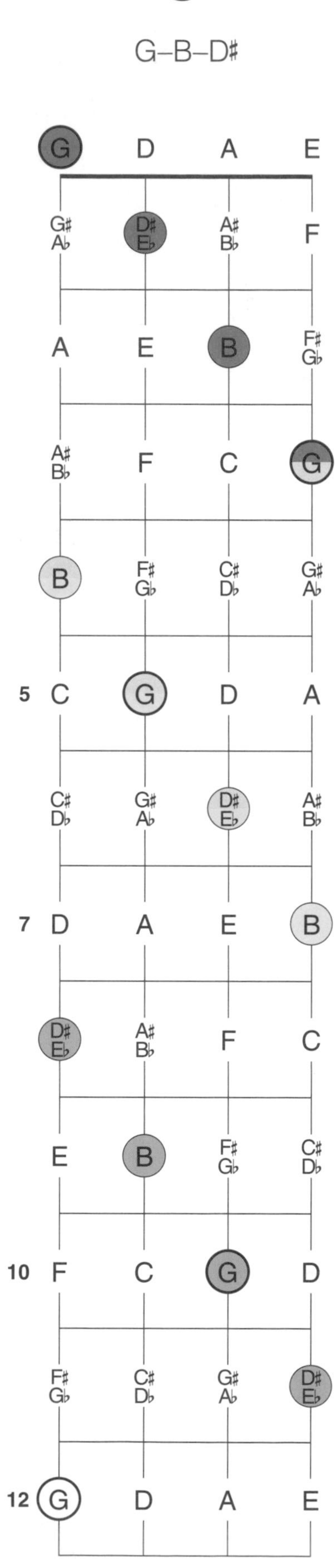

A♭+

A♭–C–E

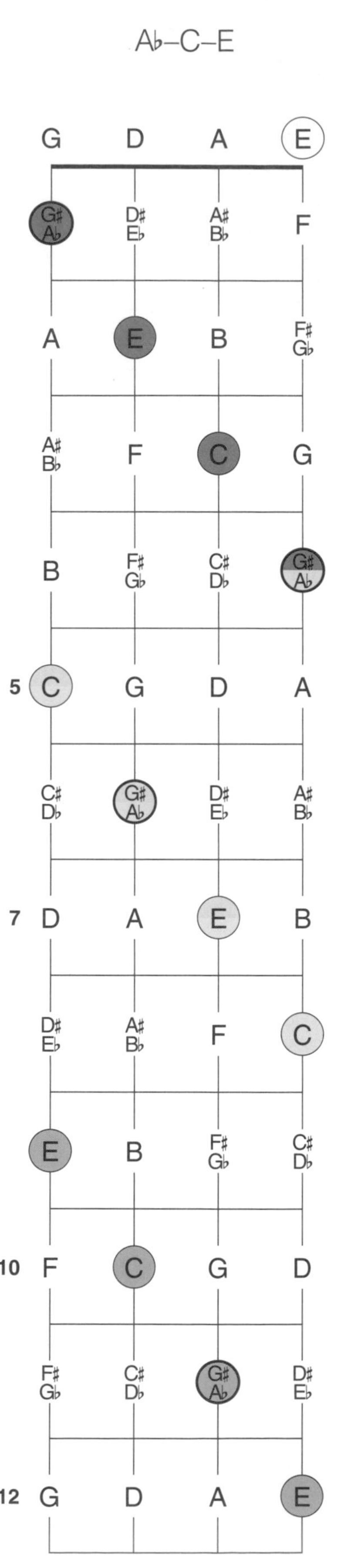

A+

A–C♯–E♯

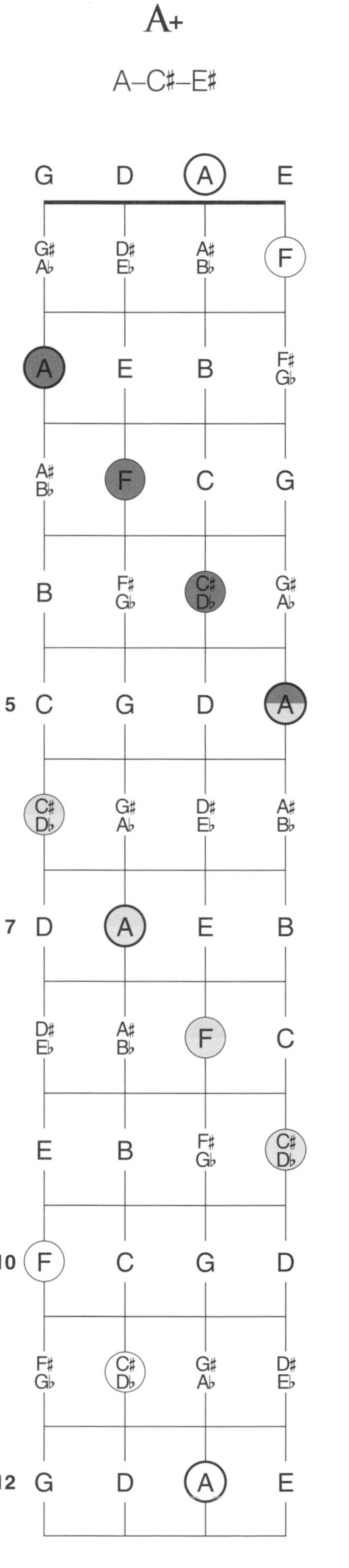

B♭+

B♭–D–F♯

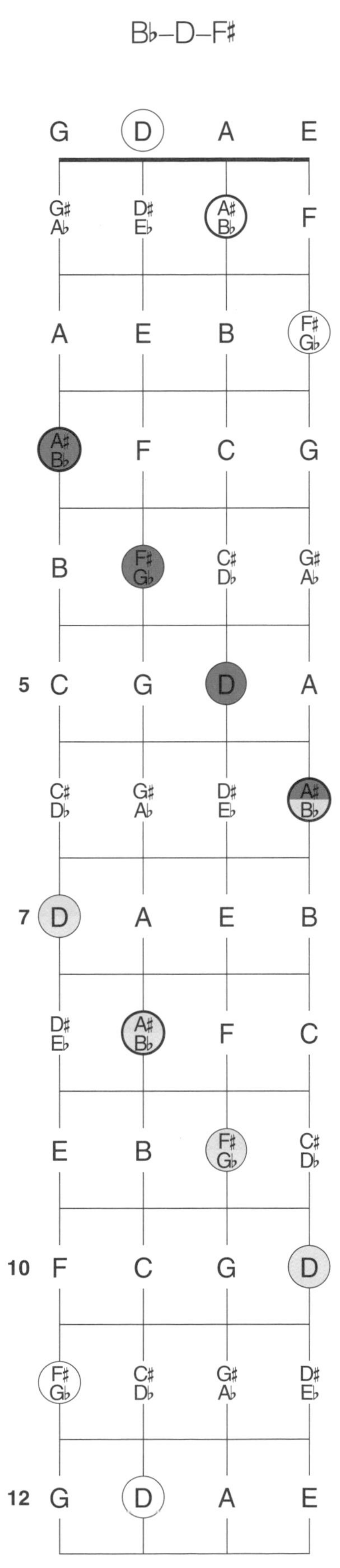

B+

B–D♯–F𝄪

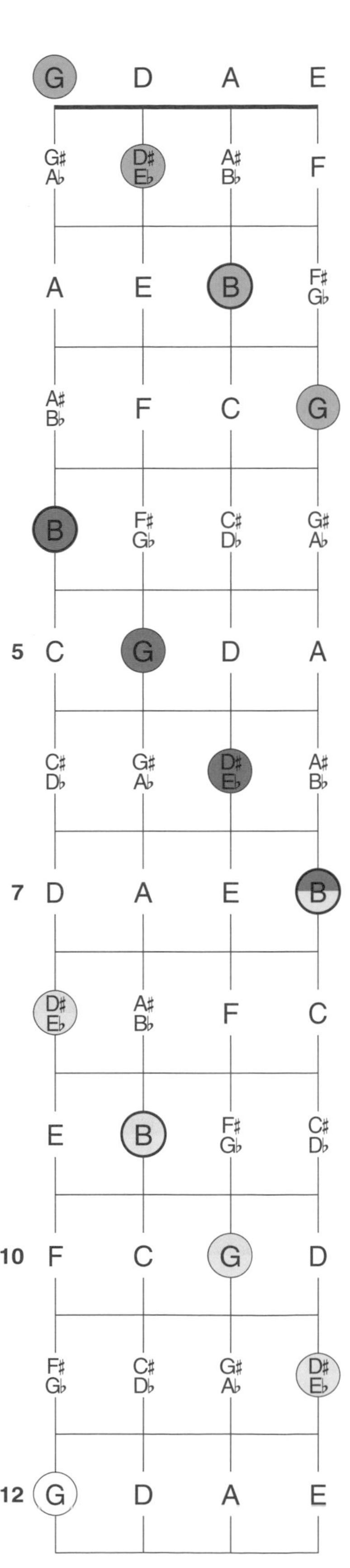

C°

C–E♭–G♭

C♯°

C♯–E–G

D°

D–F–A♭

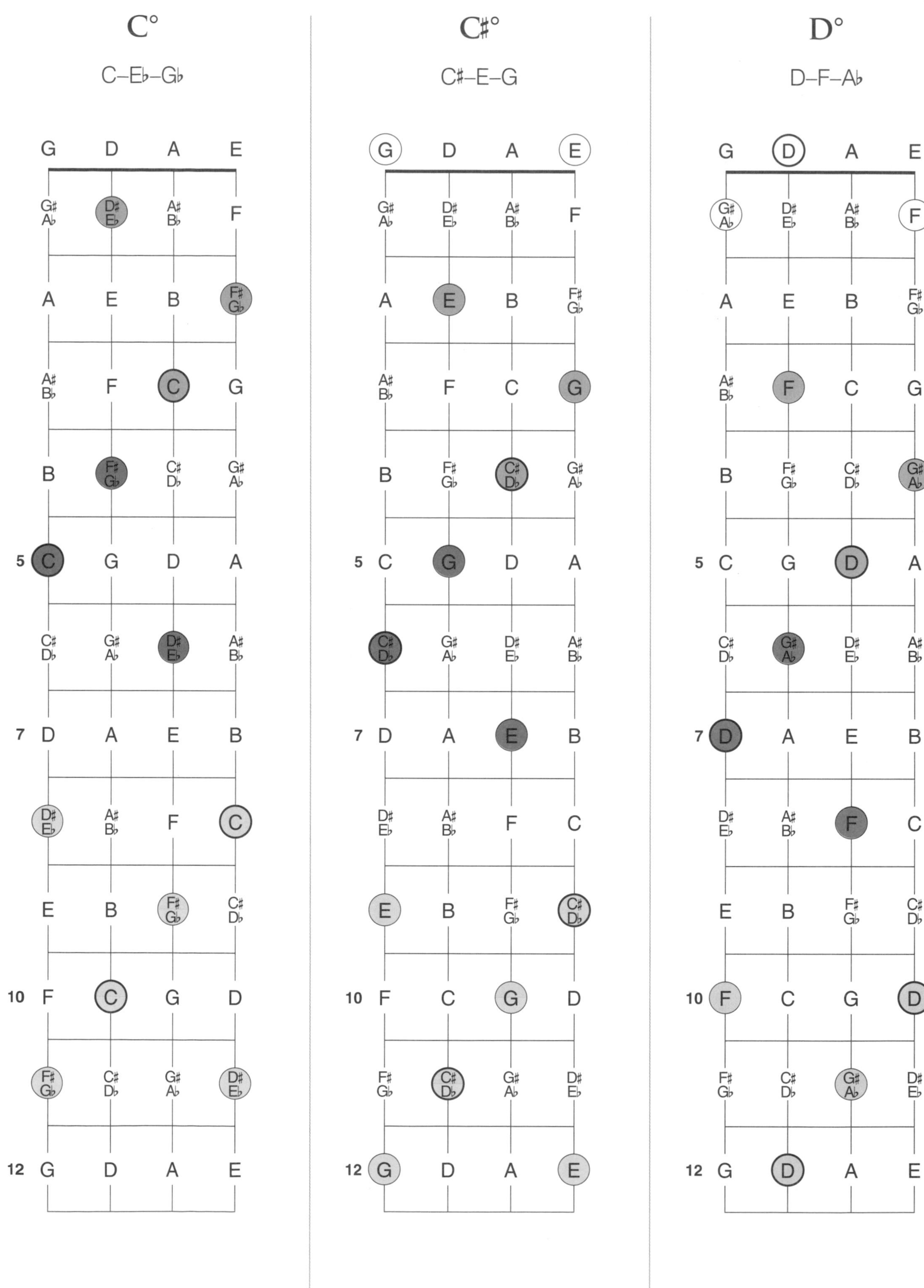

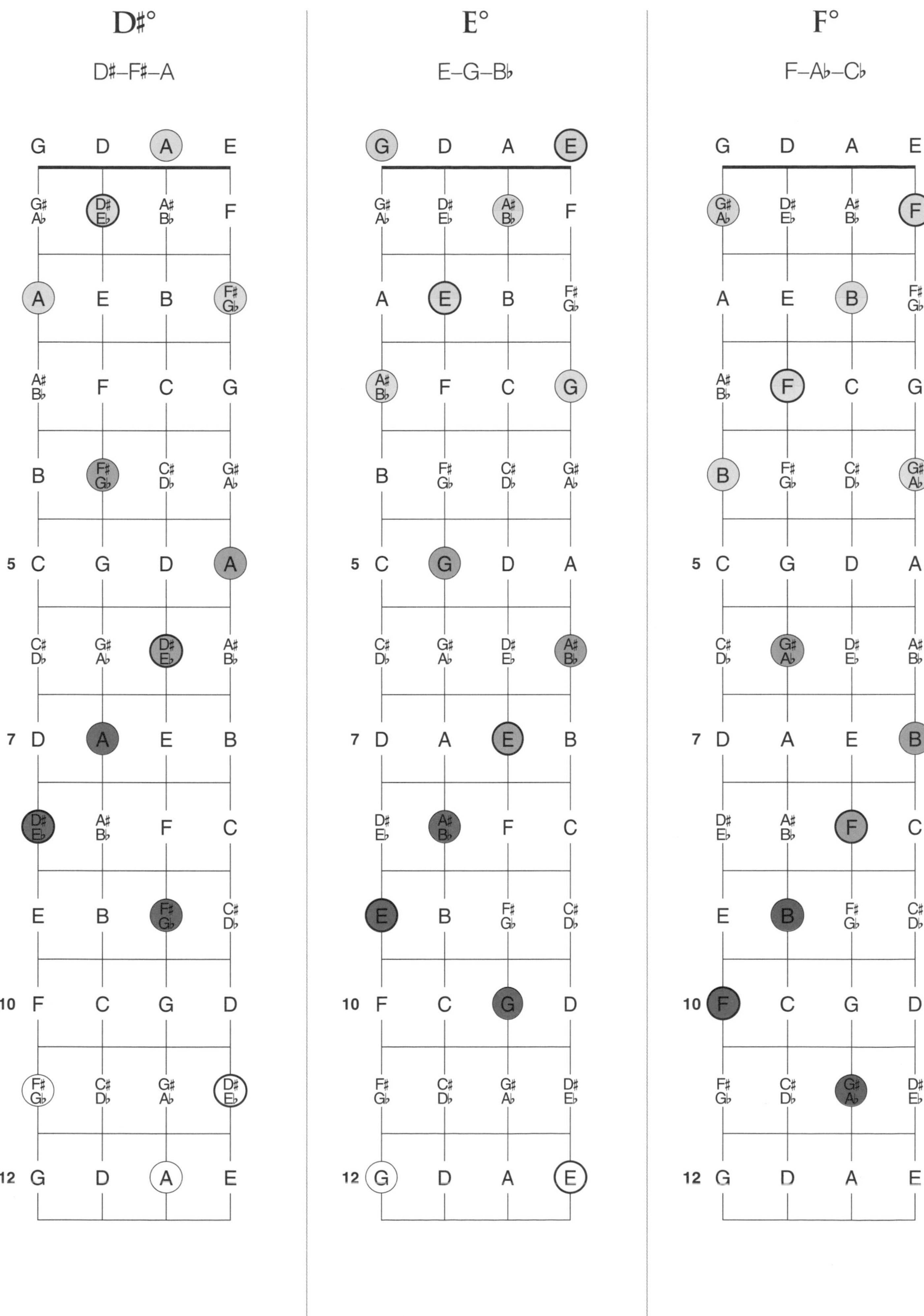
D♯°
D♯–F♯–A
E°
E–G–B♭
F°
F–A♭–C♭

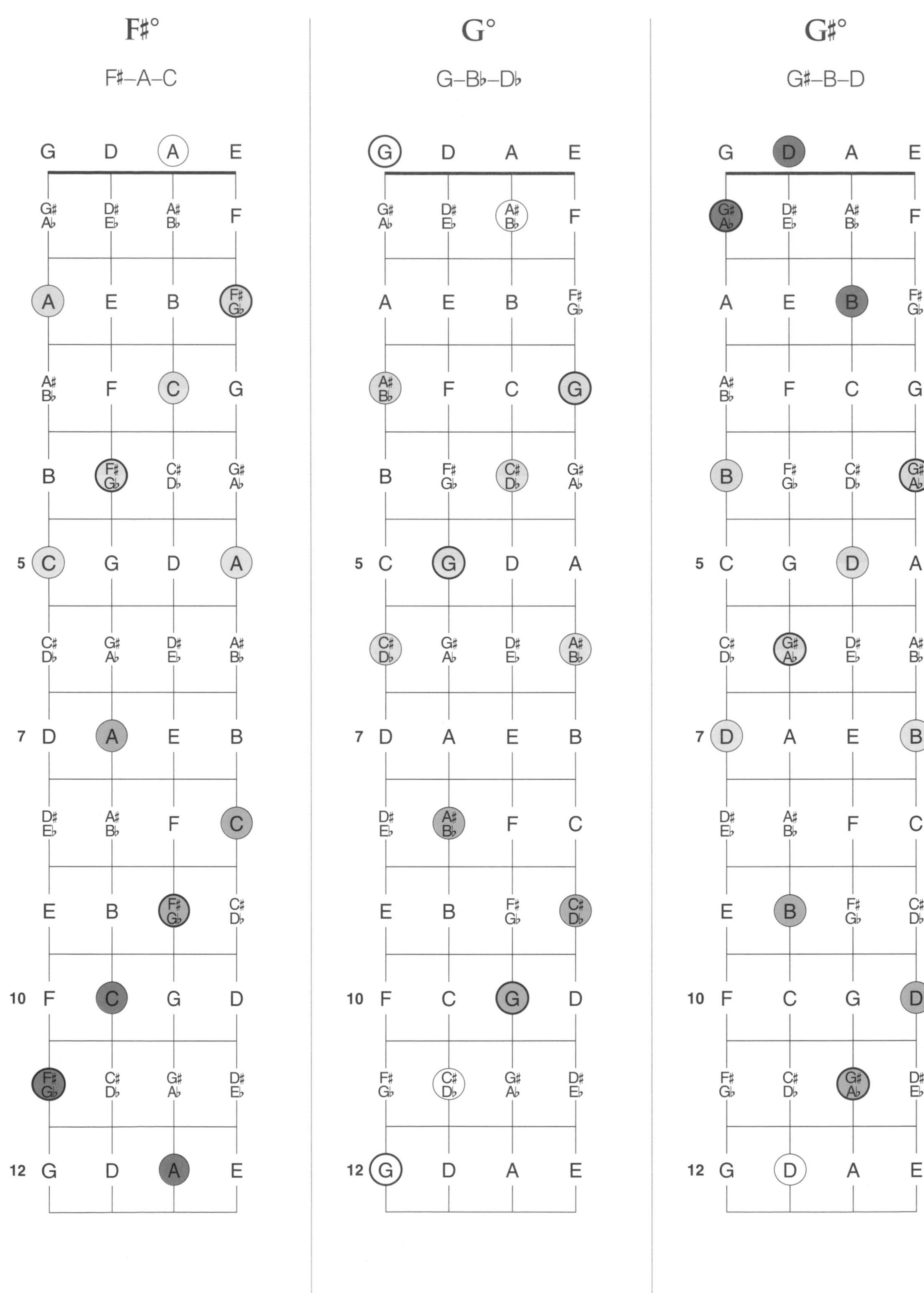
F♯°
F♯–A–C
G D A E
G°
G–B♭–D♭
G D A E
G♯°
G♯–B–D
G D A E

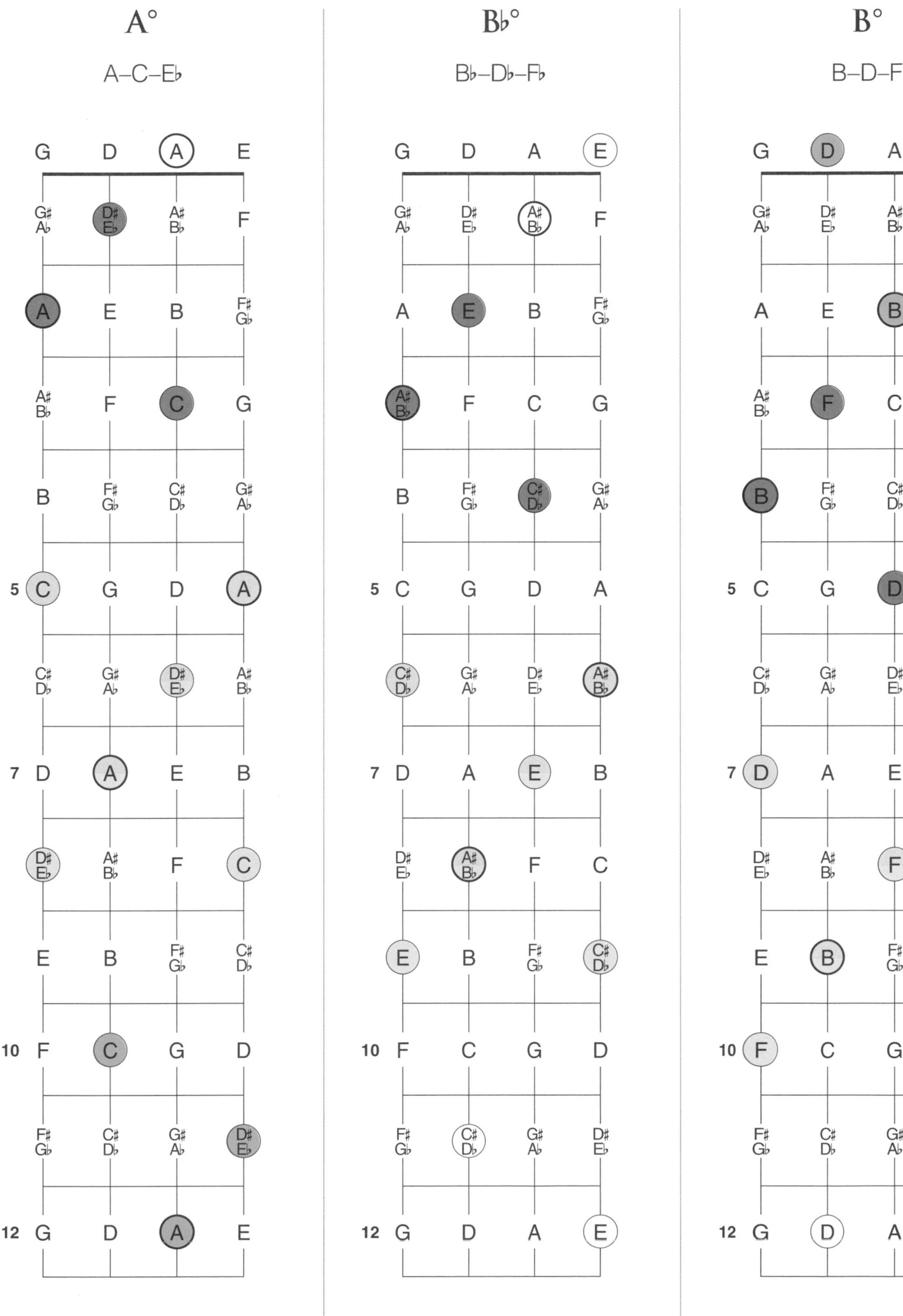
A°
A–C–E♭
B♭°
B♭–D♭–F♭
B°
B–D–F

CHORDS

TRIADS WITH ADDED NOTES

Cadd9

C–E–G–D

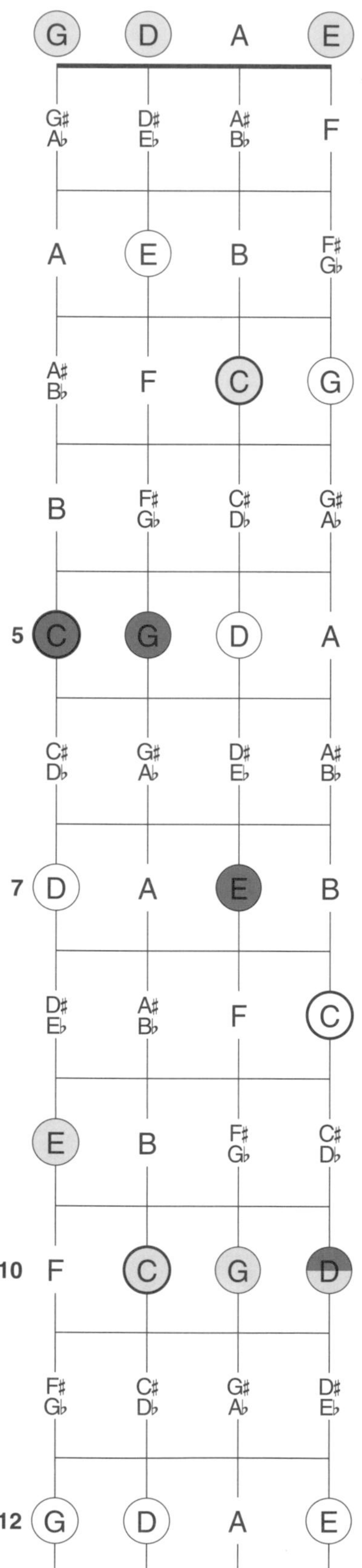

C♯/D♭add9

C♯–E♯–G♯–D♯/D♭–F–A♭–E♭

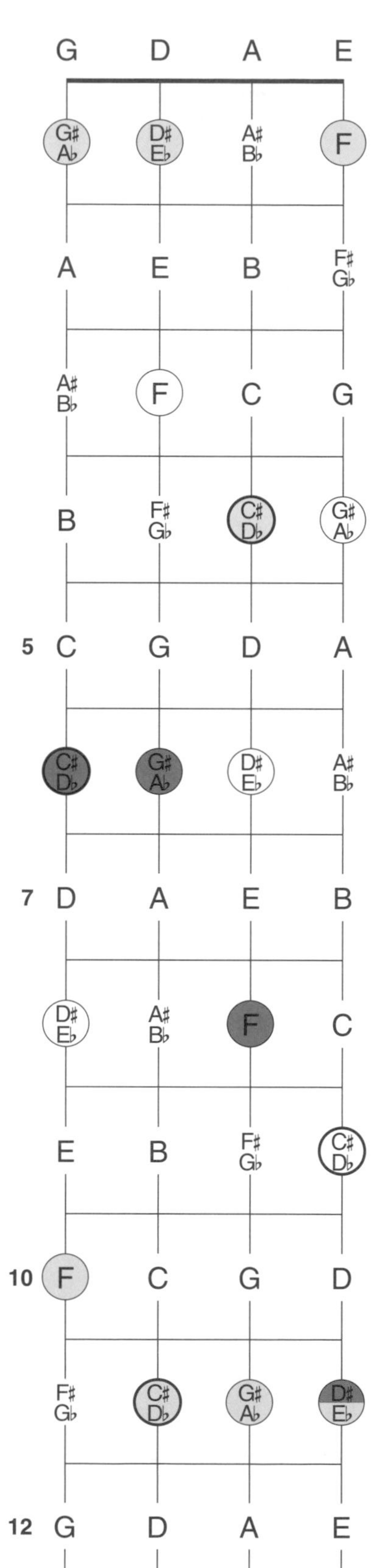

Dadd9

D–F♯–A–E

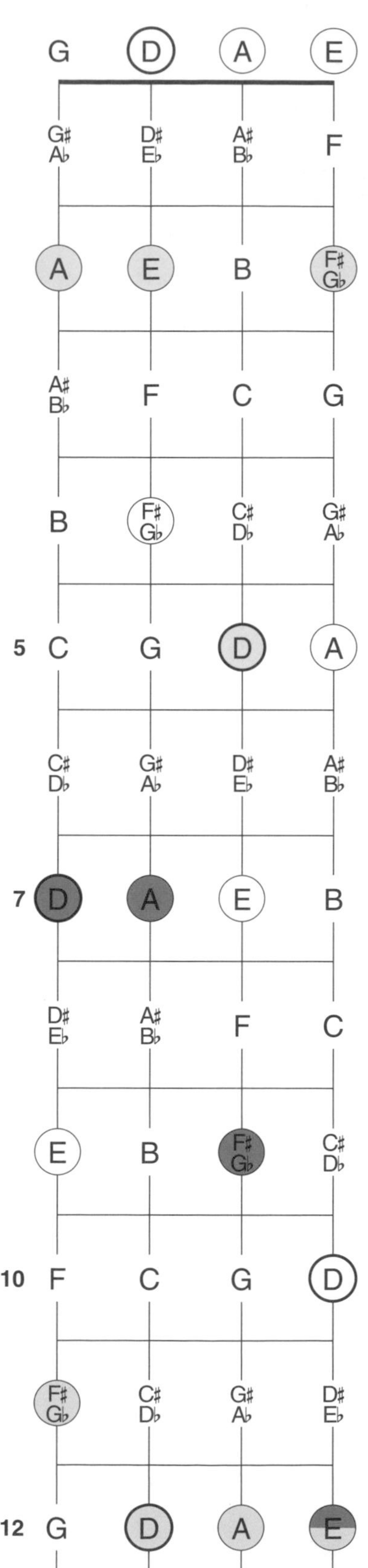

E♭add9

E♭–G–B♭–F

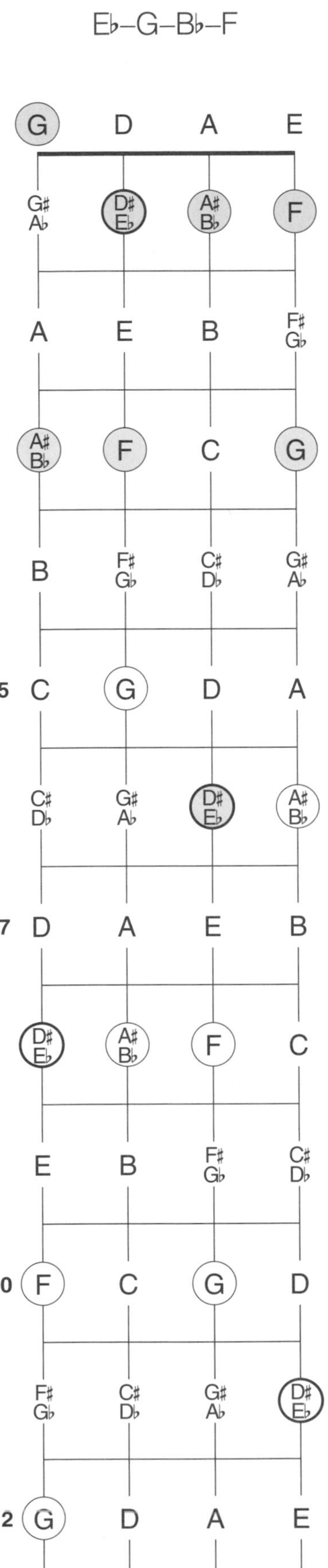

Eadd9

E–G♯–B–F♯

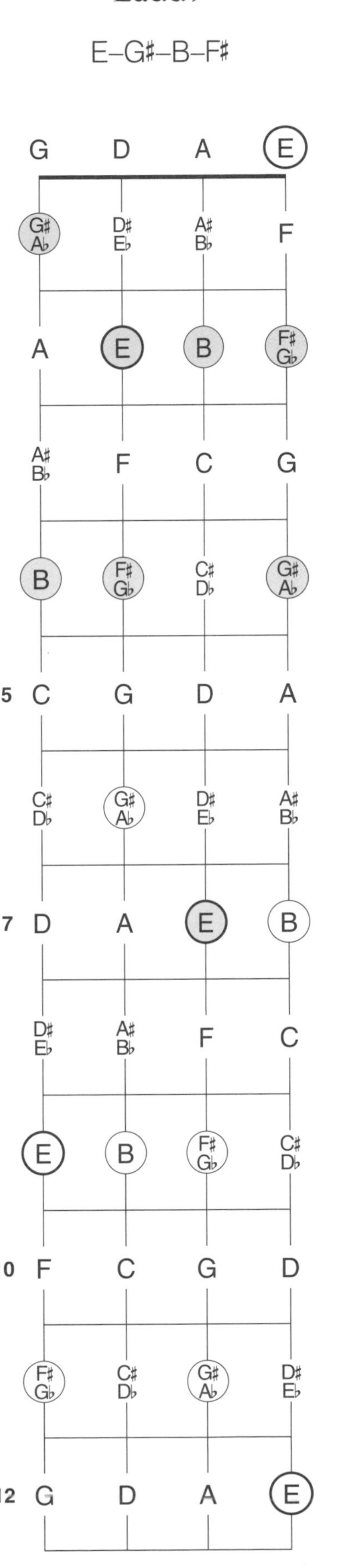

Fadd9

F–A–C–G

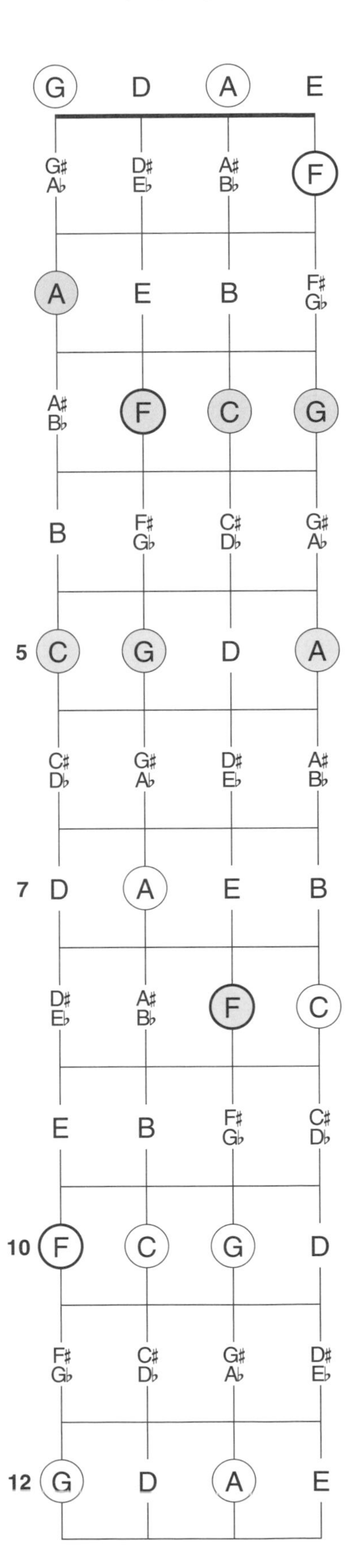

F♯/G♭add9

F♯–A♯–C♯–G♯/G♭–B♭–D♭–A♭

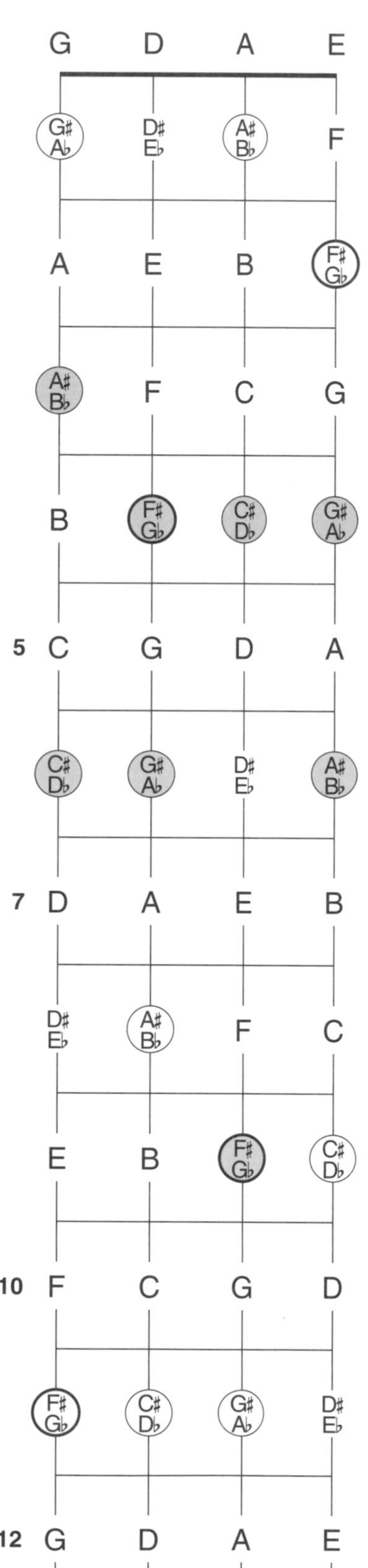

Gadd9

G–B–D–A

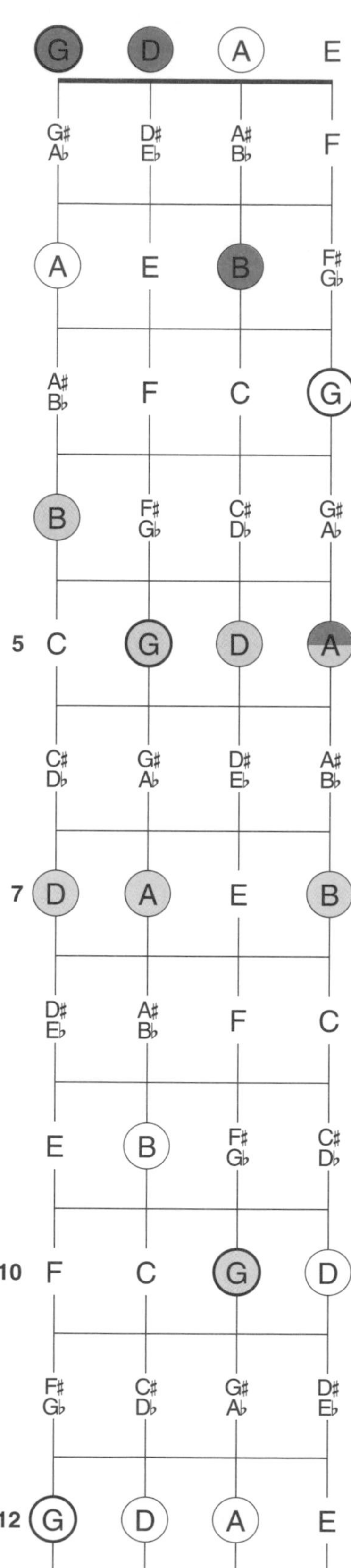

A♭add9

A♭–C–E♭–B♭

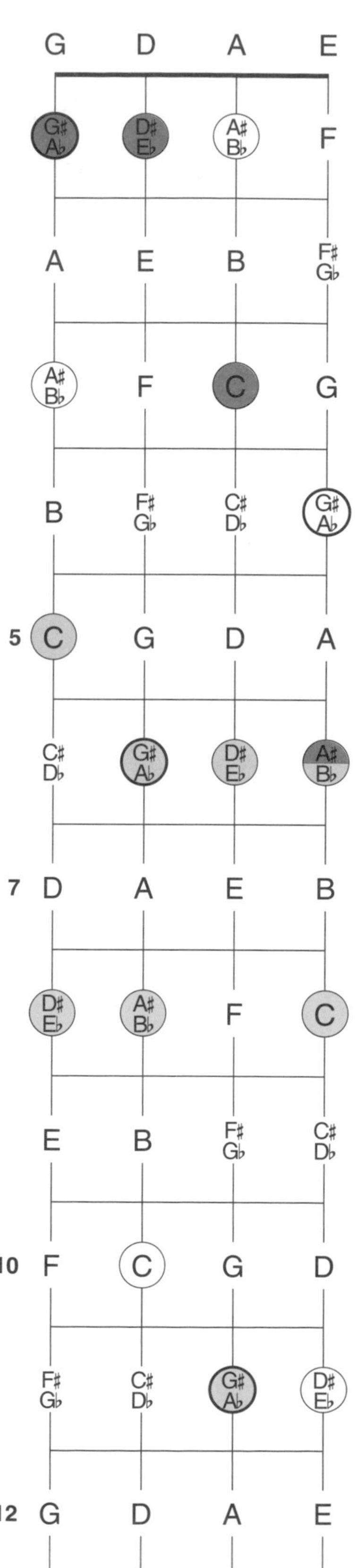

Aadd9

A–C♯–E–B

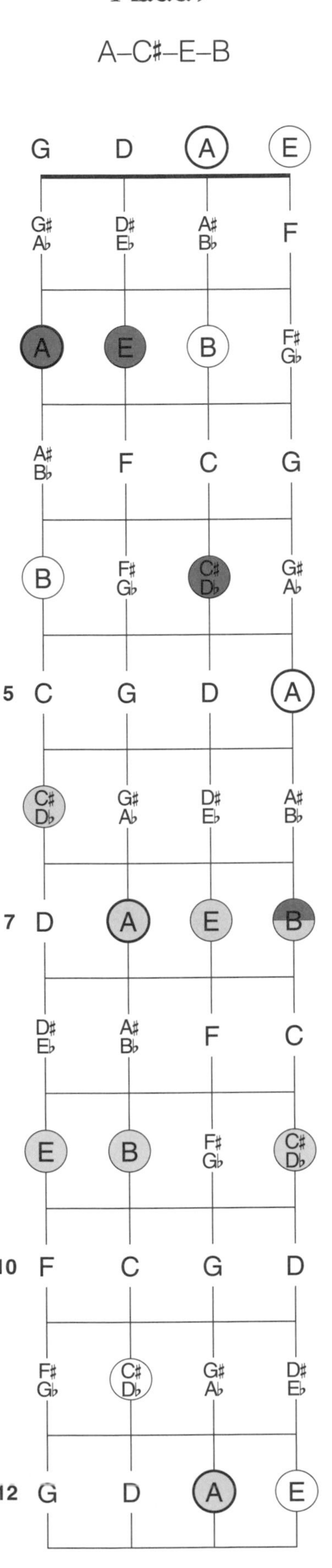

B♭add9

B♭–D–F–C

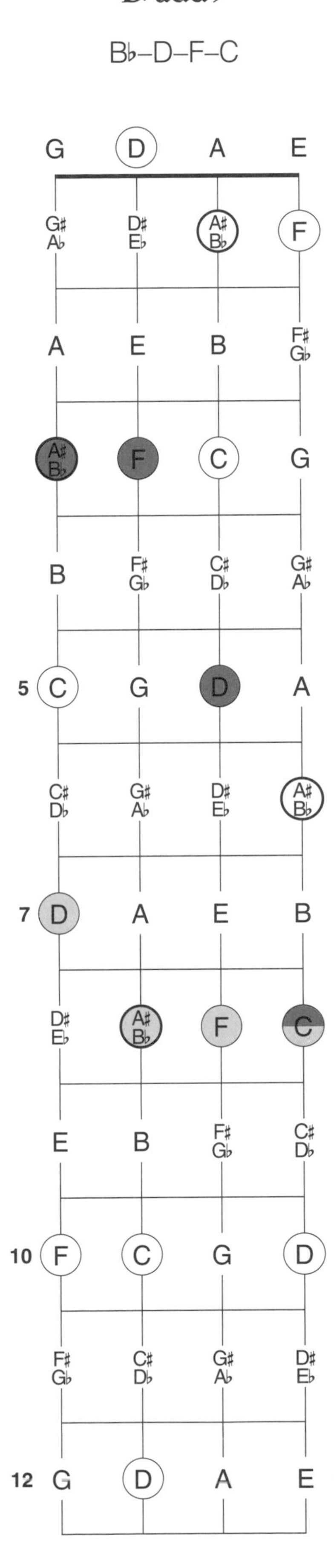

Badd9

B–D♯–F♯–C♯

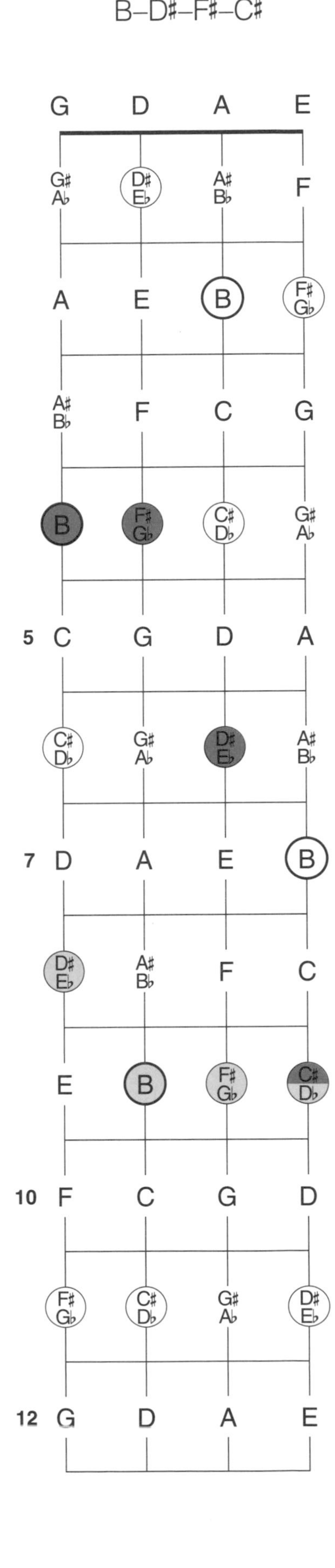

Cm(add9)

C–E♭–G–D

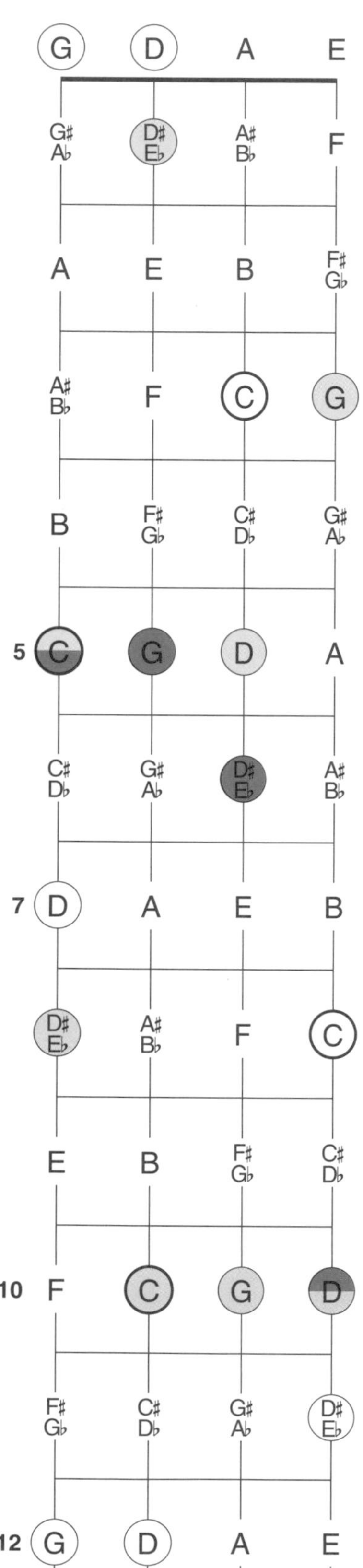

C♯m(add9)

C♯–E–G♯–D♯

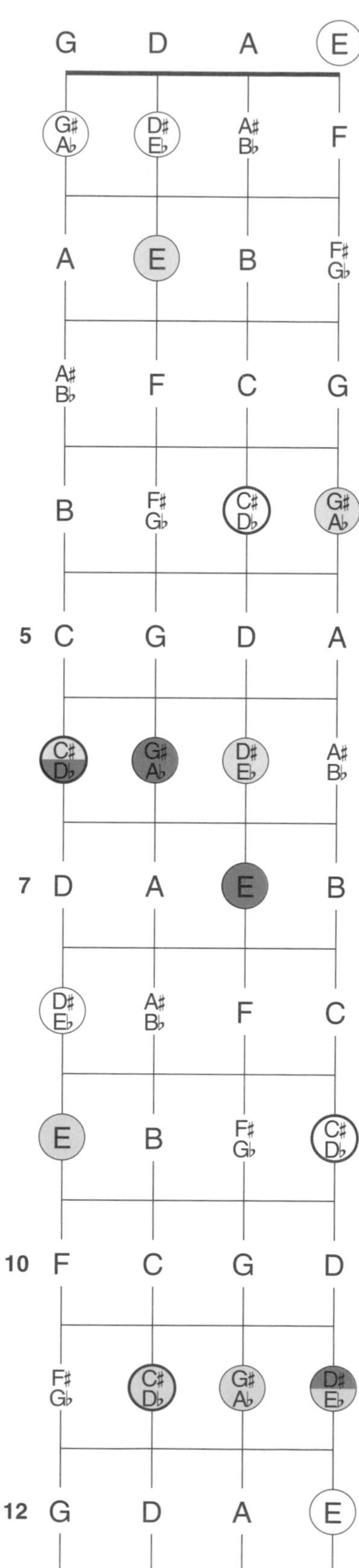

Dm(add9)

D–F–A–E

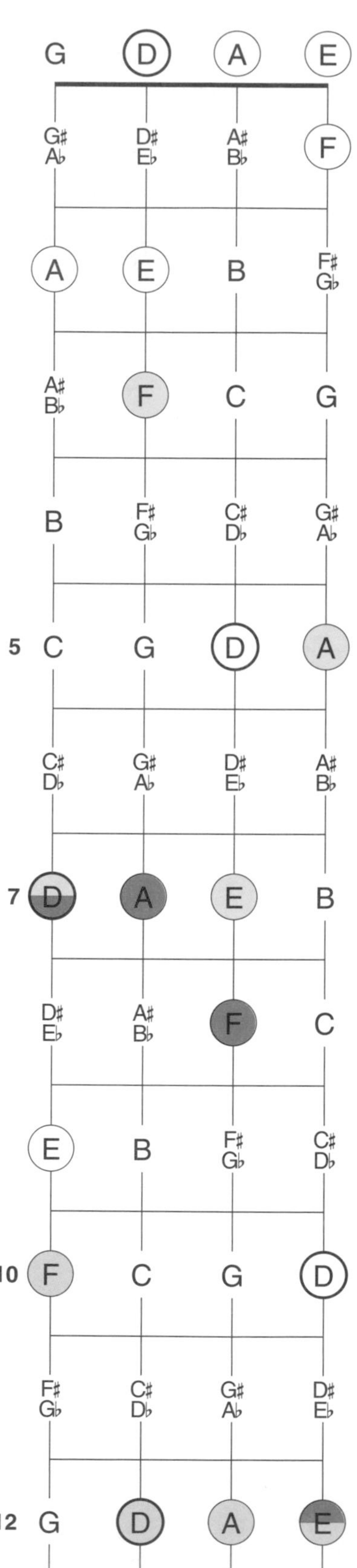

E♭m(add9)

E♭–G♭–B♭–F

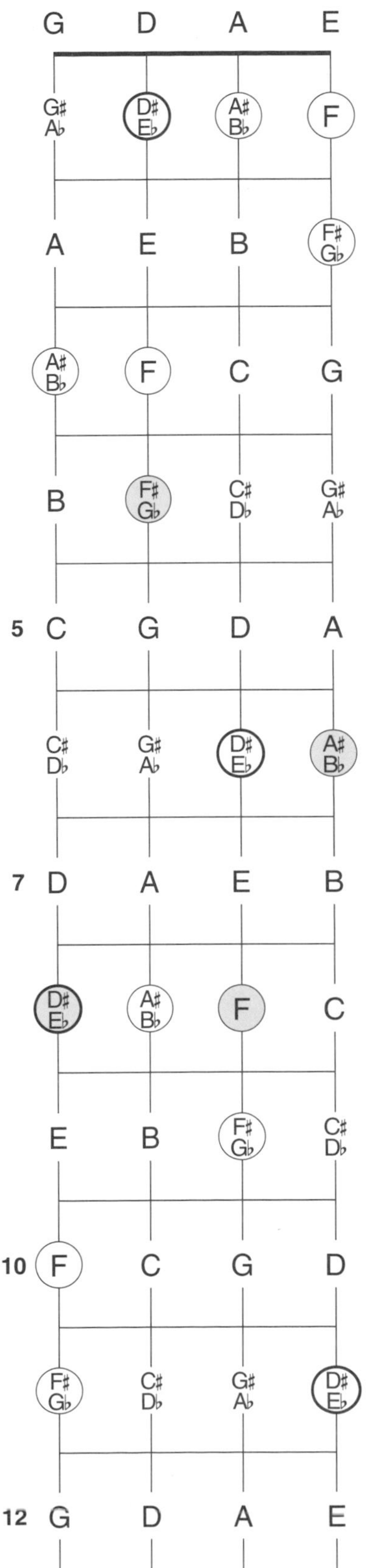

Em(add9)

E–G–B–F♯

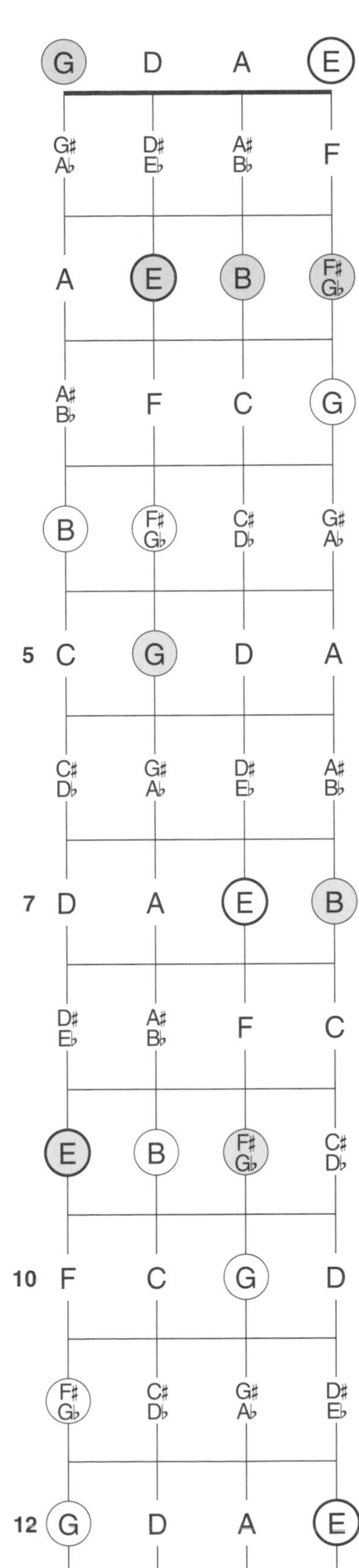

Fm(add9)

F–A♭–C–G

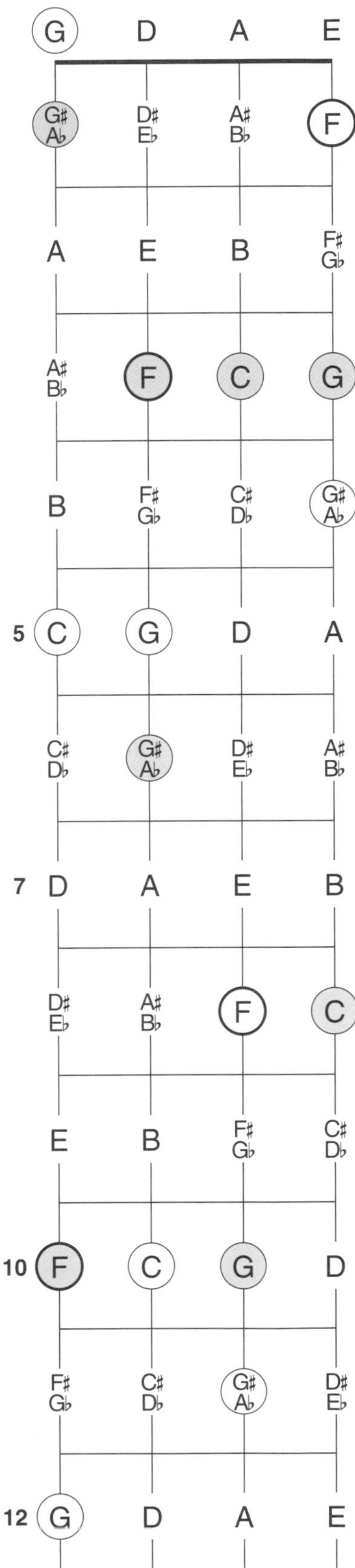

F♯m(add9)

F♯–A–C♯–G♯

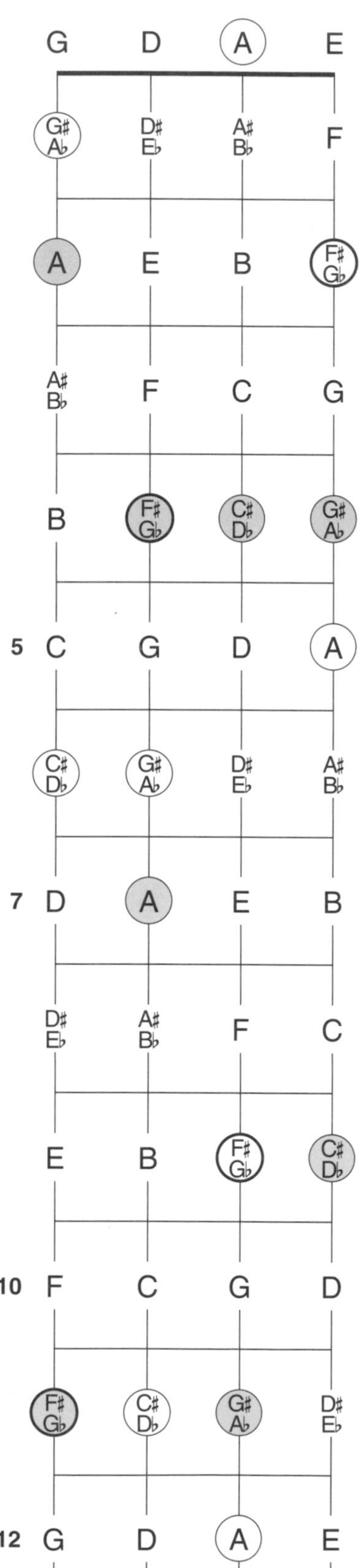

Gm(add9)

G–B♭–D–A

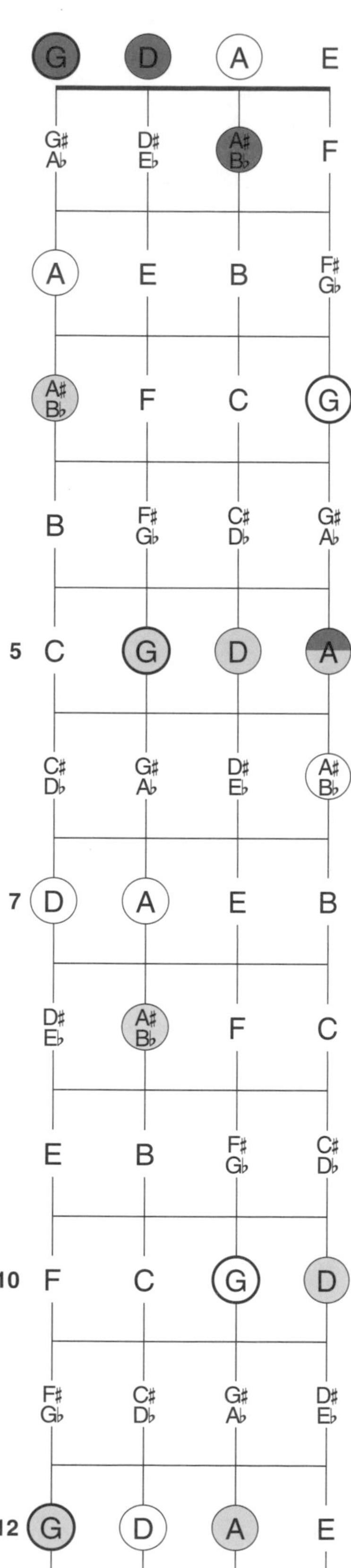

G♯/A♭m(add9)

G♯–B–D♯–A♯/A♭–C♭–E♭–B♭

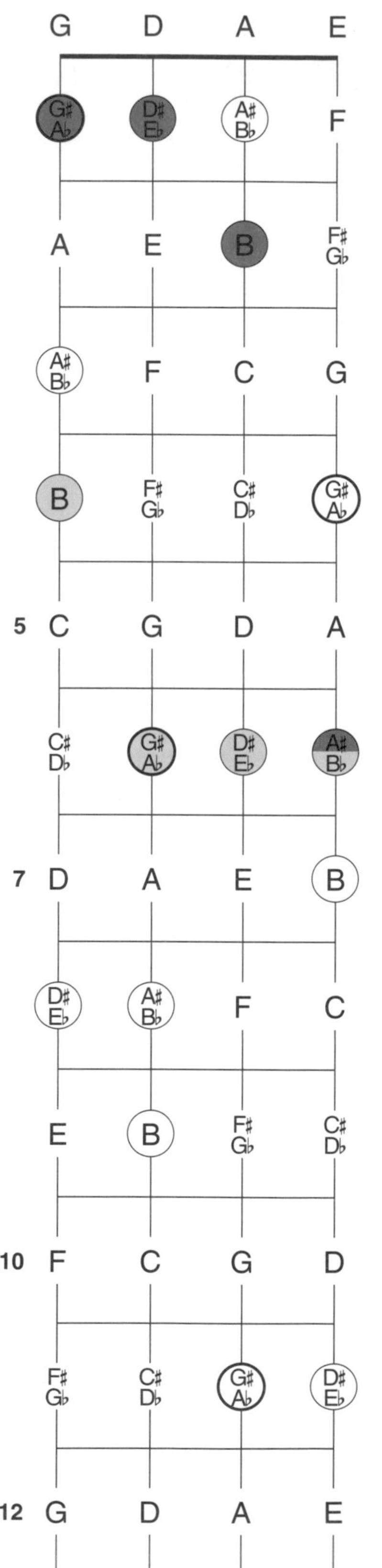

Am(add9)

A–C–E–B

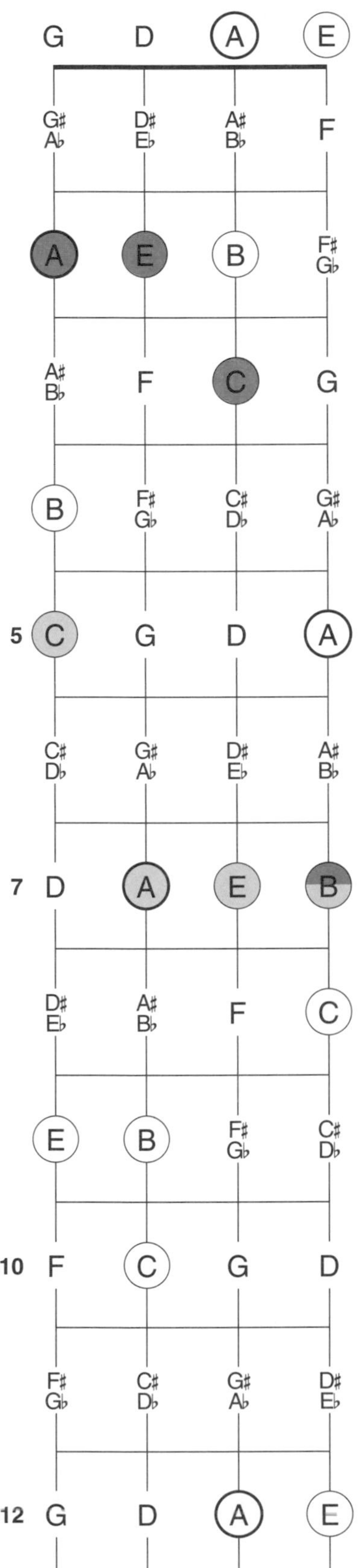

B♭m(add9)

B♭–D♭–F–C

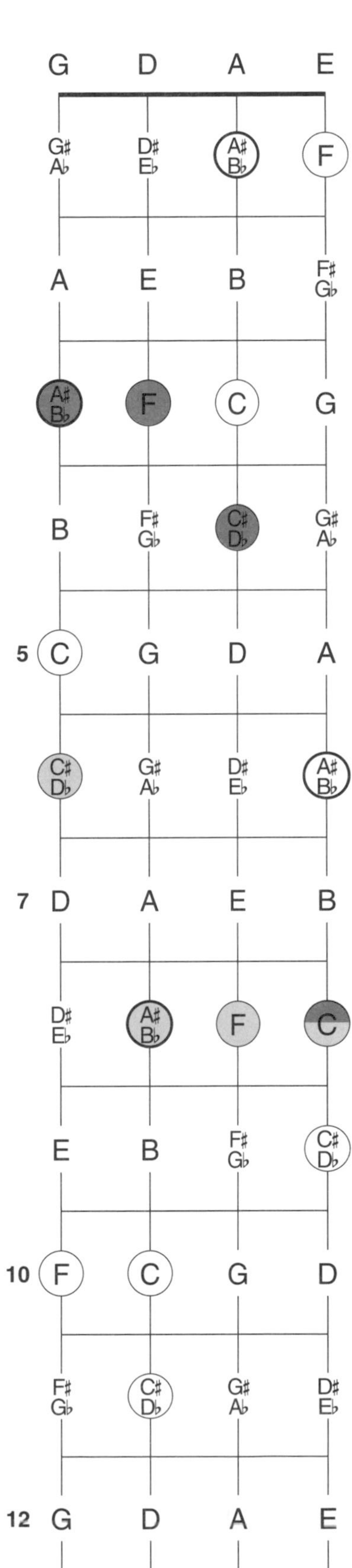

Bm(add9)

B–D–F♯–C♯

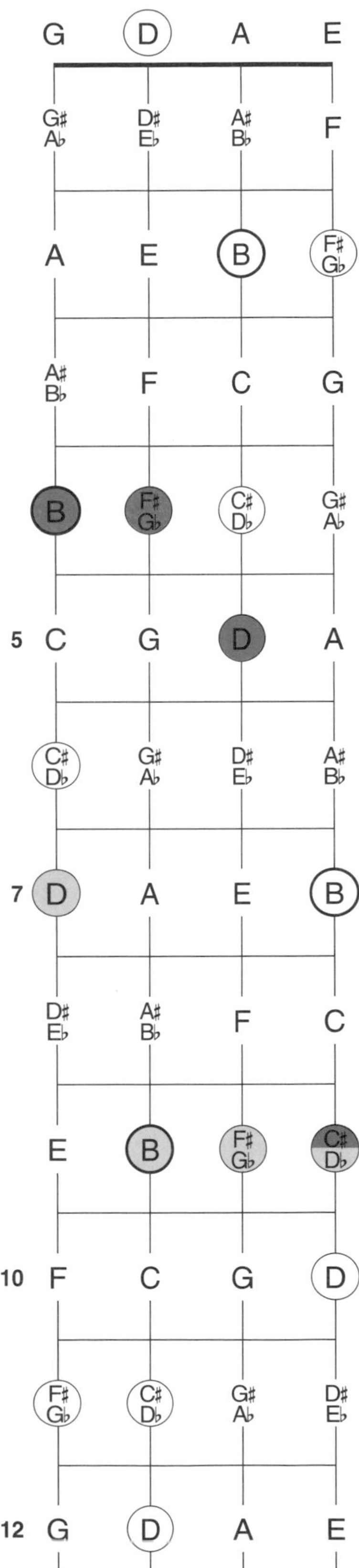

C6

C–E–G–A

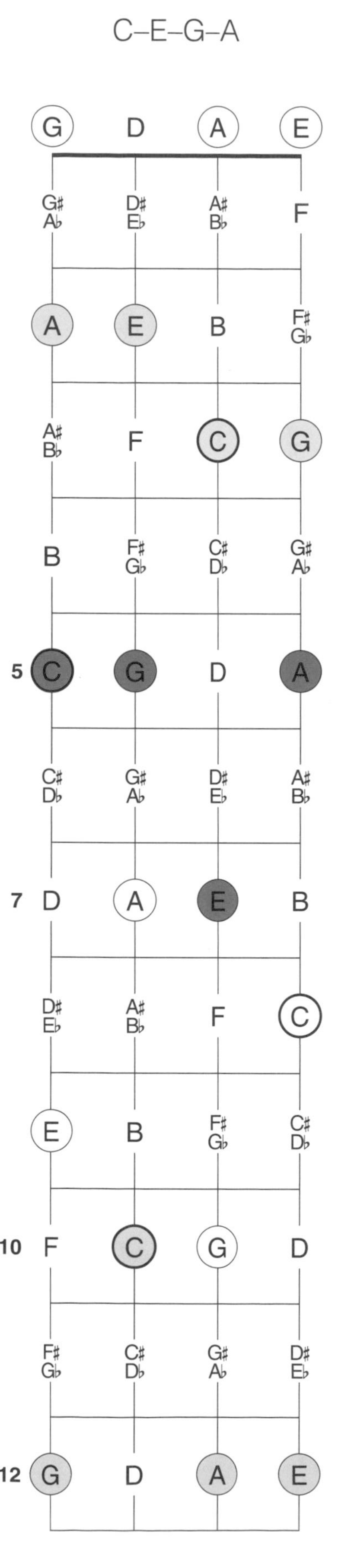

C♯/D♭6

C♯–E♯–G♯–A♯/D♭–F–A♭–B♭

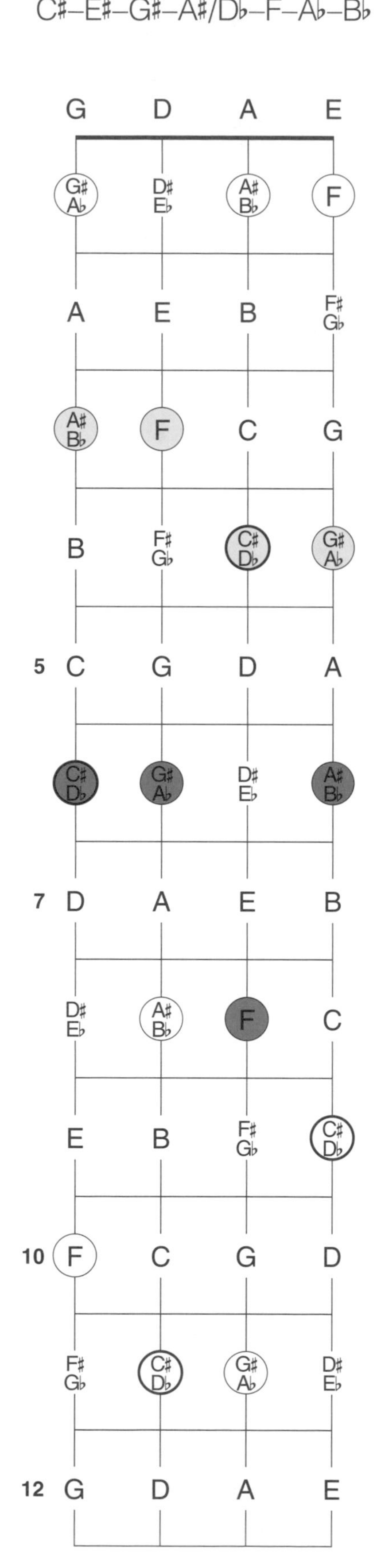

D6

D–F♯–A–B

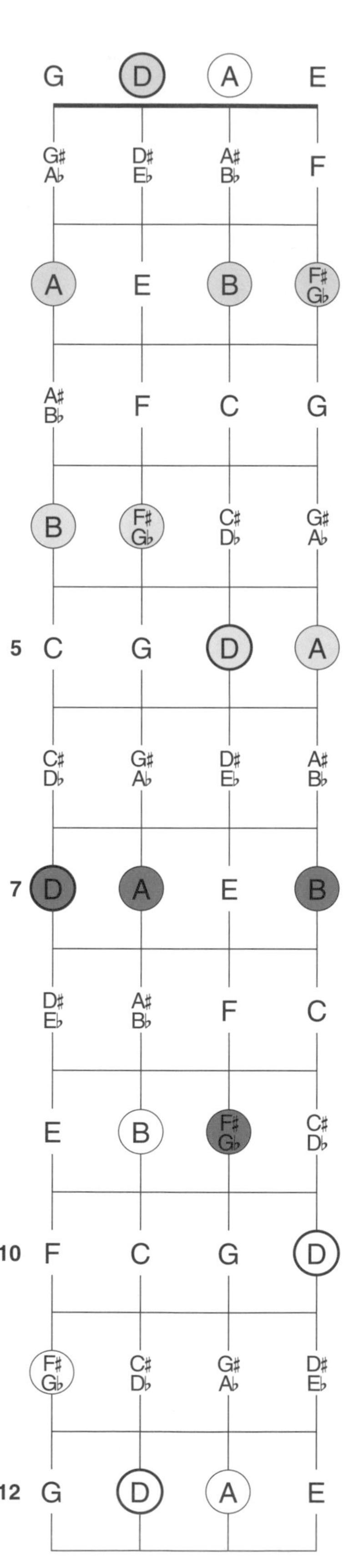

E♭6

E♭–G–B♭–C

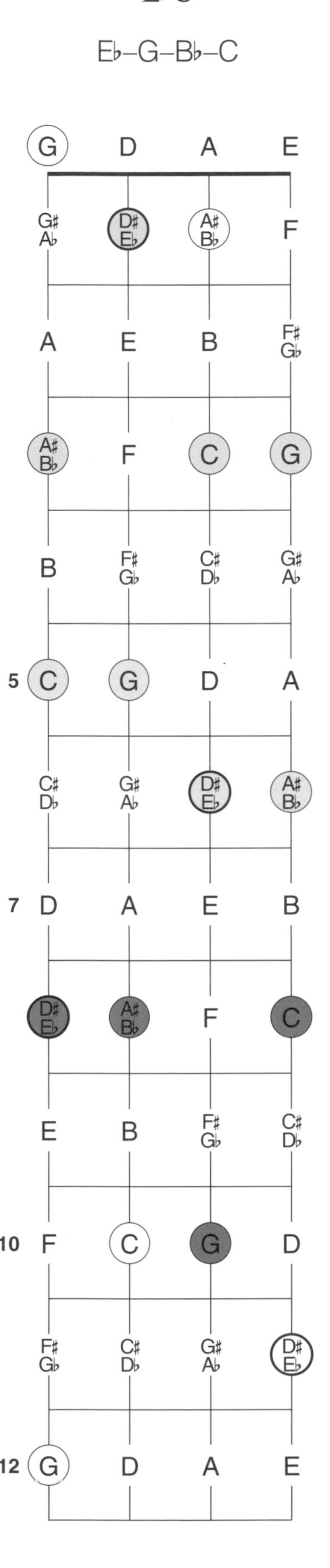

E6

E–G♯–B–C♯

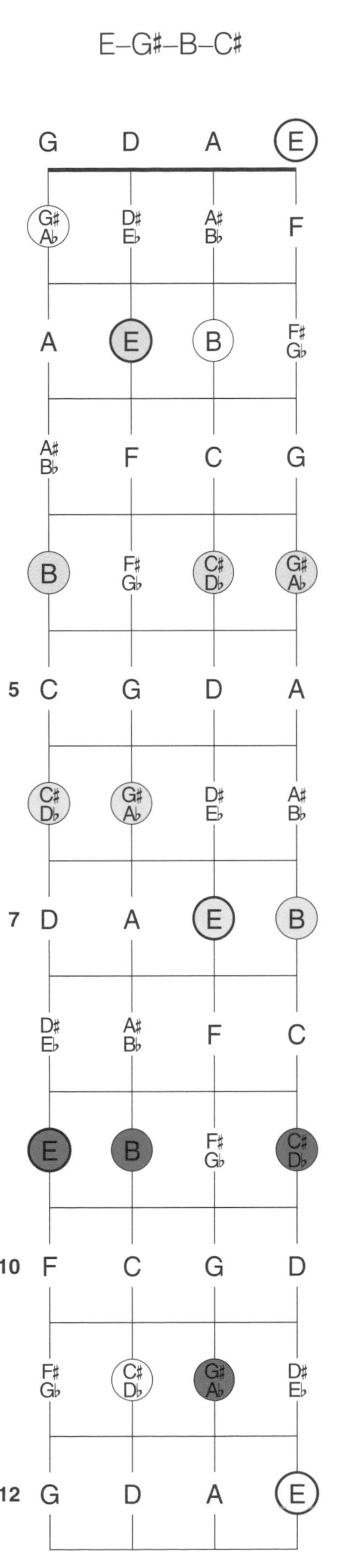

F6

F–A–C–D

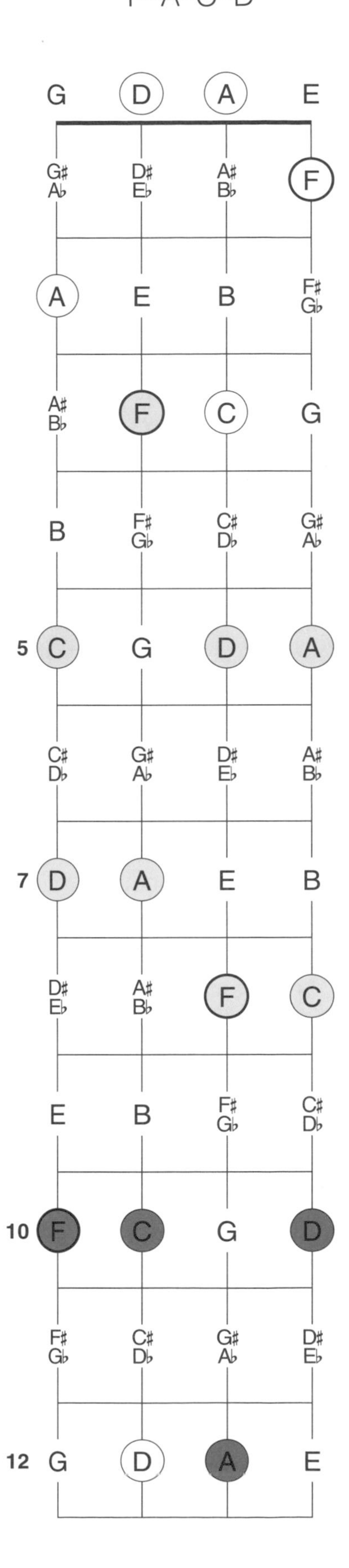

F♯/G♭6

F♯–A♯–C♯–D♯/G♭–B♭–D♭–E♭

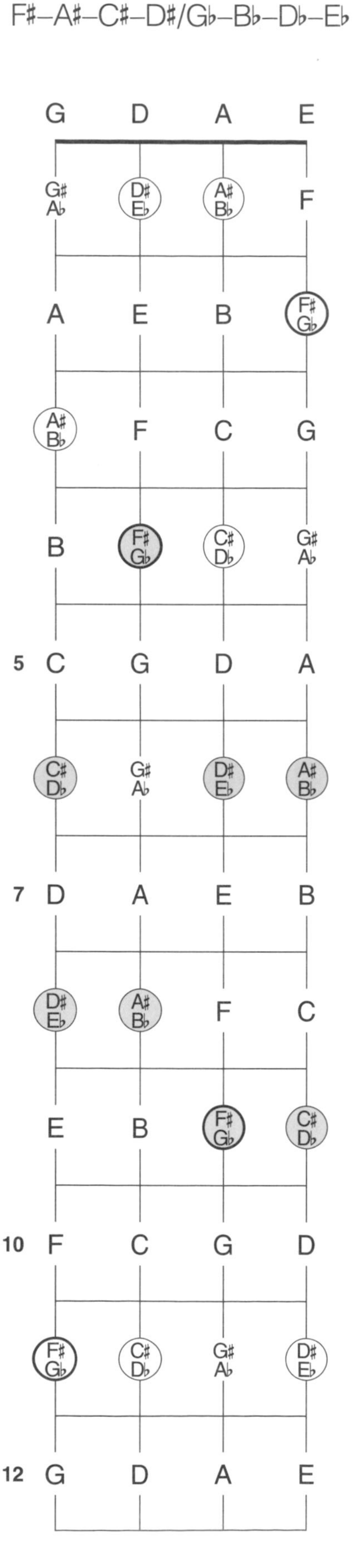

G6

G–B–D–E

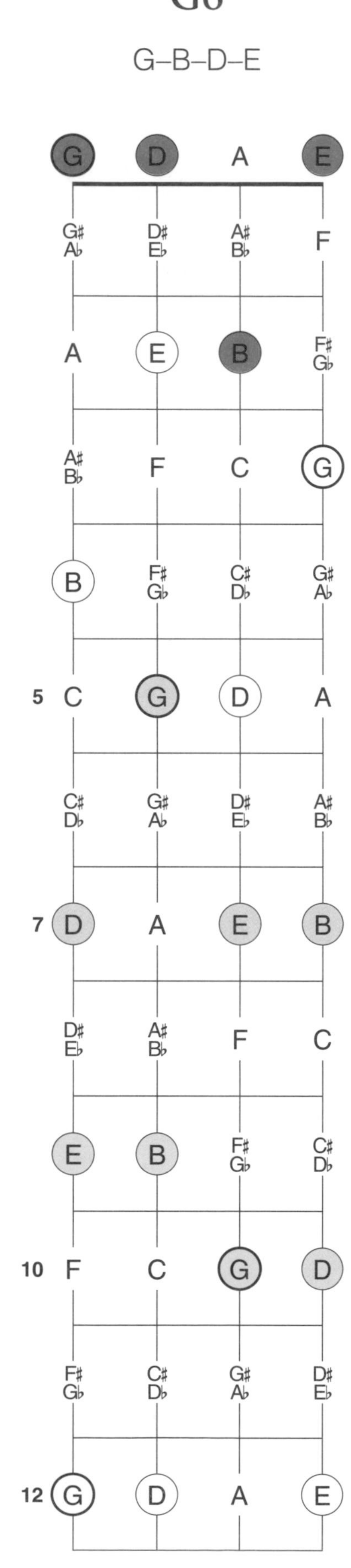

A♭6

A♭–C–E♭–F

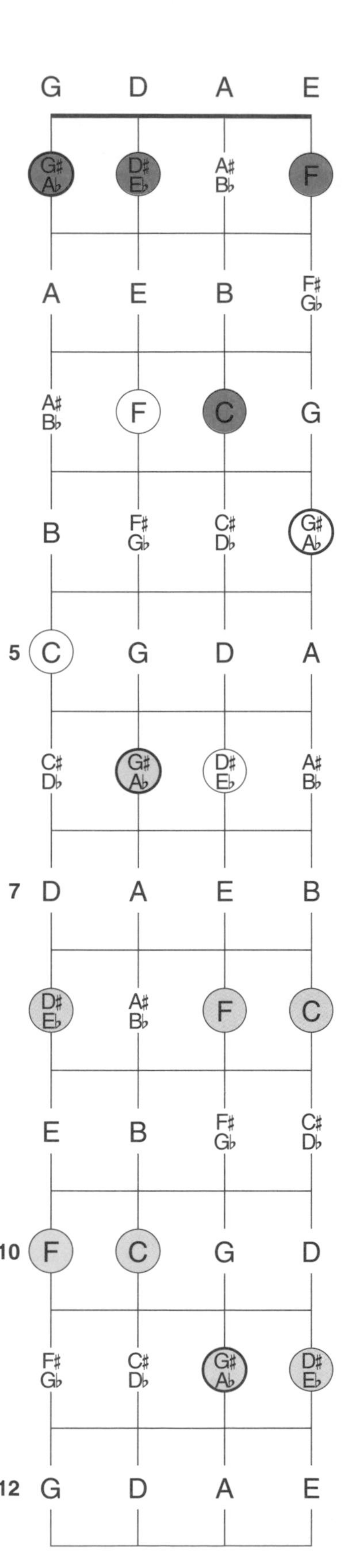

A6

A–C♯–E–F♯

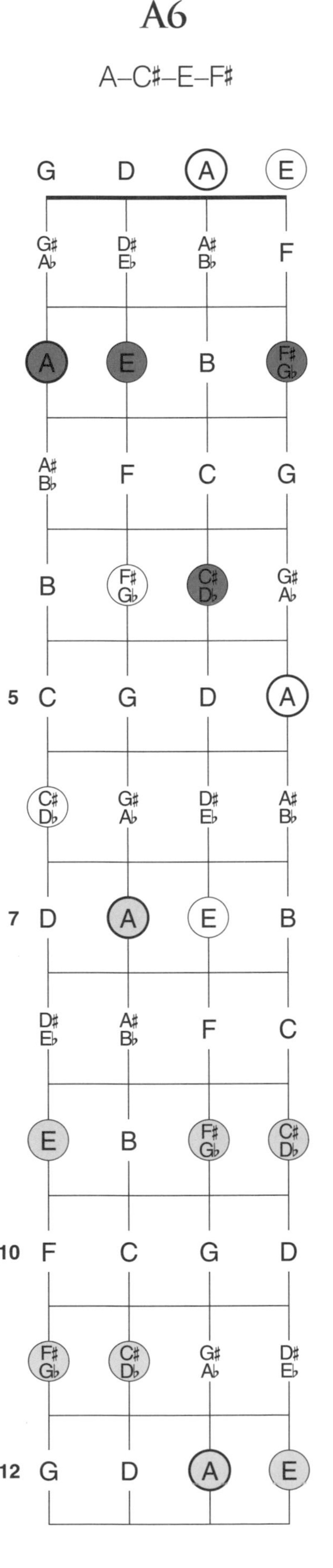

B♭6

B♭–D–F–G

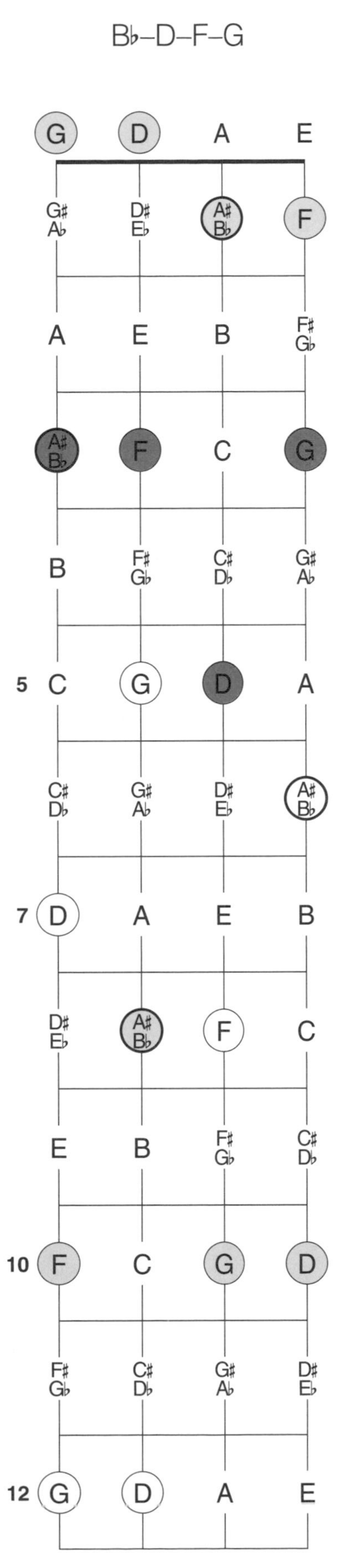

B6

B–D♯–F♯–G♯

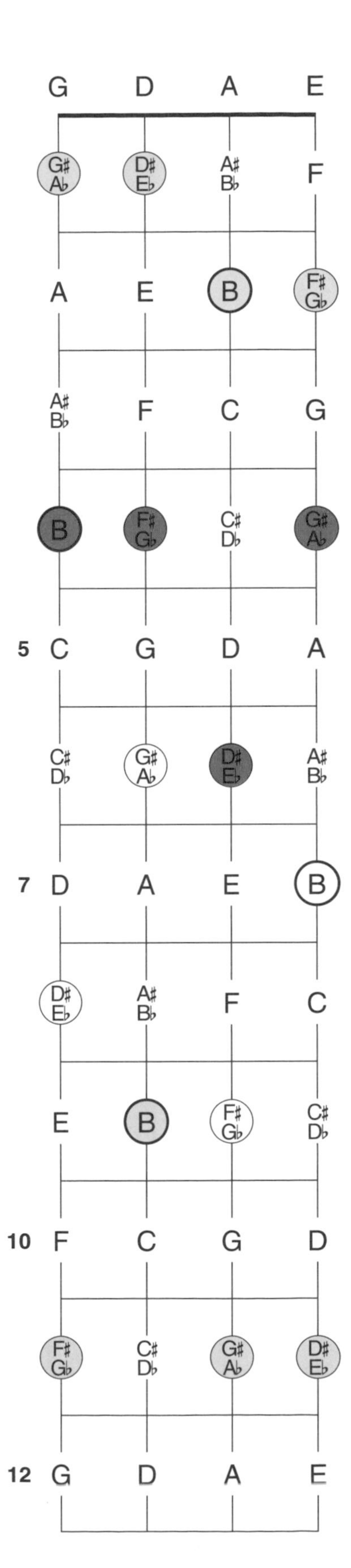

Cm6

C–E♭–G–A

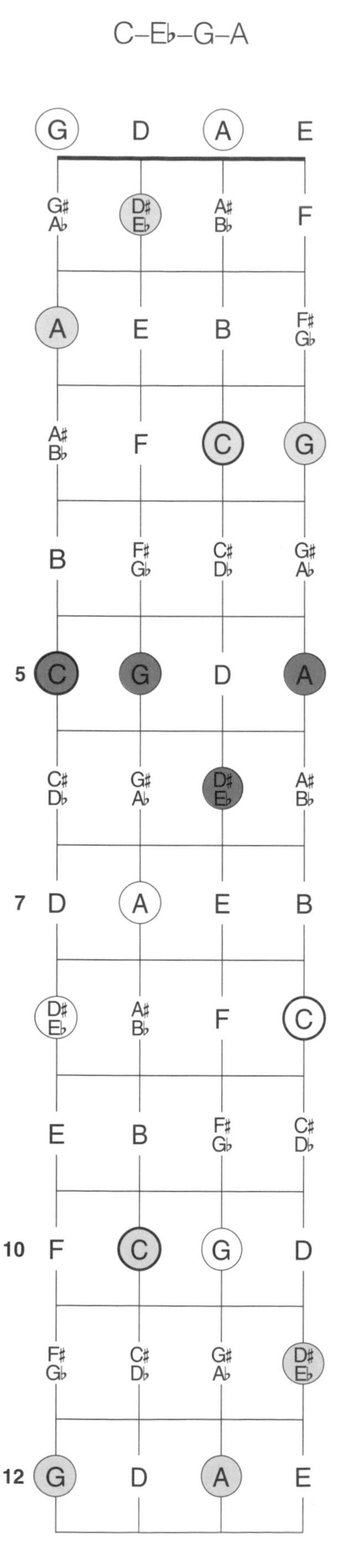

C♯m6

C♯–E–G♯–A♯

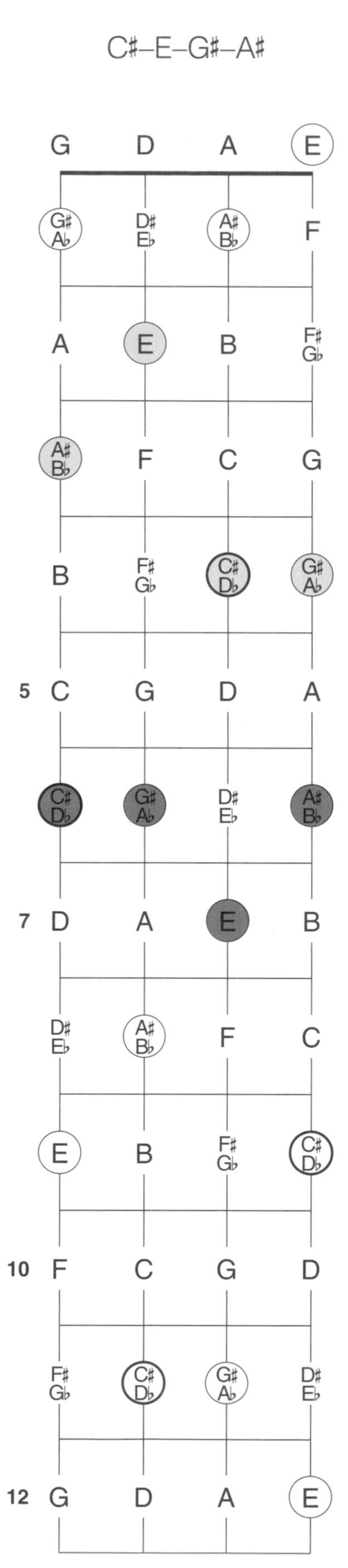

Dm6

D–F–A–B

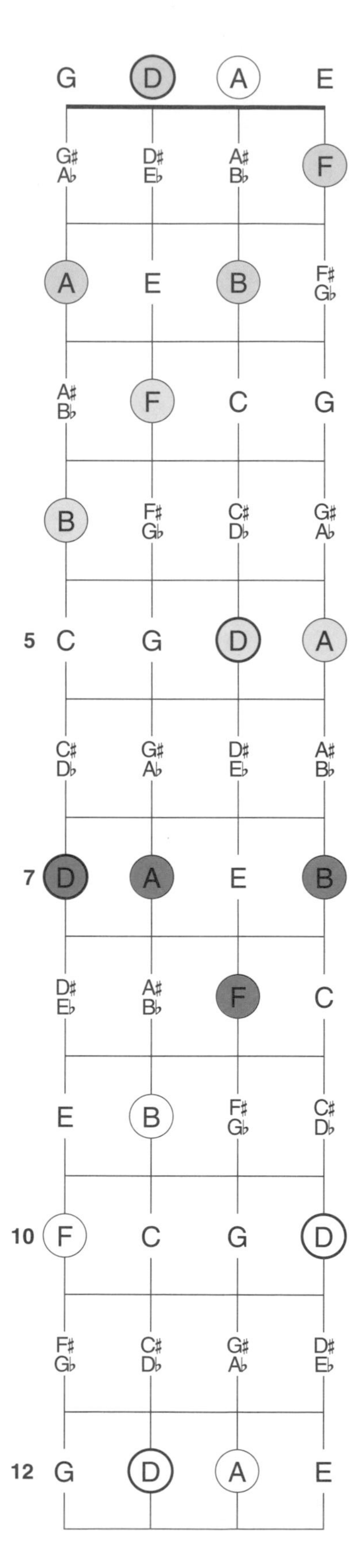

E♭m6

E♭–G♭–B♭–C

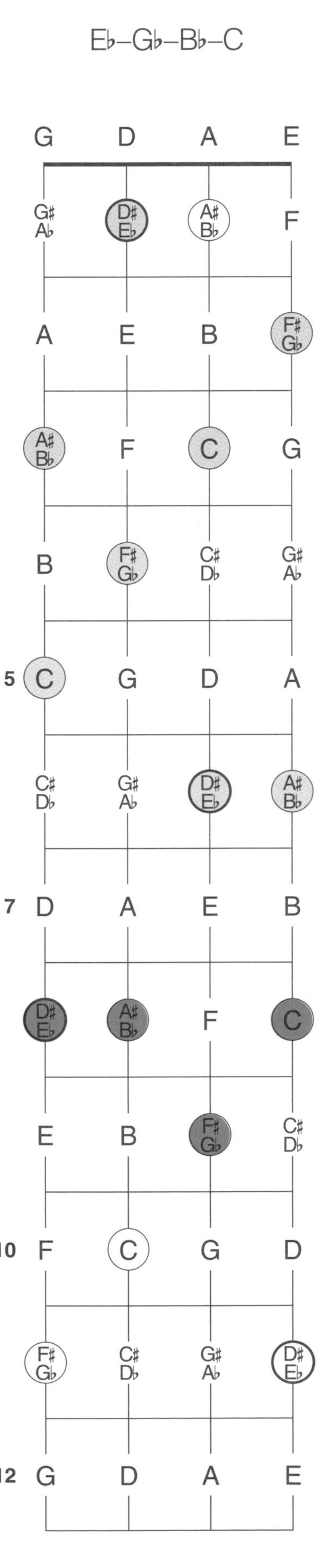

Em6

E–G–B–C♯

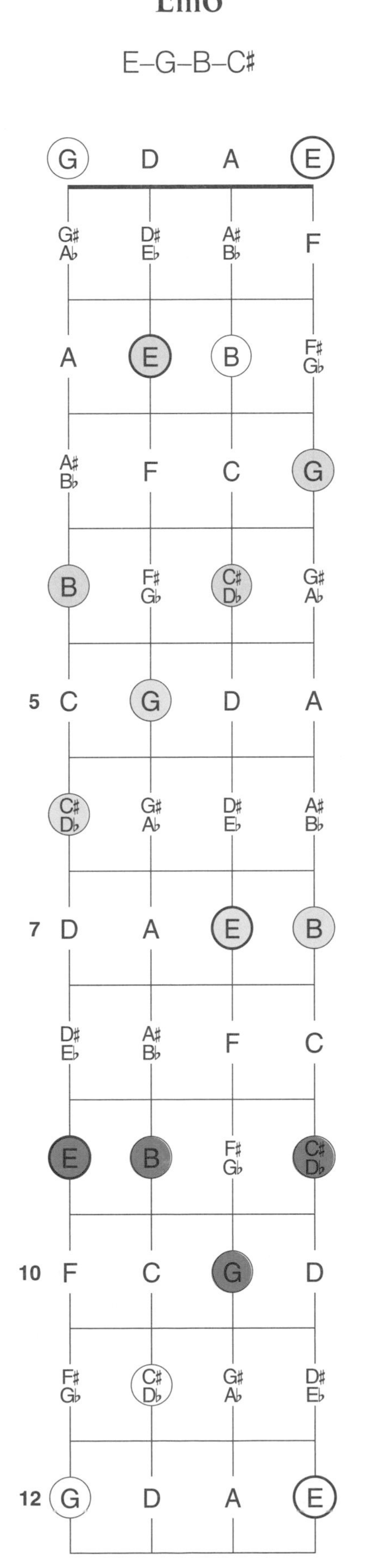

Fm6

F–A♭–C–D

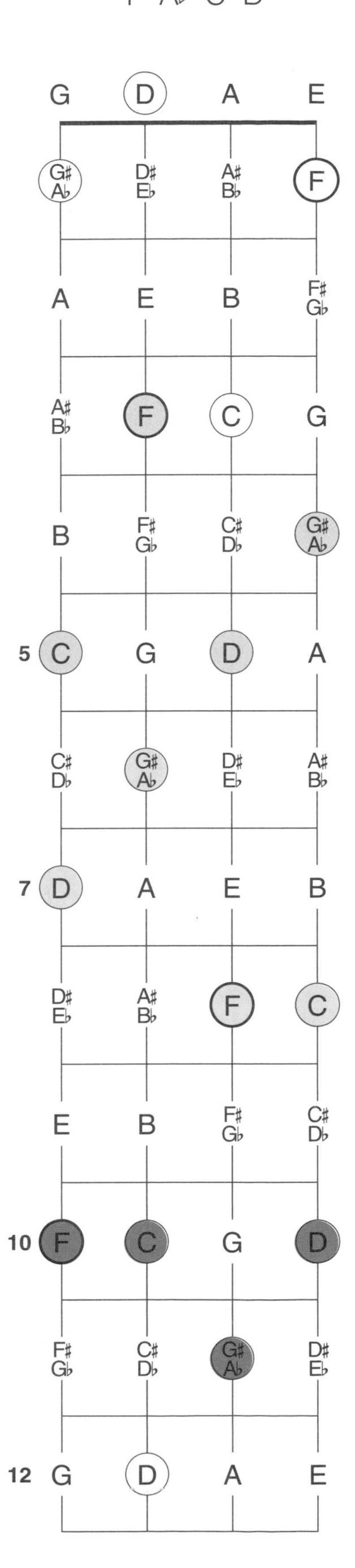

F♯m6

F♯–A–C♯–D♯

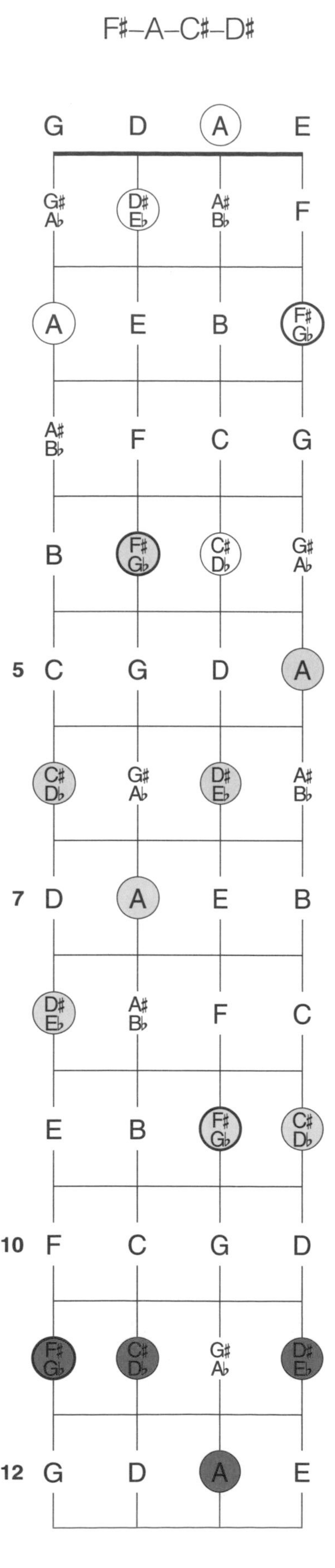

Gm6

G–B♭–D–E

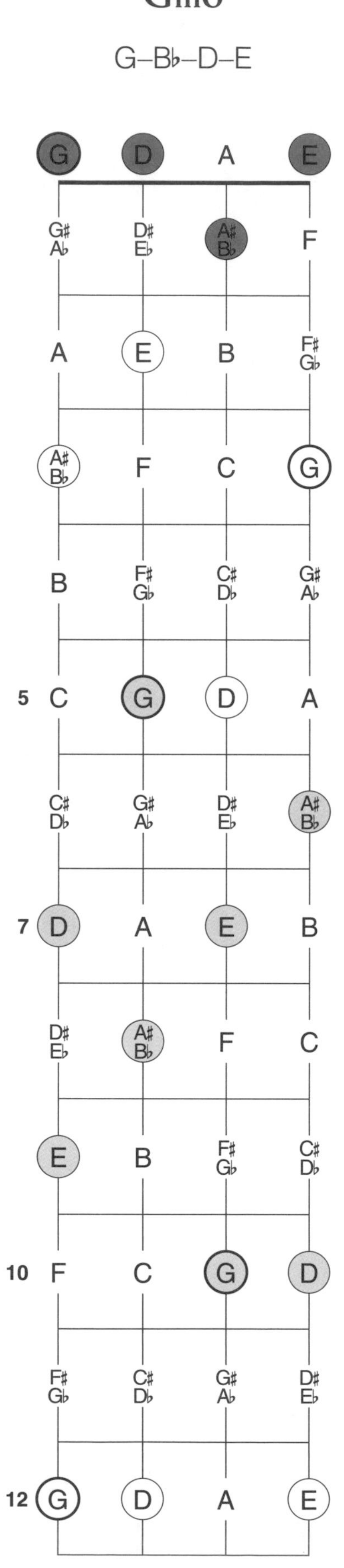

A♭m6

A♭–C♭–E♭–F

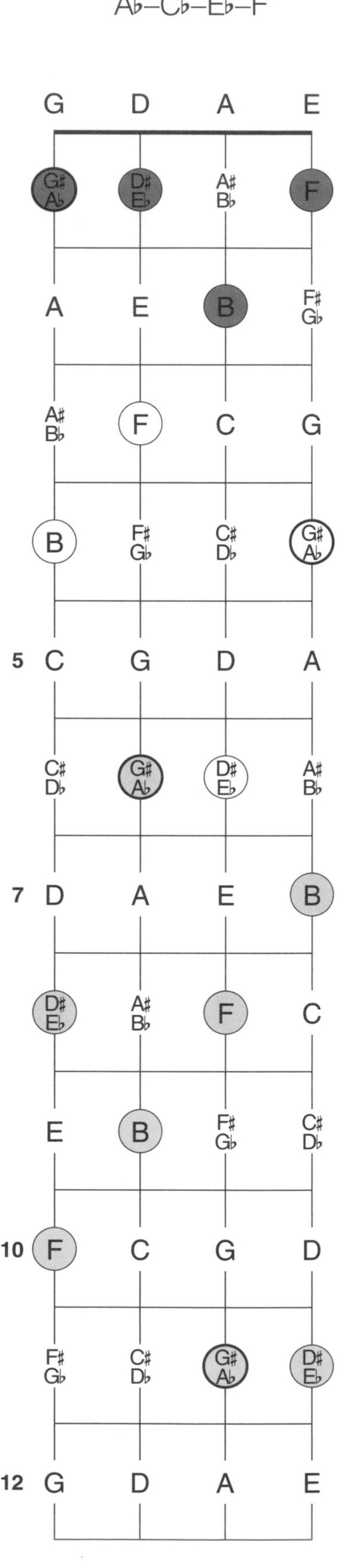

Am6

A–C–E–F♯

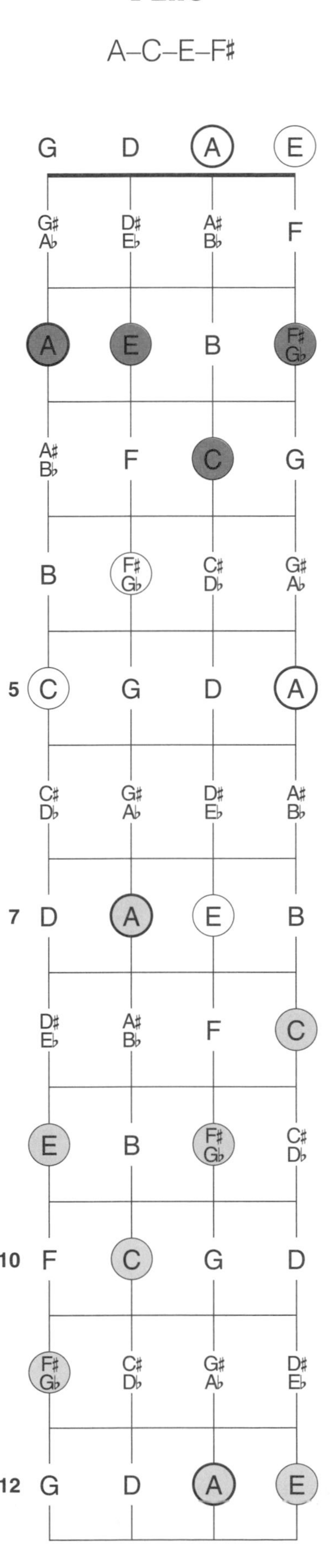

B♭m6

B♭–D♭–F–G

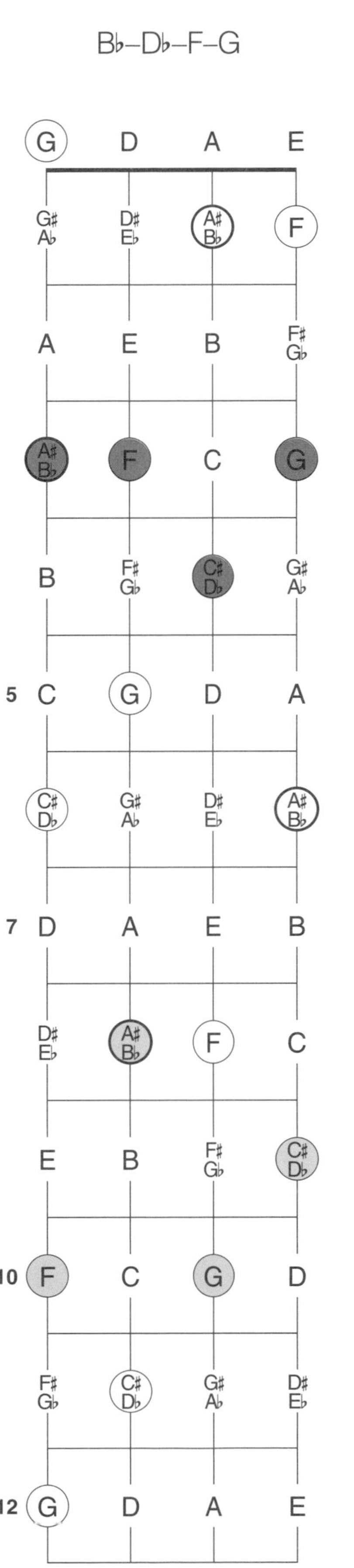

Bm6

B–D–F♯–G♯

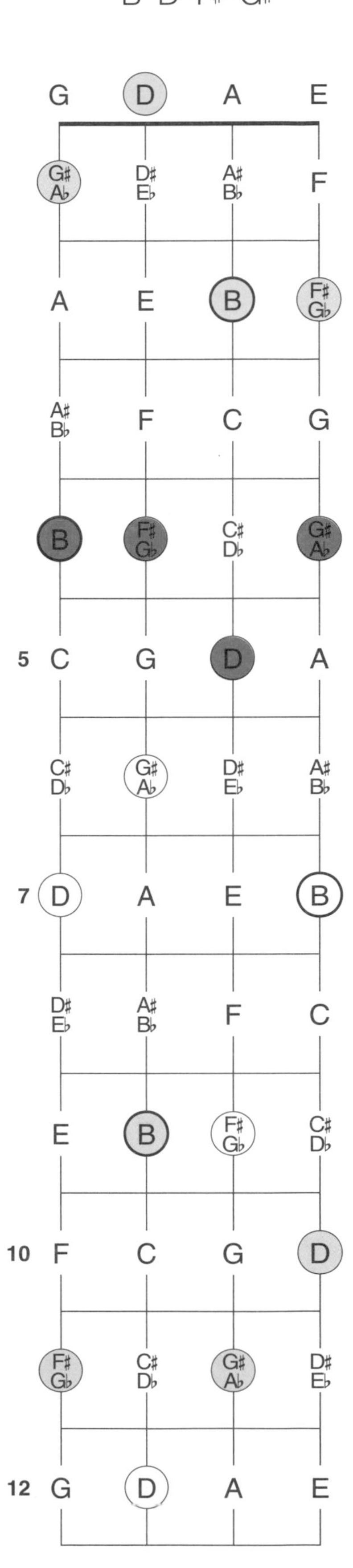

C^{6}_{9}

C–E–G–A–D

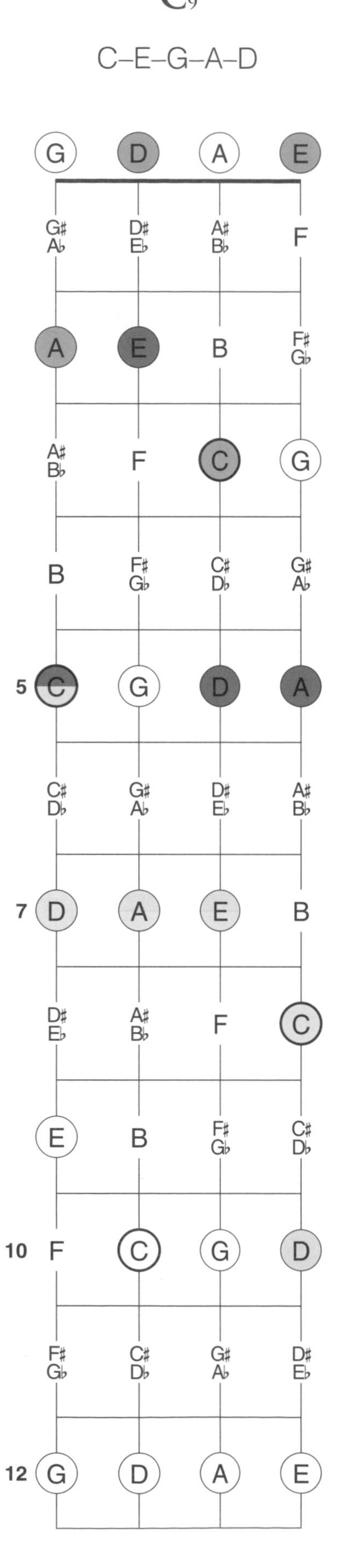

C♯/$D♭^{6}_{9}$

C♯–E♯–G♯–A♯–D♯/D♭–F–A♭–B♭–E♭

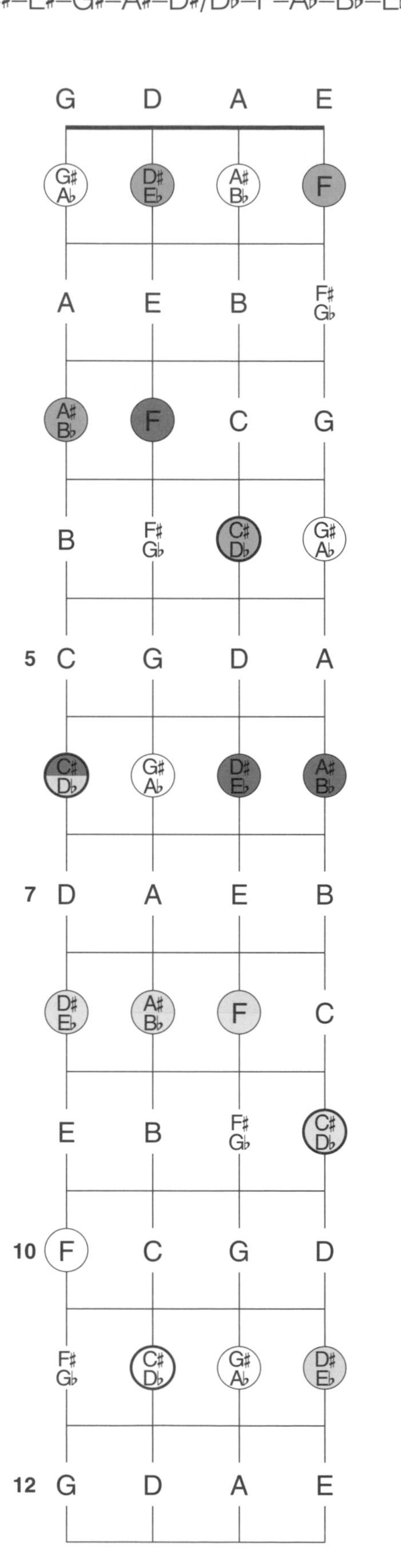

D^{6}_{9}

D–F♯–A–B–E

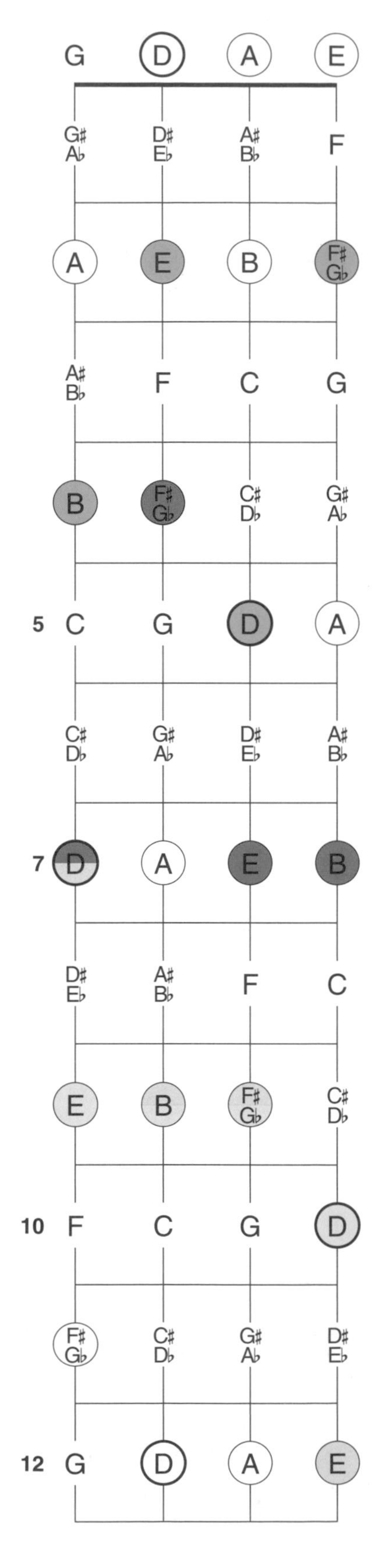

E♭$^{6}_{9}$

E♭–G–B♭–C–F

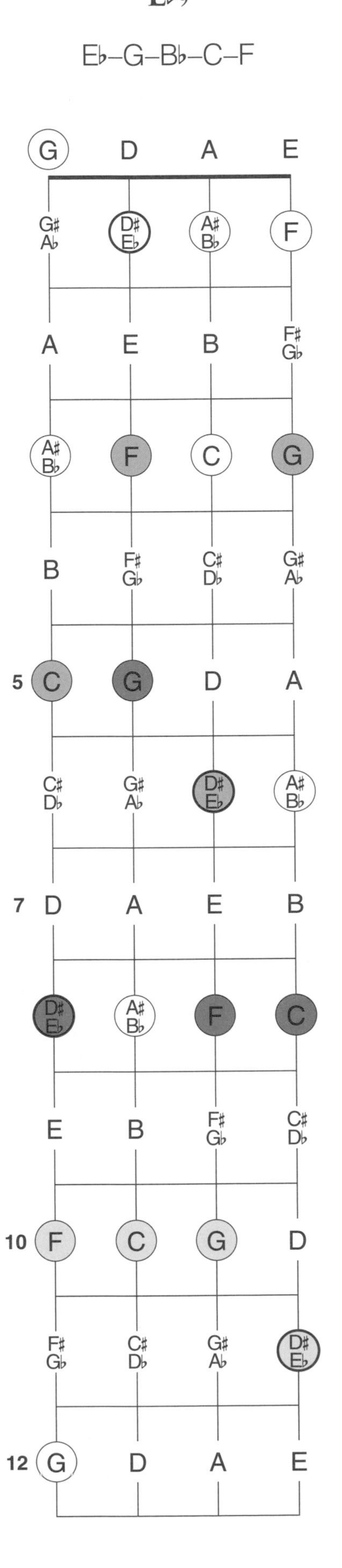

E$^{6}_{9}$

E–G♯–B–C♯–F♯

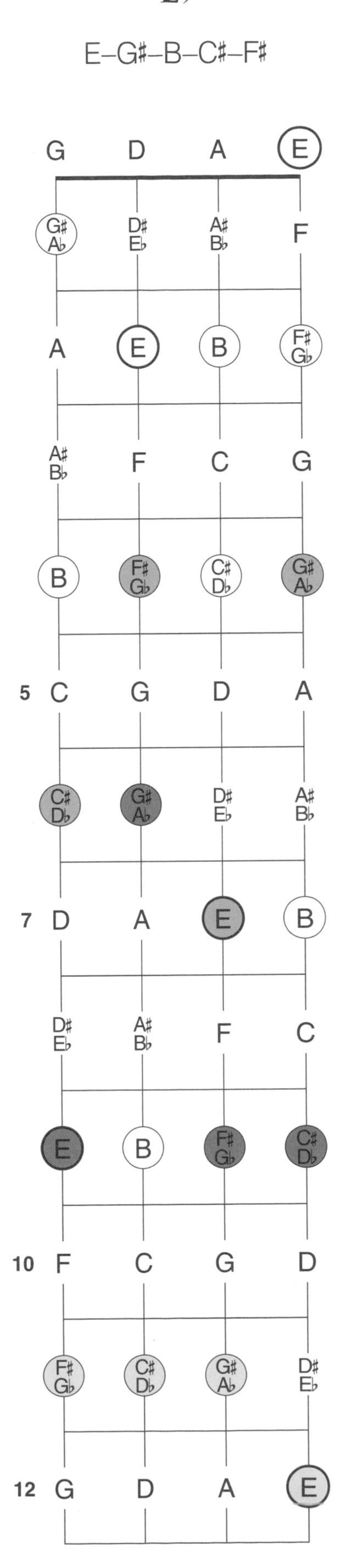

F$^{6}_{9}$

F–A–C–D–G

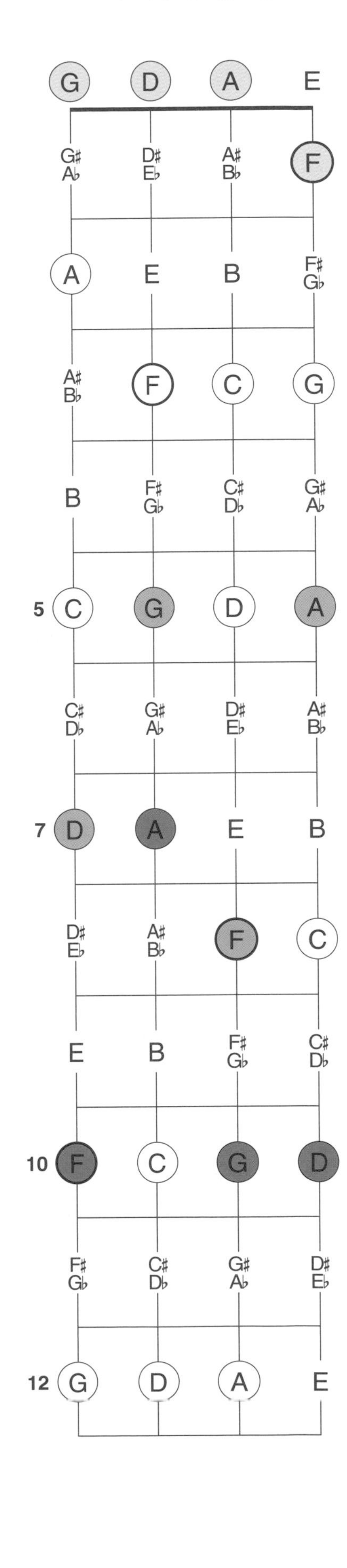

F♯/G♭$^{6}_{9}$

F♯–A♯–C♯–D♯–G♯/G♭–B♭–D♭–E♭–A♭

G$^{6}_{9}$

G–B–D–E–A

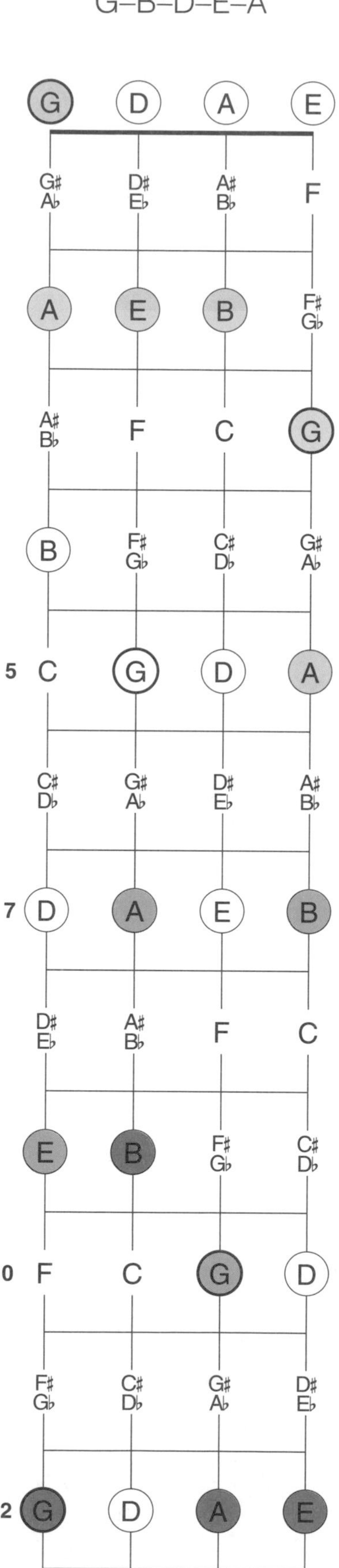

A♭$^{6}_{9}$

A♭–C–E♭–F–B♭

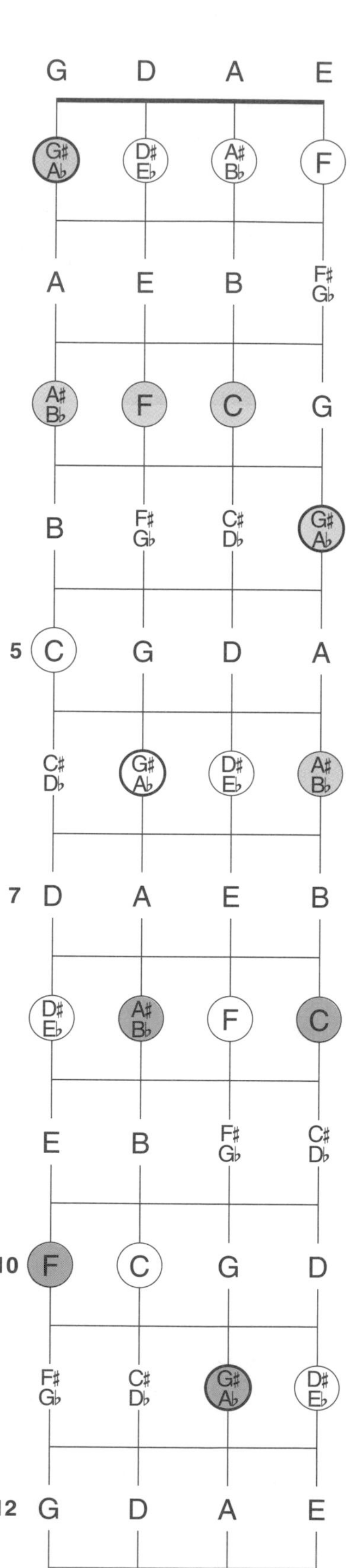

A$^{6}_{9}$

A–C♯–E–F♯–B

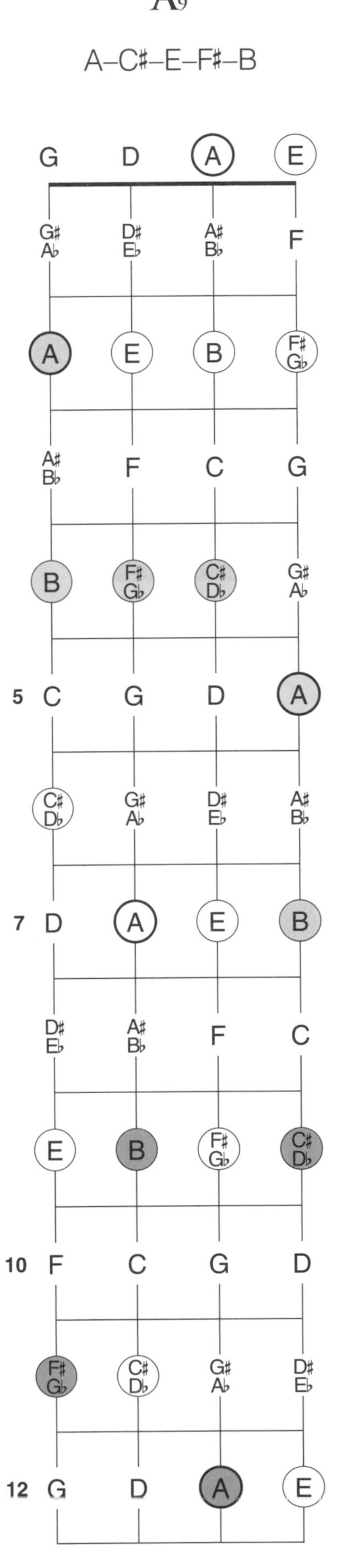

B♭$^{6}_{9}$

B♭–D–F–G–C

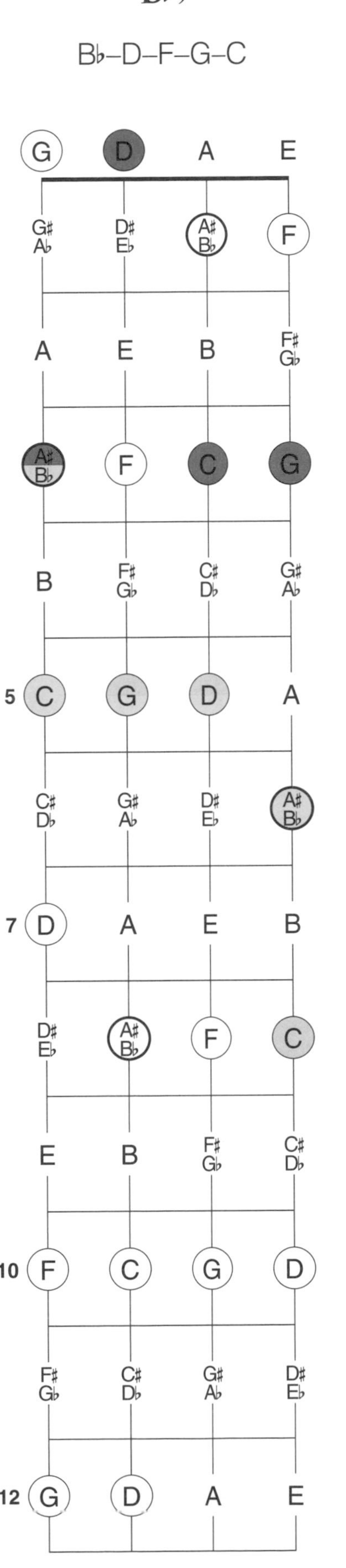

B$^{6}_{9}$

B–D♯–F♯–G♯–C♯

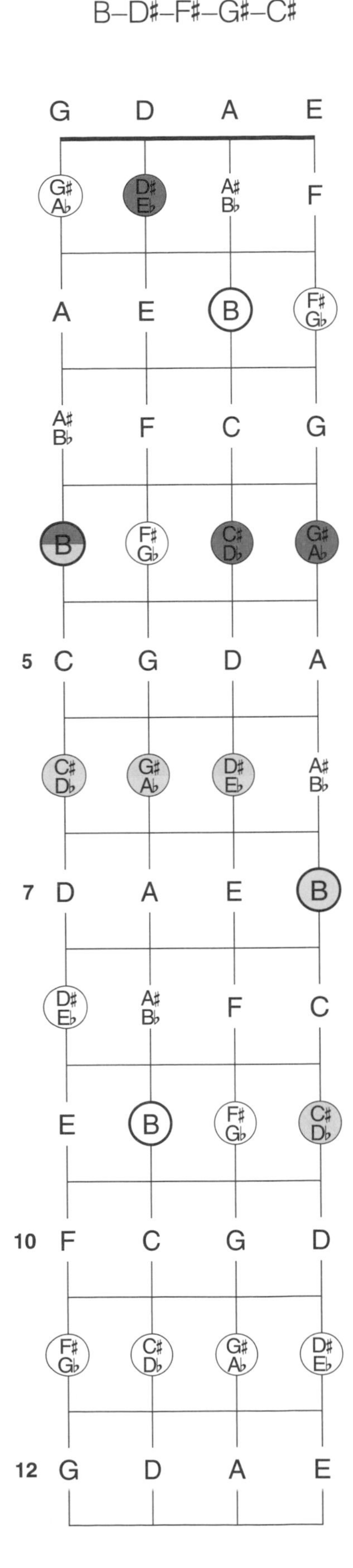

Cm$^{6}_{9}$

C–E♭–G–A–D

C♯m$^{6}_{9}$

C♯–E–G♯–A♯–D♯

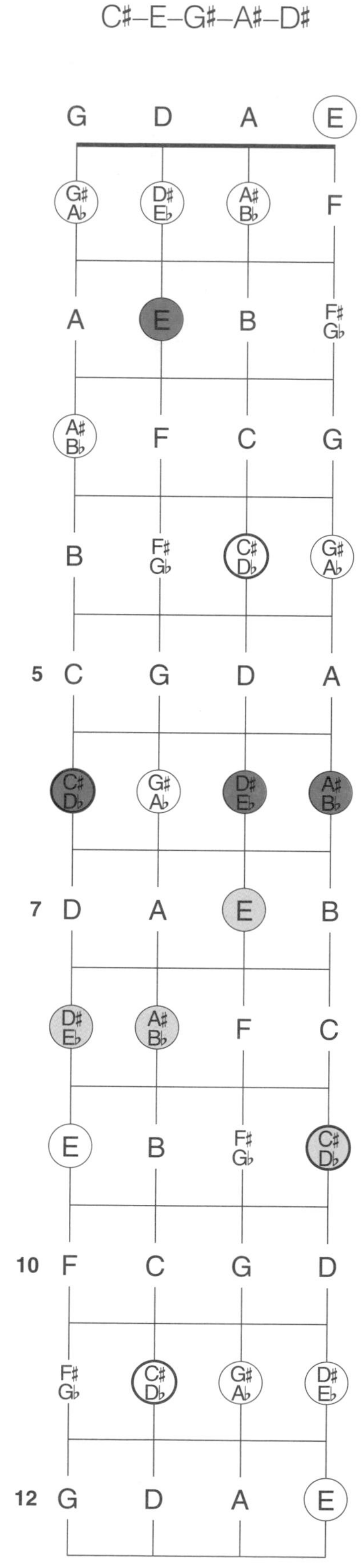

Dm$^{6}_{9}$

D–F–A–B–E

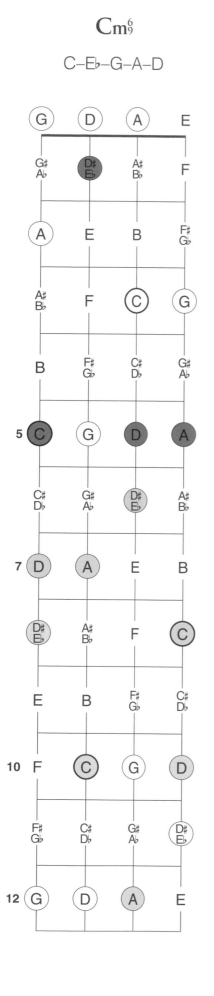

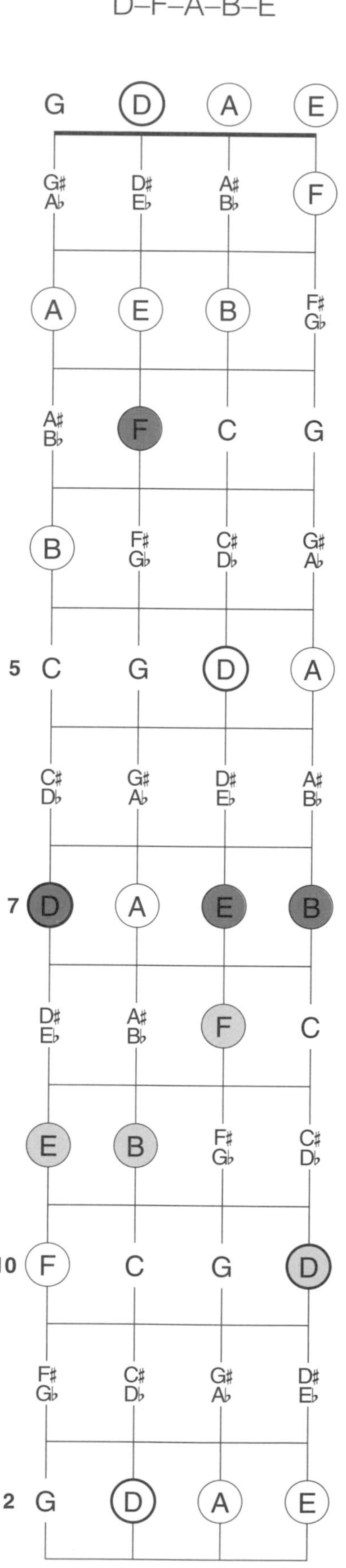

E♭m$^{6}_{9}$

E♭–G♭–B♭–C–F

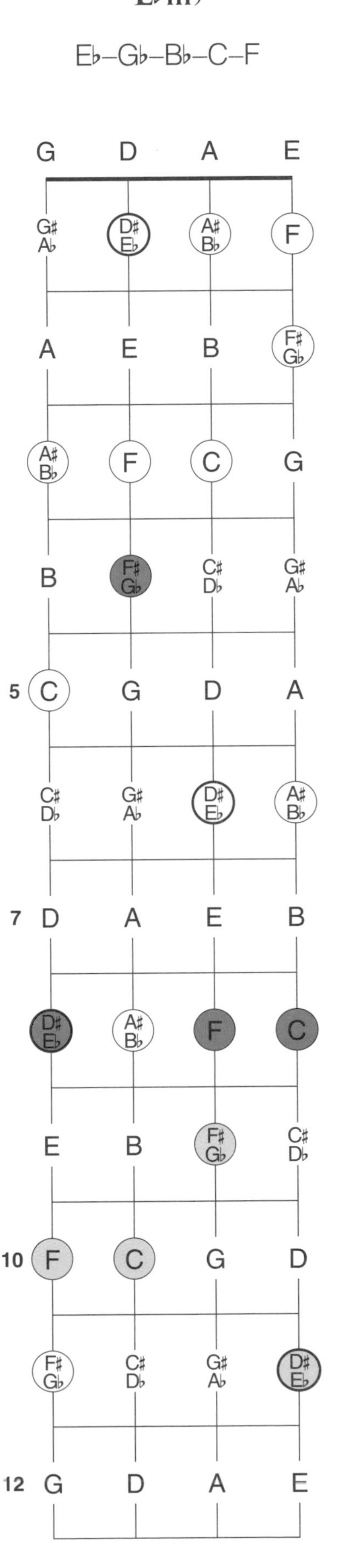

Em$^{6}_{9}$

E–G–B–C♯–F♯

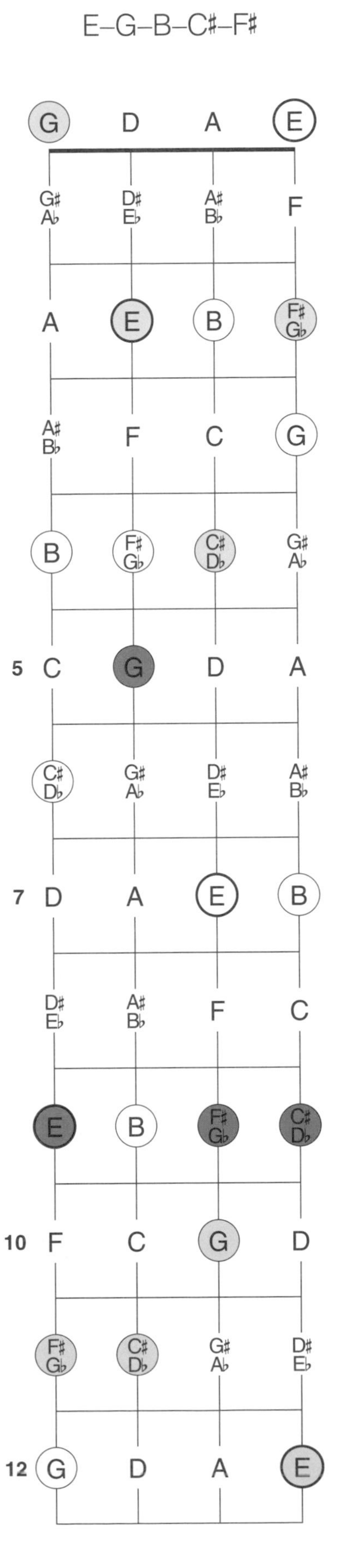

Fm$^{6}_{9}$

F–A♭–C–D–G

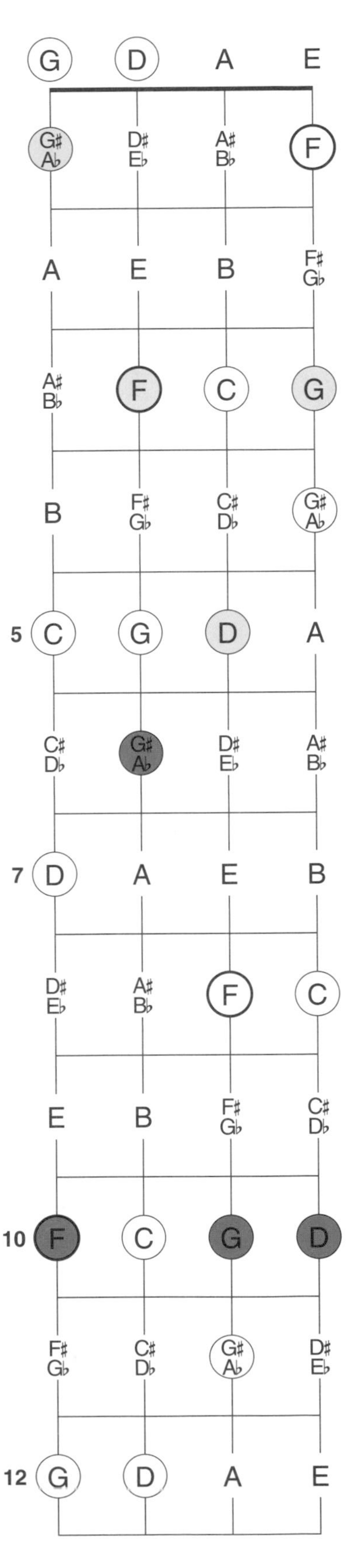

F♯m$^{6}_{9}$

F♯–A–C♯–D♯–G♯

Gm$^{6}_{9}$

G–B♭–D–E–A

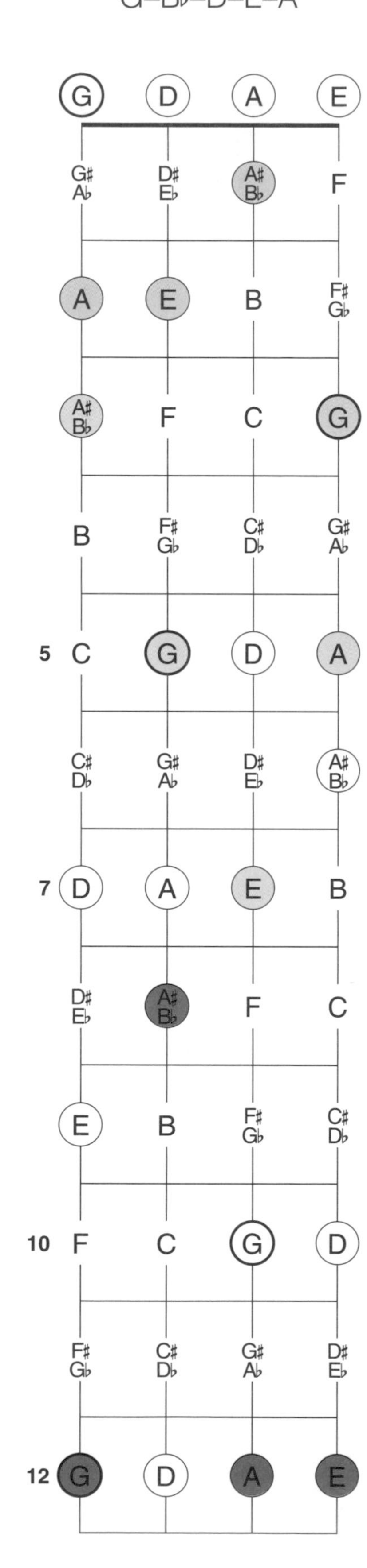

A♭m$^{6}_{9}$

A♭–C♭–E♭–F–B♭

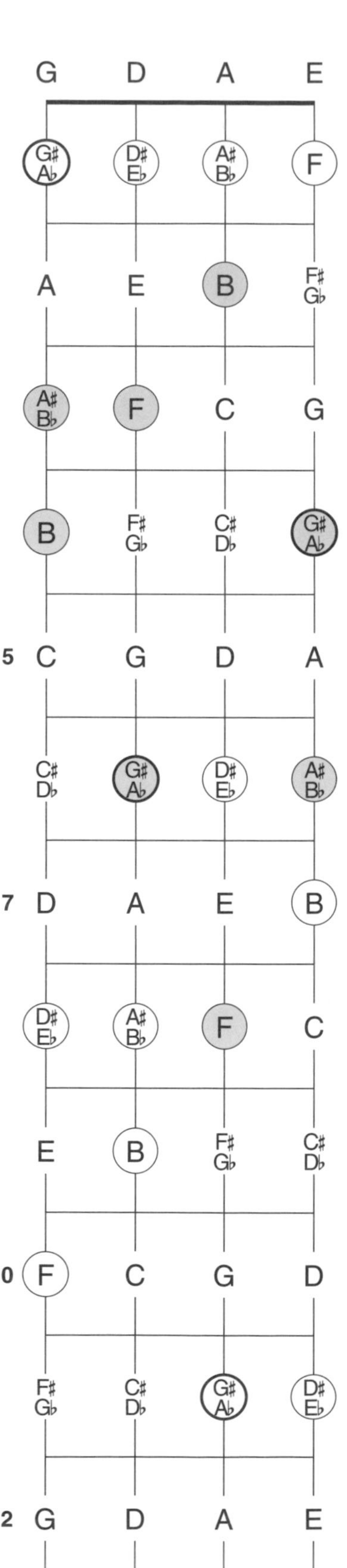

Am6/9

A–C–E–F♯–B

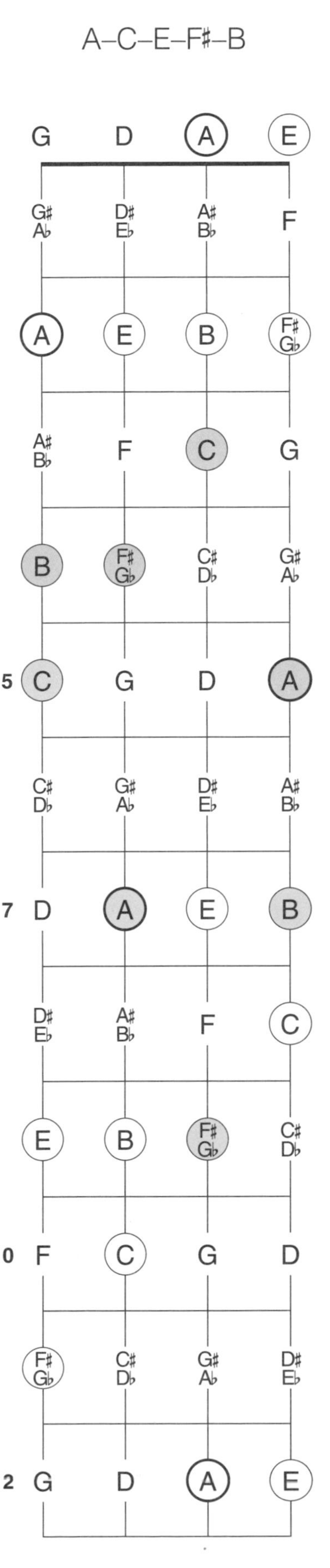

B♭m6/9

B♭–D♭–F–G–C

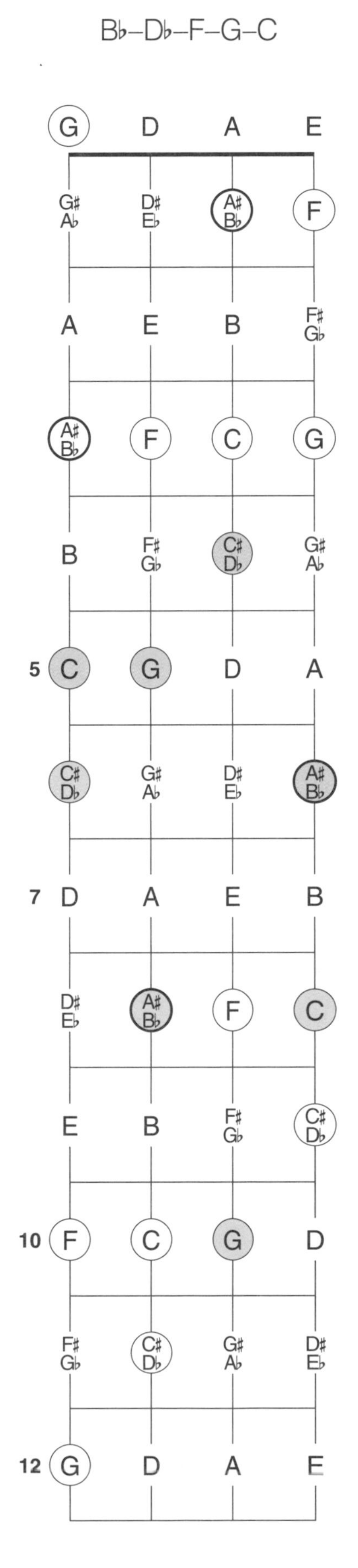

Bm6/9

B–D–F♯–G♯–C♯

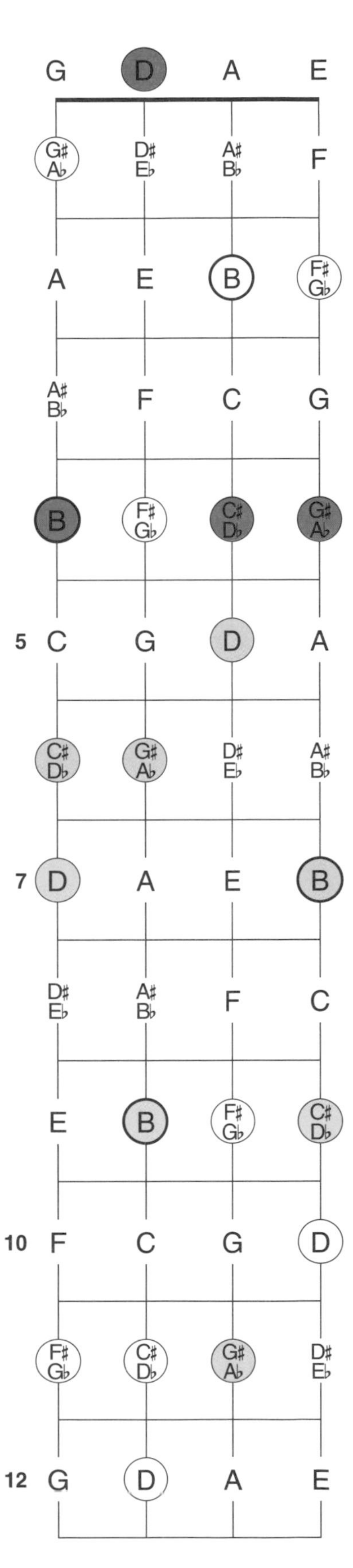

CHORDS

SEVENTH CHORDS

Cmaj7

C–E–G–B

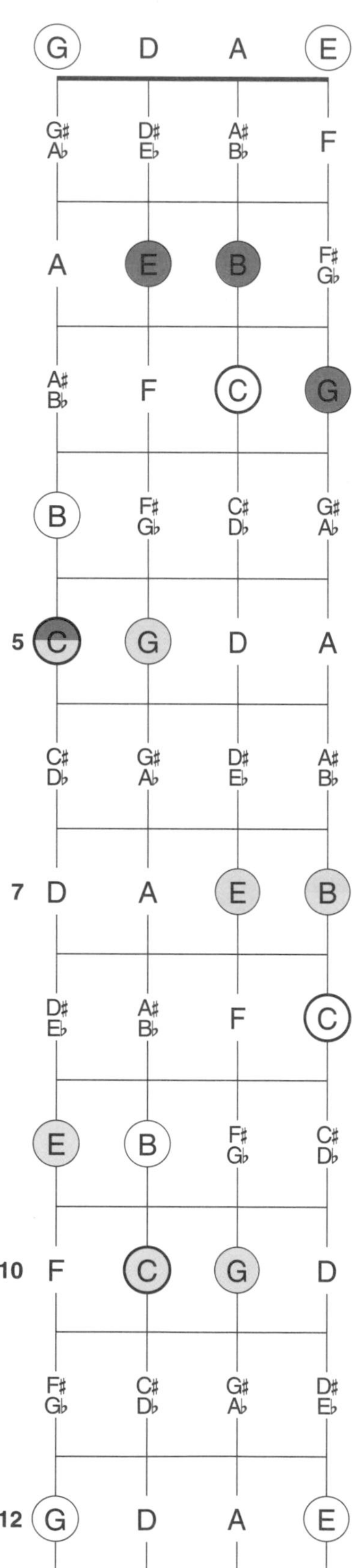

C♯/D♭maj7

C♯–E♯–G♯–B♯/D♭–F–A♭–C

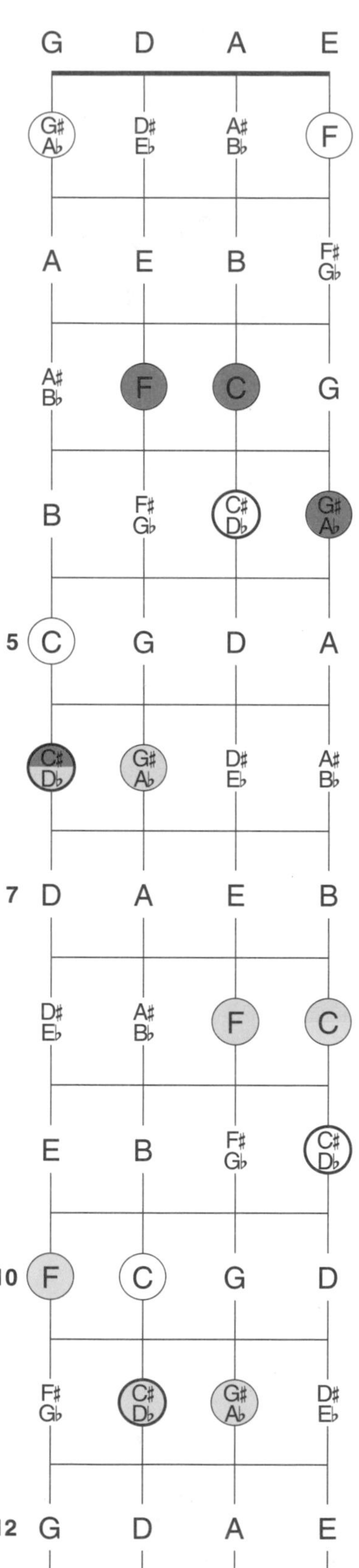

Dmaj7

D–F♯–A–C♯

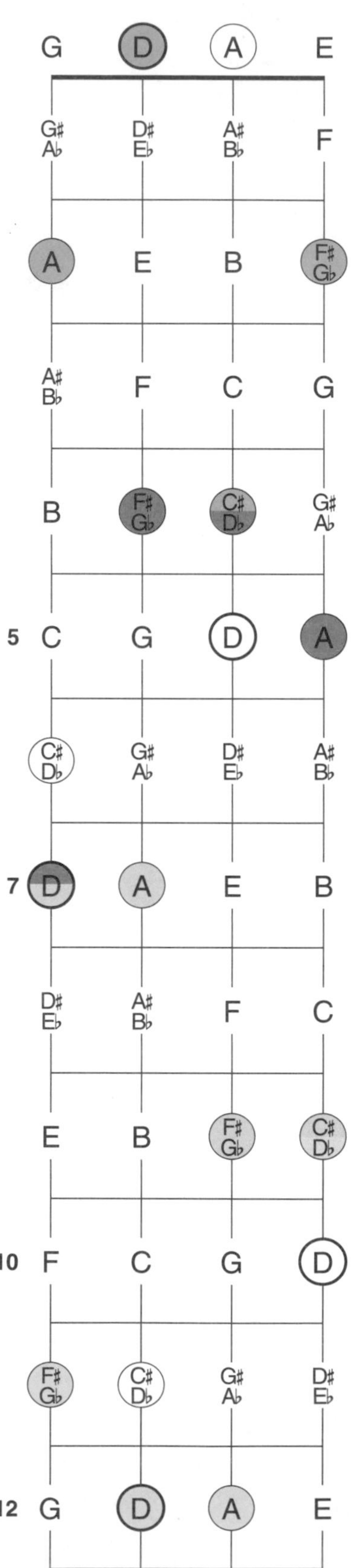

E♭maj7

E♭–G–B♭–D

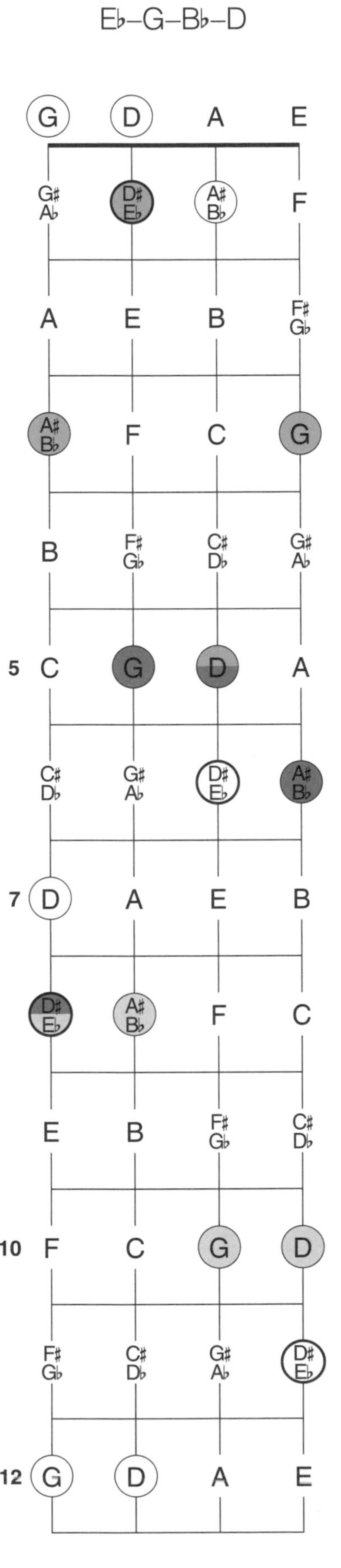

Emaj7

E–G♯–B–D♯

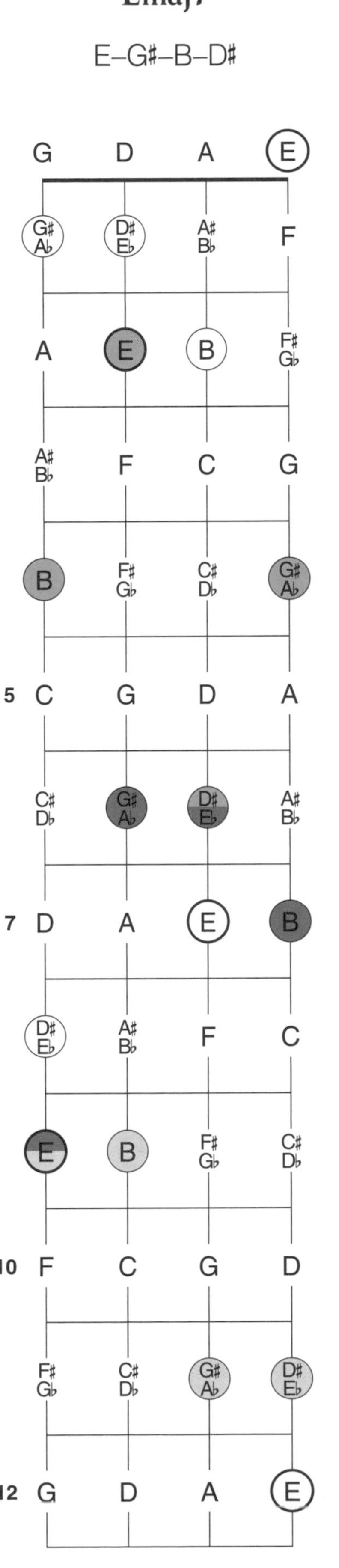

Fmaj7

F–A–C–E

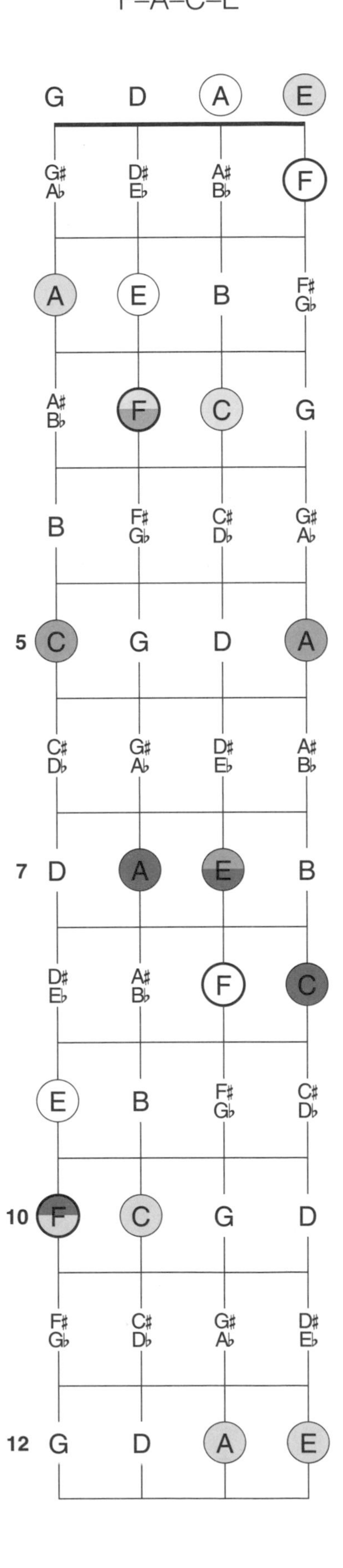

F♯/G♭maj7

F♯–A♯–C♯–E♯/G♭–B♭–D♭–F

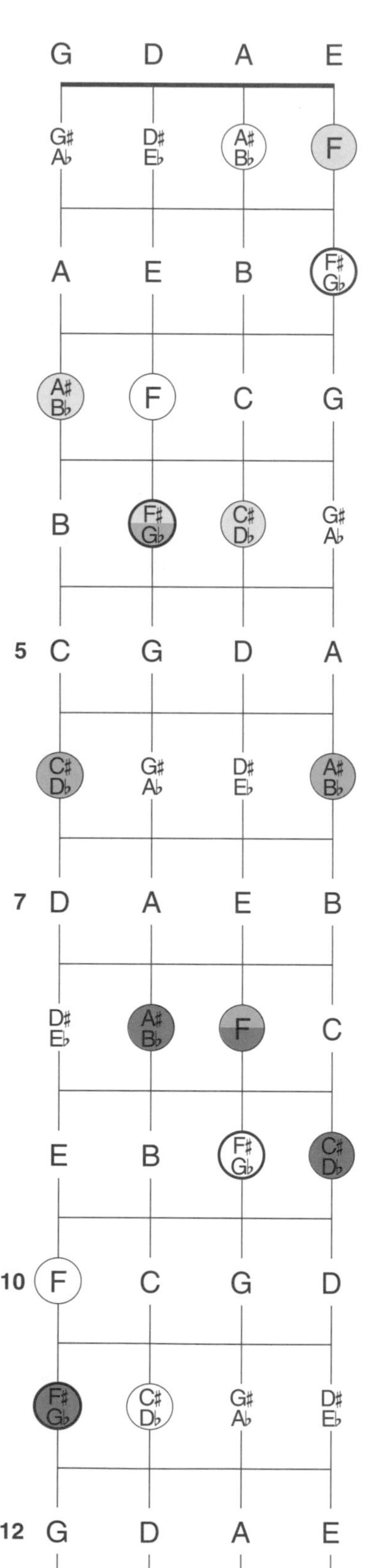

Gmaj7

G–B–D–F♯

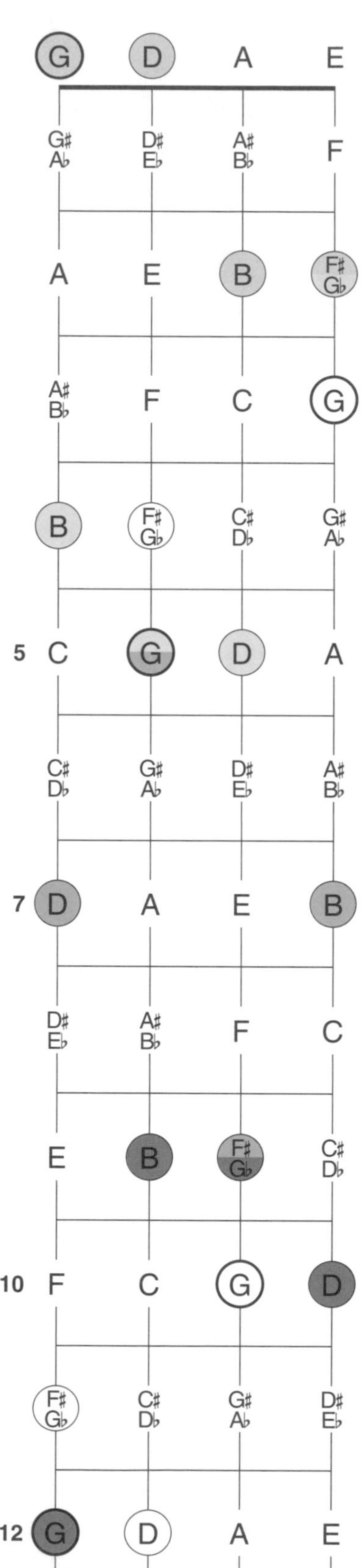

A♭maj7

A♭–C–E♭–G

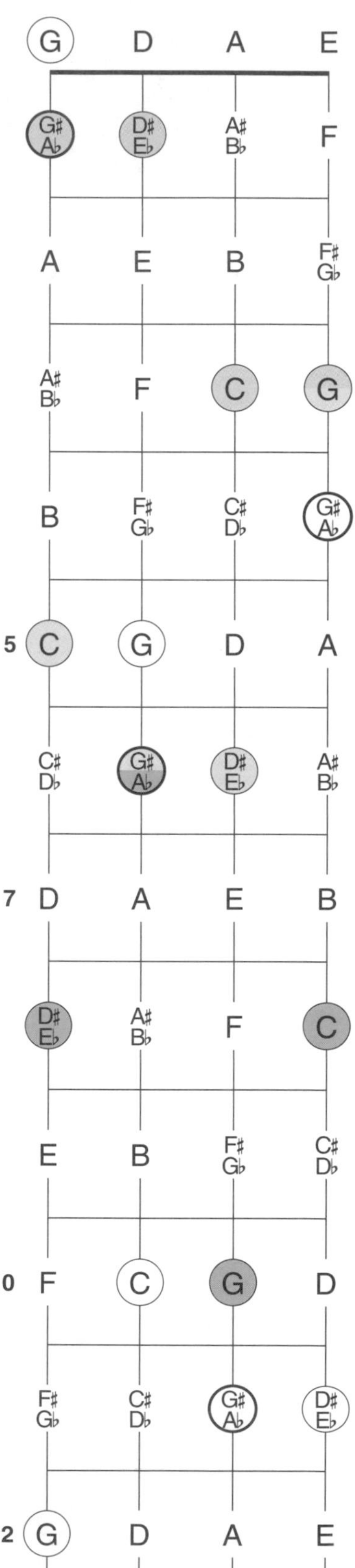

Amaj7

A–C♯–E–G♯

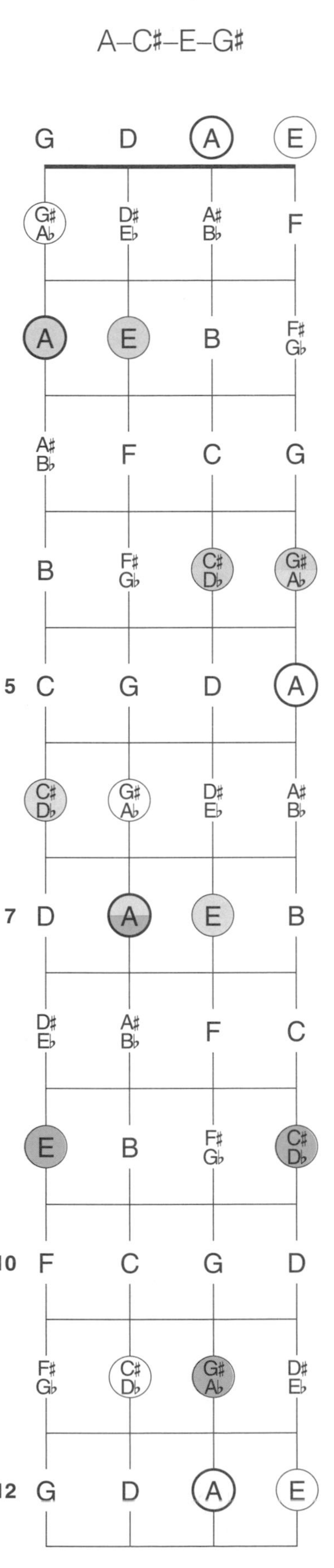

B♭maj7

B♭–D–F–A

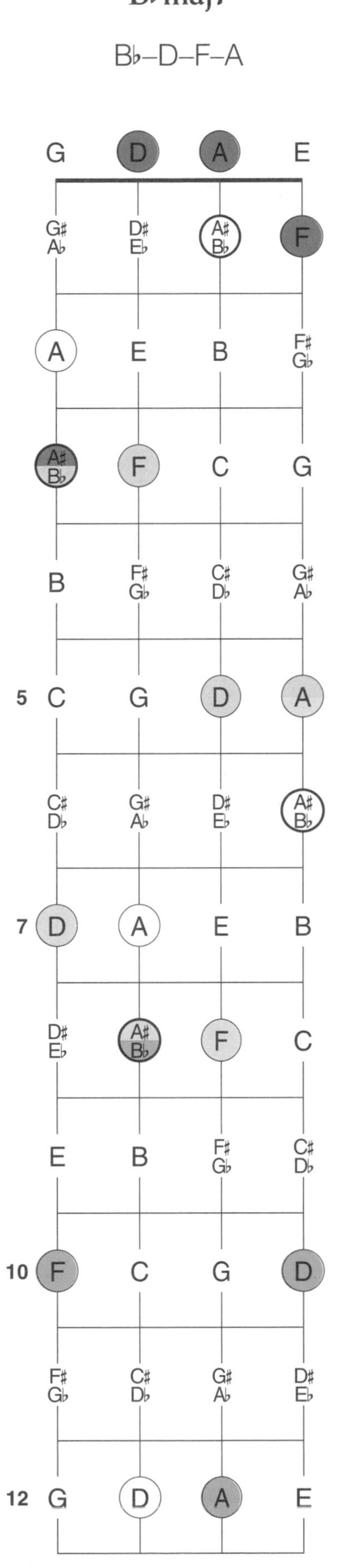

Bmaj7

B–D♯–F♯–A♯

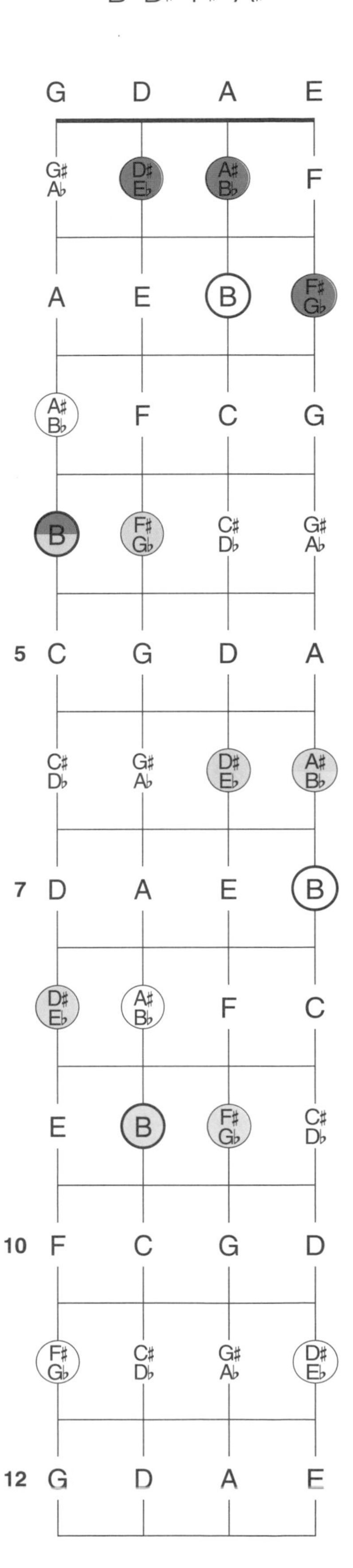

C7

C–E–G–B♭

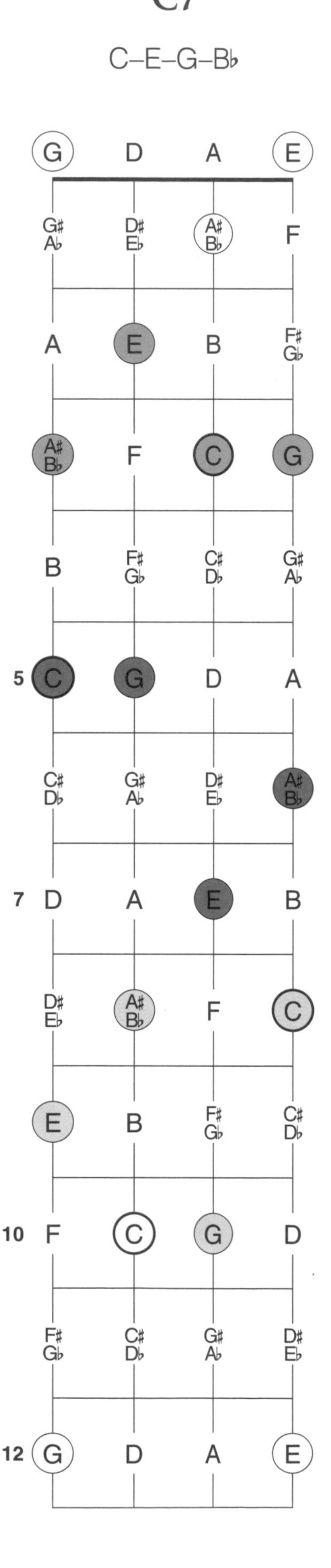

C♯/D♭7

C♯–E♯–G♯–B/D♭–F–A♭–C♭

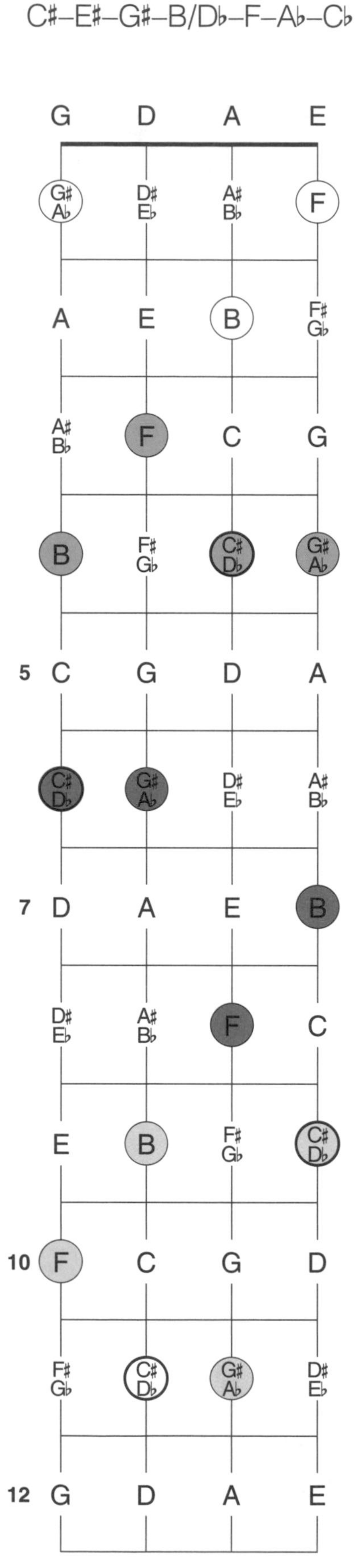

D7

D–F♯–A–C

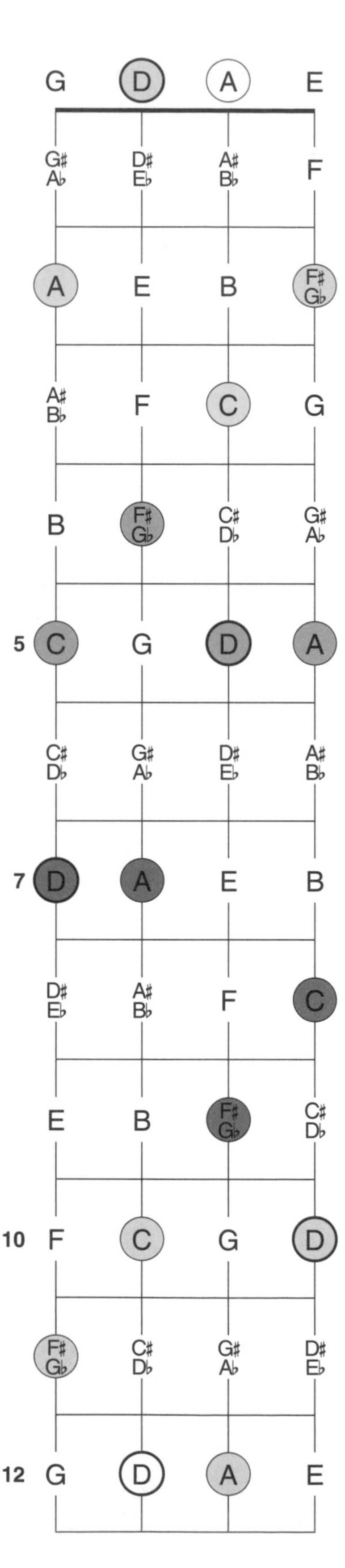

E♭7

E♭–G–B♭–D♭

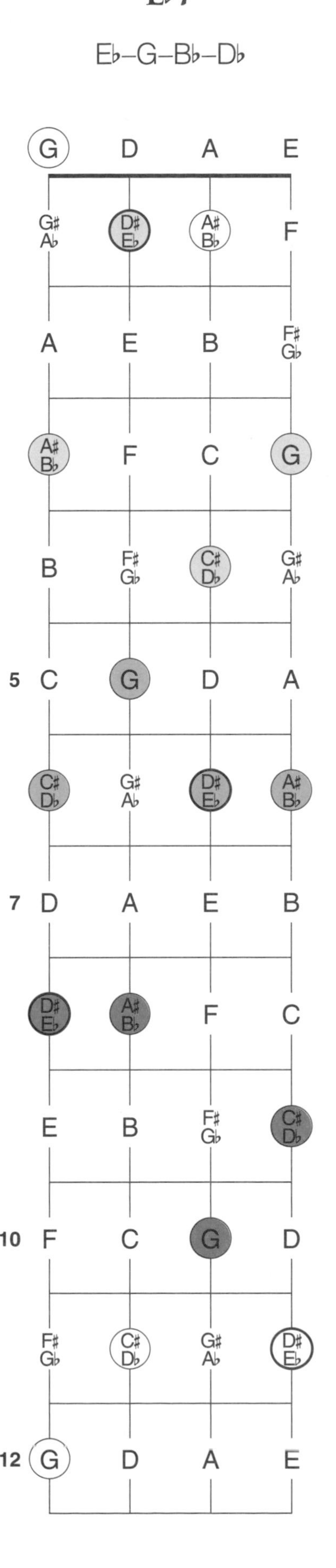

E7

E–G♯–B–D

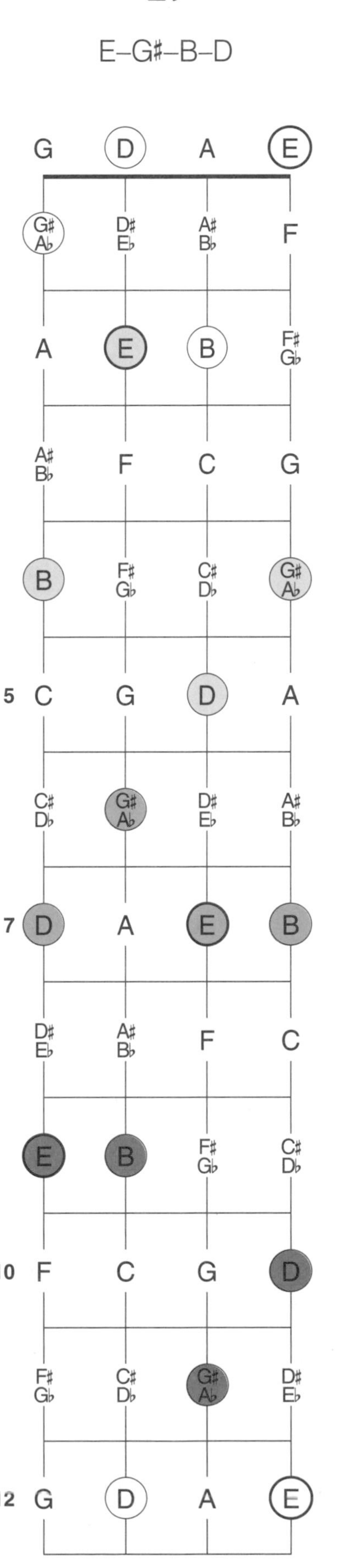

F7

F–A–C–E♭

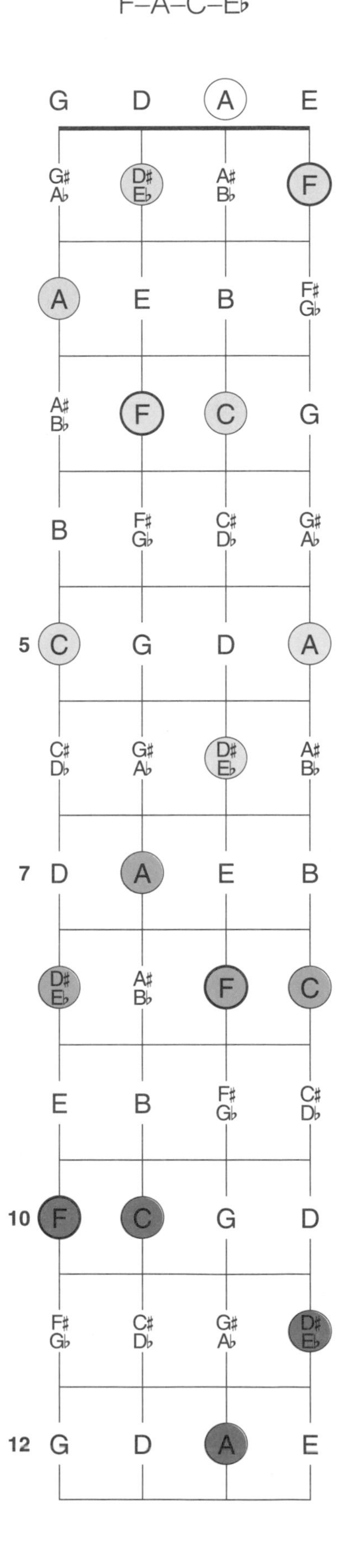

F♯/G♭7

F♯–A♯–C♯–E/G♭–B♭–D♭–F♭

G7

G–B–D–F

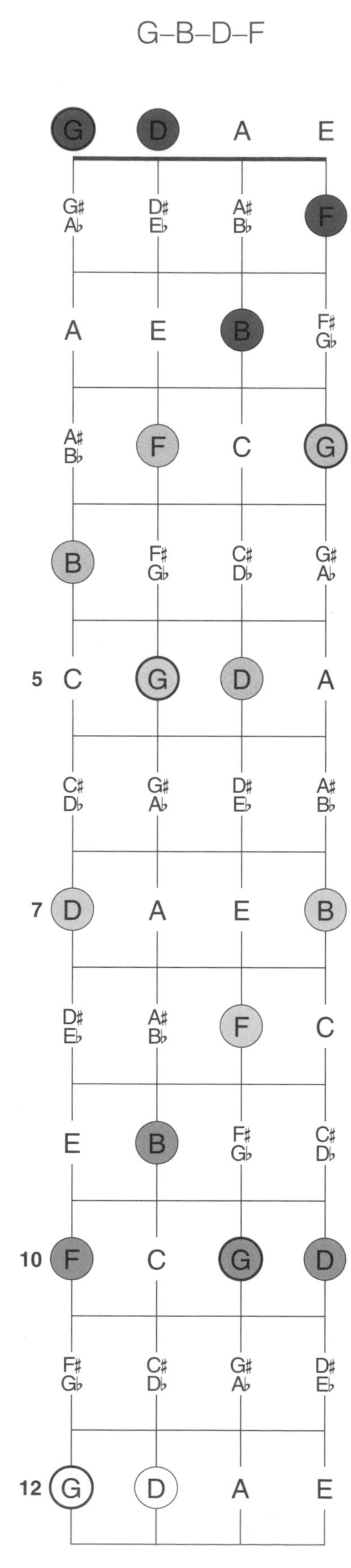

A♭7

A♭–C–E♭–G♭

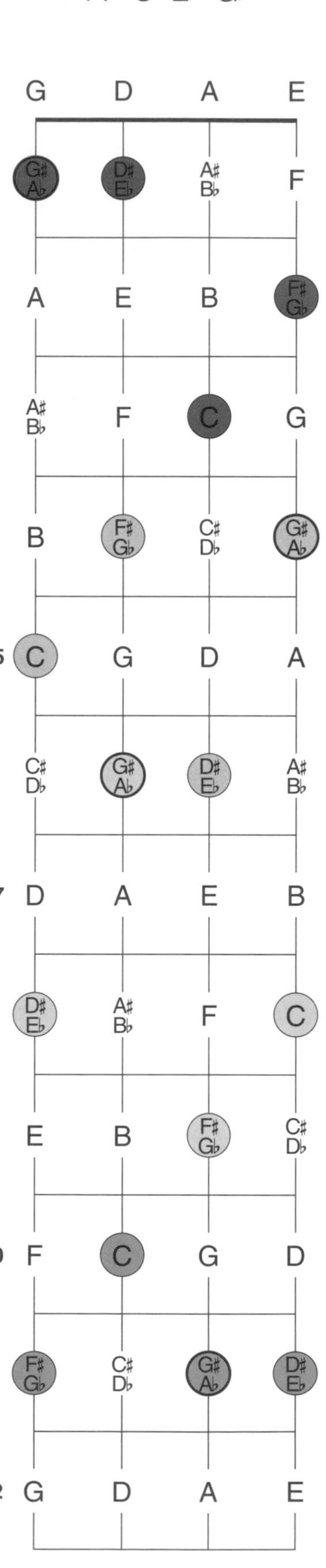

A7

A–C♯–E–G

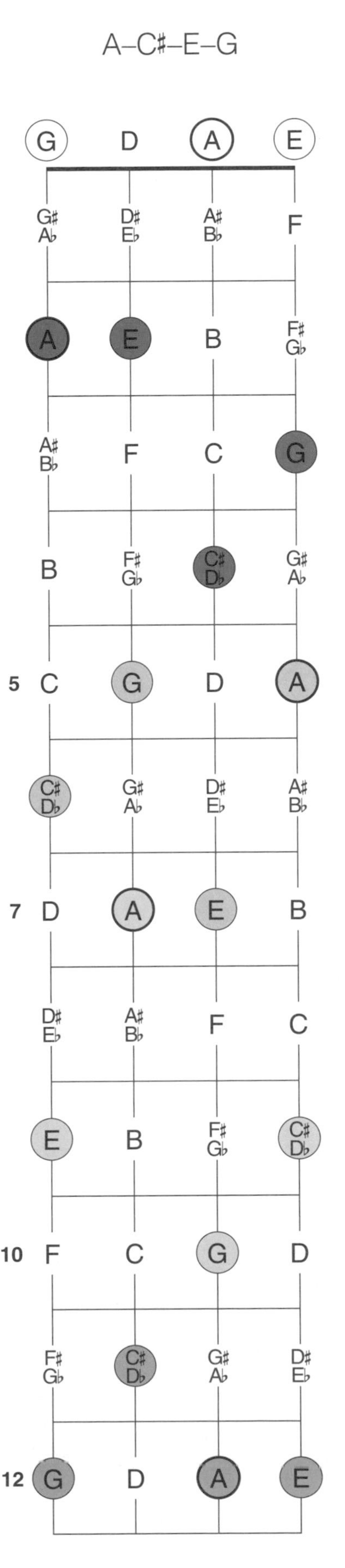

B♭7

B♭–D–F–A♭

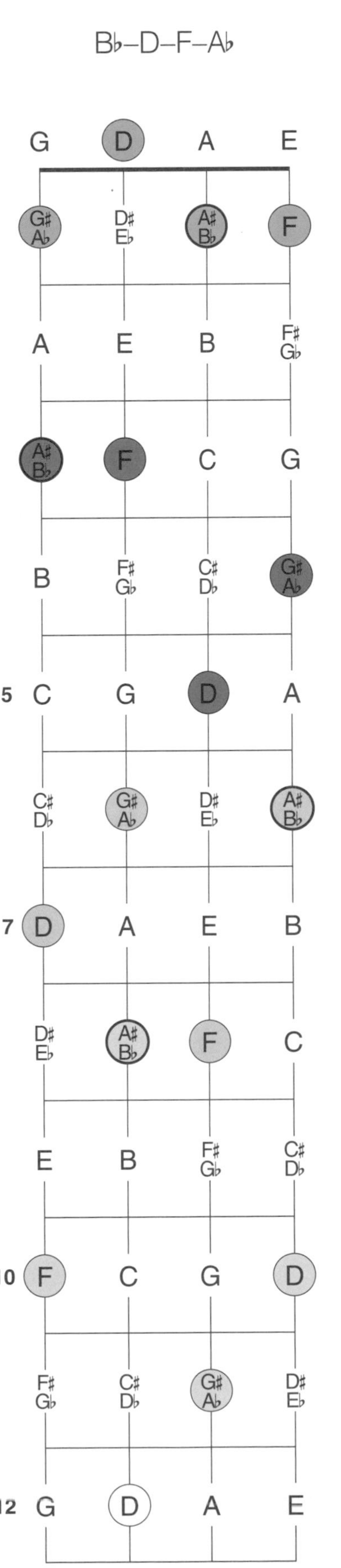

B7

B–D♯–F♯–A

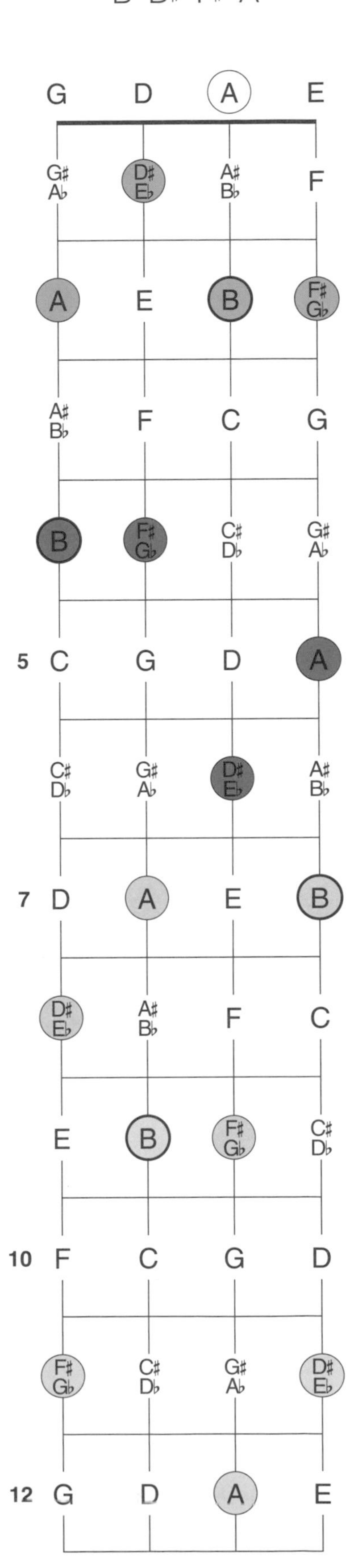

C7sus4

C–F–G–B♭

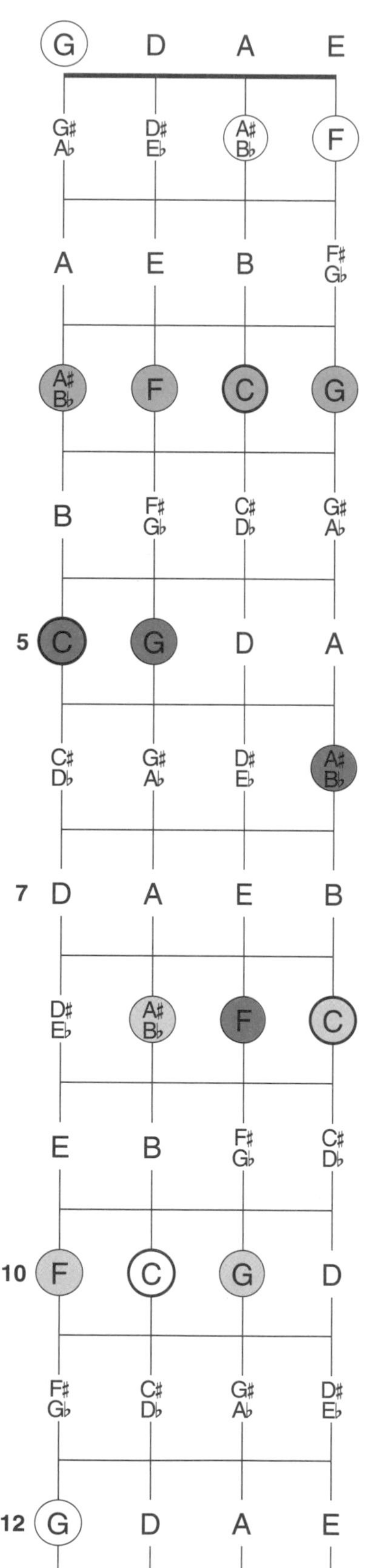

C♯/D♭7sus4

C♯–F♯–G♯–B/D♭–G♭–A♭–C♭

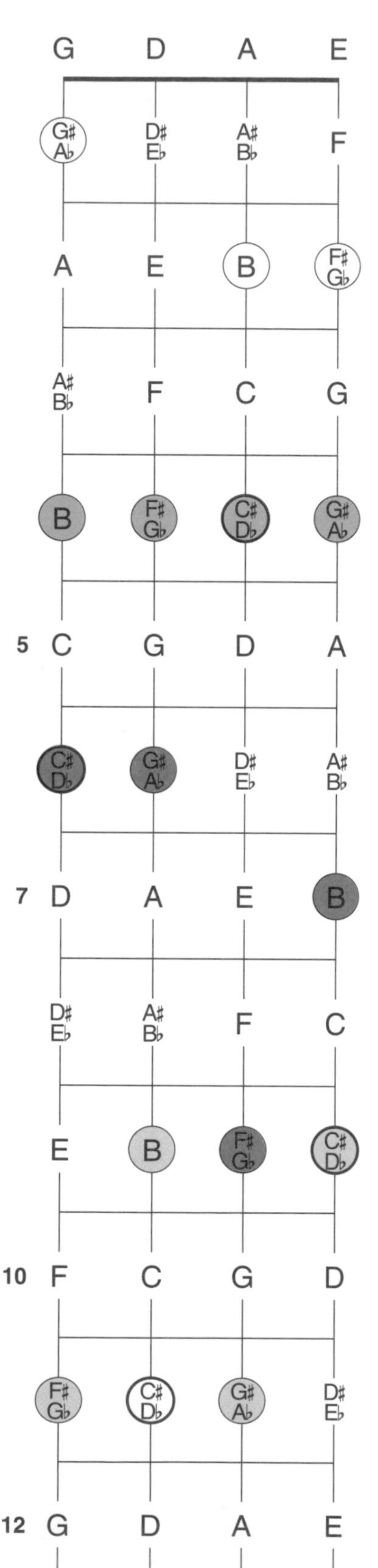

D7sus4

D–G–A–C

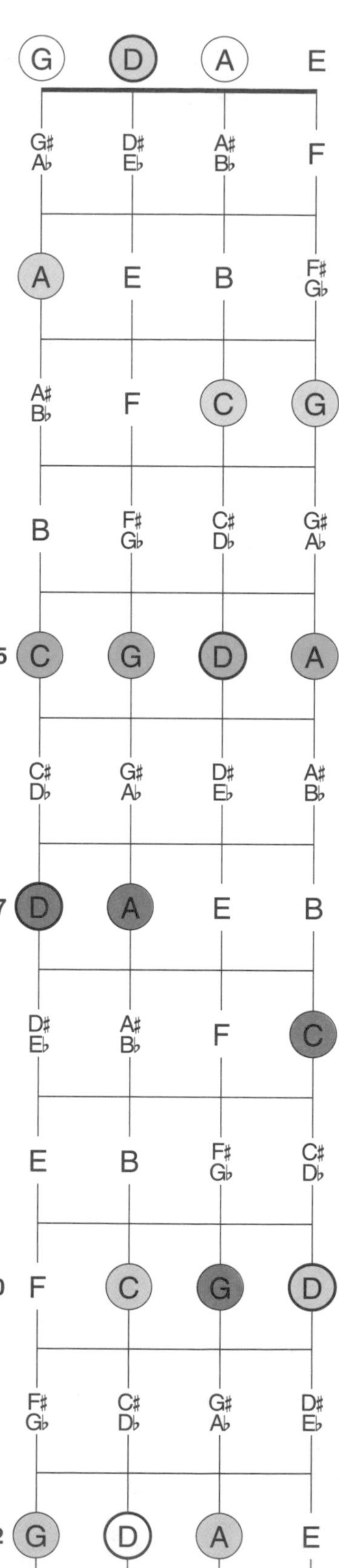

E♭7sus4

E♭–A♭–B♭–D♭

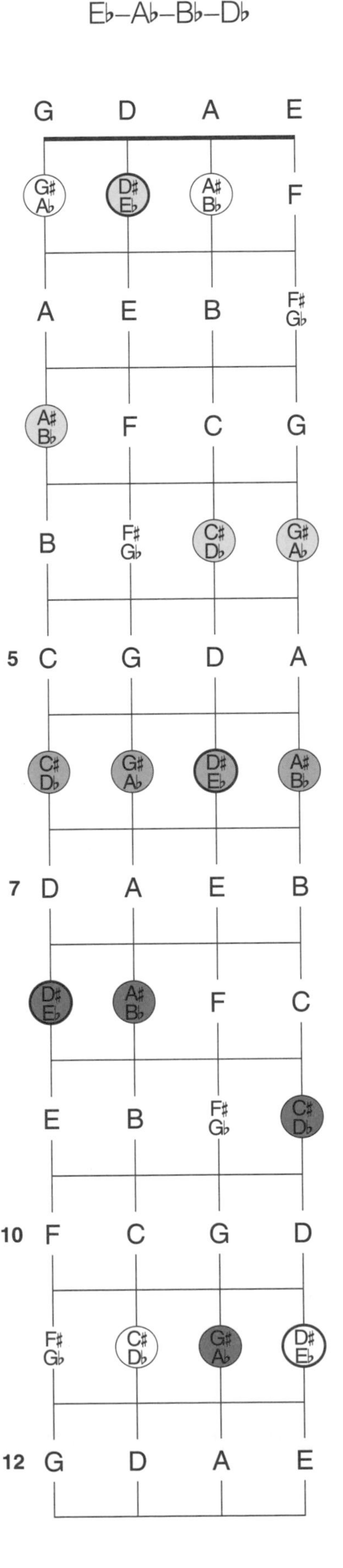

E7sus4

E–A–B–D

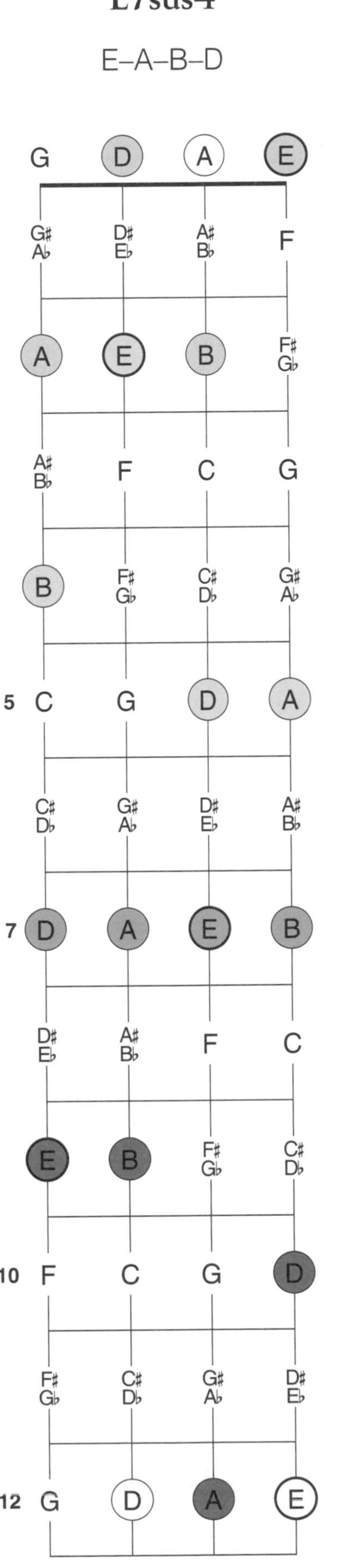

F7sus4

F–B♭–C–E♭

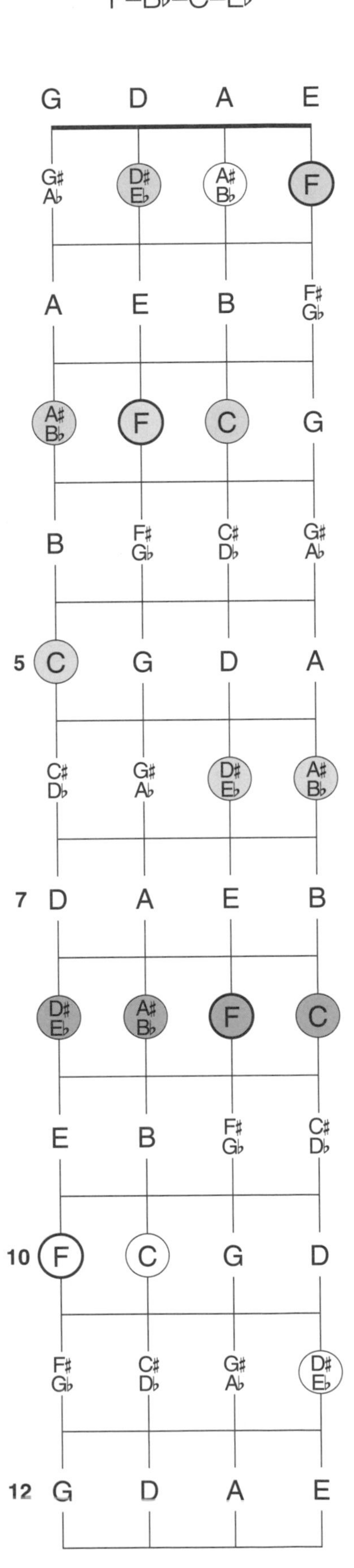

F♯7sus4

F♯–B–C♯–E

G7sus4

G–C–D–F

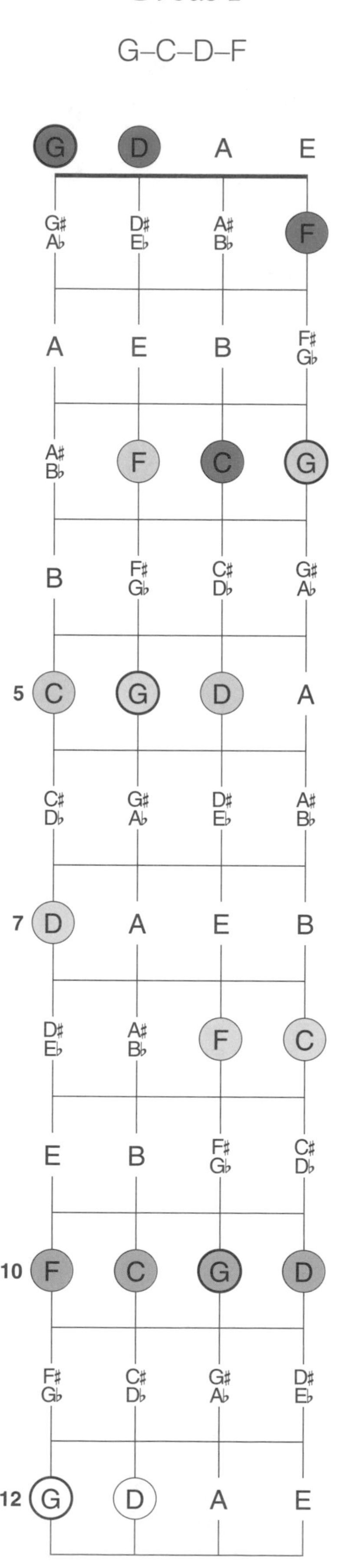

A♭7sus4

A♭–D♭–E♭–G♭

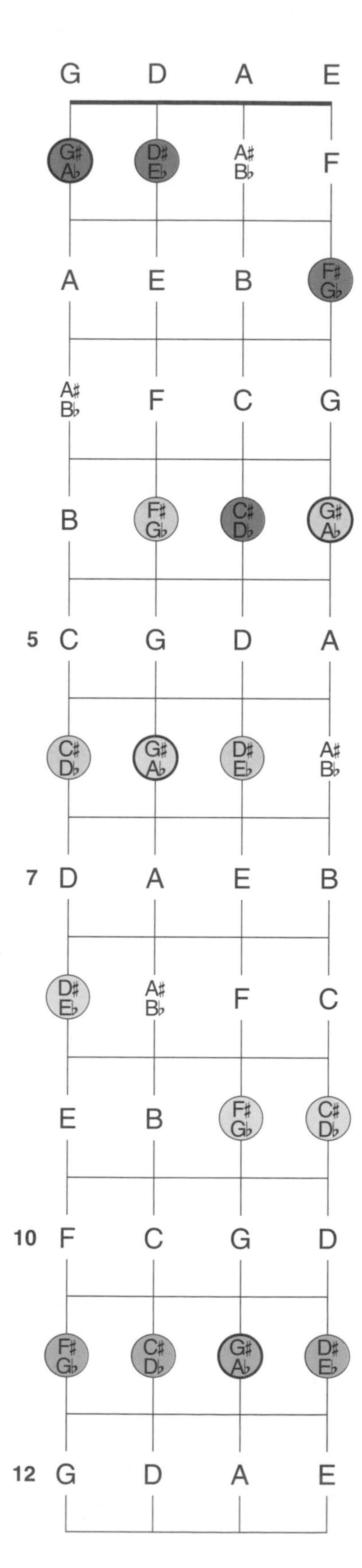

A7sus4

A–D–E–G

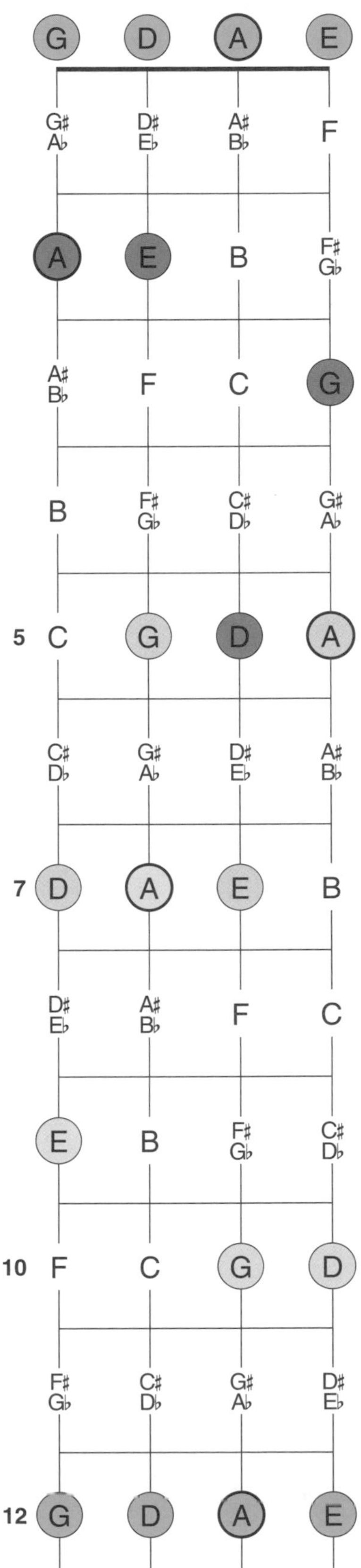

B♭7sus4

B♭–E♭–F–A♭

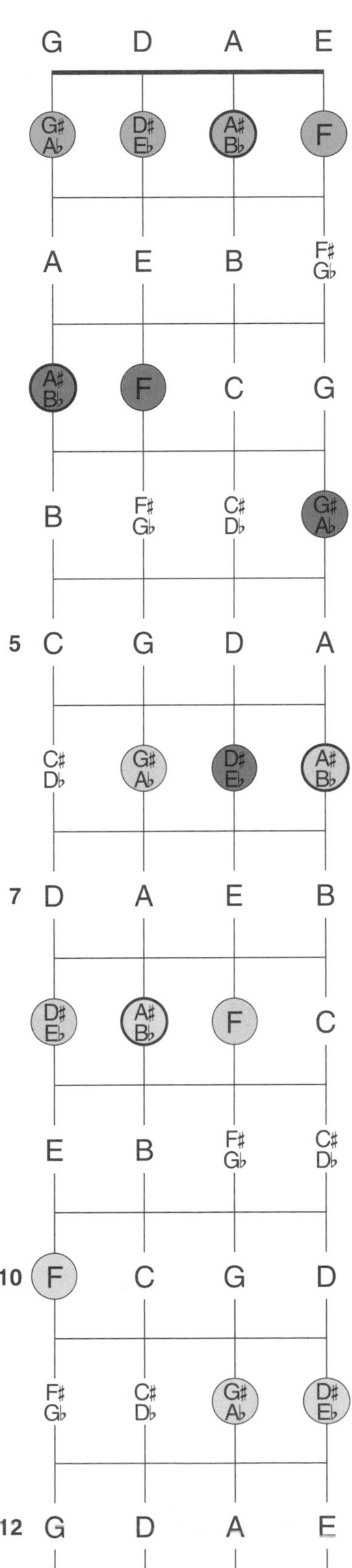

B7sus4

B–E–F♯–A

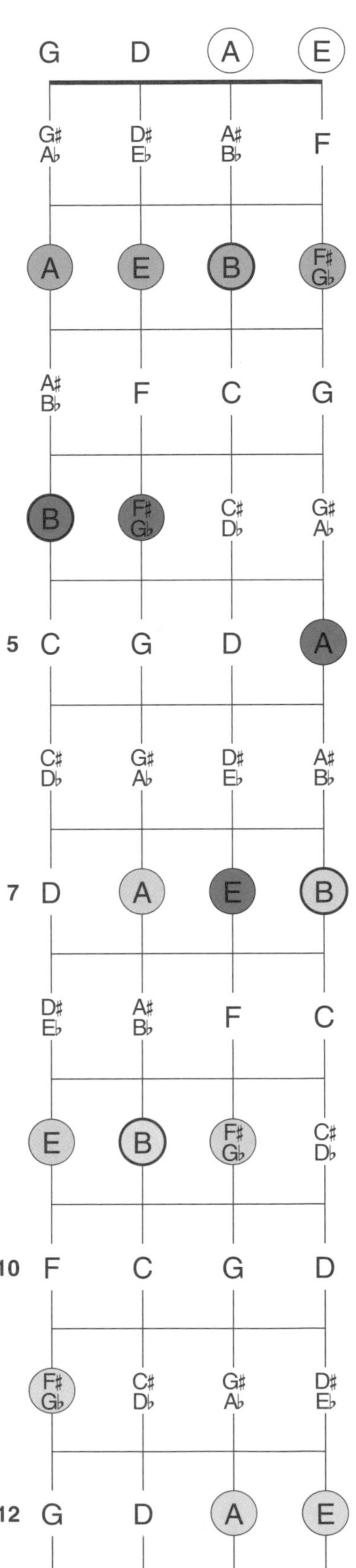

Cm7

C–E♭–G–B♭

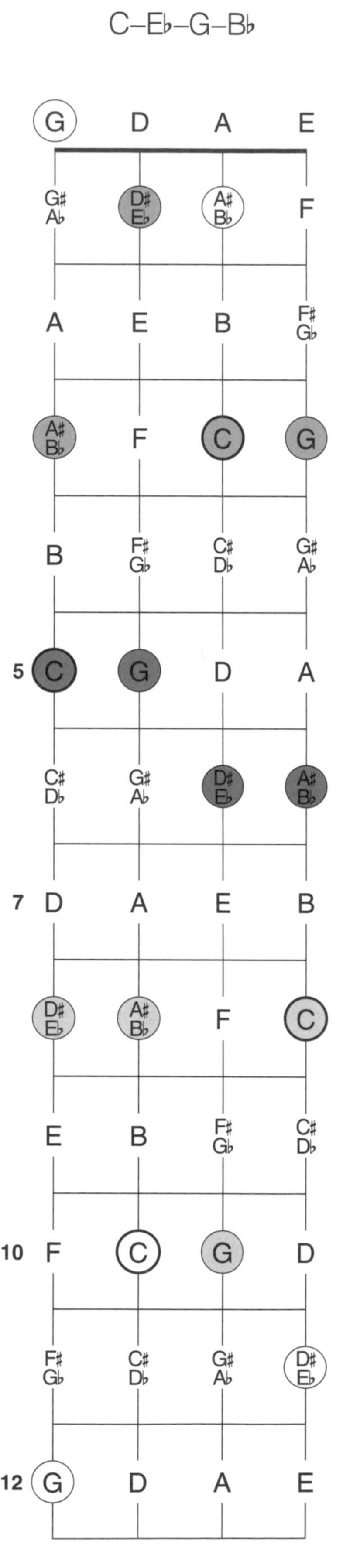

C♯m7

C♯–E–G♯–B

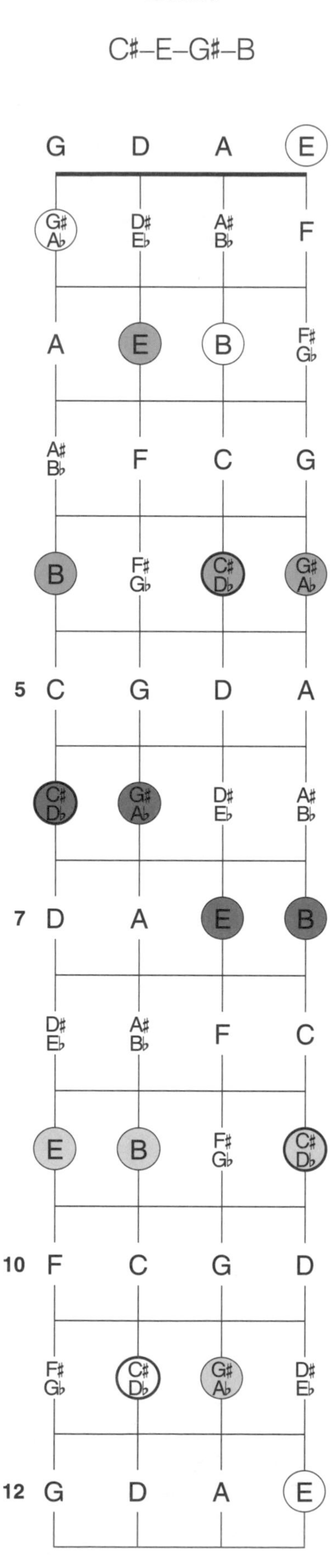

Dm7

D–F–A–C

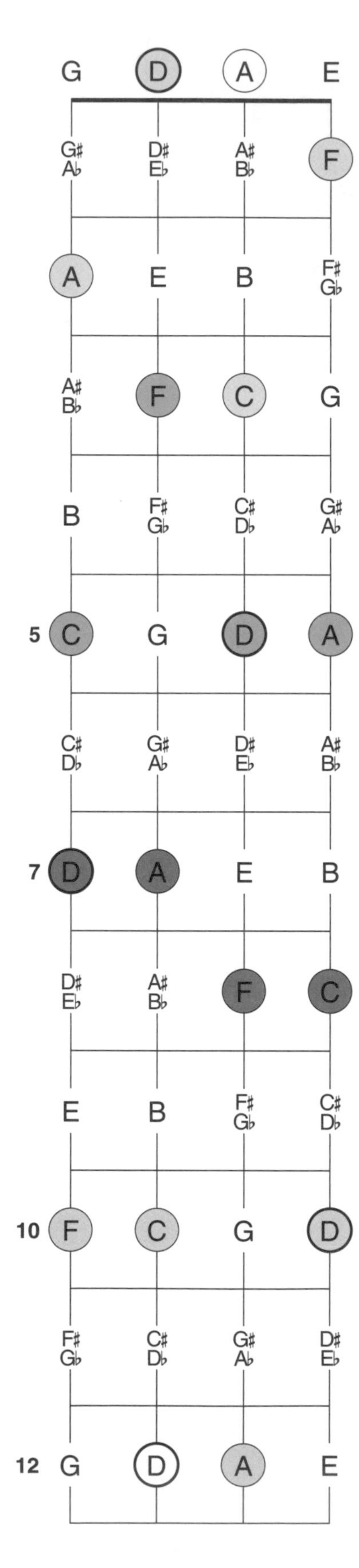

D♯/E♭m7

D♯–F♯–A♯–C♯/E♭–G♭–B♭–D♭

G D A E
G♯/A♭ D♯/E♭ A♯/B♭ F
A E B F♯/G♭
A♯/B♭ F C G
B F♯/G♭ C♯/D♭ G♯/A♭
5 C G D A
C♯/D♭ G♯/A♭ D♯/E♭ A♯/B♭
7 D A E B
D♯/E♭ A♯/B♭ F C
E B F♯/G♭ C♯/D♭
10 F C G D
F♯/G♭ C♯/D♭ G♯/A♭ D♯/E♭
12 G D A E

Em7

E–G–B–D

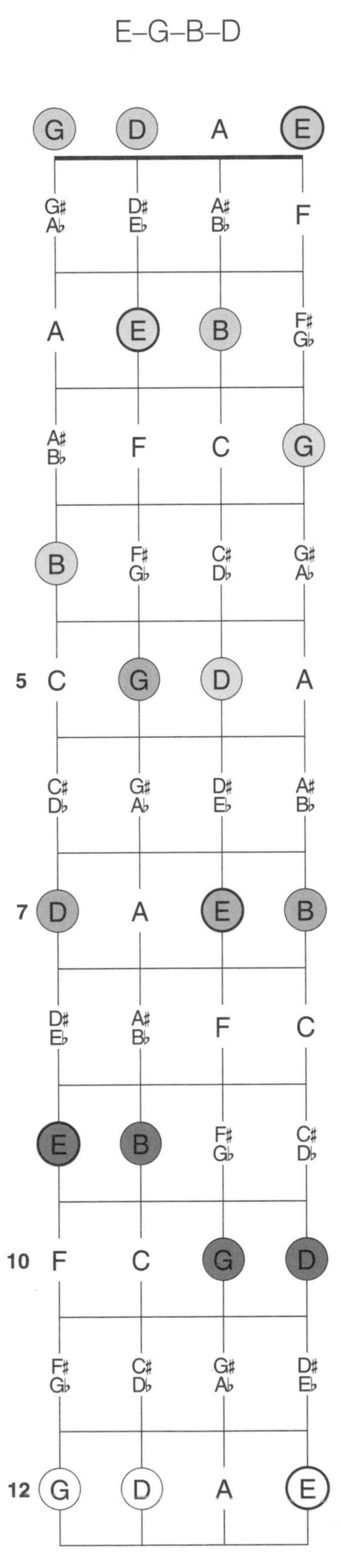

Fm7

F–A♭–C–E♭

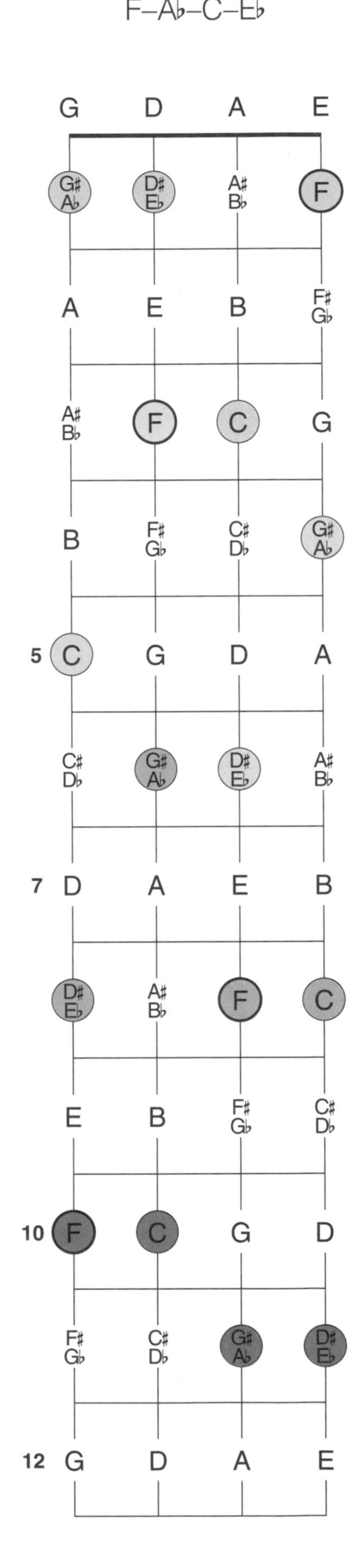

F♯m7

F♯–A–C♯–E

Gm7

G–B♭–D–F

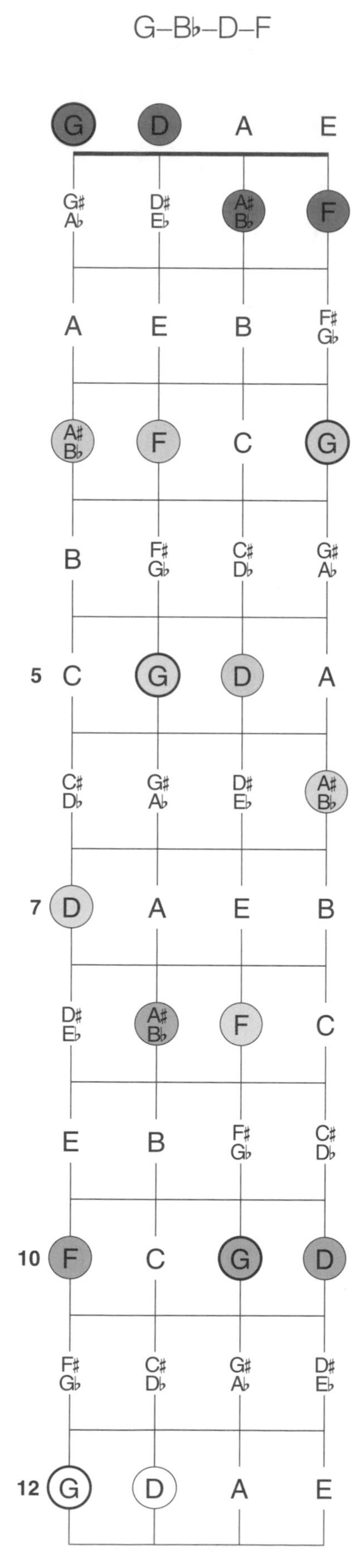

A♭m7

A♭–C♭–E♭–G♭

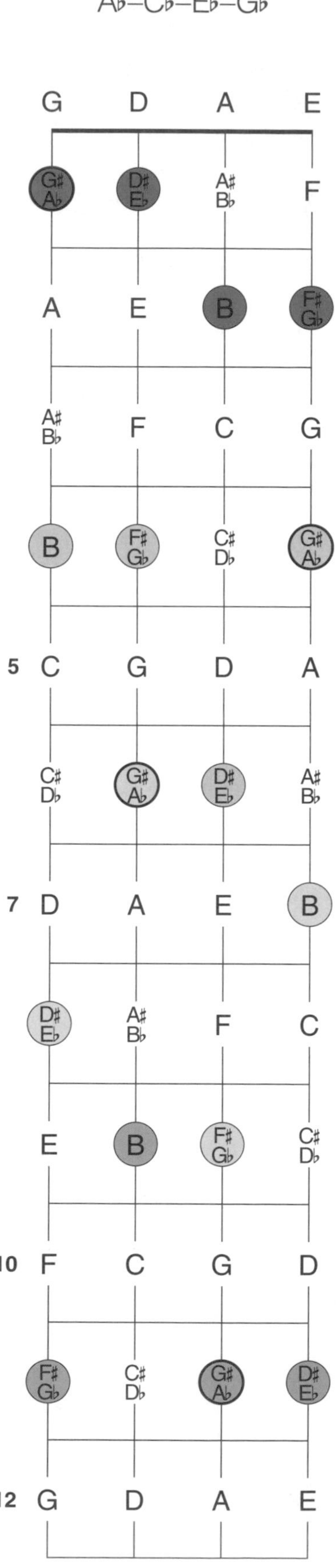

Am7

A–C–E–G

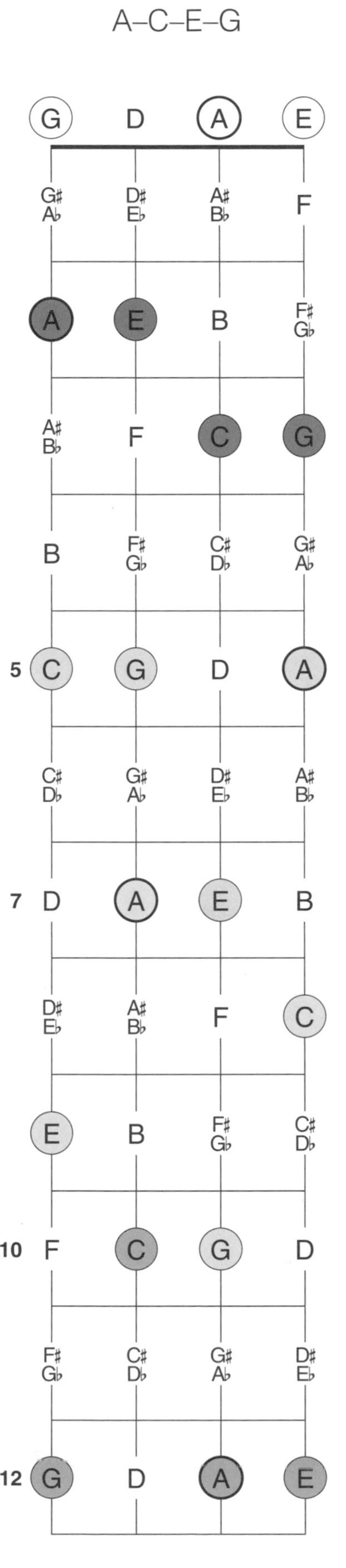

B♭m7

B♭–D♭–F–A♭

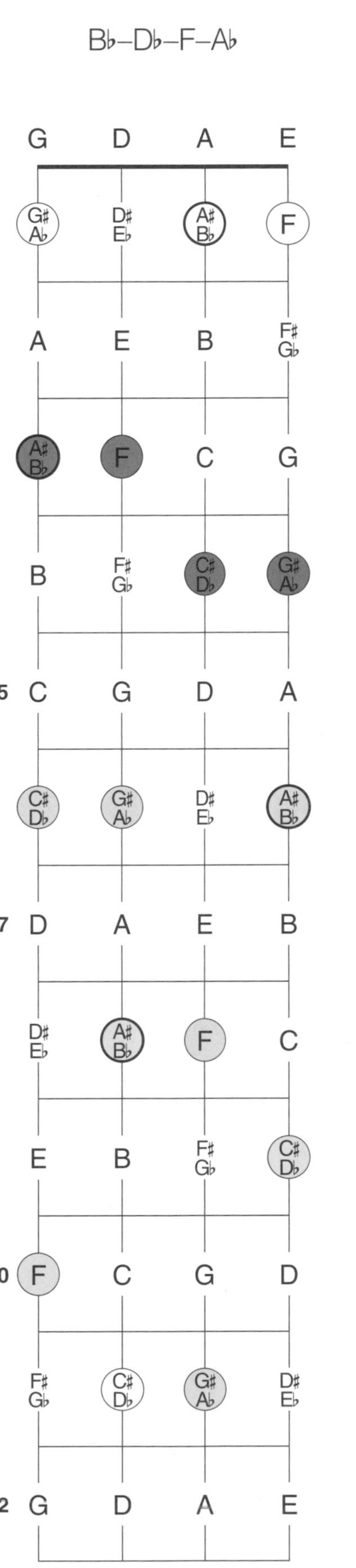

Bm7

B–D–F♯–A

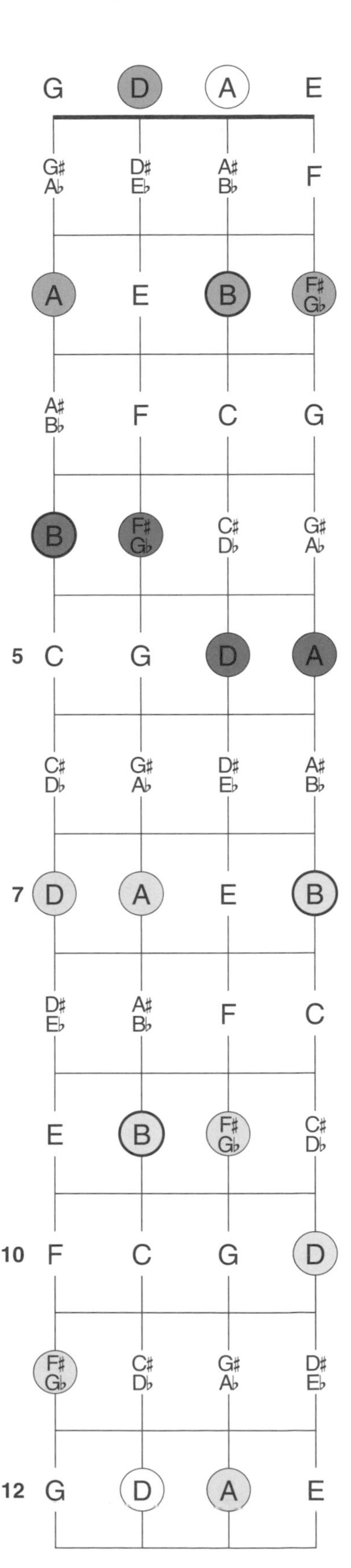

Cm(maj7)

C–E♭–G–B

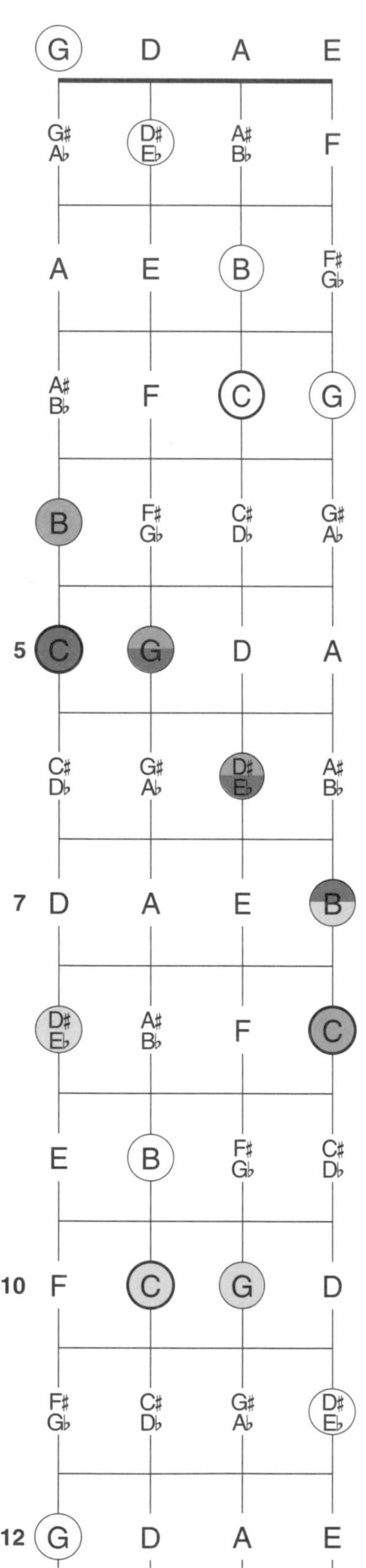

C♯m(maj7)

C♯–E–G♯–B♯

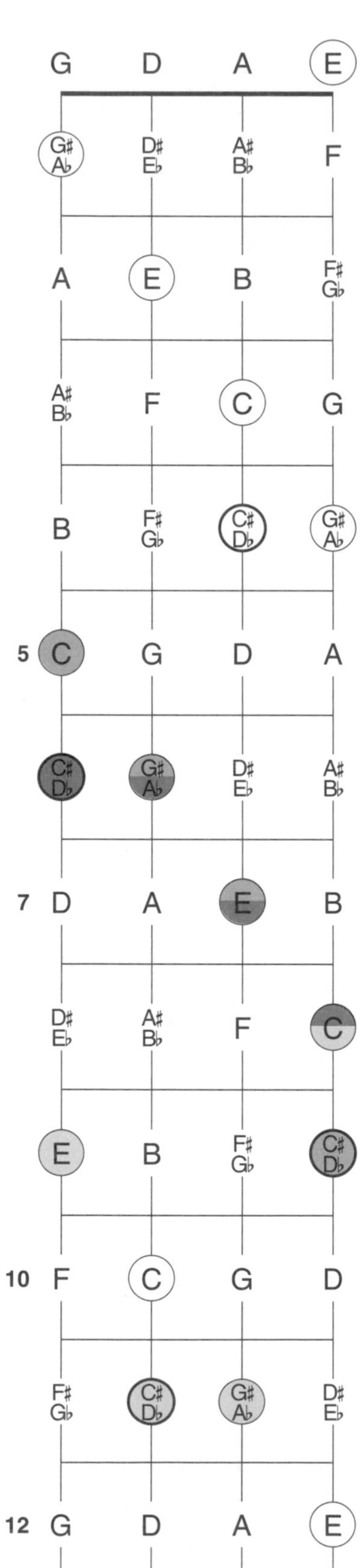

Dm(maj7)

D–F–A–C♯

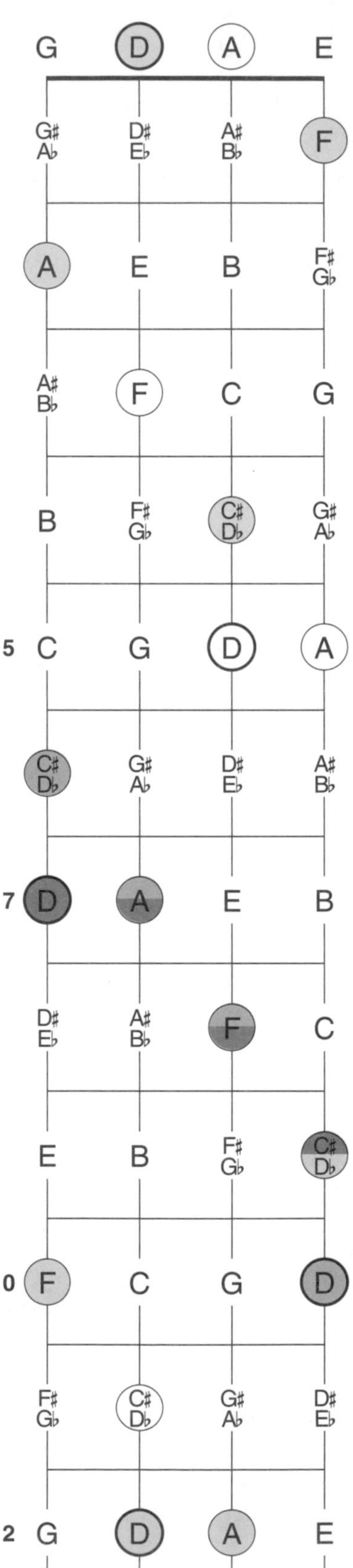

E♭m(maj7)

E♭–G♭–B♭–D

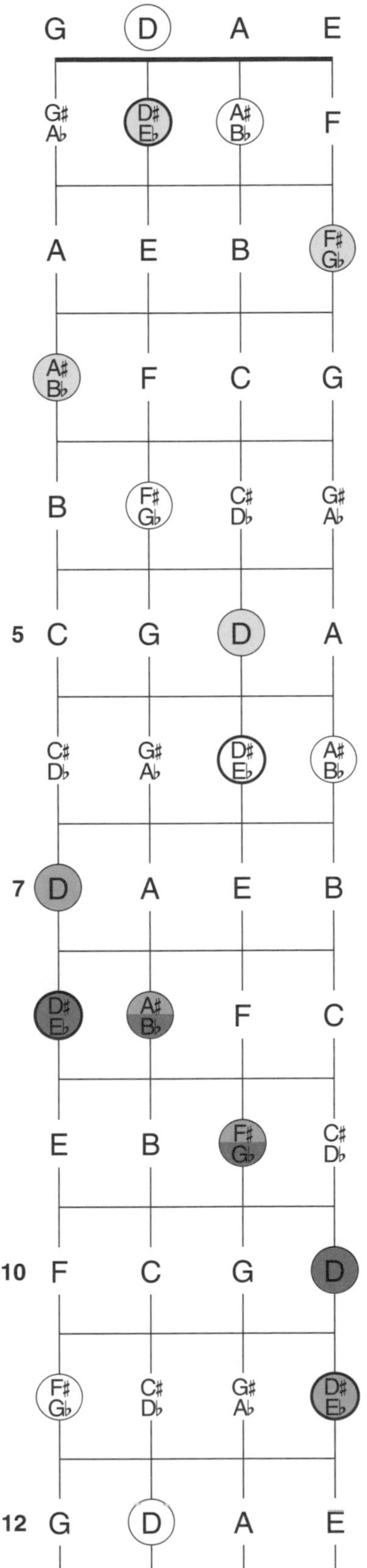

Em(maj7)

E–G–B–D♯

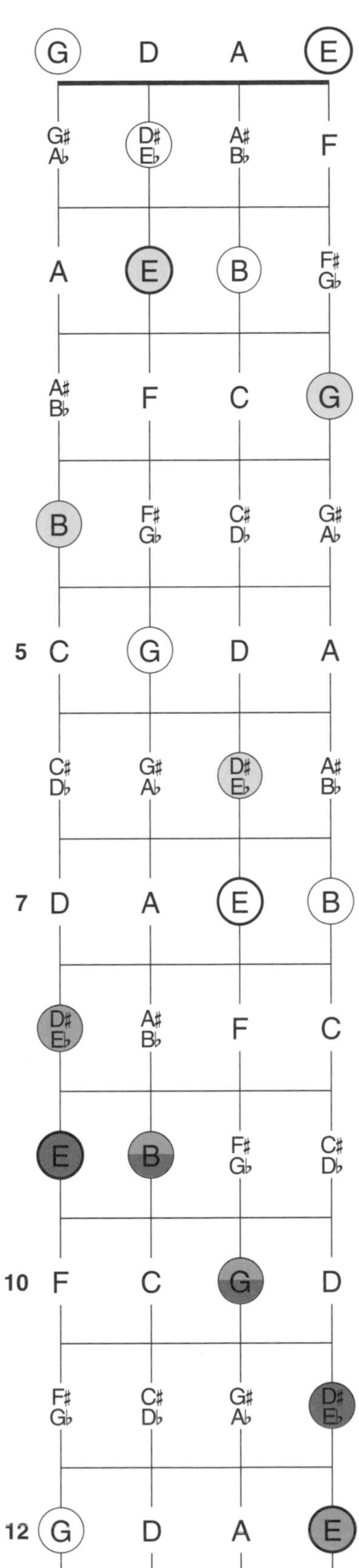

Fm(maj7)

F–A♭–C–E

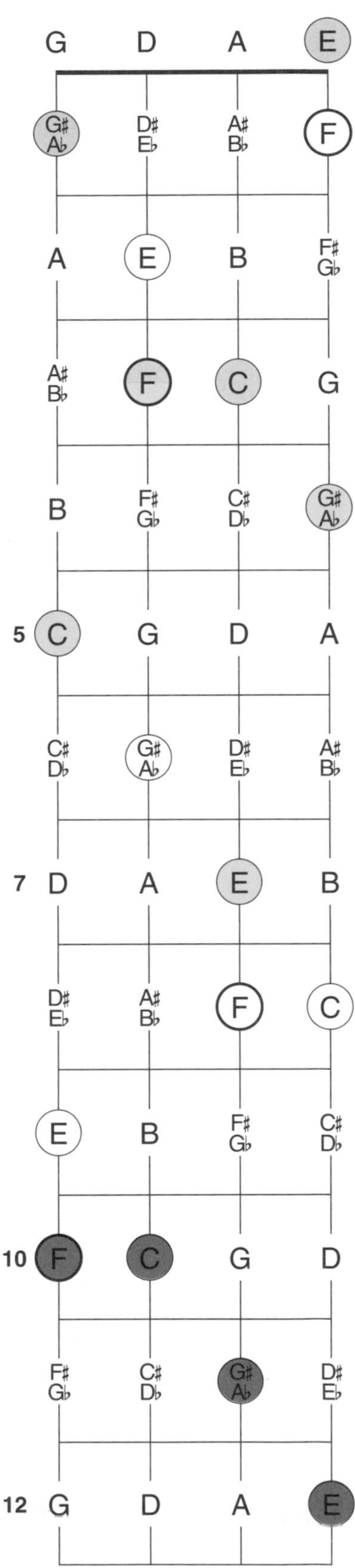

F♯m(maj7)

F♯–A–C♯–E♯

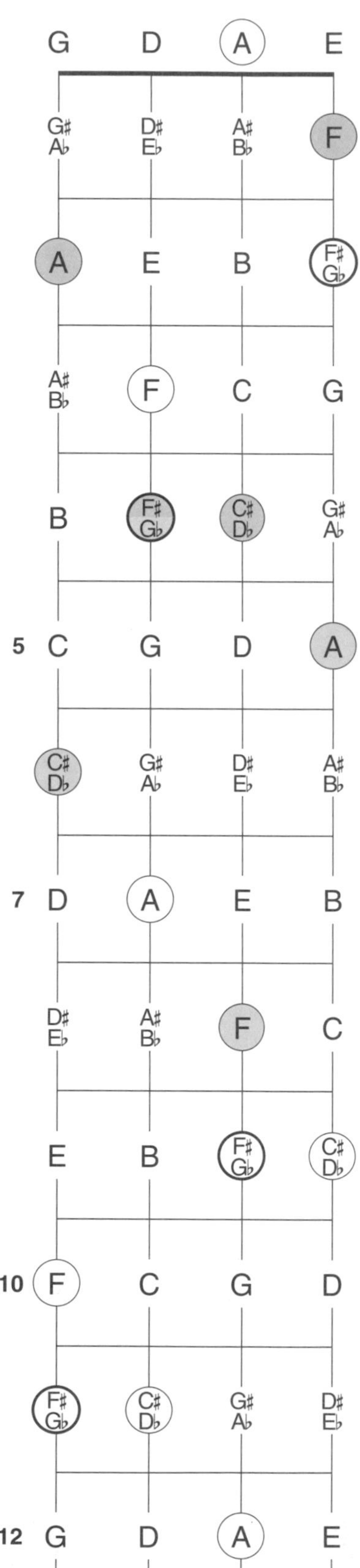

Gm(maj7)

G–B♭–D–F♯

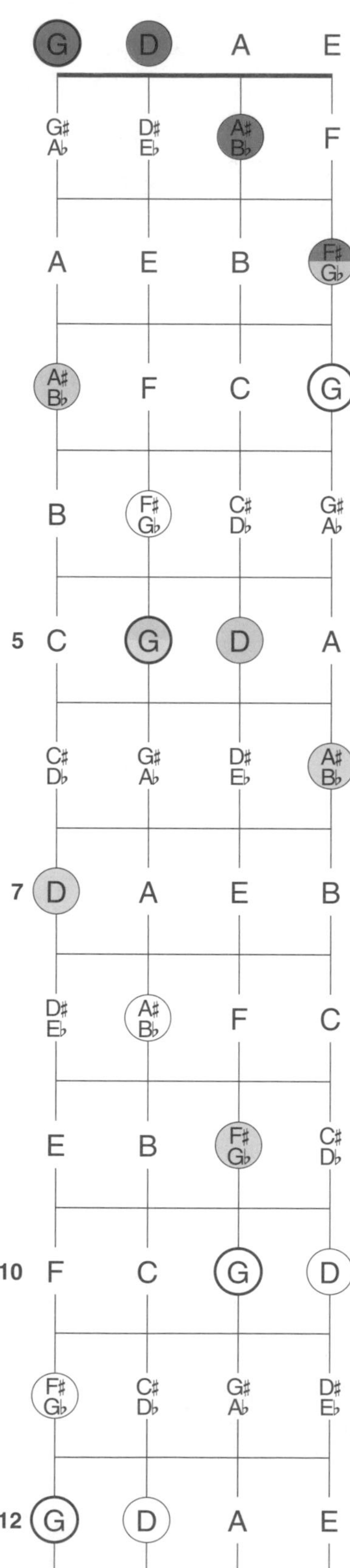

G♯/A♭m(maj7)

G♯–B–D♯–F𝄪/A♭–C♭–E♭–G

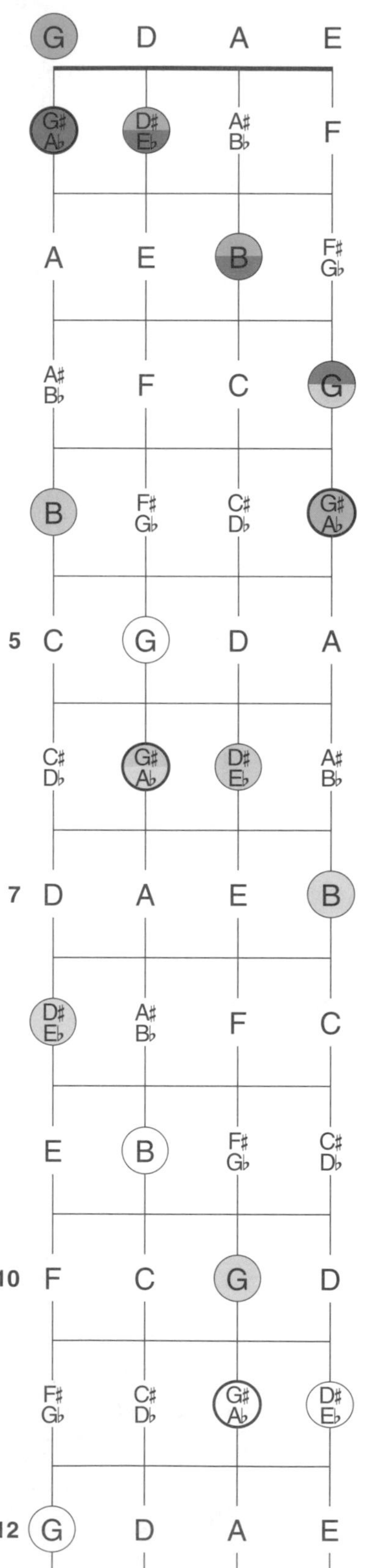

Am(maj7)

A–C–E–G♯

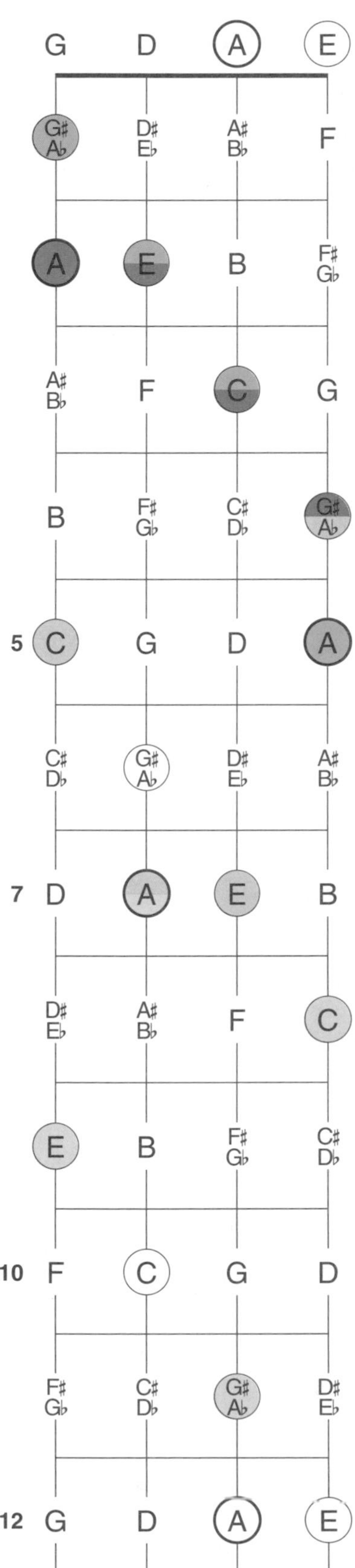

B♭m(maj7)

B♭–D♭–F–A

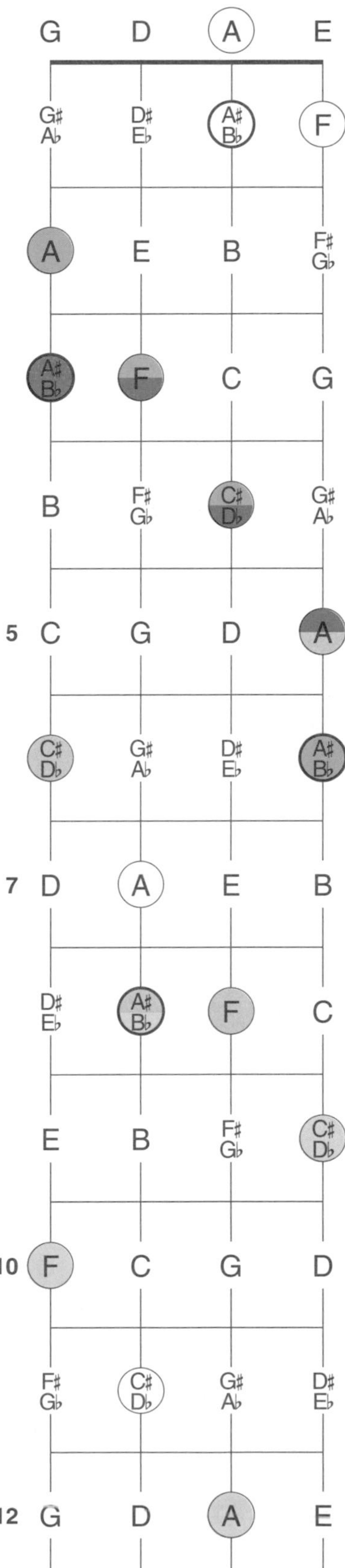

Bm(maj7)

B–D–F♯–A♯

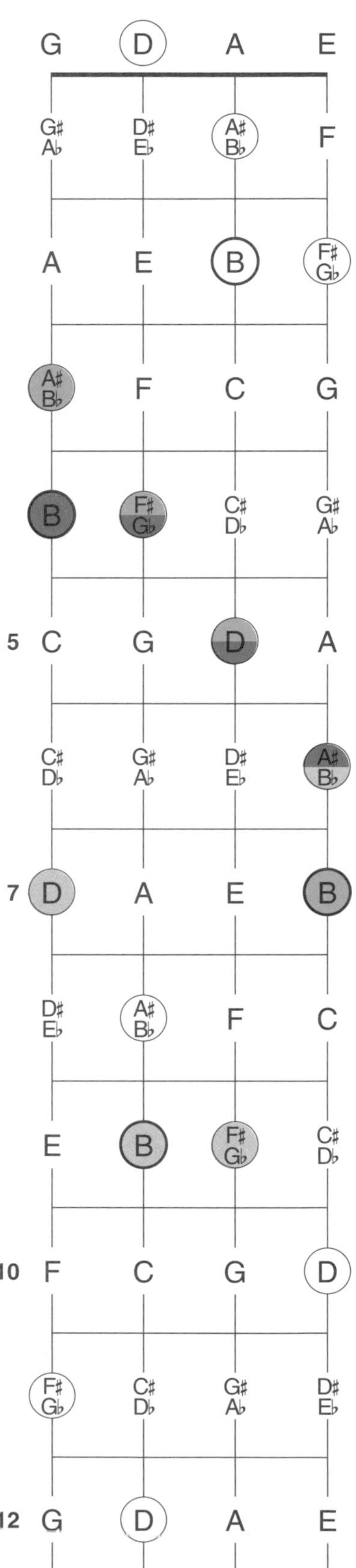

Cm7♭5

C–E♭–G♭–B♭

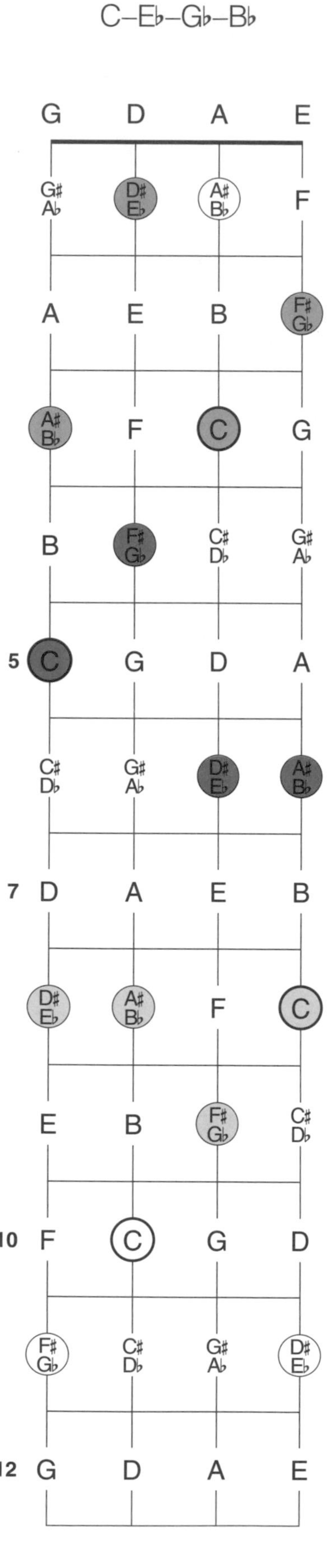

C♯m7♭5

C♯–E–G–B

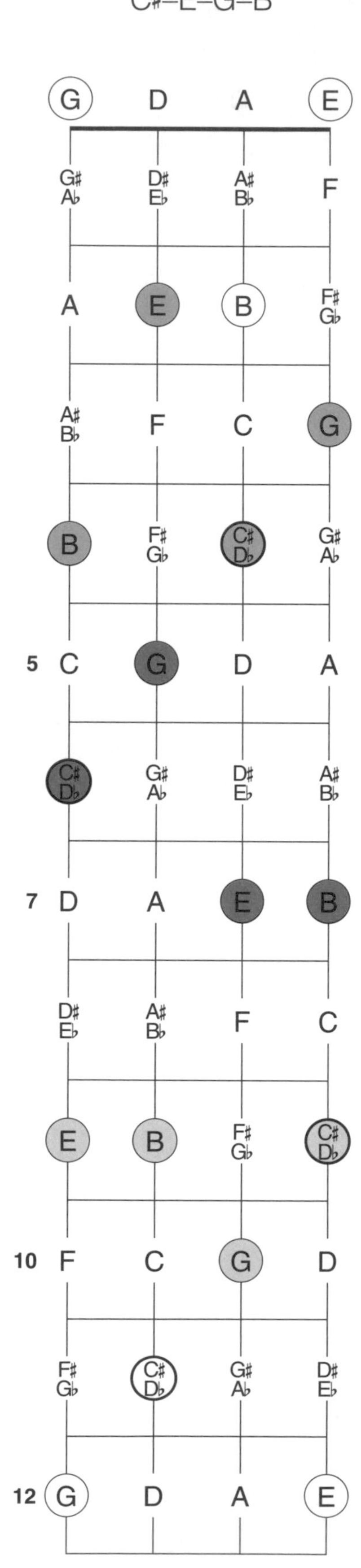

Dm7♭5

D–F–A♭–C

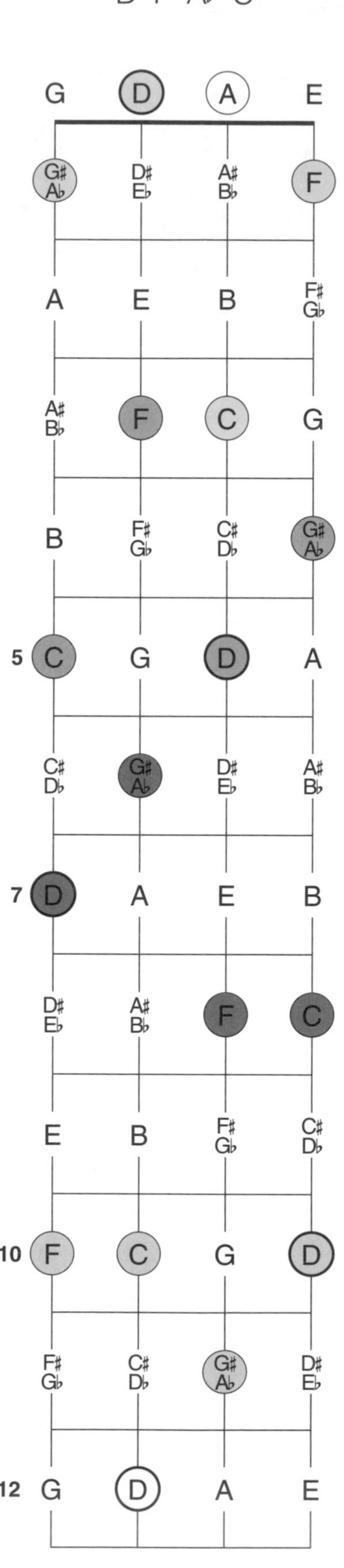

D♯/E♭m7♭5

D♯–F♯–A–C♯/E♭–G♭–B♭♭–D♭

G D A E
G♯ A♭ D♯ E♭ A♯ B♭ F
A E B F♯ G♭
A♯ B♭ F C G
B F♯ G♭ C♯ D♭ G♯ A♭
5 C G D A
C♯ D♭ G♯ A♭ D♯ E♭ A♯ B♭
7 D A E B
D♯ E♭ A♯ B♭ F C
E B F♯ G♭ C♯ D♭
10 F C G D
F♯ G♭ C♯ D♭ G♯ A♭ D♯ E♭
12 G D A E

Em7♭5

E–G–B♭–D

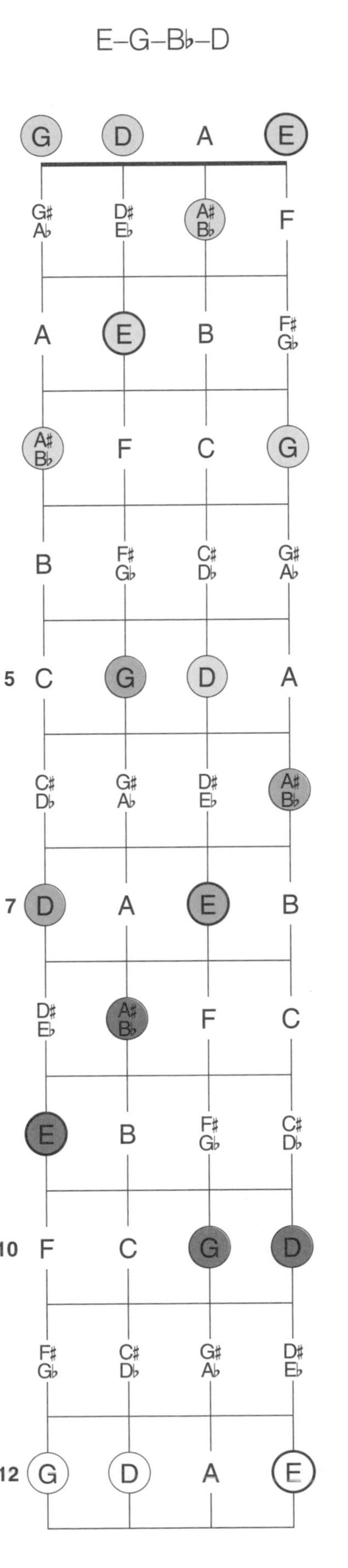

Fm7♭5

F–A♭–C♭–E♭

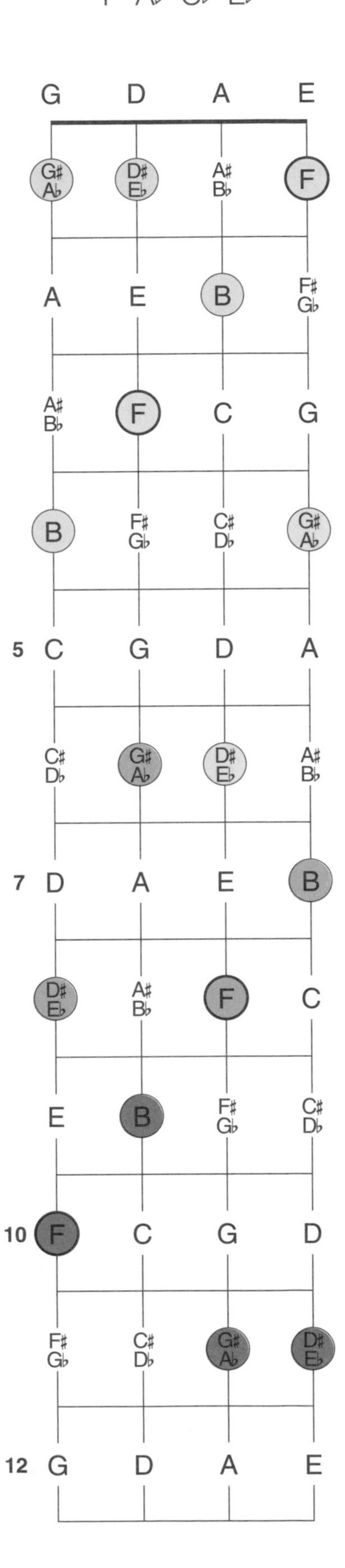

F♯m7♭5

F♯–A–C–E

Gm7♭5

G–B♭–D♭–F

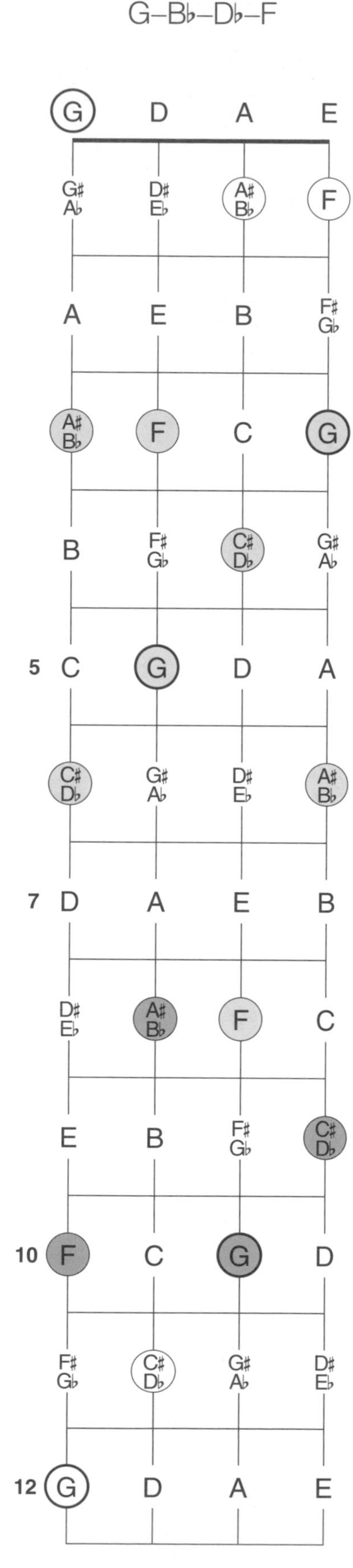

G♯m7♭5

G♯–B–D–F♯

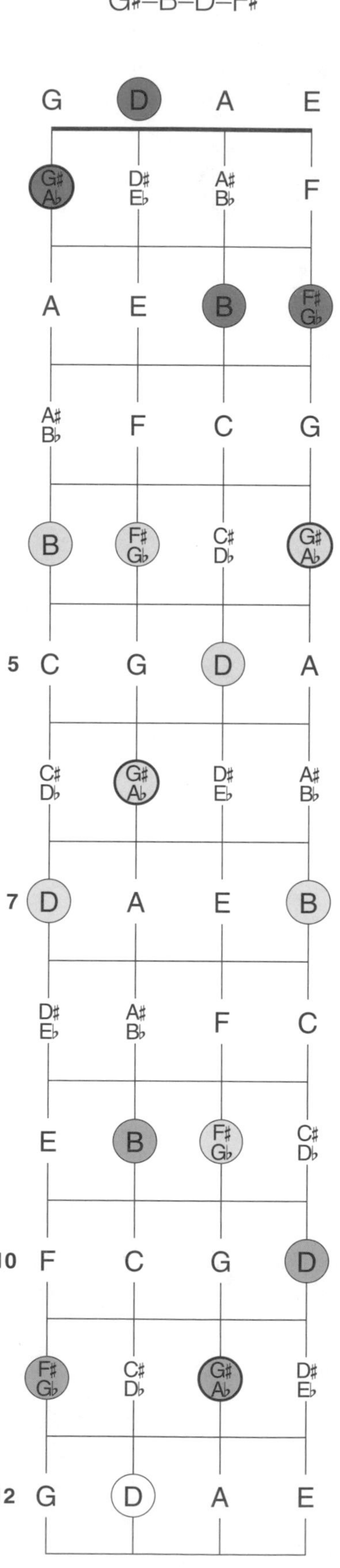

Am7♭5

A–C–E♭–G

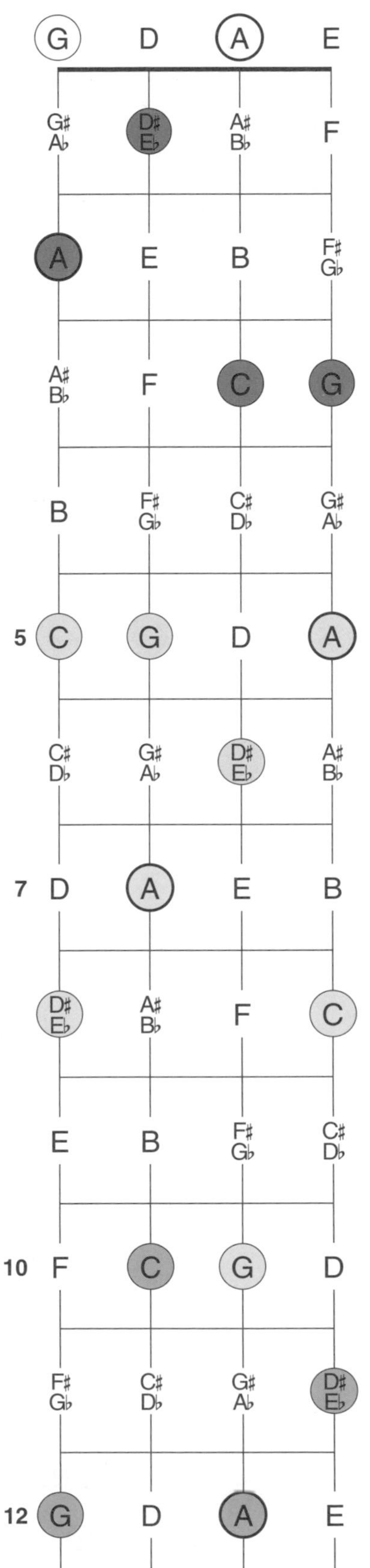

A♯/B♭m7♭5

A♯–C♯–E–G♯/B♭–D♭–F♭–A♭

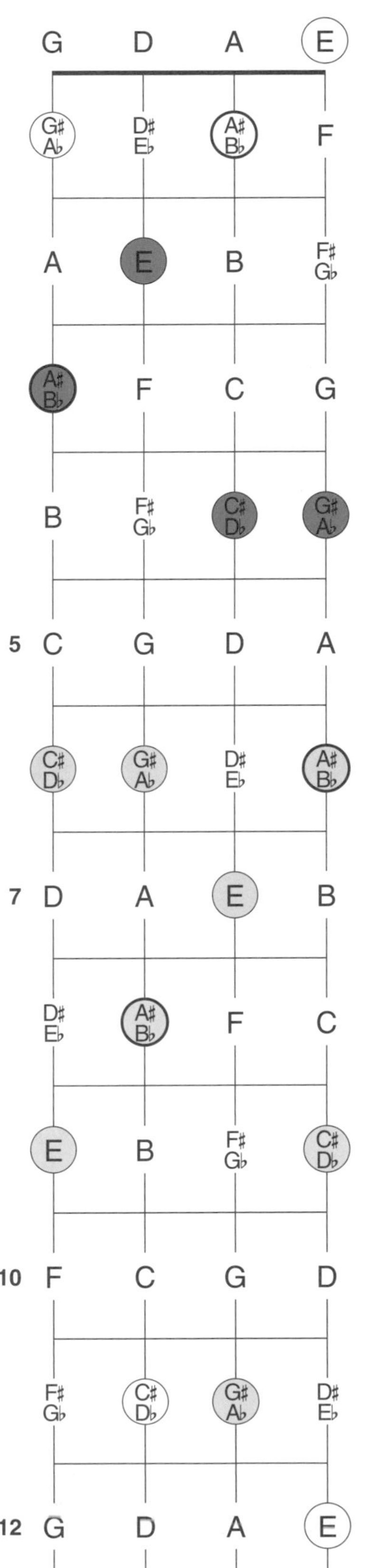

Bm7♭5

B–D–F–A

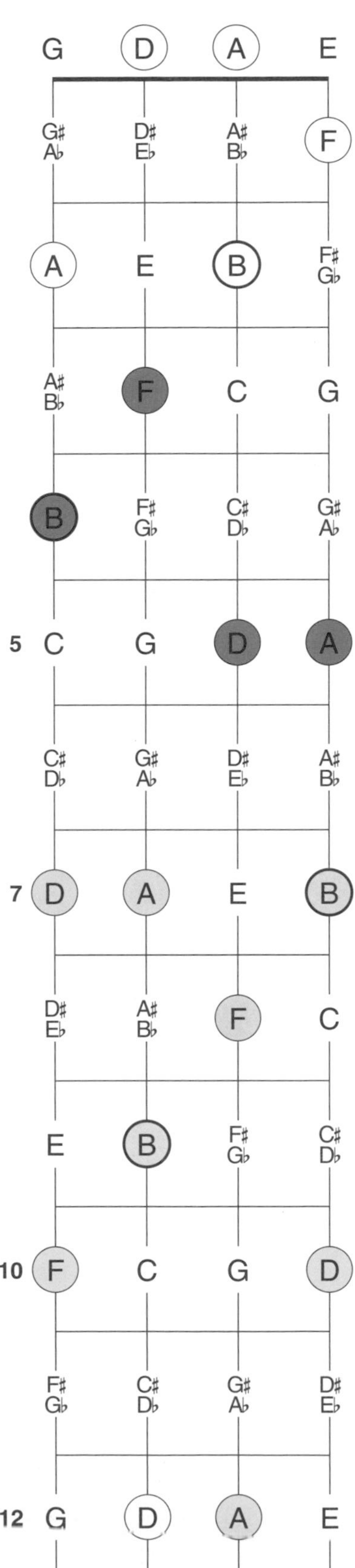

C°7

C–E♭–G♭–A

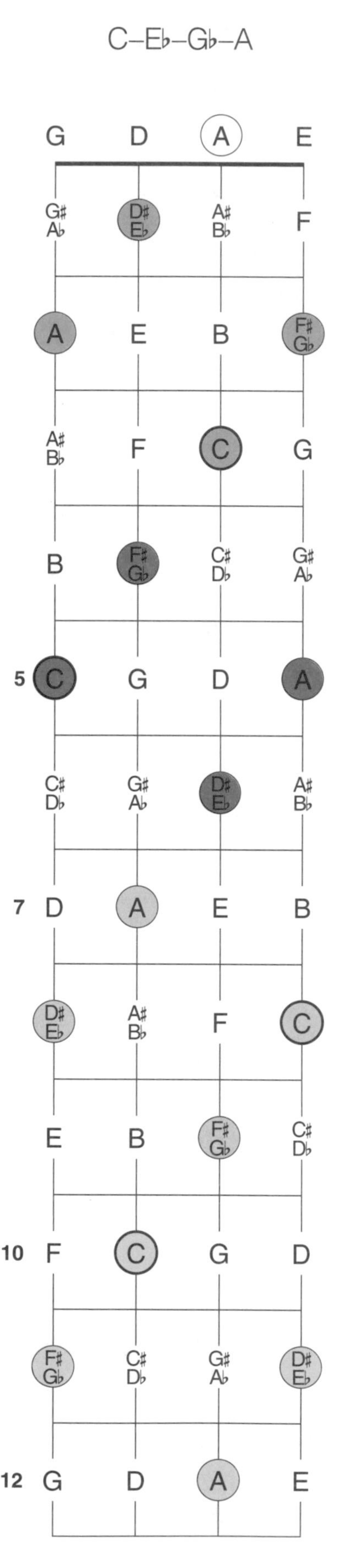

C♯°7

C♯–E–G–B♭

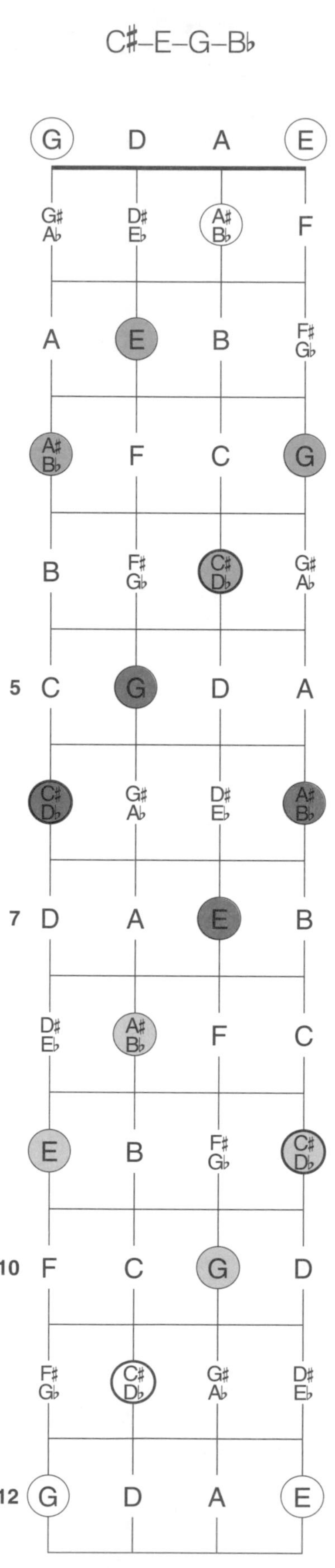

D°7

D–F–A♭–C♭

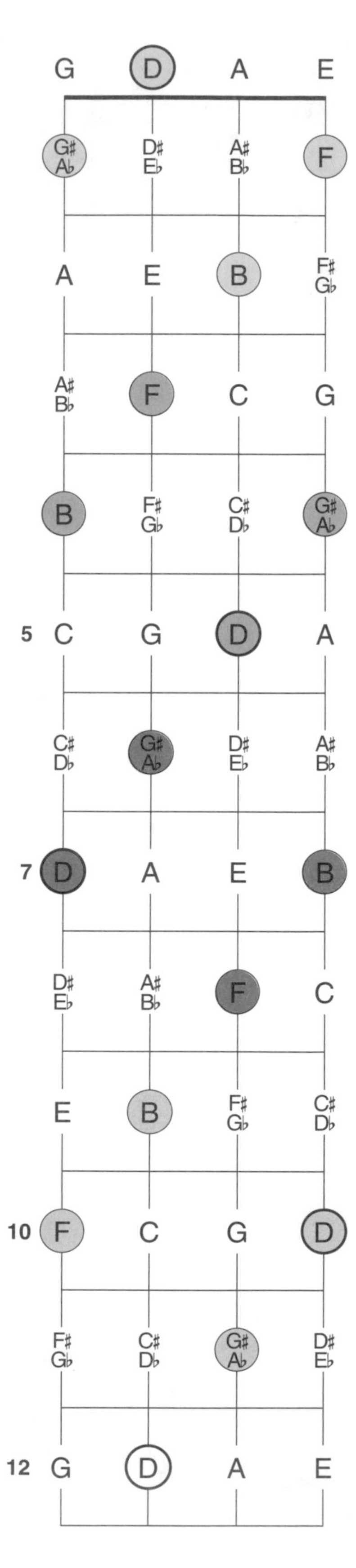

D♯°7

D♯–F♯–A–C

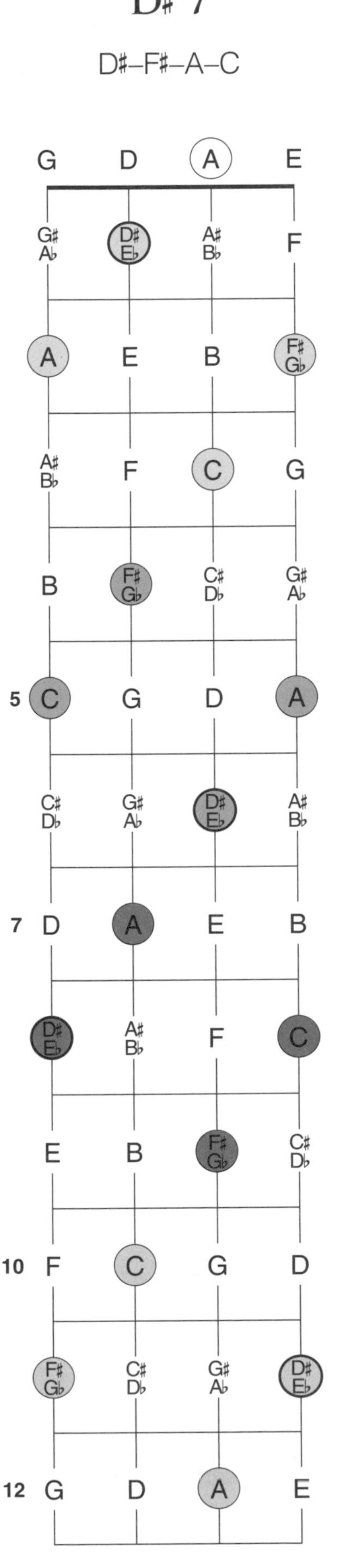

E°7

E–G–B♭–D♭

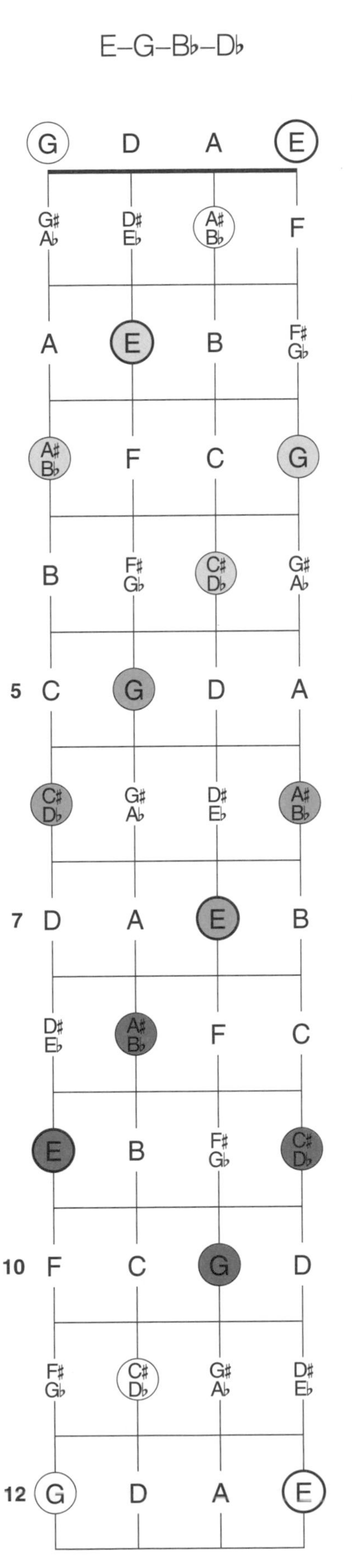

F°7

F–A♭–C♭–D

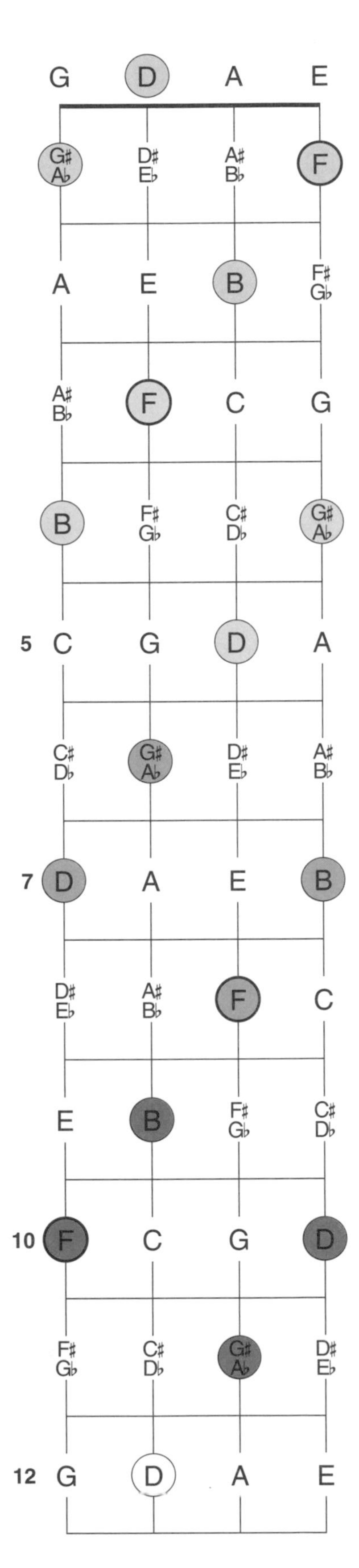

F♯°7

F♯–A–C–E♭

G D A E
G♯A♭ D♯E♭ A♯B♭ F
A E B F♯G♭
A♯B♭ F C G
B F♯G♭ C♯D♭ G♯A♭
5 C G D A
C♯D♭ G♯A♭ D♯E♭ A♯B♭
7 D A E B
D♯E♭ A♯B♭ F C
E B F♯G♭ C♯D♭
10 F C G D
F♯G♭ C♯D♭ G♯A♭ D♯E♭
12 G D A E

G°7

G–B♭–D♭–F♭

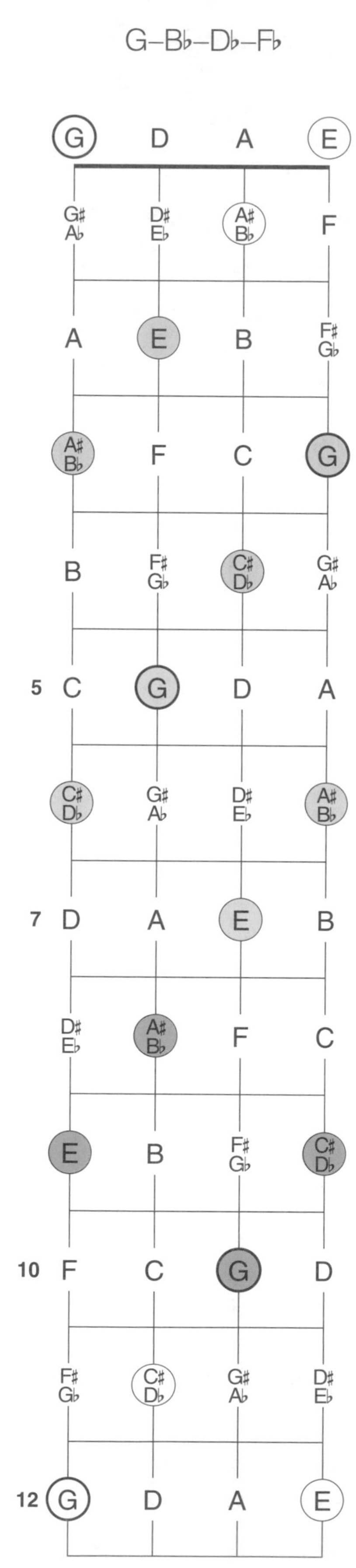

G♯°7

G♯–B–D–F

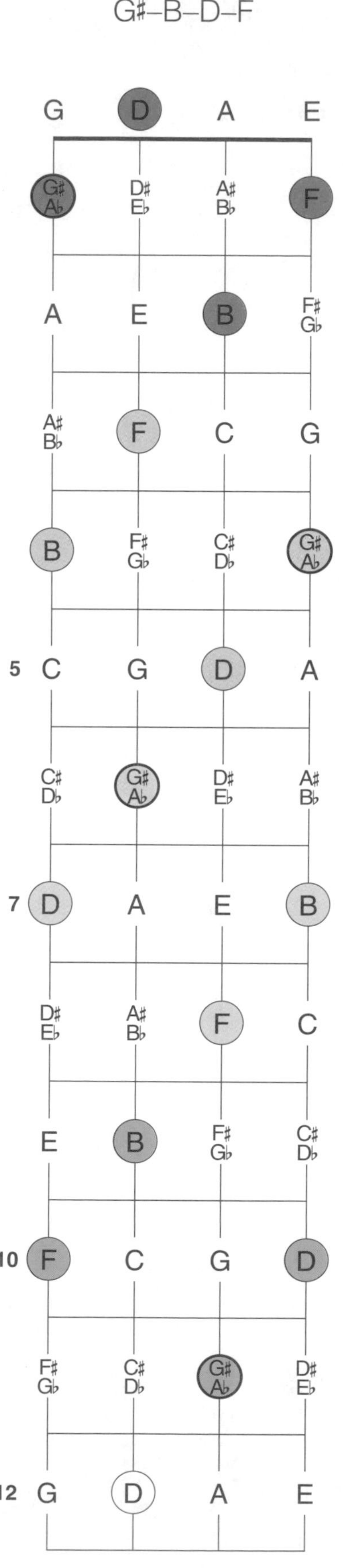

A°7

A–C–E♭–G♭

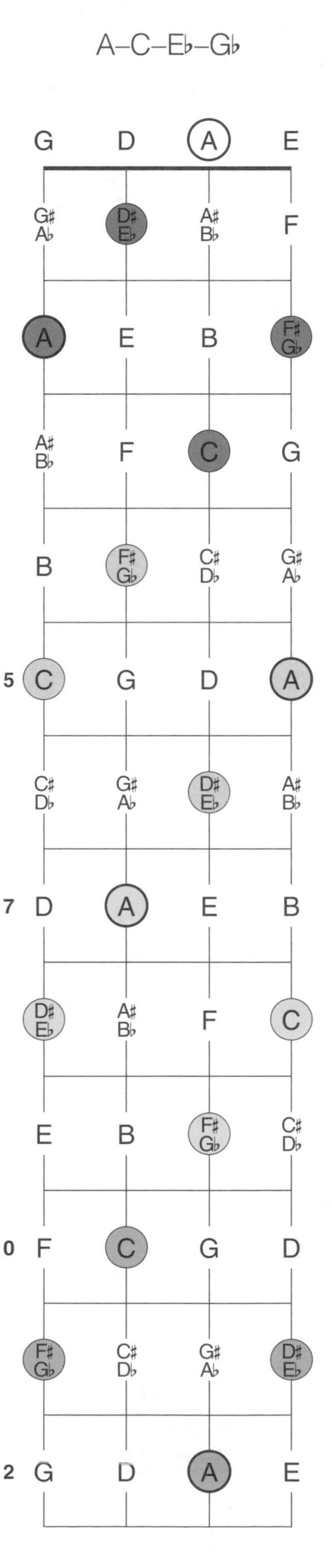

A♯/B♭°7

A♯–C♯–E–G/B♭–D♭–F♭–G

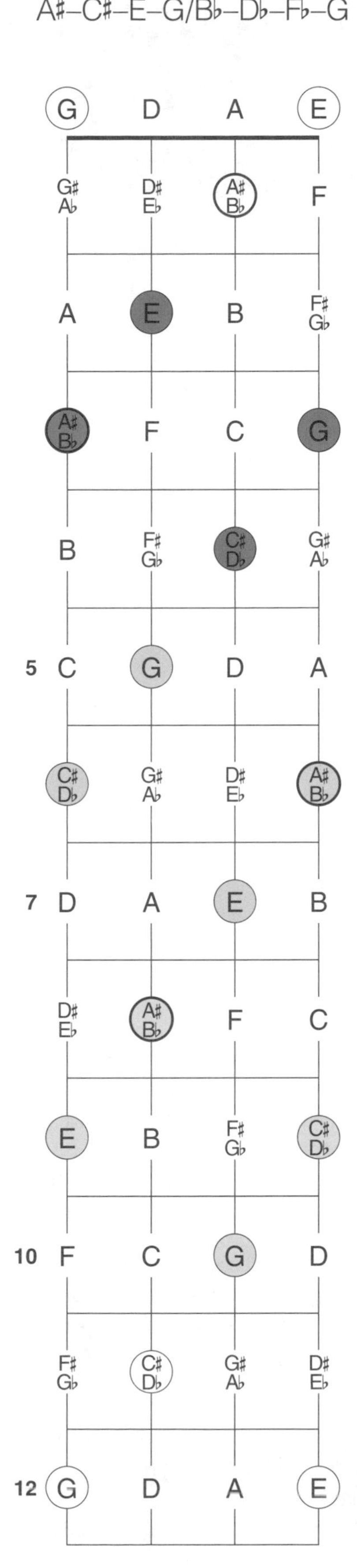

B°7

B–D–F–A♭

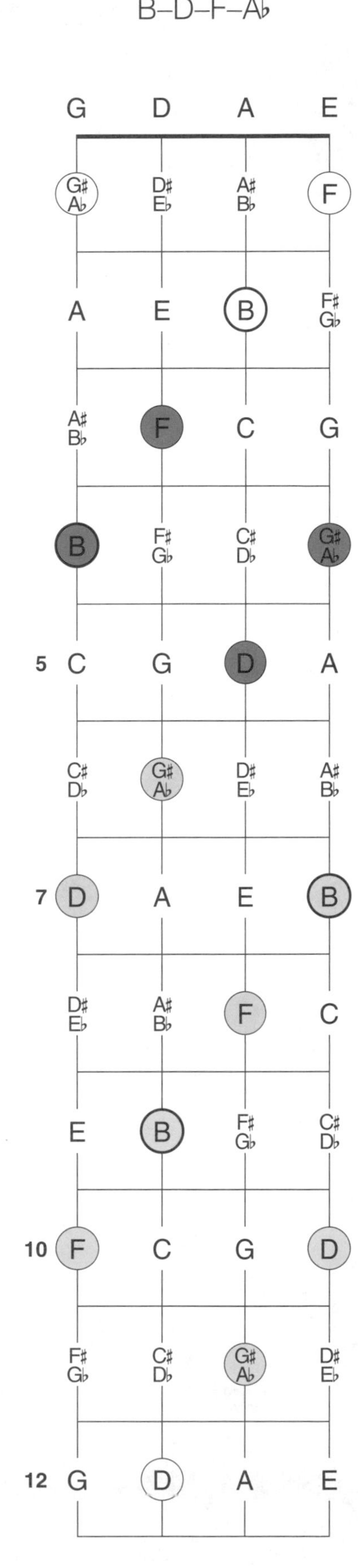

Hal Leonard Mandolin Play-Along Series

HAL•LEONARD®
MANDOLIN PLAY-ALONG

AUDIO ACCESS INCLUDED

The Mandolin Play-Along Series will help you play your favorite songs quickly and easily. Just follow the written music, listen to the CD or online audio to hear how the mandolin should sound, and then play along using the separate backing tracks. Standard notation and tablature are both included in the book. The audio is enhanced so users can adjust the recording to any tempo without changing the pitch!

INCLUDES TAB

1. BLUEGRASS
Angeline the Baker • Billy in the Low Ground • Blackberry Blossom • Fisher's Hornpipe • Old Joe Clark • Salt Creek • Soldier's Joy • Whiskey Before Breakfast.
00702517 Book/Online Audio $14.99

2. CELTIC
A Fig for a Kiss • The Kesh Jig • Morrison's Jig • The Red Haired Boy • Rights of Man • Star of Munster • The Star of the County Down • Temperence Reel.
00702518 Book/Online Audio $14.99

3. POP HITS
Brown Eyed Girl • I Shot the Sheriff • In My Life • Mrs. Robinson • Stand by Me • Superstition • Tears in Heaven • You Can't Hurry Love.
00702519 Book/CD Pack $14.99

4. J.S. BACH
Bourree in E Minor • Invention No.1 (Bach) • Invention No.2 (Bach) • Jesu, Joy of Man's Desiring • March in D Major • Minuet in G • Musette in D Major • Sleepers, Awake (Wachet Auf).
00702520 Book/CD Pack $14.99

5. GYPSY SWING
After You've Gone • Avalon • China Boy • Dark Eyes • Indiana (Back Home Again in Indiana) • Limehouse Blues • The Sheik of Araby • Tiger Rag (Hold That Tiger).
00702521 Book/CD Pack $14.99

6. ROCK HITS
Back in the High Life Again • Copperhead Road • Going to California • Ho Hey • Iris • Losing My Religion • Maggie May • Sunny Came Home.
00119367 Book/Online Audio $16.99

7. ITALIAN CLASSICS
Come Back to Sorrento • La Spagnola • Mattinata • 'O Sole Mio • Oh Marie • Santa Lucia • Tarantella • Vieni Sul Mar.
00119368 Book/Online Audio $16.99

8. MANDOLIN FAVORITES
Arrivederci Roma (Goodbye to Rome) • The Godfather (Love Theme) • Misirlou • Never on Sunday • Over the Rainbow • Spanish Eyes • That's Amoré (That's Love) • Theme from "Zorba the Greek."
00119494 Book/Online Audio $14.99

9. CHRISTMAS CAROLS
Angels We Have Heard on High • Carol of the Bells • Go, Tell It on the Mountain • Hark! the Herald Angels Sing • Joy to the World • O Holy Night • Silent Night • We Wish You a Merry Christmas.
00119895 Book/CD Pack $14.99

10. SONGS FOR BEGINNERS
Amazing Grace • Cripple Creek • Devil's Dream • Frankie and Johnny • Frosty Morning • Over the Waterfall • Short'nin' Bread • Stone's Rag.
00156776 Book/Online Audio $14.99

11. CLASSICAL THEMES
Blue Danube Waltz • Eine Kleine Nachtmusik ("Serenade"), First Movement Excerpt • Für Elise • Humoresque • In the Hall of the Mountain King • La donna e mobile • The Merry Widow Waltz • Spring, First Movement.
00156777 Book/Online Audio $14.99

HAL•LEONARD®
www.halleonard.com

Prices, contents, and availability subject to change without notice.

0418

Great Mandolin Publications

from

HAL•LEONARD®

HAL LEONARD MANDOLIN METHOD

Noted mandolinist and teacher Rich Del Grosso has authored this excellent mandolin method that features great playable tunes in several styles (bluegrass, country, folk, blues) in standard music notation and tablature. The optional audio features play-along duets.

00699296 Book Only $7.99
00695102 Book/Online Audio $15.99

EASY SONGS FOR MANDOLIN

SUPPLEMENTARY SONGBOOK TO THE HAL LEONARD MANDOLIN METHOD

20 songs to play as you learn mandolin: Annie's Song • California Dreamin' • Let It Be • Puff the Magic Dragon • Scarborough Fair • Where Have All the Flowers Gone? • and more.

00695865 Book Only $9.99
00695866 Book/CD Pack $15.99

FRETBOARD ROADMAPS – MANDOLIN

THE ESSENTIAL PATTERNS THAT ALL THE PROS KNOW AND USE

by Fred Sokolow and Bob Applebaum

The latest installment in our popular Fretboard Roadmaps series is a unique book/CD pack for all mandolin players. The CD includes 48 demonstration tracks for the exercises that will teach players to: play all over the fretboard, in any key; increase their chord, scale and lick vocabulary; play chord-based licks, moveable major and blues scales, first-position major scales and double stops; and more! Includes easy-to-follow diagrams and instructions for all levels of players.

00695357 Book/CD Pack $14.99

MANDOLIN CHORD FINDER

EASY-TO-USE GUIDE TO OVER 1,000 MANDOLIN CHORDS

by Chad Johnson

Learn to play chords on the mandolin with this comprehensive, yet easy-to-use book. The Hal Leonard Mandolin Chord Finder contains over 1,000 chord diagrams for the most important 28 chord types, including three voicings for each chord. Also includes a lesson on chord construction, and a fingerboard chart of the mandolin neck!

00695739 9" X 12" Edition $6.99
00695740 6" X 9" Edition $5.99

MANDOLIN SCALE FINDER

EASY-TO-USE GUIDE TO OVER 1,300 MANDOLIN SCALES

by Chad Johnson

Presents scale diagrams for the most often-used scales and modes in an orderly and easily accessible fashion. Use this book as a reference guide or as the foundation for creating an in-depth practice routine. Includes multiple patterns for each scale, a lesson on scale construction, and a fingerboard chart of the mandolin neck.

00695779 9" X 12" Edition $7.99
00695782 6" X 9" Edition $5.99

BILL MONROE – 16 GEMS

Authentic mandolin transcriptions of these classics by the Father of Bluegrass: Blue Grass Breakdown • Blue Grass Special • Can't You Hear Me Calling • Goodbye Old Pal • Heavy Traffic Ahead • I'm Going Back to Old Kentucky • It's Mighty Dark to Travel • Kentucky Waltz • Nobody Loves Me • Old Crossroad Is Waitin' • Remember the Cross • Shine Hallelujah Shine • Summertime Is Past and Gone • Sweetheart You Done Me Wrong • Travelin' This Lonesome Road • True Life Blues.

00690310 Mandolin Transcriptions $14.99

O BROTHER, WHERE ART THOU?

Perfect for beginning to advanced players, this collection contains both note-for-note transcribed mandolin solos, as well as mandolin arrangements of the melody lines for 11 songs from this Grammy-winning Album of the Year: Angel Band • The Big Rock Candy Mountain • Down to the River to Pray • I Am a Man of Constant Sorrow • I Am Weary (Let Me Rest) • I'll Fly Away • In the Highways (I'll Be Somewhere Working for My Lord) • In the Jailhouse Now • Indian War Whoop • Keep on the Sunny Side • You Are My Sunshine. Chord diagrams provided for each song match the chords from the original recording, and all songs are in their original key. Includes tab, lyrics and a mandolin notation legend.

00695762 .... $15.99

THE ULTIMATE BLUEGRASS MANDOLIN CONSTRUCTION MANUAL

by Roger H. Siminoff

This is the most complete step-by-step treatise ever written on building an acoustical string instrument. Siminoff, a renowned author and luthier, applies over four decades of experience to guide beginners to pros through detailed chapters on wood selection, cutting, carving, shaping, assembly, inlays, fretting, binding and assembly of an F-style mandolin.

00331088 .... $37.99

Prices, contents and availability are subject to change without notice.

Visit Hal Leonard online at www.halleonard.com

0418